Praise for *Paying Atten*[illegible]

Paying Attention makes you pay attenti[illegible]
of. Lynne Tillman takes you on a mean[illegible] old
ramshackle house of our culture. Each chapter opens a door to another room, another cabinet of curiosity, and Tillman's brain is an erudite and delightful companion.

—Marilyn Minter

Lynne Tillman writes, "Close readings aren't popular, but I like doing them." In *Paying Attention*, Tillman really *does* pay attention. In her tonal, rich, accessible voice, describing becomes a kind of thinking. These essays, from 1973 to 2025, focus on not what art is but what it *tells* us. Paintings, photographs, drawings, sculptures, novels, movies, criticism: Tillman shows us how all these forms are embedded not only in their own categories, but within a grand history of literature, philosophy, science, pop culture, politics, and, not least, psychoanalysis. Each essay, each a stand-alone story, carefully builds momentum until you see how art can tell you almost everything.

—Josiah McElheny

Diane Sawyer Gertrude Stein Eggleston and Wittgenstein! Lynne Tillman's collection of essays is a gourmet buffet of your favorite artists and others, the nuts and bolts of material practice alongside personal rumination and analytic flair. Her highways of thought go fast, connecting cultural mile markers with the great art Tillman witnessed firsthand. Lynne sees it all. Running throughout are some key quotes: "Feelings are facts" (Yvonne Rainer), "Any reality is an opinion" (Timothy Leary), and "I'm very much a part of my times" (Andy Warhol). Reading this book you realize Lynne, too, is exactly that.

—Rachel Harrison

This collection of Lynne Tillman's essays on art is a revelation. Like her great fiction, Tillman's writing about photography, painting, sculpture, and more thwarts expectation and disrupts convention; art seems new again. So does looking. Carry this book wherever you go.

—Andrew Durbin

Lynne Tillman's writing mimics the movement of her mind. Glancing like light, it's alive with coincidence, rhyme, and (free) association. Her language is both precise and wandering, and her intelligence goes deep and wide, a spotlight searching across the dark sky to illuminate philosophy, psychoanalysis, and the sheer absurdities of being human. The encounter of thought and language is never seamless: It gapes, frays, and tears, and reading her work, we sense the writer in history, connected to the moving world, yet grasping and braiding together divergent and living strands of conscious and unconscious experience. Perpetual and persistent detours provide openings to her inner world, where big ideas bump up against the everyday, and the apparently insignificant resonates like a bass guitar. Tillman created the literary field of "art writing" and in doing so, she transformed criticism and critical discourse, inventing new forms to take account of her own complicated, wry apprehension of art and life. Here, as in her other books, she continually pays, and plays out, her attention: lucid, piercing, and generous.

—Leslie Dick

If there is such a thing as an "artist's artist," Lynne Tillman regularly makes the case for the "artist's writer," from consequentially aesthetic plot points in her novels to the nimble provocations and intuitive depths brought to her artist conversations, and the absolutely necessary invention of Madame Realism, the porous critic, the one every artist wants, still capable of being shocked. Whatever the context, Tillman regularly reminds her audience that when it comes to art, there are far more interesting things to want besides wanting to be merely right.

—John Pilson

No one pays attention like Lynne Tillman does. Whether it's at a canvas, a screen, or a page, she looks, lingers, refuses to leap to pontificatory conclusions. Each sentence, scourged of in-crowd bromides, is astute, droll, long-memoried. There's so much generosity here. Inflection and insight. An incurable curiosity.

—Sukhdev Sandhu

Paying Attention

Lynne Tillman

Paying Attention

Essays on Art and Culture

Edited and with an introduction
by Elizabeth Schambelan

David Zwirner Books

Contents

Writing in Reference to Art

Elizabeth Schambelan

"I (and you) start somewhere, lean on or draw from art and life, draw meaning from others' lives and work. Where a story takes off is invariably in medias res and enmeshed in other stories."[1] And the enmeshment is unruly. It's happening on several scales at once and across dimensions, and everything has ramifications for everything else. The narrator of Lynne Tillman's "Stories Tell Stories" remarks, "It's entirely familiar that words mean as they do only in relationship to other words, and also that, by setting an adjective beside a noun, adverb beside a verb, words qualify each other." I (you) understand things with and against other things. Meaning is relational because meaning is difference. As Gertrude Stein put it in "Composition as Explanation": "It is understood by this time that everything is the same except composition and time, composition and the time of the composition and the time in the composition."[2]

Tillman also put it that way, by quoting the preceding sentence in her essay on Cindy Sherman. Another passage from "Composition as Explanation" appears in her essay on Steve Locke: "For a very long time everybody refuses and then almost without a pause almost everybody accepts. In the history of the refused in the arts and literature the rapidity of the change is always startling."[3] The only things that really signify are the things that change: composition and time, the relationships activated by citing, sequencing, splicing; by drawing from or upon. When Richard Serra famously noted that drawing is a verb, he was implying that process art is the only kind of art there is, or at least the only kind there should be. Tillman suggests something similar. "Art can be a form of consciousness, of consciousness in process."[4]

Stein, Tillman writes, "drew inspiration from cubism, especially from Picasso's and Braque's paintings; a kind of borrowing occurred, because through them she found delight and an object to translate into writing. . . . How could she break syntax as they did a flat, painted surface."[5] "Composition" can't be a verb, grammatically speaking, but it is anyway in Tillman's work. The writings in this collection break syntaxes of genre, form, discipline, disarranging and rearranging, composing in real time.

The narrator of "Stories Tell Stories" watches Joan Jonas's film *Berlin Road Movie* and thinks a dour woman "represented East Germany," but when the dour woman reappears "smiling or drinking wine, I interpreted the story differently, mildly rebuking myself for my first associations. . . . Ultimately, I didn't know what I was seeing or what story to tell myself." Stories tell stories, and *those* stories tell stories, and they don't follow neat trajectories. "Jonas attends to ineffability, to fast-moving impressions, to the unremarkable remarkable. . . . This is the *inenarrable*, which is her narrative territory: what can't be narrated." My italics. "Meanings will be inferred by viewers, and they may reside in the text, not simply or definitively, most likely as a panoply of possibility."

"You know when you're driving at night like this it can suddenly occur to you that maybe you're going in completely the wrong direction."[6] This is a line from Laurie Anderson's *Americans on the Move*. Craig Owens used it as the opening in his watershed 1980 essay "The Allegorical Impulse: Toward a Theory of Postmodernism."

"Especially wonderful, and useful, is Craig's honest reexamination of ideas he had once absorbed, followed, and believed," Tillman writes in her introduction to *Craig Owens: Portrait of a Young Critic*. "Undoing was a piece of Craig's analytical mind." The remark is echoed, or mirrored, in "Drawing from a Translation Artist," where Tillman reflects on her own work. "I am not of the 'what's done is done' variety. I am, rather, of the 'done, undone, redone, done over, done more differently' breed. . . . I accept change in forward, backward, and neutral gears." Consciousness in process drives at night, traveling highways and byways of inference and undoing.

For Owens, Anderson's road trip is "an allegory, a brief parable of reading." He defines allegory, in the simplest terms, as doubling: It "occurs whenever one text is doubled by another." He elaborates: "In allegorical structure, then, one text is *read through* another, however fragmentary, intermittent, or chaotic their relationship may be; the paradigm for the allegorical work is thus the palimpsest."[7]

Tillman translates this paradigm as pentimento: "A writer might draw a line through a word or phrase; she might keep the first word visible under the new one, like a palimpsest. . . . In writing, a superimposition doesn't fuse layers the way it does in films and photographs. A painting's surface compares better, when, say, its first or second layer shows through it."[8]

Allegory presupposes relationality, which means it presupposes criticality. "Conceived in this way," says Owens, "allegory becomes the model of all commentary, all critique." It's a model that doesn't accommodate modernist pipe dreams. "When the postmodernist work speaks of itself, it is no longer to proclaim its autonomy, its self-sufficiency, its transcendence; rather, it is to narrate its own contingency, insufficiency, lack of transcendence."[9] And, one might add, its inenarrability.

The story can't go on and goes on, can't begin and begins, in medias res. "I'm traveling mentally, the way I usually do, from a lush marsh, to a secluded road, to a chain-link fence, to a tower and abandoned railroad tracks. In the hush of these intensely static photographs, I concoct associations. . . ."[10] The photographs are by James Welling. "I find Route 81, where Cindy Sherman's Hitchhiker might have waited." The critic-as-narrator steps into allegorical space, inhabits its landscapes diegetically, tells the story, or doesn't tell it, from there.

Whatever else I do, I have to narrate insufficiency, because I can't cover all the ground I'd like to.[11] But even if you accept Walter Benjamin's thirteenth thesis on writing ("The work is the death mask of its conception"), you still have to compose the insufficient form your doomed conception will take. What to put in? What to leave out?

Which brings me to the topic of composing in the negative, i.e., leaving things out. But before I go on I should address terminology. Phrasings like "essay about" need to be qualified. "I'm speaking and looking 'at' or 'to' an artwork," Tillman commented in a 2019 interview. "I am *not* explaining it, not talking 'about' it, but addressing myself 'to' it."[12] She described Craig Owens's self-positioning: "His notion of writing alongside art was crucial. . . . He saw himself as part of the contemporary world, its art and thinking. Part, not separate from it. How does one criticize from within. . . ."

So my prepositions are not entirely apposite. And since genre is not really an operative category in Tillman's writing (though genre conventions are selectively deployed), it's debatable whether "essay" or any other genre label is apposite either. As for "criticism," Tillman rarely uses the word. Instead, she uses the phrases "writing on art"[13] and "writing in reference to art."[14] I thought I should nevertheless try to define "criticism" in this introduction, but I couldn't think of a definition that was both satisfactory and succinct, and it didn't seem like something I should dilate upon.

What not to dilate upon, which darlings to kill, what to consign to the cutting-room floor: It's an intractable problem, because every composition must have negative space to be legible as a composition, yet nature abhors a vacuum. And so does everything else. Tillman suggests that meaning itself is prone to horror vacui: "From images or words, meanings run rampant; human beings are like interpreting machines. Whether one wants to be against interpretation or for it, meanings occur, haphazard, benign or malignant, often unconsciously."[15]

Meanwhile art keeps its own counsel. "I don't expect answers from art," Tillman said in the interview. "It doesn't speak as people or other animals do."[16] This resonates with me, and, I suspect, will resonate with anyone who has spent a lot of time within earshot of art. "An artwork requires focus. . . . All art depends upon its being awarded attention."[17] This seems inarguable. But it can be hard to put into practice, because paying attention to art requires paying attention to its silences.

In her 2022 lecture "The Double," Tillman made a related point, maybe *the* crucial point about writing in reference to art. In ekphrasis, "wordlessness is doubled, uncanniness also. . . . What words are there for that emptiness, that absence."[18] "Ekphrasis" has a narrower meaning than "criticism." But I think what Tillman said is true of criticism in general: It mirrors the aphasias of its object. Whereof it cannot speak, thereof it, too, is silent.

"In writing on art, words reach for other words, phrases, idioms, and through them more images and ideas leap out. . . ."[19] This resonates, too. There's a powerful temptation to convince one's self that the agglutinative drive of language is a drive toward meaning, and that one should stuff as much language as possible into the silences of art. Tillman does not succumb to this temptation. "I always ask myself, in writing in reference to art, why is it there?"[20]

A metaphor that comes to mind in connection with Tillman's writing is a Swiss Army knife, which does not bristle with all its capabilities in a given instant, but deploys one or two at a time. The rest are retracted, but their edges glint. A term that comes to mind is "subtractive." The descriptors that seem most characteristic of her voice chime with the idea that less is more: understated, distilled, deadpan, favoring aphorism over elaboration, and, while by no means unemotional, often marked by a certain detachment, the stylistic signature of critical distance. Diana Vreeland's "Elegance is refusal" seems salient. Elegance is the ability to activate voids, to know where the negative spaces in the composition should be, and to act on that knowledge, which entails risk.

If you can tolerate the risk, then you might be able to represent complexity without simply mirroring the aesthetically problematic ornateness of reality. This to me is a hallmark of Tillman's criticism—elegant rendering of complexity. "Art of His Time," on On Kawara, for instance, encompasses emails, first-person accounts of studio visits, reflections on the atom bomb and space exploration, critical analysis of Kawara's work in relation to modernism . . . The elements are combined with clarity and sprezzatura. Tillman's *frieze* columns iterate the same intricacy in microcosm, building conceptual orreries in eight hundred words—not a lot of room in which to build anything. An orrery is a model of an astronomical system, a mobile diagram of orbits within orbits.

Speaking of taking up space, there's a very funny section on manspreading avant la lettre in Tillman's 1998 novel *No Lease on Life*. (My transitions are just as God made them.) I thought maybe the manspreading scene should be excerpted in this collection, because it's criticism, cultural criticism. There's criticism in Tillman's other works of fiction, too. For instance, her 2018 novel *Men and Apparitions* is, in part, an extended meditation on photography. Her 2006 novel *American Genius* contains critical meditations on subjects ranging from Eames chairs to national metanarratives.

But *Paying Attention* is a selection. So although it's arbitrary to incise genre divisions across Tillman's body of work, her novels aren't represented here. Neither is her short fiction, except for criticism that *is* short fiction, e.g., "Still Moving" (which originally appeared in Justine Kurland's monograph *Highway Kind*) and "21 TV Tales" (first published in the catalogue of a Barbara Kruger exhibition). Each could be described as a short story composed of even shorter stories, although the two texts are very different—the former a dreamlike tour of a small town, the latter a series of sardonic parables whose vibe lies somewhere between the brothers Grimm and Safdie.

Though Tillman eschews such monikers, she was a practitioner avant la lettre of what others have called fictocriticism: fiction addressed to art, or, criticism that includes fictive elements.[21] That her writing has influentially challenged the syntaxes of contemporary fiction is widely acknowledged. Her writing in reference to art has posed parallel challenges to criticism. Some of her methods can be concisely described. "The Last Words Are Andy Warhol" takes the form of a numbered list. In her essay "The Horse's Eye," on Carroll Dunham's drawings, she uses a droll proliferation of parentheticals to torque old-school close reading. More often, though, her syntax-breaking strategies operate and interact at a resolution too granular for brief summaries. A case in point is her meditation on Stephen Shore's photographs, "Blue Shores," an uncategorizable synthesis of chromatics, citation that edges toward textual collage, and metafictional computation ("Man + waiting car + bank = a story").

Conveying this aspect of Tillman's criticism—its innovations or departures from convention—entails capturing multifariousness and difference. The same is true of surveying her expansive critical purview (which covers visual art, film, literature, pop culture . . .) and stylistic registers. Tillman's criticism may read like a conversational anecdote, an erudite disquisition, a fairy tale, an epistle, a ghost story, an elegy, a cut up . . . It may read like criticism, but the word "like" is always operative: It's a likeness, a doubling that has a measure of unlikeness. In short, the major criteria that shaped this collection had to do with representing spectrums or ranges, panoplies of possibility. I should note that, as one might expect, I arrived at the selection of texts in consultation with their author. They include contributions to exhibition catalogues and monographs, magazine columns and features, and reviews. With respect to chronological range, *Paying Attention* aims for a parallax where the whole arc of Tillman's criticism is represented, but the past decade looms largest.

"Lived history guides these interpretations and associations," Tillman notes in her essay on Robert Gober's *Untitled* (1998–

2004).[22] Her introduction to Charles Henri Ford's diaries opens up the meaning of lived history: "The reader senses a life formed consciously in the present. . . . It is imaginatively and definitively of its time and in it."[23] Tillman's writing alongside art is also writing alongside the AIDS epidemic; the recrudescence of authoritarian nationalism; the opiate-addiction epidemic; white-supremacist police violence and the uprisings against it. It is of its time and in it, but its historicity is complex and doubt-inflected. "The past to the present can only ever be a fictional narrative, more or less accurate."[24] In "Early Years of the New Museum: An Intellectual Reminiscence or Pieces from a Consciousness," Tillman recalls how feminist commitments were translated and transmitted in her work, and in the curatorial work of the New Museum founder Marcia Tucker, in the 1980s and 1990s. These remembrances furnish a case study for a consideration of how art and culture shape and are shaped by politics, how they intervene in their times and vice versa. But then the reminiscences call themselves into question: "Memory is the single most unreliable narrator."

Although a critique of realism runs through *Paying Attention* ("What's vérité anyway?"[25]), Tillman is not a relativist. "Writing can be accurate even with the inherent obliquities of words."[26] If accuracy is possible, then there's something to be accurate about. Empirical reality is there somewhere. It's just that whether we've managed to access it in a given instance—as opposed to mistaking a mirror for a window—is always open to question. And therefore, so is the putative realism of any representation, perhaps especially our representations of bygone reality, aka history.

This brings me to a phantasmal rubric: "occasional pieces." In conversation, Tillman called her *frieze* columns "occasional pieces" and then applied that term to all the texts in this collection—with some irony, but not entirely ironically.[27]

Occasional pieces are works of criticism undertaken in and for an occasion, a moment. They're compositions in time—this time, now. But they bespeak awareness that now becomes then at every instant, and that history is ephemeral and fungible. To call a work of criticism an occasional piece is to underscore that, as the times change, art changes. An artwork is not the same work today that it was ten years ago, because it isn't seen the same way. Every encounter is a new occasion. Art doesn't stand still, and neither should its reception. "Inexplicable and unforeseeable events will produce new conditions, technologies, experiences, and incite new art. The bases for judgment and criticism will undergo upheaval, also."[28]

I find it eerie to read Tillman's reflections on influence from her 2015 David Wojnarowicz essay. "Influence occurs . . . because an artist perceives in another's work a space, or opening. . . . Influence reconceived would be a heuristic device, an emboldening or an encouragement."[29] That is how I perceived and experienced her work when I first encountered it at twenty-one or so—especially her criticism, though I didn't think of it as criticism. I just thought of it as writing about books, movies, art, etc. Until I read Tillman's writing it had not occurred to me that you could write about these things with all the artfulness you could muster, as you might when writing fiction. I was well aware of literary nonfiction, but it felt revelatory to posit criticism specifically as "literary," an arena in which writing could be art. I don't recall voicing it to myself in spatial terms, but reading her work absolutely made me feel as if I had more room to maneuver. It went deeper than questions of *how* one could write criticism. It also had to do with why one might choose to, and what the stakes might be.

One of the spaces Tillman's criticism opens up is a room in which to postulate that encounters with things might be as consequential and complicated as encounters with people.

> I engage with things as much as people. But I usually don't have fantasies about them. That probably isn't true. I watch television, I talk to it, it's not only talking to me. I'm not a sieve. It isn't, either. . . . In the laundromat, MTV's on, I see other people's clothes, I watch their eyes, mouths, how they fold their shirts, they notice me or don't, smile, don't. Music caresses, pounds, a rhythm for everything. We're doing laundry in the same time, even if we're in different cycles. It's intimate and alien. Underpants flop around in dryers. That's anonymity. Signs hang on walls and doors. . . .[30]

I think something very key about the nature of criticism is articulated here, though I don't know if I can translate it. A whole galaxy of barbed reciprocities is diagrammed: between art and life, subject and object, sign and space, criticism and story. It's a branching mise en abyme full of projections, reflections, identifications and misidentifications.

How does one criticize from within? If you take it as self-evident that criticism requires critical distance, then the question Tillman posed in the 2019 interview seems vexed indeed, because one *does* criticize from within, whether one likes it or not. If art doesn't transcend its contexts—if it doesn't achieve the autonomy envisioned by high modernism—then criticism certainly doesn't either.

Tillman's criticism is self-reflexively written from within fiction, within representation, within time. Also from within systems, laundromats, apartments, galleries, institutions, cities, networks, and friendships, and from within the cat's cradle of relationships among all these things. To me her work implies that the conflict between criticizing from within and maintaining distance can be negotiated, but it requires recognizing critical distance as something like a quantum entanglement.

I know I said I wasn't going to define criticism, but if I were going to try, I'd use the metaphor of an optical prism, something to the effect of: Criticism is just writing (or any form of expression) that uses culture as a prism. "Culture" here means any composition, anything composed by a consciousness, including, say, the position of one's body on the subway. The writer uses the composition to do to thought what prisms do to light. Namely, change it, in a way that is ideally both edifying and aesthetically compelling. This metaphor accounts for something I love about writing criticism, which is that it's never just you and the blank screen. There's a third term between you and the tabula rasa. You don't have to conjure something out of nothing. But this metaphor instrumentalizes the object of criticism—the artwork, novel, etc.—and makes it incidental at the same time. A definition that rests on it would be very flawed.

If the metaphor were to account for criticism's possibilities, there would have to be reciprocity. The prism itself would also have to be changed. Not transformed, but translated. When you translate a novel, it doesn't cease to be available in its original language. Duchamp drew a mustache on a *reproduction* of the Mona Lisa.

Tillman's criticism realizes the possibilities. The works to which she pays attention become prisms of consciousness in process. And consciousness in process changes those works, translates them.

"The unconscious doesn't obey time, which also confuses memory. . . . Maybe that's why people invented what Shakespeare, in *Richard II*, called time's 'numb'ring clock.'"[31] The newfangled mechanism offered an ordinal fantasy, promising to take over the job of keeping time, of knowing when you are. But this proved to be one of modernity's major deceptions. Splicing time into arbitrary increments didn't regulate its irrational contractions and dilations—it just syncopated them. And so ticking became the soundtrack of the dialectic of enlightenment, reason going mad. To pay attention is to get off the clock, compose in time, interpret and reinterpret. It is to write alongside and be alongside, brooking all the treachery of subjectivity, all the unreliable narrations of humans and other animals.

Addressing Chantal Akerman's last film, *No Home Movie*, Tillman superimposes one meaning of negative space onto an abyssally different one: "I could speculate: She opened a space for a viewer to impose herself. But, more, Akerman's determination not to be present on-screen signaled her wish to be absent from it forever."[32] The downside of writing alongside and being alongside is absence, loss. This is palpable in Tillman's tribute to Susan Hiller, and in her piece addressed to the art of Jim Hodges. Narrating the relationship between Hodges's work and her own story "Absence Makes the Heart," she writes:

> My story was culled from that vulnerable and empty place, which demands language to speak for humankind's passions during its cruelest drama.
>
> Maybe terrible loss anticipates, invokes, exceeds, but finally needs beauty. And I felt: Jim's work represents that collision of loss and beauty. Many of his images have figurative and actual holes, irrecoverable gaps in which he refers to absences and frailties, represents sensitivity and surprise.[33]

Tillman quotes this line from Samuel Beckett in her piece on Hodges: "All art is the same: an attempt to fill an empty space." But to fill that space completely leaves no room for meaning or experience or the distances and differences that signify. If negative space is a void, it may also be room, a room, a space in which many things might happen (no guarantees). "In art, film, writing, what is left out is as significant as what's there, because, for one thing, leaving out encourages imaginative readings. Then, there is room also for the unconscious to be activated, not just the artist's who makes the object but also and most especially the viewers'." Viewers "will see it and give it meaning, if they pay attention."[34]

Notes

1 Lynne Tillman, "Drawing from a Translation Artist." All cited texts by Lynne Tillman appear in this volume unless otherwise noted.

2 Stein, quoted in Tillman, "Cindy Sherman: Character of Characters."

3 Stein, quoted in Tillman, "Homage to Homage."

4 Tillman, "Early Years of the New Museum: An Intellectual Reminiscence or Pieces from a Consciousness."

5 Tillman, "Drawing from a Translation Artist."

6 Laurie Anderson, quoted in Craig Owens, "The Allegorical Impulse: Toward a Theory of Postmodernism, Part 2," *October* 13 (1980), p. 58.

7 Craig Owens, "The Allegorical Impulse: Toward a Theory of Postmodernism, Part 1," *October* 12 (1980), pp. 68, 69.

8 Tillman, "The Horse's Eye."

9 Owens, "The Allegorical Impulse, Part 1," p. 69; "The Allegorical Impulse, Part 2," p. 80.

10 Tillman, "Imagined Places."

11 This is a copied-and-pasted list I used to organize my notes on Tillman's criticism: (1) History, historicity, (2) the uncanny/psychoanalysis in general, (3) movement, mobility, "consciousness in process," importance of avoiding stasis and sclerosis, (4) gender/feminism/dialogue with feminism, (5) mirrors/specularity, photography, projection, (6) critique of realism, critique of authenticity and originality, critique of the possibility of unmediated expression, (7) negation/negative space/dialogue with modernism, (8) affect, eros and Thanatos, but also anhedonia, the mid and the meh, the neglected middle registers of experience. I was not so deluded as to think this introduction could cover all this ground, but I thought I might cover a lot more of it.

12 Ross McElwain, "Writing 'Alongside'—Not 'About'—Art: A Conversation with Lynne Tillman," *Los Angeles Review of Books* (May 1, 2019), accessed online.

13 Tillman, "Simply Profound."

14 Tillman, "The Double," lecture at the symposium *The Double: Identity and Difference in Modern and Contemporary Art*, National Gallery of Art, Washington, DC, October 22, 2022 (unpublished).

15 Tillman, "Stories Tell Stories."

16 McElwain, "Writing 'Alongside'—Not 'About'—Art."

17 Tillman, "Simply Profound."

18 Tillman, "The Double."

19 Tillman, "Simply Profound."

20 Tillman, "The Double."

21 Tillman's Madame Realism stories are well-known examples of fictocriticism. In a way they form a self-contained cycle, such that it seemed a question of including all of them in *Paying Attention* or none of them. They are not represented here. Those written before 2016 are collected in *The Complete Madame Realism and Other Stories* (Los Angeles: Semiotext[e], 2016).

22 Tillman, "Simply Profound."

23 Tillman, "Cut Up Life."

24 Tillman, "An Imagined Peace."

25 Tillman, "Past Shock."

26 Tillman, "Drawing from a Translation Artist."

27 To my ear "occasional pieces" has an ectoplasmic effervescence, ghosts in a gazebo whispering of summers past. It's a linguistic artifact of a time before the hollowing-out of media and publishing by hypercapitalist consolidation and authoritarian design (to the dubious extent those two things can be differentiated). I'm not viewing the bygone days of media and publishing through rose-colored glasses, just observing that there used to be more occasional pieces. And it feels like there used to be more occasions. Reality itself feels somewhat denuded by austerity. From that core association, "occasional pieces" amplifies itself to reverberate for me on the scale of a world in ruins. I speak of whatever world existed before we entered Gramsci's oft-invoked interregnum, however you want to periodize it. There was much about that world that was already ruined when it was built (to roughly paraphrase Robert Smithson, a major influence on Owens's theory of allegory). There was much about that world that deserved to be consigned to history's dustbin, though, alas, it often seems as if the things that should have been thrown out persist most hardily. I'm not mourning the past sentimentally, and Tillman certainly doesn't. But I do mourn aspects of it, and "occasional pieces" to me speaks to that sense of loss. This seems like an appropriate place to say: I realize the absence of any discussion of the current state of the world might seem more than a mere insufficiency. Frankly, I feel too overwhelmed. I will just say that the texts in *Paying Attention* model different approaches to something I've been unable to do in this introduction: situating compositions in their time, when that time feels cataclysmic.

28 Tillman, "Real Life and Living Memory."

29 Tillman, "On Influence."

30 Tillman, "Correspondences."

31 Tillman, "On Influence."

32 Tillman, "Screen Presence."

33 Tillman, "Absence Makes Art."

34 Tillman, "Simply Profound."

Paying Attention

What Makes a Celebration?

A pack of wolves gathers to celebrate the birth of a pup. They look up at the sky, eagerness in their eyes, and howl in unison. All of them welcome births with joy, and must have from their beginning, I think; and wonder what the first humans celebrated. Newly standing up, likely some covering on their naked, hairy bodies—did they celebrate their difference from other animals? Probably not. At the birth of a tiny, bloody one emerging from another's body, did they howl like wolves? To celebrate is a behavior that the human species took time to develop, though cave drawings might be a version of celebration.

From long-ago, unpictured days, humans have found ways for communally expressing grief and showing joy. Affection, attachment, love, fellowship, feelings toward others must have been transmitted with grimaces, hugs, shrugs, headshakes, gestures for all occasions. Then, events must have sprung up: a huge bonfire at harvest time, a totem pole to honor gods, sun worship at dawn, a merging of clans in something like marriage. Feelings for and about oneself and others—pride, shame, rage, jealousy—ancient texts attest to them.

There are the spontaneous or the planned or the obligatory celebrations, analogous to Claude Lévi-Strauss's idea of "the raw and the cooked," the dialectics of culture, "categorical opposites drawn from everyday experience." Of the cooked: US civil society has Thanksgiving, an ignorant and disturbing holiday, mostly enjoyed or suffered for overeating, decidedly not enjoyed by First Americans whose ancestors were massacred by white Europeans. Halloween, nonobligatory and semi-raw, is fun, most especially for children, when disguise offers them a chance to be superheroes and scare adults, while adults can regress to childhood. About which the comic Richard Lewis quipped: "At Halloween, my family dresses up as obstacles."

Few people celebrate failure, but the British commemorate a failed revolution with Guy Fawkes Day. On the street, children ask, "Penny for the guy?" A resilient irony rescues the British from maudlin sentimentality, except at Christmas.

Weddings, Christmas, birthdays, the planning for these occasions sows happiness, worry, and agitation; then come their festive, or not, results. Ask a friend: "Did you get gifts for Christmas when you were a child?" or, "Did you have birthday parties?" The response will be immediate and specific, details often vivid and surprising, or so vague and bland as to indicate trauma. Holidays can be the most ambivalent days of your life.

"I'm going home for Christmas" might begin a stand-up comic's routine, while many movies depend on family fractiousness for plot points. Getting home may be difficult, flights bumped, but being at home can be bumpier. Philip-Lorca diCorcia's 1978 scene of an overdecorated living room in Hartford is Christmas gone wild. Without people, it's an expectant, perfectly idealized Christmas. The reality of adults arguing near the tree imposes itself on the picture, while a lament can be heard: Why did we ever come home?

Sociologists claim celebrations foster social cohesion by honoring key community figures, denoting public accomplishments and private ones, such as success in love with marriage ceremonies and medals awarded for daring and courage in war. Celebrations proclaim significant moments and events, and also shape the appropriate responses—a gold watch for retirement after fifty years. They teach people when to applaud or weep, and sometimes people do both at weddings and funerals.

President Barack Obama's 2008 election night was tense, exciting, dramatic. A Black man had been nominated for president in a nation whose written constitution recognized slavery, embedding racism within it. Black communities were buoyed by possibility, and enthusiasm for Obama crossed races. Many non-Black Americans didn't feel it, not at all. And his win most likely aroused their already active and latent racism.

In Chicago, where Obama lived and was a US senator, Michal Czerwonka documented the ecstasy at his 2008 victory gathering in Grant Park. Two American flags and Obama's image on a placard wave behind a crowd of beaming supporters; in the foreground, an exultant young Black man has raised his fist in the Black Power salute. The gesture also foregrounds the civil rights movement, without which a Barack Obama wouldn't have had a chance in hell. He had run on hope, and hope animates Czerwonka's photograph. Now, it is an image of unfulfilled wishes.

Covid lockdown, masking, and being housebound, everyone felt like a prisoner. In the summer of 2020, about two months into the pandemic, whatever fears these Brooklyn neighbors felt, they ran into the streets, masks on, to escape their boredom, for a block party known as St. James Joy. "There was dancing in the street," to quote Martha and the Vandellas. Pictures of the event burst with human energy and the beauty of spontaneity, exemplifying what well-planned events can't ever do—let the moment happen, when sudden pleasure roars, when nothing else matters, it's just full-on partying.

Now, with vaccinations, apartment doors have opened. People meet and greet. There's still need for caution—the threat of new variants—but there's reason enough to celebrate the advent of almost ordinary life. The first season of *Succession* launched with an episode titled "Celebration." The eightieth-birthday luncheon for the patriarch, Logan Roy (*le roi*), was attended by his entire nuclear, or unclear, family. No one enjoyed it, especially the birthday boy. The ironic festivity united the series' disunited characters, inviting *Succession*'s viewers into the family's vicious infighting. Some birthdays are like that.

Malick Sidibé's photograph of a jolly family gathering in *Soirée familiale* (1966) sings with ebullience. The family's liveliness overflows the frame. Most of the group looks at his camera, but not everyone. Those not looking, otherwise engaged, register individuals as related to each other and unique from each other. Sidibé didn't insist, Look at me, the camera, smile, the standard gimmicks to organize group portraits. He let this family act as it wanted. Maybe they're being themselves, though one can't know. The family composition thrives with personality, a portrait of resemblances and differences.

In Frances F. Denny's *Cake, Cambridge, MA* (2013), a round, high, heavily frosted white cake is metonymic, for either a birthday or a small wedding. Cake might even be a tiny monument to the uniformity of celebrations. Sitting on a black table that disappears under it, Denny's cake is spotlighted like a movie star. But half of it is gone, likely eaten, so the cake is undone. The assumption is that it was once whole, which comments on the ways viewers narrate pictures, imagining a before them and an after them. The exposed interior might be, curiously, about interiority, what lies beneath or inside a luscious surface. Nobody's waiting for a slice, and Denny's solitary half cake says, It's over. On reflection, the party might not have been as sweet as the cake, now just a leftover.

Photography's genesis must have been influenced by people's fascination with themselves; knowing death awaits is a perpetual insult to their narcissism. Might a picture subvert eternal disappearance? "Life is a movie. Death is a photograph," Susan Sontag famously wrote. She saw a still object, necessarily of the past, the subject absent—death. But a photograph is seen by the living who enliven it with meaning. It is, instead, a fitting subject for a photograph, this stasis.

The dead are also celebrated, honored, and photographers' concepts range as widely as burial customs. Peter Hujar's elegant style in *Palermo Catacombs #11* (1963) articulates the texture and architecture of the tombs. In the sixteenth century, the Capuchin friars used these crypts when their cemetery became full. Initially, they dried the corpses, dousing them with vinegar to preserve them.

Hujar's photograph is shocking, the way death is. Hujar wants to see death, get close, focus on details. God is in the details, and maybe death is also. Their robes drape around their mummified bodies. Those faces, their icy expressions, what do they tell us? Standing up, the dead might just walk away. The liminal passage between life and death—she passed, he passed—is heightened by Hujar's inclusion of a staircase, signifying ascension and descent. The friars will walk up and down it, until, one day, they can't.

Far from Palermo, the death of a drummer, James Black, merits a traditional New Orleans jazz funeral in 1988. It's a joyous celebration. Chandra McCormick places the stark white, flower-bedecked casket, raised high by pallbearers, in the center, motoring the dynamic procession and the photograph. Some of the Black and non-Black mourners have raised their fists. So many people surround it, fan out from it, walking in front of and behind it, the coffin might be floating in the air, even though three pronounced arms do the work. James Black's life of making music has ended, and the tunes he played and loved will see him out. Exultant faces proclaim their fervent belief: James is going to a better place.

In the here and now, celebrating feels right. The vaccine—and the promise of helpful new pills—is freeing people to roam the streets, meet in bars, go shopping, see friends, dine out—even the usual seems a celebration. Nothing feels ordinary, though, while it is also very ordinary, except for the threat of the vexing unvaxxed and new variants. Still, it's a dangerous world where much more than viruses are killing people. Many would still prefer to stay home.

Etel Adnan: Glorious

A poem's jagged line breaks might suggest a cubist painting, while drawings are likely the first form of writing. The connections between art and poetry are essential and consequential in the work of Etel Adnan, painter, poet, novelist, and playwright. Her themes and passions—color, history, love, landscape, the rigors of time and vitality of experience—permeate all of her work.

Born in Beirut in 1925, Adnan studied philosophy in Paris, then moved to California, where, for many years, she taught philosophy. All the while, she was writing and making paintings, becoming well known especially for her writing, with books such as *Of Cities & Women (Letters to Fawwaz)* (1993); *Paris, When It's Naked* (1993); and *In/somnia* (2002)—all published by Post-Apollo, the sculptor and her life partner Simone Fattal's press.

Adnan's imaginative language, her ear, her intense engagement in home and history, and innovative textual play mark her poetics. She is a profound and compassionate thinker, who is prized among poets. These lines are from "Celestial City" (2009):

> The sun's setting over a setting empire
> drowns our voice
> along its course
> there's growing hunger over the
> land

By pairing the two kinds of settings—sun's and empire's—Adnan fuses the "course" of history with the sun's. Culture and nature both produce "hunger over the land," and people exist in the interstices of this dyad.

Concision of images and ideas is prominent in Adnan's literary oeuvre, just as it is in her visual work. Her paintings—landscapes of vivid, horizontal bars of colors; a glowing sun, full and round, perched on a horizon line—might appear unlike her cerebral poems, but her paintings' stark simplicity is equivalent to her writing's economy.

Differences respond to their mediums: Words do what a painting can't, a painting does what words can't. Adnan has written: "Materials, for artists, are things that mediate thought . . . condition one's aesthetic choices . . . they become in a way a *co-author* of one's work." The medium, in a wry sense, creates the message, or "mediate[s] thought," as Adnan puts it. She calls a leporello a "folding book."

In Adnan's exhibition *Seasons*, at Galerie Lelong, a leporello stands in a vitrine. Stretched open, its flattened-out page-like divisions allow it to be read like a text. A leporello, unfolded, creates horizontal movement: A viewer starts here, ends there, and time passes. Like a book, the artwork can be reread, or read from the middle to the start or to the finish.

Her 2020 paintings, the two series *Les quatre saisons* and *Planètes*, are verticals, and play differently with the eye. Tension builds from top to bottom, bottom to top. In each of the four season paintings, a band of white anchors the canvas. Black streaks arise upward from the base into dabs and strokes of seasonal color. That seeming emptiness, that band of white at the base, lifts the seasons, metaphorically, off the ground, as if cut off from the natural order.

Each *Planète* has a central, round shape; Adnan's beloved sun is here, though none is yellow or golden. Each painting's sun is different: deep orange, aqua, gray, or dark green, all set against different backgrounds: aqua on lime green, the other three on various shades of orange. Three of the suns nearly touch the sides of the painting, while the gray one is not full, a sun setting at the top of the frame. An amorphous shape lies beneath three of the suns. In one, a bicycle sits beneath it, as an inscrutable sign, although a bike suggests childhood, movement, and play.

Adnan's boldly colored tapestries dominate the exhibition. From childhood, Adnan treasured Persian carpets, and, since the 1960s, has made tapestries from her designs. None completely satisfied her. Now living in France, she has had her tapestries manufactured by the famous Aubusson atelier Pinton. Pinton has been creating tapestries since 1867, and is associated with Aubusson tapestries, which date to the fifteenth century.

Her tapestries are woven modernist paintings, and unique in her oeuvre. They are large, about six feet by seven feet, when much of her work is smaller. From afar, they appear to be wall paintings; up close, they are textured wall hangings, weavings of thick wool. Most amazing, each strand seems to have been hand-colored, and, like an oil painting, there are underpaintings—earlier color decisions or strokes peer through the surface.

Metaphorically, weaving draws loose ends together. It is a complicated form, composed of many pieces that are meant to unite. It creates a pattern of inseparable parts. Weaving is a way to consider entanglement, say, of love and hate, of small events and great ones, of an individual in culture.

Adnan titled her essay about how she came to do this work "Life Is a Weaving" (2016). "A weaving" is one of a multitude, not "the" only one. There are many ways and approaches, many versions of society and culture, many kinds of poetry and art. Life wears a coat of many colors. A Bible story could be a line in a poem, and an ancient tradition can make things new or renew them.

I want to applaud Etel Adnan. And contemplating her art, her writing, I don't want to cater to truisms about wisdom and age. It is not age that brought her wisdom. She thinks deeply and sees what others don't or haven't. Adnan uses her experience, everything she has learned and learns, and tells us about it. She is a loving explorer of life, and the world is more wonderful with her art in it.

Dana Schutz's *Boatman*

A writer can become frustrated crafting so-called art writing or the more formal term, "art criticism." Characterizing a painting—describing and responding to it, understanding and interpreting it—is vexatious. The writer is hoping to present the work adequately and articulately, but one medium addresses another, each with its own specific forms of representation. Words change, sometimes dramatically, in different contexts; on a page or canvas or wall, there are also images. Words are tricky beasts.

A painting beckons the image, the visual; it might be a landscape, an abstraction, it might be conceptual and shaping in the mind, it might be one color or many, it might be . . . It is an object that words can only approximate, but for which words may never be commensurate.

> What can be shown, cannot be said.
> —Ludwig Wittgenstein, *Tractatus Logico-Philosophicus*

Wittgenstein's dictum makes a writer's job even more paradoxical. But what does "shown" mean in this context? Treating a visual work as something that shows something suggests a consensus about what it is that is shown. In art, especially in modern and contemporary work, what is shown needs to be "said," discussed, debated, or brought into discourse. Still, what Wittgenstein means, or suggests, must be considered and reflected upon. He also stated:

> Don't explain, only describe.

Ascribing meaning to an artwork is a dubious act; the better the art, the more possibilities charge the piece. A writer can explain the materials used, say, and provide a fact-based, even historical commentary about an artwork. But to explain art indicates comprehension of why it does what it does and how it does it. Explanation relies on a critic's decision about its ontology. To explain it is different from a description of what its elements are.

Interpretation is a problem also, indebted to a critic's subjectivity, even their word choices, and can be explanatory also. An interpretation, though, has the value of an announced subjective point of view or critical position. A close reading of *Boatman* (2018) might establish a relative "objectivity," though pure description does not exist. Words are freighted; a color might be red to one, dark red to another. Still, impure descriptions are valid attempts to present the work without deciding its meanings. Wittgenstein's dictum "Don't explain, only describe" comes to help me.

I

Boatman is a complex of elements: myth or narrative, colors, shapes, figuration, abstraction, brushwork and all its formal concerns.

A close reading, as closely as I can read or register its visual elements, follows.

There is a disproportionately large head at the top, with one open eye, one closed or vacant. The nose is straight and long, painted in pink-orange, ending on top of a mouth of similar colors, though darker; the mouth is turned slightly down, might be a frown, or maybe not. One of the head's ears, deep pink or salmon-colored, sticks out from it, thrusting into the background—a turquoise-green sky with three broad streaks of white, to indicate, one assumes clouds. Red cheeks, like big dots of rouge, and short brown, slightly wavy hair that lies flat on the head fill out the rest of the face. The face is painted with heavy strokes or splotches of green, darker pink, and some black (especially the thick eyebrows, done with impasto).

The figure is likely a man, or male.

A green sky and lighter green lake or body of water are separated by a blackish-green horizon line that has large, dark petal-like shapes on either side of the line. It is and is not a horizon; rather it is indicative of a separation between sky and water. In the body of mostly green water, there are also white shapes; in this context, they might be waves or turbulence caused by the oars of the boat.

The figure wears a black vest, and both arms appear clothed in a white, long-sleeved shirt. The body with which this large head merges is a rowboat, or a human body is part of, or half of, a rowboat. The boat is foreshortened, and the man, not human at all, almost dwarfs the rowboat, which is painted in off-white with subtle stripes and yellow streaks.

There are pink-red hands, or what appear to be, or they are gloved or only mitts, and meant to hold two shovel-like oars that would row the boat. The oars are reflected on the water but they may not be in it, only above it, or suspended in motion.

On the large man's boat/body another significant element: the figure of a skinny, tiny man/boy sitting on what seems to be an endless lap. The lap area is painted black, very dark blue, and gray, with a patch of green above the putative lap, creating an illusion of depth or endlessness. The lap also serves as the boat's bottom, which is, in effect, endless or nonexistent. One of the dominant figure's fat, red hands, or gloves, the larger of the two on the right of the painting, appears to be touching or holding up the little man. The little man wears a bright yellow jacket and tie, with streaks of a darker color on the jacket. He wears red trousers. His face is gray, his eyes dark and beady, staring out of the painting toward an unseen force or the viewer. His face is uneven, one side on the right of the painting with a very high and delineated cheekbone. It lifts one side of the face, while the other side is without detail and painted a lighter gray. The little man's head is juxtaposed to the large head; it is just under the large chin. The little man's left arm and hand, palm up, are at a diagonal, gesturing toward or directing the eye toward the boatman. The little man's hand appears to be pointing to it. The painting with its boat's oars reflected in the green water is, in a sense, a still life. There seems to be no movement, the image is stationary, fixed in its merged green sky background and green water foreground. Overall, the painting seems flat, just a surface: Every element except the dark lap refuses depth. The proportion of the head is outsized, and, if the rest of the body weren't a boat, it would not fit on the canvas. The viewer's eye likely goes to it first, then to the little man, maybe. Because the colors of the sea and sky are bright, shimmering, and they encompass the head and the boat, the eye might find itself there next. The little man might come second; his presence is somewhat stealthy. He is so small relative to the head and boat. Looking at him, when I found him, was a surprise, an unexpected element, and so different, in shape and colors, from the presence that enfolds him.

II

The provenance of art isn't only in its ownership, but also its relation to earlier art and the other arts. Upon seeing *Boatman*, what struck me—my first association to it—was a resemblance to Max Beckmann's *Departure*, specifically the central panel of the triptych; not only because of the subject, figures in a boat, but also because Beckmann's style intimates itself in *Boatman*—the starkness of the image and the boldness of the lines and forms, the seemingly mythic figures.

Beckmann painted the triptych in 1932 and finished it between 1933 and 1935. It was his first one. *Departure* has been interpreted and reinterpreted many times, because of its startling figures, composition in three parts, and its relationship to myth.

A patron of his, Lilly von Schnitzler, reacted to a review of the work that called its center panel "optimistic." She wanted to buy the panel separately. She and the artist had a conversation that was recorded, from which the following is an excerpt:

> Beckmann: You want to buy the centerpiece, Lilly, but you can't have that alone, the three belong together—the center is the end of the tragedy, but the meaning can only be understood by the three parts together. . . . The King and Queen, Man and Woman, are taken to another shore by a boats man whom they do not know, he wears a mask.

> It is the mysterious figure taking us to a mysterious land.
> Schnitzler: Does it mean Acheron, is the water the river Styx, does it mean that they are dead, being taken to Hades—or to some kind of resurrection?
> Beckmann: Do we know?—The King and the Queen have freed themselves, freed themselves of the tortures of life—they have overcome them. The Queen carries the greatest treasure—Freedom—as her child in her lap. Freedom is the one thing that matters—it is the departure, the new star.[1]

If viewers were guided by Beckmann's explication of the central panel, of what the figures symbolize, *Departure*'s affect would be severely limited, and its significance blunted. The power of a work is in its reception, not in its intention; the power resides in its possibilities for interpretation, association, projection, and identification. I don't want Dana Schutz to tell me what her intention for *Boatman* was, who the figures are. Now Wittgenstein's idea—what can be shown, can't be said—is elucidated: Schutz has shown me something, and I don't know what, but words can't define it.

III

The boatman's head, I wrote earlier, was male, but the head is a grotesquerie. It reminds me of a Frankenstein, something monstrous. A face without affect gives me pause. The boatman is not human or part boat. His function—rowing the boat to the other side—brings me instantly to the figure of Charon, who brought dead souls that had received the rites of burial to their burial ground. In Greek mythology, Charon ferries the deceased across the River Styx and Acheron.

A powerful figure, this mythical presence is of ancient origin. But in Schutz's work, the head, painted in impasto, is comical and distorted, one big eye looking curiously naive, definitely wide open. And my association to that mythical creature is belied by this depiction. Still, I can't shake that old myth. It's called *Boatman*, so a man, then. The little gray-faced boy/man might be a child. In that case, the boatman might be his father, which seems unlikely but possible. I wouldn't insist on it. More improbably the boatman is his mother. If I carry on with that interpretation, this might be a clownish male Madonna, nothing sacred here, with the baby Jesus. They're heading toward death, hell, the next world. But it's a stationary image. They are stuck in the water, in the world; they are going nowhere. And it is a thing, that head. It is a thing of the imagination. It is a gothic character that resembles Charon, but instead it is a lifeless, mirthless robot. It is a mechanical thing. In his gesture to the thing, that head, the little figure is suggesting something . . . His dead black eyes are directed at the spectator, he looks out of the painting, a device often used in historical paintings. Whenever a figure points, a gesture perhaps as old as painting, it might suggest its consciousness or knowledge of the situation. Masaccio's *The Tribute Money* (1425) comes to mind. In the Greek myth, the boatman, Charon, is paid with the coin that has been placed on the corpse's mouth. The little man might be a rigid corpse, and the gesture meaningless. In Masaccio's *The Tribute Money*,

Christ and his followers do not have the money demanded by the tax man. I think, They are not going anywhere. They can't leave, they can't escape. Studying the big, monstrous face again, composed of dribs and drabs, smatters of thick paint, and many colors, I think it resembles a painter's palette. Now, the painting changes: The boatman represents the artist, carrying viewers, critics, anyone, into deeper waters, another side or position. The little figure is styled in straight lines, in his yellow jacket and tie and fashionable skinny red trousers. So different from the boatman, he is anomalous. New art, he refuses this relationship to the boatman and to myths about art.

New work often appears ungainly. The new really should, because it disrupts traditions. The eye has been acclimated or accustomed to seeing one way, then another way takes its place. To some the boatman's ferocity will be ugly—dark and dirty colors, the big face, glowering maybe, and certainly distorted. What are we facing, rhetorically, in this face.

IV

The term "narrative" often arises when discussing painting, abstract and figurative, especially in the last forty years. In the simplest sense, to narrate means to tell. Hyperbolically, in some way all work tells. The historical avant-garde had no use for that generous or too easy definition, and rebuked narrative. After World War II, it went out of style. The nouveau roman came into favor in avant-garde literary circles, and abstract expressionism became dominant in painting, especially in the US. But all forms and traditions were suspect. Jean-François Lyotard's rejection of "grand narratives" in *The Postmodern*

Condition was powerful and resonant. "Grand narratives" had shaped a glorious story for Western civilization, to itself. But in World War II, and with the revelation of Hitler's Final Solution, Enlightenment values and humanism proved to be illusory, or delusions of grandeur. Now what story could this humanity tell itself. The condemnation of storytelling has eased up since the 1970s and 1980s, though some of its critics will still argue that narratives conserve tradition and subject readers and viewers to unfortunate and untrue closures. Fortunately, from this writer's point of view, the limited idea of narrative's many possibilities has been superseded by writing and art that trounce those proscriptions.

Early paintings and frescoes told stories for the Church and represented icons of the faith. During the Reformation and the Renaissance, different stories came to be depicted, and they multiplied. Civic-minded history paintings, still lifes, horses, landscapes, portraits, common and daily-life scenes—all came to be painted.

The story of Velázquez's *Las Meninas* (1656) remains a brilliant mystery. Its complex figuration of the court and the composition's formal attributes were daring and surprising. *Las Meninas* appeared toward the end of Velázquez's life, and its radicality, its difference from the rest of his oeuvre, is a piece of its mystery. Where did that majestic work come from, how was it generated, how did it happen . . .

Boatman seems to be telling a story or stories. Two of Schutz's contemporaries, Carroll Dunham and Nicole Eisenman, also make work that, using figures and abstraction, seems to tell stories, but none of the stories is easily read or interpreted. With no one absolute tale, the works arouse aesthetic, literary, sociological, and psychological responses. In all of their work, Lyotard's grand narratives are eschewed or, if they appear, such as in Schutz's use of the image of the boatman, which may be alluding to Charon and the Green myth, they are debunked, parodied, or critiqued.

V

I have described *Boatman*, adequately I hope, but not without subjectivity. I can't say what its narrative is. I feel it tells me something, and something about it, maybe its uncanniness, captures my eye, my mind, my consciousness, and my unconsciousness. The peculiar little figure inside the larger one, the boatman, seemingly human and also a boat: Is it cradling the little figure? If so, what meaning can I extract from that? The boat itself might be a cradle. Many possibilities exist. Schutz's painting holds me. I am fascinated by it. I don't understand how these figures, colors, and shapes purchase or perform that fascination. Still, each time I look at it, I am caught in a mystery of human relations, myths, present and past cultures, and feel the power of wonder.

Note

1 The quoted text is from Charles S. Kessler, *Max Beckmann's Triptychs* (Cambridge, MA: Belknap Press, 1970).

Alex Harsley: The President Resigns

Alex Harsley's photographs hang in the window of the 4th Street Photo Gallery. Harsley opened it in 1973, two years after he had formed the nonprofit organization Minority Photographers Inc. Harsley has been photographing since he was eleven, after moving to New York from South Carolina.

For years I have been stopping in front of his store window, standing and gazing at the panoply of old and new New York scenes. Inside, he was the artist who sat at the back of the small gallery, intently working at his computer, his photographs, salon style, on the walls around him.

One afternoon, studying the photographs, I peered inside the gallery, when Harsley suddenly looked up and beckoned me inside. Now I was up close to his decades of NYC scenes, uptown, midtown, downtown—storefronts, nightclubs, musicians, parks, signs, the city during a blizzard, protest marches, ambiguous groups, strangers and friends, people looking at people or just going about their business. Harsley shot New York's streets empty, crowded, its people amused, contemplative, sleepy, pissed off, joyous. The city in all kinds of emotional and actual weather.

Harsley's adventurousness and curiosity inflect his striking images. A special intimacy animates his work: He's shooting what he feels. I feel that, for instance, in his portraits of America's brilliant musicians, Thelonious Monk, John Coltrane, Miles Davis. For the bass player in my life, David Hofstra, I bought a print of Charlie Mingus standing near his car, his bass in its cloth case, its body resting against his body. It's a disclosure or discovery of a mostly unphotographed, but nightly event—a musician getting to or leaving a gig. Picturing the extraordinary Mingus, in transition, makes this great musician appear oh-so-human.

Alex Harsley's project *The President Resigns* (1974) came about the morning after Nixon resigned on August 8, 1974. He decided to shoot all around the city, curious to see the public's reactions. He was able, uniquely, to show New Yorkers, literally and figuratively, in the very act of absorbing the news. These pictures represent that fateful event in a way I've never seen before—witnesses to how the political becomes personal.

Past Shock

Any contemporary story about the past, or even the present, acts like a fairy tale, telling us about ourselves through imagined, extreme analogies. Historical reconstructions reveal us looking back in a hall of mirrors. *I Shot Andy Warhol* (1996), directed by Mary Harron, is complicated in its depiction of a recent history, complex in its aims and ambitions, and in its filmic conception and production. It's complicated to watch, especially if you lived through the period it represents or wandered through some of its scenes.

Using or producing Warhol history—any history—is a tender, touchy project, troublingly familiar. In 1994, I spent some intense months interviewing Factory people and writing the text for *The Velvet Years: Warhol's Factory 1965–67* (1995) to accompany Stephen Shore's photographs. A weight called responsibility hangs over anyone who traffics in history. If one accepts the role of the critic, one should first be self-critical. If one uses history, one should historicize oneself. These are daunting, half-possible tasks—pulling yourself out of your thoughts while in them.

Since a return to the past is impossible, a fantasy, what does it mean to be faithful to history? Can we only recognize and record the past as a problem for the present in the present? *I Shot Andy Warhol* is seen through a prism of positions, when, (a) one already has ideas about Warhol, (b) has little information about him or the period, and/or (c) did or didn't live through it. A dramatic, vivid, uneasy movie, it leaves traces, unsettles, produces shocks of recognition and misrecognition.

After a packed press screening, I shared a cab with three friends. One said: "Andy seemed pretty nice." One responded: "I thought he was disgusting." One just listened. The friend who thought Warhol seemed nice in the movie likes Warhol's work; the friend who thought he was disgusting hates it, him. Like most things, the movie is likely to confirm some already received ideas and opinions, while threatening others.

In Michel Auder's video *Chelsea Girls with Andy Warhol* (1971–1976), Viva (Susan Hoffmann) and Brigid Polk (Brigid Berlin) are filmed in the Chelsea Hotel, talking to Warhol over the phone. Warhol doesn't know he's being audiotaped. Later, Warhol's on camera with Viva and others. Auder's video is a knowing slice of behind-the-scenes life, a surreptitious glance at Warhol. Everyone seems simultaneously devious, smug, and naive, which might be the effect of video vérité. But is there ever a "real" Warhol lurking, an Andy without preconceptions? What's vérité anyway?

Harron's Warhol is the enigmatic, charismatic leader. In a memorably charged, discomforting scene, he's seated on a couch at a party, surrounded by four women vying for his attention, his anything. He might be pleased, embarrassed, or annoyed; just a happy voyeur or narcissist. Max Weber never said charismatic leaders were nice. Deeply curious creatures, they're concocted of unfailing and dubious charm; they're disturbing figures, who are often disturbed. Jared Harris's Warhol is a blend of ambiguities—passivity, playfulness, cruelty, sweetness, indifference. Lili Taylor plays Valerie Solanas as intelligent, edgy, wry; like the others, wants to get close to him, wants something from him—in her case to produce her play.

At the Factory and in Harron's movie, Warhol's the center. He's the half-empty or half-full glass, matter for projection. Watching *I Shot Andy Warhol* is also made from projections; on the cinematic couch, each of us is a case of identification or disidentification. Once Warhol enters the movie, the narrative, like Solanas, is swayed and changed by his presence. This may be my projection. And my reading of the title *I Shot Andy Warhol* may also be. The title generates questions about the movie's attitude toward Warhol that may have been unintended and unthought; it carries the all-too-prevalent ambivalence and cynicism to Warhol and to his near death.

Based on a script written by Harron and Daniel Minahan, the movie reconstructs and plunders history, but not as a documentary. History conforms to the rules of narrative fiction. It's easy to jerk reflexively to a re-creation, to its not being what it was, really. I kept thinking: I don't know what it was. Harron's decision to portray Solanas in a fiction and as a fictional character signifies her understanding of the problems of "finding Solanas." The real Warhol, the real Solanas are the wrong things to look for. So why do we look anyway?

Recently there were three exhibitions in New York, all taking historical stock: at Exit Art/the First World, *Counterculture: Alternative Information from the Underground Press to the Internet*, curated by Brian Wallis; at the Drawing Center, *Cultural Economies: Histories from the Alternative Arts Movement, NYC*, curated by Julie Ault of Group Material; and at Artists Space, *Mr. Dead & Mrs. Free: The History of Squat Theater*, curated by Eva Buchmuller, Claudia Gould, and Anna Koós. Covering work from the 1960s to the mid-1980s, the shows are evidence of a determined, backward glance, of the desire to collect and study cultures that have, or seem to have, disappeared. Is it coherence we're searching for, attested to by past strategies or movements, not necessarily recognized at the time as movements or as coherent? What are the uses of history? To turn pieces into wholes, most especially when a present seems splintered?

In *I Shot Andy Warhol* the spectacle of the 1960s runs across the screen, scenes seen through the lens of the 1990s, and it's a wild, scary juxtaposition. Solanas—writer, lesbian, feminist who turned tricks, a paranoid who was ill before her introduction to Warhol—becomes the entryway into that difficult, turbulent time, while the Factory is a microcosm of a society and culture in revolt and convulsion.

The chaos of change in the 1960s, its sexual openness and its outlaws, finds a place in the movie's mise-en-scènes. Factory party, the backroom at Max's, the New York diner scenes. The reenactments reminded me of late, strange nights and strange places. The tableaux seemed superimposed onto the past, out of alignment, but they jarred memory from sleep and were close enough, disconcerting. They felt like archaeological sites: I was at a cinematic excavation. A weird sense of distended space and time, of continuities and discontinuities, connections and disconnections, multiplied the movie's complexity.

We're history's orphans, shaped by it, abandoned by it, searching ironically for our birth parents. Through our representation of what's no longer available, we discover our hunger for what's missed, lost. Idealized or demonized, there are our reflections, our images, on flat surfaces. Valerie Solanas, representative of an anguished, vital time in American history, is a kind of access to the period, a sad way to Warhol and the fantasy and possibilities of a now glamorous lost moment. (Her *SCUM Manifesto*, an excoriating, anti-male tract, is definitely symptomatic of the time.) The elusive, brilliant Warhol encountered Valerie Solanas, an extremely disturbed, ambitious, thwarted, talented woman. Her failure to thrive in his, or any, environment turned their meeting into a tragic collision. In all its perplexing, telling, fraught overdeterminations, that crash is a product of history, made in and about America.

Reconsidering the Genius of Gertrude Stein

Approaching Gertrude Stein's writing critically is tricky. Because she strove to reshape literary conventions—syntax, language usage, narrative order, and the sense of making sense—any comment on her choices may already be rebuffed in her poetics and practice. Stein is a trickster. This may be why, as I read *Ida* and *Stanzas in Meditation*, both reissued in corrected, authoritative editions from Yale University Press, I remembered a Jonathan Richman lyric I'll paraphrase as "Pablo Picasso never got called a jackass."

Gertrude Stein is called a genius, and it's from that vantage her writing is read—or not read, since awe and reverence are regularly met by dismissal and ridicule. Curiously, not every "genius" is equally suffocated by the label. Readers know the extraordinary reputations of Shakespeare and Virginia Woolf, but some prefer *Richard III* to *Richard II*, or *Mrs. Dalloway* to *Orlando*. They feel at liberty to discriminate.

Fewer readers imagine they can create their own Stein; many feel she is beyond their capacity to understand. Maybe this is because she has been claimed as the sine qua non of the avant-garde. But she aligned herself with her time. Being part of the "contemporary composition" was central to her work, a point she made in her trenchant essay (originally a lecture) "Composition as Explanation": "The only thing that is different from one time to another is what is seen and what is seen depends upon how everybody is doing everything." Here, Stein wielded the novelty and surprise of her prose partly to explain how novelty and surprise surface from generation to generation, and theorized why the new in art and writing may first be thought ugly, then later beautiful or classic. In that same essay, she declared: "No one is ahead of his time." (Andy

Warhol, who like Stein is both adored and mocked, once said, "I'm very much a part of my times, of my culture, as much a part of it as rockets and television." There are other parallels between Warhol and Stein, including their renown as aphorists. Stein: "Rose is a rose is a rose is a rose." Warhol: "In the future everyone will be famous for fifteen minutes." But people *have* called Warhol a jackass, and everything else.)

"For Stein," Peter Nicholls writes in his important book *Modernisms: A Literary Guide*, "language is to be grasped not as a means of reference to a world of objects which can be dominated, but as a medium of consciousness." Stein's works of consciousness depend on a reader's consciousness, and unconscious, to engage them. Otherwise, her writing is flat, the rhythms and play of her words lost along with her biting wit and clarity.

Ida was published by Random House in 1941. The Yale reissue contains reviews from the day and versions from Stein's notebooks, showing the novel's development from its beginnings in 1937. The editor, Logan Esdale, has written an excellent introduction (and notes throughout) containing necessary biographical and textual information. One learns that fame was much on Stein's mind when she was writing *Ida*—her own fame and that of Wallis Simpson, the American divorcée who became the Duchess of Windsor. Stein's celebrity rested on *The Autobiography of Alice B. Toklas*, published in America in 1933. The book became very popular and gained Stein a wide readership. With the onset of fame, Stein questioned how her work would be received because of it.

Stein constructs a cubist portrait or skewed biography of Ida, who was born with a twin, Ida-Ida, to kind parents. "It was a nicc family but they did easily lose each other. . . . Her parents went off on a trip and never came back. That was the first funny thing that happened to Ida." Odd, sad, and happy events populate the novel's pages, while doppelgängers lurk everywhere: Ida becomes Winnie, because she's winning; characters like parents to Ida come and go, and men who may, or do, become her husbands appear, disappear, reappear. Ida herself leaves and returns, often going to another state (either a place or a frame of mind). A reader experiences the pull of freedom, and Ida's contradictory desires—wanting a home, needing to escape; wanting to be known and not. Her identity is in doubt and it's not.

With these radical changes, there's a bounty of tension and release. Words appear and reappear—like Ida's husbands—but in different syntactic roles, scrambling meaning and Ida too. There's psychological and logistical weight on Ida: Whom does she know; what does she know; which dog has died; where will she live, and with whom? Most urgently, who knows her and what does that knowing do?

"Ida sat on. She said to herself. If a great many people were here and they all said hello Ida, I would not stand up, they would all stand up. If everybody offered me everything I would not refuse anything because everything is mine without my asking for it or refusing it."

There isn't a better description of celebrity affect.

Release from textual and narrative tension comes, in part, through Stein's remarkable voice, as well as from internal and external rhymes, some so childlike one might be listening to a book read aloud. "Well what did Ida do. / Ida knew just who was who. / She did. She did know." And, later on the same page: "There are so many men. / What do you call them there. / There are so many men. / They did not all know Ida. / Now then." Ida frequently rests: "When anybody needed Ida Ida was resting. That was all right that is the way Ida was needed." Reading the word "rest" again and again creates a weird sensation. The story sort of stops, and a space opens up where you can disappear like Ida, or stop too. It *provides* a rest, as in music.

Ida wanders from its theses in its second half. Interrupted by allusions to and fragments of other texts Stein wrote before or during *Ida* (like "Superstitions"), the novel turns into a repository of fleeting images and ideas its protagonist might hold. Something feels missing and amiss, even as Ida muses on missing. "Everybody began to miss something and it was not a kiss, you bet your life it was not a kiss that anybody began to miss. And yet perhaps it was." I love the insertion of "You bet your life." I made an insertion of my own: As I read, the word "Ida" started to become a pronoun and a verb: I da won't, I da will, I da wanna.

Stanzas in Meditation fulfills Stein's great ambition. Published posthumously in 1956, it's an amazing work—a lively, imaginative, modernist epic, with Stein at her playful, philosophical, poetic best as she riffs on the literary and cultural gamut. Joan Retallack's rich introduction, "On Not Not Reading 'Stanzas in Meditation': Pressures and Pleasures of the Text," reckons creatively and helpfully with the problem I'll call "Who's Afraid of Gertrude Stein?" Retallack also presents an important textual discovery from the Stein scholar Ulla Dydo: Stein's lover/wife, Alice B. Toklas, forced her to change the verb "may" to "can" throughout. (May Bookstaver was an early lover of Stein's, and Toklas—who apparently had no trouble reading Stein—was enraged finding her name so many times in the manuscript of *Stanzas in Meditation*.) In the new Yale edition, "may" has been returned, according to Stein's original manuscripts. The editors Susannah Hollister and Emily Setina, literary sleuths, have done significant work restoring this book.

I enjoy Stein most as a theorist: Her ideas startle me, in whatever form they appear. (I call myself an inexpert.) One of those ideas was that becoming a classic could kill a work of art. Readers' responses should shift, like Ida, with changing times, to make a book new(er); otherwise it doesn't truly live in the present. If Stein becomes an endpoint for literary invention—a classic—her work can't be read in the present tense. Literature can't rest on its laurels. I figure that if Stein were alive now, she'd be rambunctious differently. And she wouldn't be writing like Gertrude Stein.

Home/Not Home

Around the globe, there are over seven thousand living languages, but daily many languages die. Do Ho Suh's absorption in houses, the home, in buildings, in the interiors where people live and work causes me to wonder how many languages have words for "home" and "family." And if their inferences are similar or quite different from meanings in the American English language.

The relationship between languages and objects is like the chicken-and-egg puzzle, though it doesn't actually matter, does it, which came first, except, say, if speculating about the first and most urgent necessities of Homo sapiens—their need for artifice, to build an environment, and only then I wonder what came first.

In Europe, the use of forks didn't become common until the beginning of the eighteenth century. Photography was invented in 1839, with many innovations before it, decades before anesthesia. Much, much earlier in time, in the Great Rift Valley in Kenya, where humankind is meant to have begun, though there is controversy about that, the sun bears down; the heat can be brutal. A people's need for shelter, to be protected from the sun, animals, storms, would have, I think, been immediate. Clothing came later, it is theorized, with the invention of the eyed sewing needle that allowed Homo sapiens to make layered clothing—maybe even underwear—and, with this novel needle, the ability to layer their clothes allowed them to expand into colder climates during an ice age.

Who would live in the shelters, singly or as groups, and how were the inhabitants chosen. Housing might have been cause for fighting, as it is now—not with fists but money and laws. Individuals would return to their dwellings, safer from the unknown. After millennia adult children commonly, maybe universally—that's a step too far—

would leave the farm, say, and start their own families. They might expect to return to the family house whenever they chose.

Everything in prehistory about human evolution is understood only through remains, bones, cave drawings, and tools.

Home and family came to be fused as a mental and emotional picture. While some can't leave home, others can't leave fast enough. It's said home is where the heart is, but home is also where the heart is broken. In Do Ho Suh's art, his aesthetics, a house is a structure, a carapace, and home is an image, an idea, infused with emotions, memories, and forgetfulness. His images congeal into other pictures, mental ones. In the mind: a bedroom, the bed, that picture on a dresser, if you have one; a kitchen stove, where your mother cooked, if she did, a certain pot that had a crack in it; a living room or den, if it existed, where family gathered, talked, watched TV, and argued.

Suh makes presentations of the ordinary, reminding you that, when living long in a place, you no longer notice what's in it. Suh remakes a house's accoutrements. These will become the remnants that scientists study, hundreds of years later, to see how people lived.

The "homeliness" of a stove, a sink, a toothbrush holder is precisely evocative of home, the seemingly insignificant details resonate in the unconscious's memory palace. The appearance of what hasn't been seen in many, many years can be shockingly tender.

Suh's representations of "home" are canny and uncanny. What if home is not where you feel at home. Conversely, what is home when you are not at home; and what is home when it is in fact lost.

Do Ho Suh's sculptures, drawings, fabric works, rubbings, tracings, and installations propose the existence of the tangible and its intangible remains. His structures are oxymoronic, because objects take form and are there, but they are also not there. No longer functional, but common, uncannily home, Suh's nonfunctional representations incite affect, psychological associations; his spectral objects offer a sense of embodiment but also deny it.

Here "home" is dialogical, because there is no solution to what home means or is.

***

As a young man, Suh hoped to study marine biology, asking himself: Why do all fish look different? Fish can be viewed in bodies of water, the deeper an ocean floor the greater the visibility with less sediment. Transparency permits seeing through, a quality Suh must have treasured about the oceans, since it is essential in his work.

To be able to see through even fragile walls is a metaphor. Walls create artificial boundaries, built structures obviously rely on walls for load bearing, to hold up floors, say, and walls make separations in houses and offices. In Western architecture, walls are not meant to be seen through. Spaces formed by walls designate a hierarchy in family, business, and other relationships: the boss's office, the master bedroom.

Viewed psychologically and metaphorically, a wall blocks action and resultant insights as it constructs a variety of separations. Obstructions and separations incite quandaries, interactions freighted with mystery, and misunderstandings. Behind closed doors and walls, acts and words are expressed that might cause chaos, say, arousing emotions difficult even to define. Invisible, psychic walls, or boundaries, are erected, strong and weak. People, of course, are not transparent and can't see through concrete walls; they can only hope to perceive others' boundaries and set their own.

In the fabric architecture work, Suh re-creates, in his inimitable style, larger structures—public ones. One is called *Reflection* (2004), but across the entire series shadows augment the sculptures, and, in that way, create other or adjacent objects. The shadow suggests closeness, ominousness, and sadness, of which the object is usually unaware. Suh's work reflects on itself, without sinister intent, not as a prosaic haunting, but in recognition of human consciousness: Actions will have consequences. They shadow the acts.

A "reflection" implies a multidimensional, multifaceted concept. A thought, a meditation, an image in the shadow of another object, a face in a mirror—a reflection is never the thing itself, or a shadow of itself. Suh knows that—it's essential to his art. He can only call up the thing, bring it to mind.

In contrast to concrete walls that allow for privacy and secrecy, Suh's structures flirt with limited visibility. His materials—rice paper, silk, polyester—deny complete transparency, only some light let in. To viewers, mystery might accrue, but a mystery is not the same as a secret. Still, one can cause the other, and certainly in families and homes some of what occurs will be unspoken, secret, mysterious.

Suh's father was a traditional Korean painter, and the family house was of traditional Korean architecture. These houses' interiors are built in layers, with rice paper, fabric, screens, moving walls that can be open or shut. Movable walls and sliding doors create changing shapes, allowing for different uses of space. Japanese and Korean architecture is practical—no space is wasted, for one, while ventilation and access of movement in a small space are facilitated. There was insufficient space to build differently.

In the Japanese filmmaker Yasujirō Ozu's films, people move in and out of such rooms with great fluidity and gracefulness. Their entries and exits are nearly seamless and nearly silent; quiet fills Ozu's scenes after the characters have left it. Wearing slippers, they seem to glide away, augmenting the pregnant silence left after a conversation.

Something like that is evident in Suh's pieces. What happened in the rooms or buildings is left in them. It is why, perhaps, he doesn't allow viewers to be able to see it all. Also, much that happened in a home or room is beyond recalling. The flirtation with vision, the flimsy or fragile materials blocking it like an analogue to a past event: sometimes it is just on the edge of return.

***

> If you write "loving" and "rubbing" in Korean, it's the same word. You can pronounce it "loving" or "rubbing" either way.
> —Do Ho Suh

Rituals are said not to exist in American life, but they are everywhere, just not as usually defined: specific meals on holidays; attending every Mets opening baseball game; writing on bras at sweet sixteen birthday parties; coming out as gay to your parents; dropping to a knee to propose marriage; weddings when the bride wears something borrowed and blue. These are not formal ceremonies, not religious duties, say, but they are, for many, close to religion and belief, and benefit the spirit.

Ritual is an actor or agent in Suh's work. In *Rubbing/Loving* (2015–2016), his rubbing of the family house will eventually realize it as a trace, skeleton. He will have spent years effecting this haunting embodiment, and few people, I imagine, would feel such urgency—to cover their family house in mulberry paper, then use charcoal to rub every surface, every window, door, mark. A rubbing of a house creates a ghost of itself.

Objects are impalpable, though in current debates about post-humanity, it is proffered that objects have feelings. I'm agnostic about this, because I have no reason to accept or not accept the theory. I do wonder what its possible imminence means.

Barring certainty, I'd say Suh's objects are impalpable. They may be touched, literally, by him, felt psychologically by him, and aesthetically and emotionally by viewers. Memories inhere in a home, and a house is also a container of ideas. If the family house as it's being rubbed has feelings about Suh's movements, what might they be.

A built house surrounds bodies, while a home ideally embraces its inhabitants. With rubbing, Suh embraces it, whatever its responses might be. His body touches the house, he leans toward it, his hands caress it. He feels and sees marks, indelible ones, and traces those. The walls might be scarred, and every scar might have a story. He rubs those into the mulberry paper.

> When complete, I try to be the beholder of my own work.
> —Do Ho Suh

In doing these rubbings, pictures and moments might be reawakened. Muscle memory resides in the body and in neural routes of brains, the way song lyrics do, remembered by people with Alzheimer's and other forms of dementia. The mind/body remembers what the conscious mind might not.

His body is touching another body, an inanimate body. If Suh is intimate with the house, it is a one-way intimacy. And can that be named intimacy, or is it love for an object that cannot love back. In this way, his devotion, attention, and love is unrequited. This too relates to the image of home and family, not necessarily its reality.

Inherent in Suh's movements—his touching with hands and fingers—is eroticism. In the rubbings, longings reside. A return to the family and home by this closeness and these gestures can never return Suh to what it was. Seeking it, going back home, can be futile. A home/family's embrace can comfort but also create anxiety, while being home again can elicit feelings of loss. Nothing is or can be the same, and so one longs and longs for the impossible.

Suh desires closeness even in this impossibility.

> There is always a distance.
> —Do Ho Suh

***

In 1996, Suh returned to his school, Kyung Shin High School. It had been the first modern, Western-style school in Korea and the oldest. He scanned all of the extant yearbooks, the earliest dating from the 1930s when Korea was under Japanese occupation. Male students then had to wear Japanese-style military cadet black uniforms. Because Suh's grandfather had been a political activist in the resistance, fighting for Korean independence, Suh's education was free. For *Who Am We?* (1999) hundreds of faces of students were transformed into wallpaper, hundreds of faces of anonymous young men.

"I placed them in a grid," Suh says. "And I saw somebody who looked like my father. I thought that was so weird. And it goes back to my interest in fish: Maybe we're not that different."

That wallpaper—the first work of Suh's I saw[1]—was seminal to his art: a return to the past, the significance of remembering, a plethora of faces blending into each other, an ocean of faces. No face is more striking than another, no one more individual than another. The wallpaper, the totality of images, viewed from a distance, looked like dots and marks as if pixelated. And, like memory, blurred.

With the distance of time, remembering is work. An aroma or the fragrance from a flower might conjure a long-ago event, but what was it. People think—I have—I'll always remember this. Then don't. The past grows more distant too, memory is obscured, much of the past obliterated. Oddly even a once vivid and important event falls into vagueness. The memory is fuzzy.

Looking for the past is like peering through Suh's silks and rice paper. Something is there, but the object is cloudy, undefined. Those feelings are present in his works.

These feelings transform from the personal to emotions common to humanity, such as we know it.

After Suh's father's death in 2020, he sorted out his files and letters. He found a document listing his father's educational credentials, and discovered that his father had gone to the same high school he had. But his father had never told him. Secrets, everyone says, go to the grave.

So curious. Suh doesn't know why. It often happens that, after a parent dies, many questions arise, and can't be answered. Time passes. Questions remain. Irrational, indefinable, potent thoughts and feelings come, memories arise randomly, all living at the heart of Do Ho Suh's project.

The heart is a metaphor and, linguistically, a synecdoche, a part for the whole. Suh's expansive project imagines our emotional lives embedded in objects. His art articulates sensations and feelings central to an everyday existence, to those bits and pieces present and past. Long-ago memories can get lost or become vague. There are so many gaps, and words don't seem to capture them. They usually arrive like fragments from Super 8 movies or creased candid photographs. Memories suggest the preverbal period of life, before words described events and defined them.

Stepping out of my guise as a critic, who writes alongside art, as the late art critic Craig Owens put it, I feel close to Do Ho Suh's work, his aesthetic. To me, a fiction writer, each piece could be a story in which I am the protagonist, and I can write or assemble my own narrative. With his generative art, Do Ho Suh opens the door wide for others to enter their own house. His work is beautiful, irresistible, thoughtful, and created with a generous spirit. Its affects are without limit, depending on a viewer's subjectivity. To me, his artwork senses and proposes the inevitable history of being human.

Notes

All quotes from Do Ho Suh are from a conversation with the author.

1 In 1996, Do Ho Suh was my student in the Critical Issues course I taught at Yale, where he was studying for his MFA. A later version of the wallpaper was expanded to encompass many more people's portraits from various sources in Seoul.

Absence Makes Art

Artists concoct things to protect themselves, to stop, elide, even erase, inexplicable terrors and compensate for anguishing losses. Making work comes from wishes and hopes, also. Maybe for the maker, art functions as a talisman, I mean, in an unconscious sense. The desire-to-make is an insistent neediness. To be driven to write or paint or photograph emerges, even erupts, from unbidden feelings, metaphorical and actual deaths, when, for instance, as a child, you realize that you're not alone, and then look for consoling objects to install in those raw places. Satisfactions may abound, but, forever, generating art will uncover resilient dissatisfactions, incapable of cure. Ruptures are primary sources, everyone's primary colors.

In the mid-1980s, Jim Hodges and I met through a mutual friend, Tim Hailand. Hodges and I would see each other at openings from time to time, and it turned out that we liked each other's work. One day last year, he asked me to write a piece for his exhibition at a contemporary art museum in Santiago de Compostela, Spain. There's a thirteenth-century church on its grounds, he told me, and before I wrote anything, he wanted me to see the extraordinary medieval city, the last stop on ancient Christian pilgrimages, and the art center where he'd install his work.

Before I went, Jim visited me in my apartment, and as the sun set, we discussed our histories, psychologies, our ideas about art, and felt a sympathy, or connection—two people working in different media, with congruent aims. But there was a great difference between us: Jimmy's an optimist.

I traveled to Santiago de Compostela in February 2005, then I visited him in his studio, to tell him what I felt, what I saw, my responses to the art center's space, each room sized and shaped differently, each a problem and a possibility. Its architect, Siza, had cleverly related the building's levels to the vertiginous garden behind it, so the floors shifted subtly and sometimes dizzyingly, maybe altering a museum-goer's perceptions. We talked about the old church on its grounds, and how Jim might use it. I'm an atheist, but declared urgently: "We all have our personal altars." Right then, Jim decided to project *New AIDS Drug* (1991) on the church's altar. Later, he showed me a timeline for his work that he'd fashioned, part of his conceptualizing of the exhibition. He started at 1985, with early work, his beginnings, creating a chronology of images but also a sort of lineage. Each picture on the central axis had two or three offshoots, smaller pictures or footnotes. I was struck by his beginning with the past.

In my fiction, especially the novels, I want endings to return to beginnings, for the reader to wander back imaginatively and connect images, words, and ideas, for the novel to reverberate in the mind. Jim's work revels in and unearths the significance of pastness, of what's gone, lost, what's left, discarded literally, or stuck in memory; then, through a work, he claims it—for now. Sometimes I think: If the past inside us were unedited, so that every moment would be available, what kind of lives would we lead, entangled in the enormous weight of memory. Yet, realizing how much I've forgotten always troubles me; we lose so much. But then writers can be compared with Freud's hysterics, who can't relinquish the past.

Looking at Jim's floor work *what's left* (1992), I could write a short story. I want to know: Where's the body? Who wore those jeans? A person, a man, must have hurriedly undressed—for sex, for a shower, he was late, had to change fast, for a party, a tryst, or a funeral. No, he committed suicide—but this happened a while ago, because the web is elaborate, woven over time. The silvery white brass adds a starry night to my story of him. There's something quintessentially Jim Hodges in this piece, with its mix of formal elements, materials, his use of sculpture and drawing, its quality of lightness and heaviness, its references to a human body and daily life. Tough, casual, worrying, the collection of clothes lies on the floor, shapelessly shaped, dropped or thrown there, but because the lacy web attaches it to a wall, where it may continue to develop, it's both fragile and enduring, too. It's like the brain, whose cells renew and whose neurons generate startling and complex links and relationships.

Several times, Jim exhorted me: "Write whatever you want. Anything." Whatever freedom is, though, it isn't easy, because there's a necessity to use it completely. So, for the artist who has it, it's not creativity that matters; it's the freedom-to-do that does. It's the sole and singular element entailed in art-making that makes it exceptional. In a way, no matter the materials, craft, talent, and skill, all an artist has is this highly specific freedom. Most jobs don't allow it, art-making depends upon actualizing it. Why this, why not that, what's best, what for, what will it mean if anything? Artists may choose to ignore the market and maybe not find buyers for their work, or accept its parameters, and notice, or not, possible subliminal effects on their production.

Jim allowed me all the space I needed. I tried to write a new story, but each time I'd start, I'd think: I have the story already: "Absence Makes the Heart"—even the title seemed right. The story's baroque narrative, its ceremonial quality, corresponded to Church ritual, pomp, and pageantry. The female protagonist who says "Don't leave me" wears a purple gown. There's an elaborateness, lushness, and poignancy in Jim's art and, in my story, an excess of emotion. The filigree and hide-and-seek spaces in Jim's work, especially, evoked other, strong associations: I wrote "Absence Makes the Heart" out of emptiness, the absolute void that shocking death leaves. Invariably, death comes as a shock, even though it's expected.

My father, Nathan Tillman, died on August 7, 1984. His absence had strange, surprising, and even baroque effects on me and I began writing the story a few weeks after he was cremated. I was in London, and I can still remember the rectangular wooden table at which I wrote, the window in front of the typewriter, and how empty the room felt. Loss actually felt physical, and most terrifying was that I had been left alone and that, now with my father gone, no one or nothing could protect me. It didn't matter that I knew he couldn't. My story was culled from that vulnerable and empty place, which demands language to speak for humankind's passions during its cruelest drama.

Maybe terrible loss anticipates, invokes, exceeds, but finally needs beauty. And I felt: Jim's work represents that collision of loss and beauty. Many of his images have figurative and actual holes, irrecoverable gaps in which he refers to absences and frailties, represents sensitivity and surprise, openness and anxiety; his lines are sensuous and mysterious, so that, in the interstices, emptiness becomes solitude, or, more, transforms into lustrous potentiality. I suppose I could claim *In this lifetime* to support this notion: Here's a photograph of a leafy tree where tears and rips allow spaces for wonder and renewal. That's Jimmy's optimism.

Some people are generous and leave big spaces for others. As an author, I hope I am; I know I want to leave space for readers, so they can put their imaginations to work and make a story theirs. As a visual artist, and one who is remarkably attached to words and music, Jim does that for viewers. Making art comes from a process that goes on in the mind and body all the time. Sometimes an artist or writer can find a way to enter or excavate experience, an inchoate sensation, drag out, shape, or compose words and images in a form that narrates or displays, more or less coherently, these disparate and as yet inarticulate ideas. A construction may suggest smart or dumb, fluid or intractable thoughts and emotions to others. Maybe the object will contain, propose, or invent visual, verbal, psychological, formal, political, and other meanings. If this occurs, elegantly, like a scientific theorem, with beauty or beautiful ugliness, intellectual or visceral, with logic, nonsense, or wonder, by abstraction or figuration, through terror, uncertainty, absurdity, it does so because of its execution in a chosen form, which is, in a sense, freely chosen. But, always, art and literature exist recognizably within their historical and cultural spaces.

In any medium, art's about decisions, problems, followed by insight, which arrives after much thought—a belief in the right way to do it—and the more decisions an artist realizes need to be made, the more freedom-to-do there is and the more responsibility. Engage possibility and find ways to make it happen best, I tell myself, but aware of my limitations, my habits of mind, I recognize that I won't see or discover every one. More and more, I trust my imagination to pull me through. Though some theorists over the last sixty years have disdained the concept as hopelessly tainted by idealism, I feel comforted in believing that Freud also meant imagination when he wrote about fantasy. In any case, it's a necessary and restorative page in my operating manual.

Absence makes the heart and art, too, but could I give Jim an "old" story? What was an old story? Was it used up? Yet there was Jim Hodges's story—of his evolution, continuous and discontinuous, as an artist—and it, too, was an old story. I hesitated and hesitated and then decided I had to, because the story couldn't be ignored, it kept returning to me, and finally I had to trust my sense that I could do nothing better. And when Jim and I met next, in a café in my neighborhood, I brought him my first collection of stories, also titled *Absence Makes the Heart* in which the old story sat. I was so nervous, so I'm not sure how fast I handed it to him (later, when I asked, he told me "instantly"), but to my terror and delight, he began reading the story right away. I walked out of the restaurant to let him do it alone, because I was too anxious to watch him and imagine his response to every word. But sometimes I spied on him through the café's open door. The end of this story: "Absence Makes the Heart" appears in the book. What I feel best about is that return to the past present, that recovering the old may renew it, even transform it, and help it live, perhaps more fully.

That's what I decided was the ending, it's what I felt. But then, I was given a gift, a book, Franz Lidz's *Ghosty Men*, about the Collyer brothers, wealthy American eccentrics who lived in an unfathomably chaotic and filthy house in Harlem. "New York's Greatest Hoarders," they never threw out anything. I opened the book and its epigraph was from Samuel Beckett: "All art is the same: an attempt to fill an empty space." What I feel best about now is having chanced upon an old—and the perfect—statement for what I've been trying to say.

Being human offers Homo sapiens variety, or some elasticity, in social life, though sociologists claim that people's personalities disappear with no one else around. Imagining this evacuation, I see a person alone in a self-chosen shelter, motionless on a chair, like a houseplant with prehensile thumbs.

Diane Sawyer, an unctuous American TV news anchor, once asked a mob assassin: "But haven't you ever thought, How can I do this? Who am I?" The man looked at her with incredulity, then said: "I'm a gangster." Now, it's true that people (aka human beings) named themselves human and also defined humanity, but this tautological affair entails neuroses: Do we have a natural state? To say there isn't one doesn't quell anxiety, and "just act natural" and "be yourself" remain resilient punch lines to the shaggy-dog story called existence. There are instincts and drives, the basics from which Sigmund Freud theorized—but, oh, the complex array of acts that might satisfy these!

The bandwidth of human behavior includes self-image recognition and cerebration, prized differences from other animals (both premises are currently under investigation). With bigger brains, people have concocted notions about self-reflection and self-awareness, which allowed for "I think; therefore, I am." Not "I think what; therefore, I am what?" One would have thought that might matter.

Human beings have, like other animals, sexual and excretory organs that either share the same orifice or sit near enough to confuse identification by children. In evolutionary terms, apparently, there have been no great improvements. Also, shit still stinks, which, given the horrors humans commit, seems appropriate.

Dominique Laporte's *History of Shit* narrated the lengths to which people have gone to cover up the smell. But the body finds its way, discharging ugly odors, keeping humans close to their "uncivilized" ancestors. Human violence keeps people as close, maybe closer; it too has likely never changed, only the tools. But violence can't be covered up with perfume. In part, theories about essence and construction, nature versus nurture, address, directly and indirectly, motives for aggression and cruelty, ethical behavior—or its lack—and the power of the irrational in the human animal.

In the 1950s, the American ethnomethodologists Erving Goffman, Harvey Sacks, and Harold Garfinkel examined tiny units of social life, such as conversation among friends. Seemingly meaningless conventions screamed disaster if not followed: No "hello" back to a friend jeopardizes the relationship. Little miscues caused rips in society's seams. They studied gender, declaring masculinity and femininity as performances in need of consistent routines. Other people surveilled others for lapses that endangered identity, but worse any hope for a life without torment.

Humans act differently in wars, in crowds; they act differently if they think nobody's watching. Punishments and limits—prohibitions on murder, incest, cannibalism—mostly keep people in line, otherwise, humans would be no better than animals, humans like to claim. But all mammals teach their kind and follow rules; they form societies often less violent than ours. Apes, chimps, elephants—the mothers commit years to training their offspring. Wolves, male and female, are ecstatic at the birth of a cub; all guard their young. So, that's no insult: We do behave like animals. At parties I observe people acting much like dogs, except for sniffing rear ends, which is generally done in private.

"Acting like a human" is a matter of opinion, too. "Did I do the right thing?" can translate into "did I act right?" Some people act better than others; even when being honest, some people aren't convincing. Yet con artists are great at appearing sincere. Being honest or "yourself" isn't necessarily a "natural" state, since the human capacity to dissimulate must have always had a necessity for species survival.

I admit to wonder and consternation when people bemoan the loss of authenticity in art, in identity, in life. Andy Warhol is regularly blamed for its supposed absence. He's blamed for everything. I don't know what pure state, unmediated existence, or moment in history to which people can or should return. Homo sapiens call themselves makers and doers, and they never leave well enough alone.

Some people are actual actors. Theater has been around a long time, because it serves several purposes. For one, people can watch others being human, portraying emotions and actions, their consequences and vicissitudes. Which brings me to Ryan Gosling in the film *Blue Valentine*. Gosling embodies an unusually sensitive human to a degree I find unnerving. He plays the husband in this anti-romance romance—a so-called regular American guy, but one I had never seen on screen or stage. Not a rebel like James Dean or Marlon Brando, standard bearers of "acting real." No, Gosling's character is content to love his wife passionately, to adore and care for their child; he is ambitionless, happy to have a lame job. This life is enough for him, and he believes it should be for his wife.

Gosling's character might or might not exist off-screen. Still, an artifact, a movie, has proffered a novel image for Americans raised on Horatio Alger and other long-running constructions. In *Blue Valentine*, Ryan Gosling enacts a "real human being" better than most human beings do. I might one day meet such a person. Probably not Mr. Gosling, who would, most likely, not live up to my expectations.

Cut Up Life

Dear Poet
Charles Henri Ford
Did the lake overturn
when Narcissus fell in
became opaque
a mad lake—
Oh poet dear
please make it clear
and let it recover
the reflected image
of that foolish lover—

Amazedly
Florine Stettheimer

Charles Henri (né Henry) Ford made his entrance on February 10, 1908, in Hazlehurst, Mississippi, to Gertrude Cato and Charles Lloyd Ford. It was his idea to change the spelling of Henry to Henri. "I was tired of being asked if I was related to Henry Ford," he says, "and a young girl wrote me on lavender paper in red ink and made a mistake that I liked so I kept it."

Ford's parents, and his father's brothers, owned hotels in various small cities in Mississippi and Texas—Ford was born in a hotel that burned down soon after—and his early life was peripatetic. His mother, whom he compares in his diary with Hamlet's mother, Gertrude, was an artist herself and seems to have been a dramatic, beautiful, and compelling character. This primary love led the way to Ford's two great loves—Djuna Barnes and Pavel (Pavlik) Tchelitchew.

Ford met Barnes in New York in 1929, before he left for Paris in 1931, and lived with her in Morocco, where he typed the manuscript of her novel *Nightwood.* "She couldn't spell," he says. His most enduring relationship was with the Russian painter Pavlik Tchelitchew. They lived together for twenty-three years. Ford and Tchelitchew met in Paris, in 1933, at an opening, when Ford was twenty-four and Tchelitchew, thirty-five. Of the meeting Ford notes in his diary that he wrote Parker Tyler at the time: "I've found a genius." In a powerful way, the diary circles around and is about Pavlik, "his great heart," and their complicated love and long relationship.

His younger sister, Ruth Ford—the diary's "Sister"—was a well-known actor. She debuted in Orson Welles's Mercury Theatre production of *The Shoemaker's Holiday* in 1938; performed in plays by Tennessee Williams; had a lead in Jean-Paul Sartre's *No Exit* (translated by Paul Bowles in 1946), and received a nomination from the London Drama Critics, in 1957, for her performance as Temple Drake in *Requiem for a Nun*, which she had adapted into a play with William Faulkner. Ruth Ford was married to the Hollywood actor Zachary Scott, who died in 1965, and lives in the Dakota, four floors below her older brother.

> I loved the Blues before I loved the Poem. Somehow the two loves were from the same source. So it was natural I called my poetry review *Blues.*

Precocious and ambitious, the young poet launched *Blues: A Magazine of New Rhythms*, in 1929. William Carlos Williams and Eugene Jolas were two of its contributing editors and Kathleen

Tankersley Young its associate editor. For nine issues, Ford solicited and published writing from Ezra Pound, Gertrude Stein, Kay Boyle, Harry Crosby, James Farrell, H.D., Kenneth Rexroth, Mark Van Doren, Louis Zukofsky, Edouard Roditi, Erskine Caldwell. He was the first to publish Paul Bowles.

From Mississippi, Ford moved to New York to write poetry and lead *la vie bohème* in Greenwich Village. Ford had published Parker Tyler, the poet and future film critic and writer, in *Blues* and was corresponding with him. They met in person in New York—"I could hardly see his face, he had so much makeup on," Ford says—and soon collaborated on writing *The Young and Evil.* Called by some the first gay novel, published in 1933, banned in the United States and England, it is, like Ford himself, unapologetic, unashamed, poetic, candid, and determinedly free of conventions.

> It's not doing the things one wants to do—even if considered a vice, like opium-taking—that makes one age, but doing things one doesn't want to do.

A kind of surrealist free verse, the uninhibited novel was influenced, in part, by Ford's mentor Gertrude Stein, who took him up when he was first in Paris. When Ford fell in love with Tchelitchew, Stein found less reason to see him; she and Tchelitchew had one of those famous, furious partings of the way. But in *The Autobiography of Alice B. Toklas*, Stein writes of Ford: "He is also honest which is also a pleasure."

Along with *The Young and Evil,* Ford is perhaps best known for *View*, the international art magazine he edited in New York, from

1940 to 1947. The Europeans Marcel Duchamp, André Breton, Max Ernst—forced into exile during World War II—the Americans Maya Deren, Meyer Schapiro, Joseph Cornell, Florine Stettheimer, Man Ray, Paul Bowles, and many more found a home in *View*'s pages and on its covers. Not coincidentally, Ford begins his diary a year after he stops *View* and ends it shortly after the death of Tchelitchew in 1957.

Since finishing the diary, Ford has produced or invented the "poem poster" (shown at the Ubu Gallery in New York in 2000); published many books of poetry, including a limited-edition, unique collage book, *Spare Parts* (1966), and *Out of the Labyrinth: Selected Poems* (1991); directed the feature-length movie *Johnny Minotaur* (1971; shot in Crete, starring Allen Ginsberg among others); and exhibited his photographs, most recently with fellow Mississippian Allen Frame (at the Leslie Tonkonow Gallery in New York).

You have to enjoy what you're doing and do it every day.

Ford has made a habit of doing what he wants to do, and his life is dedicated, as much as anyone's can be, to poetry, art, and the pursuit of pleasure. He usually adheres to a self-imposed, rigorous routine, and now, just short of ninety-three, he writes haiku poems and makes collages daily. When I visit him on a brilliant fall day, October 1, 2000, one of the day's haikus is on his desk:

Men too have a
change

of life
didn't Marcel
                Duchamp
   have it twice

***

I first read Charles Henri Ford's diary in the late 1970s, and again in the late 1980s, when I urged him to have it published. He didn't want to bother. He was writing poems, making collages and photographs; not one, as the reader will see, to look back with longing or regret.

> Those were not the days. These are the days. My days are always these.

> I find it pointless to have a nostalgia about the past.

> I: "Would you like to be in Rome . . . where all the pretty boys are?" Pavlik: "Don't turn the dagger in the wound."

Poetry, genius, love, fame, friendship, beauty, family, character, sex, psychology, youth, and Pavlik, always, are variously appetizers, entrées, or desserts on Ford's menu *du jour et de la nuit*. His diary is riveting. As it moves from theme to theme, the reader senses a life formed consciously in the present, one lived spontaneously, interrupted and interfered with by memory and the pressure of unconscious thoughts. The reader feels the moment's vitality and presence, and the sorrow at its loss, but not because Ford insists on it. Emotion—disappointment and sadness—is there in the way he writes the day, flying from an idea, sex act, or fantasy, to a line in a poem, a report on dinner talk, a death, an argument, to a question about aesthetics, a worry about Pavlik—then it's all gone, except the memory of it, what he's written down.

> A passionate schoolboy who knew what he wanted—and got it. (In the pissoir.)
>
> A shadow falls, a fragment of night; a day goes, a fragment of death. Life and the sun tomorrow.
>
> Many beautiful machines—Tanguy painted. But the most beautiful machine is and always will be the human body.

His diary is beautiful and homely, an epic poem about the dailiness of art and life. It's filled with insights about himself, love, sex, his illusions, delusions; there's silliness, homages to his heroes—Isak Dinesen, for one—and acerbic or reverent considerations of his contemporaries. Tchelitchew comments that Jean Genet, whom Ford finds "solemn and humorless," is "*un moraliste—comme Sade*"; Ford refers, less perceptively, to "messes signed by Jackson Pollock." The diary is loaded with gossip about history's celebrated, with whom Ford has had lunch or met at an opening. When he introduces Djuna Barnes to Tennessee Williams at a party, she asks Williams: "How does it feel to be rich and famous?"

Diaries confirm that life is in the details, and in its passions, all of which Ford includes, all of which are inevitably subservient to time.

Ford's diary is profound not because it marks time passing or spent, but because it is imaginatively and definitively of its time and in it.

> I asked Parker (in a letter) if he thought posthumous fame is any fun and he replied it might be to posterity.

> Go back to music, rhythm, as Yeats did, for a renewal of inspiration in poetry. "Go back" in the sense of renewal—

> Pavlik's summary of how I spend my time: "fornication and fabrication."

Like histories, diaries are accounts of the past. Unlike histories, they are not written retrospectively, and subjectivity is their central claim to truth. Faithful to the subjective, the diarist's words, Ford's eyes and ears, conduct the reader through the world he inhabits. The reader finds the way back as it was to Ford. His irrepressibility, his understanding of the power of transience—in sex, art, love—his appreciation of the ephemeral, and his desire to have it all, anyway, for as long as he can, carry us with him.

> Years of work, a burst of glory, and it's all over.

> Up at six and found a feather in my bed, as though, while I was sleeping, I'd been a bird.

> Pavlik told me—in 1933—that I had been sent to him because his mother died.

What is called history comes to us as a transcription of the evanescent. A radio announcer's excited play-by-play of the Tony Zale–Marcel Cerdan fight becomes a monologue written by a surrealist. The now-famous 1948 *Life* photograph of poets at the Gotham Book Mart—Ford, the Sitwells, Marianne Moore, Tennessee Williams, Delmore Schwartz, W. H. Auden, Elizabeth Bishop, Stephen Spender, Randall Jarrell—was first, in the diary, an occasion for a gathering. The photograph documents the group, contributing to the historical record—these poets were there, those not, some are forgotten now.

Ford's commentary about the group offers another record, a personal view that instantly affects the august photograph. He complains that Gore Vidal is in it, that Vidal is not a poet, and the reader can see the tension the photograph does not image. And then there are Ford's musings about Christine Jorgensen, the G.I. who in 1953 underwent the first highly publicized man-to-woman sex change operation.

> Why is everyone always foolish enough to think that a sexual partner will make life happy?
>
> I took a terrace walk and saw the most brilliant falling star. I always make the same wish: Love.

A diary tells us what its author was thinking about then and how it was thought. It is different from a history, because it is an itinerary of lived attitudes, a catalogue of attitudes. Attitude is in the air we breathe, and we don't always think about what we take in and give out. Ford's ideas are his and not his, and, as a matter of history, the expression of attitudes allows a return to the past that so-called objective accounts can't. Ford lets us conspire with him, breathe with him.

> A record of himself is all any man records.
>
> Being jerked off—if done by the right person—leaves no regrets.
>
> Characteristic of our age (Henry James' *The Turn of the Screw* a forerunner)—more and more interest in the perversity of children . . . to shock now, the child must be involved—Example in painting: Balthus, more shocking than Dali. . . . The child is all.

The contemporary reader may be surprised by Ford's anxiety about the effects of masturbation—"I recover from self-abuse"—or disturbed or pleased by his ecstatic evocations and lust for teenaged boys, by his openness about his desires generally. Maybe the only thing in life that doesn't change, apart from the certainty of death—though these days that seems to be changing—is desire. Only its articulations and the environment in which it is felt shift. Ford's freedom or constraints, his prejudices or lacks, gauge his moment and ours.

***

> But I look too good to ruin: I wish my twin would come along and I'd kiss him.

> I don't know how my character will come out in these notes and memories, but I think we usually are to others what we are to ourselves.

The literary diary is a strange form. Was it written to be read? Maybe. Probably. Is it self-conscious? Necessarily. Ford's diary was written to examine himself and others, and in a way, its self-consciousness is its raison d'être. Preciousness is stripped from its self-consciousness by Ford's sardonic, unflinching self-criticism—he's regularly concerned with his character as well as Pavlik's. (The diary pulses, too, with the impact of psychoanalytic theory on contemporary thinking.) But Ford is unselfconscious about his devotion to the cause of aesthetics and the examined life. And is, in his fashion, devoted to love, writing a love story with its own deliberate ideas about heart.

> No one will ever mean more to me—inspire me more—than Pavlik. . . .
>
> The fatal image: Vito's profile as he looked over the terrace yesterday. There it was and there's nothing one can do about it. I wasn't born to live alone.
>
> Pavlik's great heart stopped beating at ten to eight (July 1957).

Ford's diary ends with questions. Does he love Vito? Does Vito love him? Anyway, what is love. Pavlik has died. Ford's days will change.

His life has come to the reader in bits and pieces, a collage, or, like his poems, a cut up. It ends the same way.

> "This ravaging sense of the shortness of life . . ." (V. W.)
> I don't have that. I sense, rather, that life will be long—
> too long.

Charles said something, on that brilliant fall day, about being fortunate or having had good fortune. I teased him about becoming soft. He said, I think a little sheepishly, "Well, it's the right time, isn't it?"

> I shall continue this document until the end of the next year, then I vow to continue it no longer. It's a secret vice. Vices should be public.

Note
All spoken remarks from Charles Henri Ford are from two recent conversations with the author. All other quoted material is from Ford, *Water from a Bucket: A Diary, 1948–1957* (New York: Turtle Point Press, 2001), unless a source is cited.

Cindy Sherman: Character of Characters

I

> Nothing changes from generation to generation except the thing seen and that makes a composition.
> —Gertrude Stein, "Composition as Explanation"

Cindy Sherman keeps changing the way the world looks, and how it looks at itself. Her photographs have, since the 1970s, fused with the "natural" scenery, the environment, and seem now to have been here forever.

Sherman was born in Glen Ridge, New Jersey, in 1954, and grew up in Huntington, Long Island, New York, a child of the suburbs when suburbia was burgeoning. This is usually where the story of the American 1950s starts: After World War II, the United States became a world power. It was a time of optimism, expansiveness, and growing prosperity: TVs in every house, two cars in every garage, and the reign of Detroit and IBM. Meanwhile, Hollywood movies invented America not only for Americans but also for the world.

This version of history ignores another America: discontent, poor, but also aroused after the war. Black American men who had fought against racism abroad, in a segregated army, returned to Jim Crow America. Women who had worked in factories were displaced when the soldiers returned. Frustration and unrest were also by-products of the war, along with the Cold War, the nuclear arms race, and a manufactured paranoia about domestic communism.

In 1963, when John F. Kennedy was assassinated, Sherman was nine; she was a teenager when Martin Luther King Jr., Malcolm X, and Robert Kennedy were murdered. Figuratively, she grew up with the Vietnam War, the civil rights movement, the second wave of feminism, the gay liberation movement, and with Warhol, hippies, and rock and roll. The 1960s ended and the 1970s began with America's loss in the Vietnam War, Watergate, and President Nixon's resignation. By then, American optimism had been shredded.

Sherman came of age in the mid-1970s. She attended college in upstate New York, switching from painting to photography, which wasn't unusual: Art-making was changing almost seismically, with artists reevaluating image-making, the relationship between art and politics, between text and image. All of culture was under scrutiny, like T. S. Eliot's "patient etherized upon a table." Humanism was interrogated by feminist theory, psychoanalysis, and deconstruction. Identity politics, postcolonialist theory, and issues of representation, to name a few, challenged artists indirectly or directly. In any case, different things were happening in their studios.

My mercilessly partial gloss on living history serves as a background or a small picture of Time. Maybe it's a historical prop against which to foreground Sherman's life and work. Were this partial history a board game, I'd suggest: Cindy Sherman starts HERE, during an extraordinarily charged intellectual, political, and aesthetic period.

II

> Composition is not there, it is going to be there and we are here.
> —Gertrude Stein, "Composition as Explanation"

Sherman started with portraiture and depicted solitary girls and women dressed up, made up, performing womanliness as a convention and disguise. She acted the parts, concocted the poses, subtly transforming the girl next door into vamp and superstar. Soon she pictured her characters in situations for which she built the props and sets: Her studio became her own movie house, where she mounted photo-dramas. Her characters—abject, frightened, complacent, bewildered, sexy—and their states of mind, economic position, or sexual feelings might be gleaned from their enigmatic expressions and surroundings.

Sherman mined images of femininity and masculinity from Hollywood, fashion, and advertisements. Through her mind's eye, anyone could appropriate or become any image. Images were available, everywhere. Appropriation, in Sherman's world, began at home, a fact of life as well as a new artistic strategy: Being an original was highly unlikely, and no longer urgent. Uniqueness and the "original" were, for postmodernists, dubious requirements and values for art.

Sherman concocted ever more elaborate environments and stranger backgrounds: faces obscured under gooey muck, prosthetic body parts hung in space. She emphasized distortion and disturbance. She made things very hard to look at. Grotesque-looking beings appeared to be survivors of terrible wars. Worldly women existed unhappily or stoically in exaggerated displays of wealth, or as muses, with warts, in art history.

Sherman knew how to achieve a look, *the* look. A knowing artfulness and determined vision enabled her to represent the photographic illusion—of glamorous, confused, desperate, or whimsical women—then destroy it. She achieved "realness," entirely through artifice. By the late 1980s, she had contributed toward making Aretha Franklin's 1960s anthem "A Natural Woman" a curious assertion.

III

> It is understood by this time that everything is the same except composition and time, composition and the time of the composition and the time in the composition.
> —Gertrude Stein, "Composition as Explanation"

After Andy Warhol, Marshall McLuhan, and the advent of postmodernism, surface was no longer superficial—face value had value. The surface signified, because people existed in, and as, images to themselves and to each other. People had images, which made meanings and produced consequences: Pretending and posing could be true, but not Truth, not an essential Truth. That didn't exist. And, just as there are no lies on an analyst's couch, because an analysand's misrepresentations are revealing, Sherman's art attested that people's hopes of being someone else are also a reality. Fantasies do become realities.

Sherman's decision to dissolve "human-being-ness," to create degraded, horrifying figures, confronted human pride and disrupted the facade of socialization people believe separates them from other animals. Her bald moves built even more space for a viewer's unconscious activity, which might account for the experience of feeling struck dumb in front of her work.

Her representations showed disorder, nonhierarchical chaos; her explorations of human adaptability pictured endemic discontinuities. In her art, the state of being human suggests endless, terrifying possibility: Anything might happen in Sherman's work, as well as in life, and it does.

The human species skates on thin ice if it imagines that identity is stable, that chance and randomness don't play their parts, daily. What Sherman's characters wear—for instance, haute couture—

can only cover their naked bodies, never protect them from harm. Her work undermines and frustrates the great wish for security, and also for continuity, an illusion our hapless species needs to believe. Her fragmented, mutating faces and bodies rip at the fabric of identity, relationships, institutions, and treasured traditions in art.

IV

Photographs don't tell any more than they show; they don't explain or speak. They are entities, objects. What they show is perceived by viewers, in part, as projections and through identification. Photographs do ineluctably display something, but that thing is a matter of interpretation.

Sherman's work foregrounds the picture itself as a template on which viewers can seek themselves, deny recognition, or recognize others. She doesn't create windows to see through or beyond; her impenetrable surfaces resist that type of entry. Instead, Sherman figures into her compositions the reality and position of a viewer: The viewer becomes an intrinsic element in the photographs. The pictures intimate a person standing there, looking at them. It will be said that all pictures need a viewer to complete them. But not all pictures incorporate the viewer the way Sherman's do. She constructs a photographic entanglement by the method with which she manufactures the images.

Playing all the roles—camera, subject, object—she is also initially a viewer, the picture's very first viewer. She performs inside and outside of the frame, as seen and seer, even seeker. Her several positions conceive a "subjective" and "objective" framing. When

Sherman stands outside of the frame, she can experience it as a viewer might, and can physically register as a viewer, to imbricate, imaginatively, a viewer inside the frame. She creates a dynamic object relationship among the elements. If Sherman were a novelist, I'd propose: She has incorporated the reader into every text, by allowing for a subjective space for the reader/viewer.

It's often written that, because Sherman plays parts before the camera, her photographs are about her identity. They are not. If they were, the work would not be as generative as it has proven to be. It would sit in frames, not doing very much, and would not be so influential, or "great." By great, I mean expansive, effective, with depth, intimacy, and immediacy.

Her photographs are not about her. They are about us. Human beings want to look at themselves, and the ubiquity of the camera and its photographic products demonstrates that obsession. People construct ways to look at themselves and others. It is an incessant desire, impossible to satisfy, which creates more pictures. Humans stare at each other longingly, or with disgust, anxiety, curiosity. People watch people, as if everyone might live in a zoo or be a zookeeper. People police themselves: Species survival might require knowledge of every kind of condition that could be endured or character and behavior that might be encountered. Sherman's art registers the relentlessness of people to see who they are, or who they might be or become. And what will happen to them.

V

> Seen thus, in her sacramental black silk, a wisp of lace turned over the collar and fastened by a mosaic brooch,

> and her face smoothed into harmony with her apparel, Ann Eliza looked ten years younger than behind the counter, in the heat and burden of the day. It would have been as difficult to guess her approximate age as that of the black silk, for she had the same worn and glossy aspect as her dress; but a faint tinge of pink still lingered on her cheek-bones, like the reflection of sunset which sometimes colors the west long after the day is over.
> —Edith Wharton, *The Bunner Sisters*

Edith Wharton created fictional figures with words. Cindy Sherman creates visual fictions. In hers, figure and ground might collapse or contradict the other, and disturb the eye with disjunctive objects. In her photograph *Untitled #512* (2010–2011), there's an unlikely pairing, of character and terrain. A tall, dark-haired woman stands on a rocky plain: She is isolated; the place appears barren. No plants or trees, just boulders, earth, and a person. The woman, in her thirties or forties, wears a long, elegant cloak that, like her hairstyle, indicates she might be a flapper. Somewhere, it could be the roaring twenties.

Her cloak is a pale, pinky beige, satin or silk, trimmed with white feathers. Her feathery collar nearly covers her chin. One shoulder is drawn up, suggesting reticence or secrets. She wears white leather, strapped shoes, her legs positioned as if she were modeling her outfit. Her facial expression is impassive, but sharp and deliberate as she stares at the camera, the viewer. Like her cloak, the ground is a subtle tan, with brown. There's a crevice not far from her, with fluffy white material in it. Like clouds or cotton, the white stuff is as decorative as the feathers on the woman's coat. The tonality of the picture encourages a rapid and fluid movement of the eye, from figure to ground, which join formally. But the woman clashes, an out-of-place figure looking out. A misfit in a misbegotten place. Even a hallucinatory figure in a dreamscape. A flapper who creates a flap.

The longer I look at the image, or project and identify, the more I think of the persistence of gender and gendered relations. To what extent does gender shape what I see and order the visual imagination, and more, the world? The space itself is gendered: It's the Wild West, an uninhabited frontier to be conquered, etc. She isn't the Marlboro Woman, though she certainly might be commenting on the Marlboro Man.

VI

> So far then the progress of my conceptions was the natural progress entirely in accordance with my epoch as I am sure is to be quite easily realized if you think over the scene that was before us all from year to year. . . . There is the long history of how every one ever acted or has felt and that nothing inside in them in all of them makes it connectedly different.
>
> —Gertrude Stein, "Composition as Explanation"

From what Sherman has seen, learned, and experienced, she has made "a new composition." She has drawn on Stein's "the thing seen" imaginatively, and, with her own particular consciousness and extraordinary visual sense, she has forged a singularly distinctive, unforgettable, and distinguished art. I only wish I could see how people will react to it a long time from now.

Introduction to *Closer*

Closer was first published in 1989. I read it then, a story about teen gay boys obsessed with sex, discontented seekers, wanting and rejecting each other, sullen and smart boys, passive rebels mostly on drugs. I remember, back then, laughing at the absurdity of their exaggerated listlessness: *Closer*, a disturbing and stark comedy of contemporary manners, a society of boys on self-destruct, a satire of some kind.

Almost thirty-five years later I am again reading *Closer*, the same words, sentences, structure, the same chapters in the same order. But the whole has been thrown up into the air and come down as something else. Mostly I don't remember the novel, just the atmosphere of it, and what I do remember is not necessarily what I read in 1989.

This second reading—call it my first reading.

The chapter "John the Beginner" starts *Closer*. John is in high school, as are all the others in the book, except for Philippe, an older man, a predator or a lover or both. John hates his face, is still loyal to punk. He is disaffected, like the other boys in the novel, and a teen artist who "didn't know what he was doing." He draws portraits of "the best-looking students because they were fun to deface." Soon, John's anti-interpretation, anti-art stance about his work infuriates his teachers, whose brilliance they once praised. The youthful artist, and Dennis Cooper the author, doubts art's significance. This doubt occurs throughout the novel. John thinks, "What if his drawings weren't really important at all except as places to put his confusion."

John's doubts about art's validity intimate *Closer*, in part, as a metafiction. Portrait of the Artist as a Young Gay Man. Cooper wonders about the validity of a novel to explicate the lives of these boys. Novels are, like any other art, Cooper suggests, places to put confusion.

And *Closer* is confusing, generatively so, because of the complexity of the characters, their emotions and the lack of them. Their own confusion, as I read, turned into mine, a reader's. I don't identify with the boys; and don't need to, though some readers always look for identification, which may or may not occur; it is a mistaken approach to any art I think. I read also for disidentification. They are not I, and I encounter other ideas and worlds.

In every boy's chapter—John, David, George (two chapters), Cliff, Alex, Philippe (he has a chapter but is an adult), and Steve—there comes an insistence on fucking or being fucked. They finish, go on to the next activity, as if the sex hadn't happened, or at least it is not remarked upon.

Their affectlessness is not explained, and making general sociological or psychological analyses seems pointless, worse, reductive. Cooper doesn't make their ways of being reasonable—oh yes, absent parents, fathers more present than mothers, they have no power over their children's lives. Cooper writes outside of usual explanations—they are new, they are in their own cosmos. He is writing them into existence on the page, as experiences.

John says he's a better artist than a person, and George tells John his life is his art. Their sensibilities might evince approaches to how to live as an artist or jejune expressions about being artists.

George Miles enters the novel in the first chapter. George is the beautiful boy of the novel, most wanted, most likely not to succeed, most preyed upon, and most loved, especially when he plays dead. John makes drawings of George. Later they fuck or John fucks

George "and [keeps] his eye on the last and definitive portrait [of George]." Their sex, whatever it is, occurs and ends.

Cooper writes casual, seemingly uninteresting and even meaningless sex, though I'm not sure I can be confident of what meaningful sex is. The sex scenes rebuke pornographic versions of boys having sex. Cum shots, moans, lustful breathing, nothing like this happens. How the sex is written might make some, none, or many readers desirous. It is quite perfunctory. And I'm not a young gay man, and they are, of course, different from each other. I also don't need to be one kind or any particular kind of person to read *Closer* and feel the story.

The artificiality of porn is discussed by two of the boys, Alex and Cliff, who are plotting their own porn film. More teen artists. Watching porn, looking at porn drawings, they plan to shoot George Miles surreptitiously, while he is being fucked by Philippe in a ritual in which George plays dead. The sexual ritual that Philippe inflicts upon George—or that is wanted by George—is, at the very least, ambiguous. It appears to be a sadistic encounter, because George is passive, playing dead, but maybe George wants this, he wants to be dead. He takes LSD like candy, and needs it to function, like to go to school. By playing dead, being taken, and not partaking, he might, in his mind, be registering his art. Images of dead people abound in art history.

Miles's skin, his beauty, his passivity—Philippe lusts for him, and wants to be as far inside him as he can be. He opens George's ass and anus wider and wider. He wonders if he might love him. Later, Philippe brings a friend for a threesome. The friend is menacing. Much of the novel plays with casual menace, a sense of foreboding—

it seems that none of the boys are safe. In a crucial scene, Philippe's friend, alone with Miles, moves beyond the limits of play, if that's what this is. George awakens from the threat of death as if from a dream or a nightmare, Cooper emphatically and dramatically enunciating the perils of erasing the boundary between fantasy and reality. George doesn't really want to be dead-dead.

Getting inside George is a metaphor and an actual event. Cooper's suggestive title, *Closer*, alerts readers to the novel's philosophic position. Philippe gets deeply inside George Miles, maybe to know the mystery of the other. And it might seem logical to believe one gets closer to another human being, when one body enters another's. Yet getting inside, Cooper understands, is not getting closer. Not necessarily knowing the other, not finding intimacy, which is more complex than that. It is almost ironic that penetration happens as much as it does without it.

In the last chapter, "Steve the Forefront," Steve doubts his ability to know anything. "Trouble is, I only know about death from song lyrics and movies, so I don't know how to react." Will life become "real" for him, or will it always seem a simulation. And about being closer, Cooper writes: "People don't really know one another unless they're speaking. As soon as they shut up, no matter how close they've been, that understanding is gone. They become cute, ugly, tall. . . . I find this frightening most of the time." That's Steve speaking, after he's had sex with Keith, "which was very expected and pleasant."

Cooper fuses a so-called reality, having sex, with powerful fantasies about it, and about pretty much everything else. The novel rides on the sharp edge of ambiguity. Sex is sex, its own event or experience, and then it's over. Sex doesn't change the boys' lives. Should it? What do they want. Where is pleasure for them. If sex isn't the answer, what is?

The question is important, and I think it is also important to know the time and context in which Cooper wrote this powerful, outrageous, often funny, highly crafted novel—the height of the AIDS crisis. Back then, Cooper was criticized for representing sex in ways that seemed to give permission to unprotected sex. Back then, fantasy itself was dangerous.

Cooper isn't a realist writer. He knows fantasy and lust and danger are also a part of reality. He tests and contests it, writing of strange desires, the unknowable, and mysteries, refusing conventions that appear to show life "as it is." The boys are Cooper's creations, they are close to boys, not actual boys. And that is, after all, what fiction is: verisimilitude.

Dennis Cooper is a remarkable and fascinating writer, a great stylist, a unique thinker, who, through his fiction, risks being misunderstood and often is. His novels put belief, conventional wisdom, and credibility in jeopardy, and he can make readers very uncomfortable. It reminds me of Wittgenstein's statement: "I don't know why we are here, but I'm pretty sure that it is not in order to enjoy ourselves."

Hilary Harkness: Queer Visions

Contemporary art is often criticized for its irrelevance, uselessness; it doesn't directly have an effect on, or defend against, famine, floods, poverty.

> At least 65,000 years ago, Neanderthals used red pigments to paint marks on the walls of deep caves in Spain. In Ardales cave near to Malaga in southern Spain they colored the concave sections of bright white stalactites. In Maltravieso cave in Extremadura, western Spain, they drew around their hands.
>
> —Paul Pettitt, "Neanderthals: The Oldest Art in the World Wasn't Made by Homo Sapiens"

Whatever purpose or function might have meant to our millennia-ago species ancestors, they drew and used colors; the Neanderthals' markings appeared before the arrival of Homo sapiens, who went on to make figures. Before acquiring spoken and written language as we know it, they demonstrated a need to represent, to communicate in images, signs, or codes. That necessity existed along with the birth of early human beings.

What artists make now and why are some of the questions I pose to myself. No one can say with certainty what motivates an artist; there are almost innumerable conscious and unconscious reasons to do anything, or nothing at all. It could be in opposition to prevailing norms and power structures. It could be to escape them.

Hilary Harkness's paintings are original, startling, precise, fantastic, colorful, serious, and curious works. The iconography is intricate and detailed. She paints surprising scenes and nonexistent realities; she refutes James Brown's song: "It's a Man's Man's Man's World." These are new worlds of difference in which her figures are rigorously painted, her characters in unique compositions.

About her painting *Rearguard Action!* (2000), Harkness says, "The figures I'm depicting represent both genders as 'generic female.' Why shouldn't large breasts symbolize virility?" Nonbinary, they are thin, elongated, sometimes wearing sailors' caps, short shorts, and bikini tops. They replace "men" in war and are soldiers.

Harkness configures a world of seemingly lesbian women in which their pronoun, "she," is the generic—"he" transforms or is absorbed into "she." These female-appearing figures, or "soldiers," represent both sexes.

> In terms of the feminist struggle specifically, I have had a vehement refusal over the last decade, with one or two minor aberrations, to allow images of women into my films at all, since I do not see how those images can be separated from the dominant meanings.
> —Peter Gidal, quoted in Mary Ann Doane, "Woman's Stake: Filming the Female Body"

> If representations of women are presently lending themselves so well to sexism and oppression, is it possible to create images of women that are non-objectifying? Is there a peculiarly feminist way to represent women, and if so, what is it?
> —Cynthia Eller, "Divine Objectification: The Representation of Goddesses and Women in Feminist Spirituality"

The representation of women, of the female body in particular, has compelled a pitched battle, fervent since the late 1960s—who can do it, how should it be done, is there a right way, and should it be done at all? The language of painting has its own unwritten dictionary that artists have augmented since cave paintings. I mean, the trajectory of art and artists' concerns has traveled very far from its beginnings. Women have been portrayed as virgins, angels, whores, pictured reading books, sexily lounging, occasionally painting pictures, cut into bits and pieces, nude, clothed . . .

> I think for an artist to make something transcendental, it has to in some way be related to reality, so an artist has to be interacting with people, or the world, in some kind of way.
> —Hilary Harkness, quoted in Sheila Heti, "The Process: Hilary Harkness"

Harkness's series of military ship paintings—behemoths of the sea, fighters in World War II—are architectural feats and imaginative spaces for her novel females. Composed of many levels, each ship is structured with platforms or levels, divided into cubicles or predellas, minute paintings within the entire, larger work. In them, sailors/soldiers perform their duties, play, tease each other, masturbate, have sex, shower, go to the toilet. They're mutable beings, the way the male/female character Orlando was in Woolf's eponymous novel, in which a polymorphous perversity was enjoyed.

Producing work in San Francisco after graduating with an MFA from Yale, Harkness wrote about her sense of "isolation from an affirming LGBTQ community" and "creative exile," and one day saw "out her second-floor apartment window . . . fanciful post-apocalyptic all female scenes." (See *Drunk Girl Observing a Flower*, 1999.) In *Sinking the Bismarck* (2002), her microscopic shipboard residents proffer an opposition to so-called reality; they make their own universe. They recall the figures and landscapes in paintings by Hieronymus Bosch, especially *The Garden of Earthly Delights* (c. 1500). Bosch conceived of worlds in which his imagination was total and overwhelming, where his motivations, desires, fears, and fascinations dominated, and their meanings created a fertile ground for possibilities.

I'd submit that Harkness's work, like Bosch's, also depicts what is not actual but is fertile ground. It might be what is wanted, might be what could be loved or feared, it might be the future or the past—the painted objects and acts cannot be instantly interpreted. The paintings' effects and affect are dependent upon the viewers' projections: Ultimately, viewers will decide the meanings.

> The creative act is not performed by the artist alone; the spectator brings the work in contact with the external world by deciphering and interpreting its inner qualifications and thus adds his contribution to the creative act. Destruction is also creation. It's the viewer that makes the work.
> —Marcel Duchamp, quoted in Calvin Tomkins, *Duchamp: A Biography*

Artists do destroy while they create, though the slate is never clean of art's history. Harkness's paintings contend with and disrupt conventions in narrative paintings, using fantasy and realities, possible and improbable ones. She entertains and plagues stereotypes, often with comic effect, which have been embroidered into psyches for centuries. In our messy image-laden culture, common representations of women show them as benign, unlikely to cause trouble, but Harkness's figures act out, act up, and cause trouble. They are troublemakers.

The usual, pervasive imaging of women is a subtle form of violence that eradicates women's agency, unlike but just as insidious as the obvious violence to women that goes unimpeded, normalized in society, such as rape. It was said and still is that women brought it on: She really wanted it, but she was passive and didn't know she did.[1] Instead, Harkness paints action figures.

> There is art and there is official art, there always has been and there always will be. An artist puts down what he knows and at every moment it is what he knows at that moment.
> —Gertrude Stein, *The Autobiography of Alice B. Toklas*

> The creator of the new composition in the arts is an outlaw until he is a classic.
> —Gertrude Stein, "Composition as Explanation"

Harkness's series on Gertrude Stein and Alice B. Toklas tells a very different tale about them. Shown as sexual beings, they are women who love each other, love others, fight with each other, and sometimes feel hatred for each other. "Through the Gertrude Stein and Alice B. Toklas paintings," Harkness says, "I explore the power struggle at the center of their relationship."

The paintings concentrate on some recognizable figures, such as the two women at the center and Ernest Hemingway, who played a role in their lives. Unlike Harkness's battleship series, the characters are differentiated from each other, each an individual portrait.

Harkness paints lush, lusty figures—in purples, pinks, yellows, vivid flesh tones—in sensuous and curvaceous lines. The interiors are vivacious; they are specific to a significant subculture in the early twentieth century. Stein and Toklas ran a celebrated literary and art salon in their flat, its walls covered with great art of the time. Stein was a powerful cultural and literary figure, and today an icon of experimental writing.

Alice at Loggerheads (2009) is an Alice B. Toklas at odds with any other image of her—pictorial or written—I know: Stein's lover, companion, and, in a sense, her social and business manager. Harkness sees Alice "as a powerful woman in her own right—however, she deployed her immense powers for Gertrude's gain and left little to nothing for herself." In fact, when Stein died in 1946, while she left her painting collection to Alice, that ownership was complicated by Stein's family's claims, based on Stein's confusing will. Stein's family allowed Toklas to keep some of the art treasures, but Toklas lived a very long time, until 1967, and the money ran out. She died in poverty.

In the painting, Alice is alone at a café table. Her white blouse, with black lines drawn on the front, is open enough that a breast is exposed. Her head rests on her fist, her elbow on the table. Alice is dark-haired, wears red lipstick, her eyes framed with kohl, and she is lovely, perplexed, in contemplation, or daydreaming. A half glass of deep red wine, next to a half-full wine bottle that contains a shark fetus, sits on the small table, as well as two seashells face down. Basket, the couple's legendary poodle, is in front of the table, only part of his white head visible. Behind Alice, the background is painted a medium-to-dark brown, and on the left, the background is painted a purplish blue with a large white bird and a few white cloudlike shapes. It seems like freedom.

With its accoutrements, the portrait of this relatively unknown figure in literary and art history—known because of her "marriage" to Stein—responds to centuries-past portraits of women. There is not a plethora unless counting those of Mary and the baby Jesus. Unholy women whose portraits were painted came from royalty, the aristocracy, or from immense wealth.

Another relation to, and antecedent of, Harkness's *Alice at Loggerheads* is Lavinia Fontana's *Costanza Alidosi* (c. 1595). Her dog on her lap, sitting on a red velvet (it appears) high-backed chair, surrounded by a drape of green velvet, Alidosi wears an elaborate gown. She is not smiling. She appears to be looking sternly or seriously at the painter, another well-born woman. Alidosi may be bemused or dubious, her small dog lounging on her lap. Near her, a table with a vase of flowers, an open bracelet or necklace, and on the dark background on a wall, a painting with an arch and a semblance of a vista in the distance, an older painting perhaps from the Renaissance. These objects and details annotate aspects of her and her life, just as a large face-down shell on the café table might relate to Toklas: may be the actual Alice, closed to view, living in Stein's shadow. Or perhaps, in *Alice at Loggerheads*,

Harkness places seashells on Alice's table for their historic symbolic value, encouraging other readings.

Seashells have long been associated with love and fertility; seashells have also represented female genitalia. At the time Toklas and Stein were together, a lesbian couple having a child would have been considered outlandish and even unimaginable, socially frowned upon and illegal, like their union. As important, the technology wouldn't have been available to enable it. But what might have Alice desired if she had been free to desire? Harkness's paintings allow for depictions of what may be women's unconscious, prohibited fantasies.

In another painting, *Woman with the Hat* (2011), Alice holds Hemingway's decapitated head, his bloody brain and viscera dripping out. A bane in Alicc's life with Stein, Hemingway was disgusted by Stein's lesbianism and her submission to Alice, about which he wrote in his memoir *A Moveable Feast*. Hemingway's homophobia must have been apparent to Toklas, if not Stein; ultimately he was banished from the salon. It's notable that Alice is holding his head, as if it were the head of Holofernes hanging from Judith's hand as painted by Artemisia Gentileschi. A woman deploying her power, strong and able to overpower an enemy, is a trope or subtext in Harkness's work. It is notable, in *Sinking the Bismarck*, that seemingly female sailors help sink the single most deadly weapon in the German navy's arsenal. The *Bismarck* had ruled the seas, destroying many Allied ships and troops, until finally it was destroyed.

> Unless there is a new mind there cannot be a new line, the old will go on repeating itself with recurring deadliness.
> —William Carlos Williams, *Paterson, Book II*

There's something otherworldly in Harkness's paintings, the way in which objects are juxtaposed or appear in unlikely places, even surreal. But she is not a surrealist. Her battleship paintings remind me of yet another elder's art, Pieter Bruegel the Elder's *The Triumph of Death* (1562), when armies of men—and some of the troops' skeletons—battle to the death; it is a work about a reality—war—with death the phantasm.

Stories abound in her paintings, but none is a legible narrative; they occasion wonder. Harkness's supposedly realistic portrayals of Stein and Toklas are not "real life" but the way the painter sees into their lives. The paintings require a viewer's imagination—they might even be fairy tales.

This may be apocryphal, but the tale goes that Albert Einstein was asked by a young mother how to make her son smart. He said, "Have him read fairy tales." Then, she asked, "What should he read after that?" Einstein said, "Have him read more fairy tales." Einstein knew that intelligence is produced by enabling the imagination, and that imagination coincides with lofty aims—to discover a vaccine or invent the iPhone—and, most especially, the desire for new approaches to society and culture.

Harkness has an inspiring imagination, unlike any I know. In her work, there is painterly sophistication, narratives, realism, surrealism, fantasy, mordant humor, ambiguity, and playfulness. In her worlds, a viewer cannot discern a single point of view or attitude. They embody the mystery of unknown futures. Maybe, they say, maybe this might happen, and this will be the way people think.

Harkness's paintings are beautiful, sumptuous, witty; they partake of aesthetic and cultural risks, actively and deliberately queering environments, like life aboard a military vessel. She appropriates, does, re-does, and undoes images of women. She asks: What if women weren't the other sex. What if, as Simone de Beauvoir titled her seminal work, women weren't "the second sex."

Note

1 See Susan Brownmiller, *Against Our Will* (New York: Simon & Schuster, 1975). Brownmiller's seminal work rigorously challenged these pernicious attitudes, but rape is still epidemic in the US.

Love Story

Derek Jarman's *Caravaggio* (1986) is not a *Masterpiece Theatre* version of the life of a great painter. Its sets are minimal and sometimes anachronistic, as are some of the props and the dialogue, alluding as much to Italian neorealist cinema as to the Counter-Reformation. In its approach to art history, in which the painter Caravaggio is sometimes referred to as the last great Renaissance master, Jarman's *Caravaggio* is insouciant, but not shocking if one believes that history is a matter of interpretation, of fighting over meaning, of imposing meaning. As Jarman himself puts it, in an interview in the English film magazine *Afterimage*, "The past does not exist. It is what we interpret. . . . When Caravaggio painted biblical scenes, they were always of people of his period. . . . It's only a recent tradition that creeps in by way of someone like Poussin who does it properly and makes it look like Rome. . . . It seems to me very old-fashioned and unthinking the more recent way of visualizing films [about the past]."

As if to insist upon this dead or nonexistent past, the film opens with a shot of the dying Caravaggio. His face is scarred; one eye open, the other shut. He's gone, it appears, and this dying body frames the film and is its present tense, after which all other scenes are of the past—flashbacks. Or Caravaggesque scenes, tableaux, parading before the spectator's eyes as if they were Caravaggio's own death-rattle phantasms, the feverish visions of a dying artist.

Jarman uses certain agreed-upon facts of Caravaggio's short and controversial life and career for the film's narrative. Cardinal del Monte, Caravaggio's patron, appears first in the film where he appears in art-history texts about the painter's life—beside the hospital bed of the young Caravaggio. Jarman also represents the artist Baglione, who wrote about Caravaggio in his *Lives*, published in 1642, and Scipione Borghese, a nephew of the pope, who was a patron of the arts as well as a cardinal. How these, and other, historical figures are represented is another matter. Baglione types insults on a manual typewriter or sits like Marat in a bathtub, penning attacks. (In his book *Caravaggio*, Howard Hibbard writes that since Baglione "was himself a painter in Rome during this entire period, we have to take all his statements seriously." Jarman's approach—he is also a painter—seems the reverse: Can we trust anything Baglione has to say about a fellow painter/competitor?) Scipione Borghese looks like a Mafia capo; the pope whispers to Caravaggio about the painter's naughtiness as if the two were in sacrilegious cahoots. With these representations Jarman challenges received ideas about the past, which is itself already a series of representations.

In the broadest possible sense, *Caravaggio* translates a life into film. Thus all the elements that go toward making it a film called *Caravaggio*—its cinematography, its lighting, its dialogue, its art direction, its editing—represent Jarman's conception of Caravaggio. The aspect of Jarman's art that most intrigues me is the fiction he employs to tell Caravaggio's story. Jarman invents a character called Jerusaleme to be the painter's helper/son and builds a complicated fictitious relationship among three people, based upon two documented events: Caravaggio's murder of Ranuccio Tomassoni, and a court case involving Caravaggio in a fight over a woman called Lena, who was most likely a prostitute.

After the scene in which Caravaggio is shown dying, with his helper Jerusaleme in attendance, the first flashback is to Caravaggio paying money to a poor family for a six-year-old boy (who turns out to be Jerusaleme). The next scene is of the boy and the painter in his studio; the boy plays with Caravaggio's *Medusa*, using it as a shield as he runs around the room. Next the boy climbs into the lap of Caravaggio, who strokes his hair tenderly and rocks him in his arms. Jerusaleme is mute, dumb. Like a fool that Shakespeare—whose dates are roughly equivalent to Caravaggio's—might have created, he watches devotedly over his master's life as he grows up with him. Through his silence he acts as Caravaggio's silent partner, standing in for the ineffable, the unspoken. At times he literally appears to be Caravaggio's other half. Another interpretation: His presence in Caravaggio's life challenges the conventional view of the painter as a violent man, and perhaps challenges a view of homosexuals that would not allow them to be good paternal or maternal figures. Or perhaps his silence represents the impossibility of bringing back history. The mute is an unsettling presence in the film, as much an audience to the events as the maker who tries to film dead events and people.

Jarman's film attempts to match and parallel his sense of the painter's style. His choice of actors to play Caravaggio's models is idiosyncratic, as was Caravaggio's—he used poor people, street toughs, prostitutes to pose for religious subjects. For lighting Jarman incorporates Caravaggio's innovative chiaroscuro, making a rich color film that's reminiscent of black-and-white Hollywood films of the 1940s, with their emphasis on shadow, white whites, and black blacks. But unlike classic cinema, where there is either a good girl or a femme fatale or sometimes both, in *Caravaggio* sexual jealousy and pleasure are spread generously in a different kind of sexual economy among the three protagonists of the fictitious love affair that Jarman gives us.

Jarman could have fashioned an ordinary triangular relationship, where one of the lovers does not get a share of the love in circulation. Instead, he has constructed a relationship of complicated feelings, actions, and looks that turns into a treatise on sexuality and sexual politics in the artist's time, and our own. In classic cinema, according to Laura Mulvey in her oft-quoted "Visual Pleasure and Narrative Cinema," one of the three looks of the cinema is the look of the male protagonist at the female protagonist, which fixes her as the object of the gaze. In *Caravaggio*, in almost every scene in which the three lovers—Ranuccio is a street fighter with whom Caravaggio falls in love and who models for him; Lena is initially Ranuccio's lover—appear together, each character looks from one to the other. The male characters are as much fixed by Lena's gaze as they are by each other's and she is by theirs. When Caravaggio kisses Ranuccio on the mouth, Lena is present and watching. When Caravaggio presents Lena with a beautiful ball gown to wear to an art opening (called an unveiling), Lena's kiss of delight for Caravaggio turns into one of passion, as Ranuccio watches in the background, somewhat out of focus but in the frame. After they break from their embrace, both turn to look at him, which is followed by a shot of his looking at them. In fact when Caravaggio first approaches Ranuccio, Lena is there, and what could have been a close-up of Ranuccio alone as looked at by Caravaggio is a medium shot of Ranuccio and Lena as looked at by him. This structure of complicated looks is repeated over and over again.

Ultimately Lena leaves Ranuccio for Scipione Borghese, telling Ranuccio in front of Caravaggio, "You have Michele." She is pregnant, and when Ranuccio asks whose child it is, she answers, "Mine." She smiles and proclaims that her child will be very, very rich. Ranuccio appears stunned; Caravaggio watchful, reflective. The next scene is of Lena's drowned body floating in a river. (From the script: "Like Ophelia, she is dressed in a scarlet gown which streams out from her, turning, turning, an image of peace and beauty at rest.") From the moment of her death, the film spirals from death to death. Ranuccio tells Caravaggio that he killed Lena for him, "for love," and Caravaggio slits his lover's throat. Soon after Caravaggio finally dies.

Jarman's *Caravaggio* imagines a time that Foucault theorizes about in *The History of Sexuality*, a time when sexuality was less scrutinized and less controlled. Caravaggio, like Shakespeare, partook of the spirit of his age, an age that allowed for sexual ambiguity, in which sexuality and identity were not so closely aligned that one could not sometimes be with men or with women. Shakespeare's sonnets and comedies, in particular, attest to this. And while sodomy, according to Foucault, has always been treated as an aberration, it was the act rather than the person that was aberrant.

The killing of Ranuccio by Caravaggio is a stunning and disturbing act. It says, for one thing, that Caravaggio will not love over this woman's dead body. It's a scene that Thomas Hoving, in his review of the film for *Connoisseur* titled "A Question of Vulgarity," finds more violent than all the killing in Sylvester Stallone's *Cobra*, which Hoving contrasts to Jarman's film. *Cobra*, Hoving writes, "isn't vulgar or cynical. It's a straightforward, taut, well-crafted celluloid romp. The slaughter is so clean and unaffecting that you cannot take it seriously. . . . I wish I could say as much for *Caravaggio*." Hoving continues: "No one knows whether Caravaggio was homosexual. Nevertheless, the director has seized upon this speculation as if it were the absolute truth, and the film *slithers on* from there" (italics added). I mention this review, not for its insights, but for its patent homophobia. Jarman has called *Caravaggio* "a public statement" (*Afterimage*), and it seems to me its statement is in part directed toward comments such as Hoving's.

I've chosen to concentrate primarily on *Caravaggio* the love story rather than on *Caravaggio* the artist story, which is also a significant part of this elegant and intelligent film. Jarman cuts from scenes of the painter's life to the scenes he painted from life. Some of the most arresting images in the film are the groupings of models, absolutely still, holding their poses, which by now are famous through Caravaggio's paintings of them. Jarman did not film the paintings themselves; instead, they are represented in the film by posed tableaux, and by Christopher Hobbs's paintings of the paintings. Caravaggio's friends, lovers, and patrons have been incorporated into these tableaux: Cardinal del Monte poses for *St. Jerome in His Study*, and Ranuccio Tomassoni for *The Martyrdom of St. Matthew*. By showing Caravaggio at work on these tableaux, Jarman constantly animates the paintings by moving into the artist's life to demonstrate where his work came from. When the streetwise models for *Concert of Youths* break their pose, they kid Caravaggio about his relations with Cardinal del Monte. For Jarman's Caravaggio, the life that informed his art is more valuable than the art itself; midway through the film Jarman has Caravaggio say, "How can you compare flesh and blood with oil and ground pigment?"

What I've written about, however, is what *Caravaggio* "meant" to me. And so I add my interpretation to other possible interpretations, all of which are based upon Jarman's representations of other interpretations, and participate in a seemingly endless love affair and battle with meaning.

Stories Tell Stories

Early in the twentieth century, simultaneous with new approaches in linguistics, the Soviet filmmaker Lev Kuleshov explored how meanings in film occur, through sequencing and editing. The Kuleshov effect shows that viewers gain more meaning from the juxtaposition of two shots in sequence than from one isolated shot.

It's entirely familiar that words mean as they do only in relationship to other words, and also that, by setting an adjective beside a noun, adverb beside a verb, words qualify each other. Sequencing in film changes meaning radically. The brain causes it, but in each viewer the effect joins with overdetermined processes, which include individual psychology, environment, history, culture. This concatenation of elements, and others, results in, let's say, a person's version of reality, and a viewpoint, from which people construe or "make up" different stories to tell themselves and others. People don't see the same movie—or experience the same reality, for that matter.

Berlin Road Movie (1971) relies on the Kuleshov effect, using unsettling jump cuts and shots augmented by duration, repetition, and looping. The film is in black and white, and color, about nine and one half minutes long. Shot from a vehicle, likely a car, out the front window, it positions the viewer as another passenger riding in a car along a country road, trees and fields on both sides. A pickup truck is in the distance. Gradually, the car/camera gains on the truck, until the viewer can see a figure in the driver's seat.

After thirty-nine seconds, there's a jump cut. Now the film is in saturated color, of the face of an elderly woman, a bright pink scarf on her head tied under her chin, and she's in a burnt-yellow sweater. The woman wears large-framed glasses, her skin is weathered, wrinkled, her mouth set downward, and from the way her lips curl in, and cheeks sink, she appears to have few front teeth. The woman is looking away from the camera, toward something out of frame. The shot—a moving portrait—lasts several seconds.

The film returns to the road.

The camera/car has passed the pickup truck; then another car speeds past it. The car is heading toward a vanishing point at the end of the road. It takes about forty seconds to arrive there—as if the car were going through a tunnel, there's a light at the end of it—when the film cuts back to the woman's face. She is looking down, and smiling. Then, the road again. Three minutes and twelve seconds later, more or less, a cut to her face. She isn't looking at the camera, but her head is lifted up, and thc camera stays longer on her face. She glances, very briefly, at the camera, then quickly looks away. The film cuts back to the road, as the car/camera goes through a village, where there is some slight traffic, two cars, a bike. Three minutes and forty-four seconds into the film, the woman appears again, in profile, drinking a glass of wine, it's a tight shot, her sharp chin at the bottom of the frame.

The road again, the village again, two cars with headlights on, it may be raining, a bike, a motorcycle. At four minutes and twenty-five seconds, there's a cut, again, to the woman's face: She rubs her nose. Her eyes stare into faraway space.

Then, surprisingly, the film loops back, repeating the long opening shot. But now the first cut to the elderly woman shows her looking directly at the camera, and then looking away, smiling and drinking wine. This episode is followed by the car/camera riding toward the horizon, through the same tunnel of trees, into the light. Repetitions continue, the order changes, some shots last longer. Those shots of the woman the viewer has already seen combine with other already-seen shots, but differently.

Watching the film the first time, without stopping it, the way it was intended to be viewed, I found myself riding in the car, moving forward, toward some place. I recalled that I had once been driven along that same road, through East Germany to West Germany. There was only one road, the scene was pastoral, and the journey seemed like a visit to the Old World: I had those thoughts as I watched Joan Jonas's film.

When the elderly woman entered the picture, literally, my thoughts changed: She represented East Germany, a person Jonas most likely met on the film-journey at one of the rest stops provided by the East German government. She lived nearby. She manifested, even in her face, even inscrutably, East Germany's history. She knew the war. I read into her. The set of her mouth, at first, grim, bespoke almost instantly an attitude I held about life in the East before the Wall came down. Grim.

The film moved on.

When the elderly woman appeared again, smiling or drinking wine, I interpreted the story differently, mildly rebuking myself for my first associations. Her smile, the red wine, and the pink scarf composed a very different image. Now smiling, her image countermanded my prejudice, preconceived idea, or stereotype. Now, on the screen: a woman, the image of a woman, who was enjoying herself, drinking a glass of wine, at lunch or at the end of the day—after work? Like anyone in East or West Germany, I thought, she had her good days and bad ones. Ultimately, I didn't know what I was seeing or what story to tell myself. I couldn't make up a story. The film stymied that. For one thing, there existed no third term, no other object—person or thing—to help build that story.

From images or words, meanings run rampant; human beings are like interpreting machines. Whether one wants to be against interpretation or for it, meanings occur, haphazard, benign or malignant, often unconsciously: Only consciousness of one's responses affords any freedom from them. Jonas's work, her version of storytelling, has its own methods that abjure easy summary.

The structure of *Berlin Road Movie*, relative to Jonas's more mature work, is simple: a portrait and a road contrasted, big movements and small ones, short and long. Later videos and films—and performance and gallery installations—play with more complex structures and elements. Building a coherent story from any of them is an effort of will: Interpretations don't come easily. At least not to me.

Jonas sometimes borrows from myth, fairy or folk tales: In performances or in videos, the actors or Jonas herself might be costumed in ways reminiscent of figures from them. But Vladimir Propp's *Morphology of the Folktale* (1928) delineates how far from them Jonas's work actually is. Like Kuleshov, Propp played a key role in the early twentieth century, and his semiotic work underlies the fields of narratology. Propp considered fairy tales as "tales of magic" and "wonder-tales." About folk tales, he theorized that all "are constructed on the basis of one single string of actions or events called 'functions.'" His structural model insisted that "function, and not theme, motif, character, plot, or motivation, is the fundamental unit of analysis," and that "functions are independent of how and by whom they are fulfilled; from the standpoint of structural analysis . . . the deed itself alone matters. . . . The number of functions available to fairy-tale–tellers is thirty-one."[1]

Propp's rigorous, important analysis is a heuristic device for understanding how narrative sometimes functions. It doesn't apply to Jonas's oeuvre, because of her refusal of logical or causal structures. She concocts visual events, gestures, and movements, and sets them in collision. Jonas attends to ineffability, to fast-moving impressions, to the unremarkable remarkable, to looking and not knowing one is looking—upon realization, always a curious sensation. As in an action painting—she began as a painter—Jonas applies colors, strokes various objects into a scene, or masks them, against a background that changes. She lets things happen in the foreground that don't determine other happenings, say, in a video or on a stage.

The completed piece may defy reason or explanation, and the result can't be told or narrated easily. This is the inenarrable, which is her narrative territory: what can't be narrated. Her stories don't necessarily add up, the way a life doesn't, though meanings will be inferred by viewers, and they may reside in the text, not simply or definitively, most likely as a panoply of possibility.

Flannery O'Connor wrote, "Mystery is the great embarrassment to the modern mind."[2] Joan Jonas risks everything in her work: She looks at human mystery, the murky stuff of life, not for the love of obscurity or ambiguity. Her art also doesn't demystify. In that unpredictable wilderness, gnarly feelings can separate from motives or goals, people come and go, strange things happen without beginnings, and events don't have discernible endings. There are no absolutes or inevitable conclusions. More important, there may be no need of them. Jonas's great project says, in so many ways and approaches: There is no embarrassment in not knowing.

Notes

1 Manuel Aguirre, "An Outline of Propp's Model for the Study of Fairytales," The Northanger Library Project: Tools and Frames (October 2011), accessed online.

2 Flannery O'Connor, "The Teaching of Literature," in *Mystery and Manners: Occasional Prose*, ed. Sally and Robert Fitzgerald (London: Farrar, Straus & Giroux, 1969), p. 124.

Nothing and Everything to See Here

Entranced by looking through a lens, to the eyes and face hidden behind a camera's eye, the world can become a photograph, an image and only that.

You talkin' to me? You talkin' to me?

Travis Bickle stares at himself in a mirror, stands at an angle, makes himself fierce and big, and wills himself to be a killer, a menace, a nightmare. Scorsese's Bickle, his *Taxi Driver*, is cinema's idiosyncratic, unique subject—a self looking and being looked at. Not looking benignly, not at all. Bickle has a purpose.

Bickle is a metafictional character who describes a movie within a movie, performing actor and audience. Bickle poses to please his mirror image, the self as audience. Then, Scorsese sends him into the streets, a malevolent superhero.

A camera eye mimics a human eye, with which it forms a symbiosis, though which mother, which child is moot. Looking is accessible, while shielding the looker from being taken for, literally, a roving eye—or a person's inner eye, private eye, second eye. It permits avid, even dangerous curiosity. The machine allows looking but is not big on forgiveness.

Often, walking in a city or town, I avert my eyes. But I am inadvertently or deliberately looking at someone, a stranger. And why, the stranger wonders, is she looking at me.

You lookin' at me?

I can see a question in their eyes, my glance may not appear to be innocent, not devoid of unwanted curiosity. It is not entirely innocent of wanting to know. It registers everything I cannot control, I know nothing about them.

I don't know how people, strangers and also friends, see themselves. I cannot control how they see me. Or what I appear to be. I have glanced their way, and now I look down. The street is recently tarred, and parts are slick with oil. My shoes stick to the surface, and, as in dreams, I cannot move. I am stuck, I can't get out of this moment.

Anne Collier has lifted an eye from its comic-book existence, enlarged it, and now it is alarming. Large, wide open, sightless, it only appears to be seeing. It seems to see something in its periphery. Its gaze is not straightforward. It is not looking at you, viewer, but you are looking where it does (*Woman Crying Comic #39*, 2022).

Are you lookin' at me?
I'm not looking at you.

Mascaraed, long black eyelashes form canopies over sky-blue eyes with very white whites. Her two tears—she's a crying woman—resemble those infamous "hanging chads," oblong tears or rips in election ballots. Now the homonym "tears" as a noun meets "tears" as a verb below the eyelid: She's crying, she's being torn apart. Collier's crying eye-woman, and women, underlies that image's prominence in popular culture.

A crying woman is blameless, weakened, not a femme fatale or bad mother or wanton woman or slut or bitch. A crying woman is vulnerable. Defenseless, she has lost her cool. No Travis Bickle, the eye-woman has laid down her arms. Disarmed, she is no danger to anyone. Maybe only herself.

In *Crying (Painting)* (2021), a much larger eye, with one falling teardrop, is not extracted from a comic. The big brown painted eye nearly touches the sides of the vertical canvas. The eye seems to be glancing to the side, again, not looking at its being looked at by a viewer. It sits beneath a thick brownish/black eyebrow, almost a straight line. The line is a slash of paint. It frames the sad eye, and turns the eye severe. Is the eye glowering and crying, is there fear there, or just melancholy?

Jesus said, "The eye is the lamp of the body. If your eyes are good, your whole body will be full of light" (Matthew 6:22). One scholarly interpretation interprets "good" as Jesus meaning to perceive correctly. "The eyes are the windows to the soul" has been attributed to William Shakespeare, Leonardo da Vinci, the philosopher Cicero, and also the Bible. Recent studies in psychology indicate that the position of eyes—squinting, open-eyed—suggests people's emotions. But which ones.

Caught looking, I shift my eyes, look down, chin to chest, but the damage has been done; an inadvertent glance in their direction cannot be erased. Looks can kill.

I can't always keep my eyes down, I need to cross a street, and, when I look up, say, at a traffic light, someone might be coming my way, and our eyes meet. Then I might look down again or smile to establish an innocence, a benignity, of my glance. That smile is reciprocated or ignored. I was spit at once.

"Let me speak objectively. I'm being objective." Hints of photography arrived in the late eighteenth century; photography was fostered by positivism—the concept that the world could be known by empirical evidence, observation, and science.

A person behind a camera or grabbing an image from the screen is never indifferent, objective, neutral. What is their mood when they take or make a picture. People carry attitudes, the French would say, a *parti pris*, a biased or preconceived point of view. I wonder if it is possible to see without preconceptions, which are embedded in perception.

In the eyes of the law, when a person is considered to have reached the age of majority and not under the power of anyone else, they are presumed to be in "one's own right" or "sui juris." To be able to judge for oneself in the eyes of the law, though justice is blind, her eyes covered. She need not see to judge, and yet it is "in the eyes of the law" that one is judged competent to make up their own mind.

The eyes witness events, and cannot be trusted. Justice must be blind, but witnesses need to be able to have seen what occurred.

I don't know what objectivity is, I know what it is supposed to be. Psychologists devised the Thematic Apperception Tests, which use pictures to show clients or patients to gauge their responses to them—a person in a bathtub, say. Does it suggest to them danger, rest, relief, is the person terrified of water, and where will that knowledge lead. Imprecise, of course. And then there are Rorschach tests to test how a person projects into an abstract image.

I suppose the wish for objectivity is why dumb scholastic tests were devised, requiring Yes or No and True or False answers—to test subjects without bias. The tests have been found not to be free of culture and society's values, educated and other, but loaded with it all.

The eye's function in art and literature is to add or evoke meaning and emotion to a setting, a face, to an event. Projection and transference are aspects of looking that incite Anne Collier's interests; matters of perception, ordered by cultural, aesthetic, social, and psychological conduits are invested in all of her work.

Often used, often incorrectly, "projection" and "transference" indict objectivity. Freud's theory of transference, in lay terms, indicates that what one perceives in another includes the perceiver's personal history. I believe such and such about a person because in that person I see or experience, without conscious awareness, my sister or father. While projection means, I imagine what I am thinking the other is thinking, that my thoughts are their thoughts. Projection produces great mischief in conversation and friendship. It is why people don't understand each other; in fact, why people don't hear the other.

In her visual investigations, sometimes Collier sets faces and eyes behind bars; uses filters to build or inflate moods, enhancing or detracting from the eye's putative meanings. Blue or yellow or green creates atmospheres, suggests emotional states. A blue mood, green with envy, yellow for a sunny day or for a coward. People see color in and through their own eyes, that is, their own brains.

You lookin' at me? You talkin' to me?

In *Woman Crying #20* (2021), one half of a woman's face almost takes up the entire picture. The surface is gritty, the face framed in black; it's a dark image, the eyebrow slash darker and straighter. The woman is crying, her dark eyeball nearly covering all of the white in the eye. She may be furious or . . . What is her affect? It's hard to say. I can only project into it, which is a product of one of Collier's beautiful and curious artful manifestations.

The corner of the "dark lady's" eye is highlighted in white, and also a tear below her eye and several tears have formed a whitish rivulet on her upper cheek. Like the eyebrow, her half lips are dark as if a deep purplish red.

See what I mean?
See what she means?

Collier works with photography's effects, its ruthless recasting of objects of all kinds. This crying woman is so different from the ones in color, say. Through beautiful images, she also depicts the way a camera and its devices shape and reshape and do and undo physical realities. Is that what I really look like, someone might ask. One might as well ask, Is this the way life is, or the way the world is. A sophisticated viewer of photographs knows their manipulations. Yet, and even so, a photograph works on us, because it touches our senses and what we don't know about them, or ourselves.

Collier is wary of photography's tricks, and in her work also indicts the photographer's eye, as in an advertisement for Sigma cameras. Her use of the ad comments on the commerce that employs women's bodies to sell products, for one. But also, she focuses on the photographer as a purveyor of these images, and the camera as an instrument of objectification. That Collier deliberately hangs this image on a gallery wall declares and signifies her understanding of how she might also, in her practice, objectify others. Doing this, Collier is performing an act of meta-photography, photography about itself and its ethics, its methods, uses, virtues, and vices. Her art does and undoes itself, visits and revisits itself, and becomes something all its own, unique and fascinating.

Still Moving: Eight Stories

. . . I am
bound more to my sentences
the more you batter at me
to follow you.
—William Carlos Williams, "January"

Estranged mountains bulged under the sky, the big sky, the endless sky. Anyway, no one could see an end to it, which reassured her, since so much seemed to be coming to an end. It felt that way.

But it seemed impossible—the universe dropping off, ending, there would be an end, and then there would be nothing, a no more, a vacuum of no more. Her imagination couldn't let her go there.

***

A new train set changed the living room into her playground. Just a little engine and two cars, red and green, going around the metal track, but the little girl imagined more, because the trains followed the curves, stayed on the track, and kept circling and going, going. Her father sat beside her on the floor, like her, beaming.

A very long line of freight trains took a long time to pass. She knew it would come to an end, and was patient at the railroad crossing. The cars of many colors—yellow, red, green—lumbered by, boxes on wheels, while the train's lonesome whistle kept calling, Here I come, here I am, here I go.

Freight trains, at all times of day and night, wailed through hundreds of small towns, just a gas station, a luncheonette, maybe a beauty parlor, towns undone by human failure and natural disaster, flood, drought, towns with no product but the wind blowing.

Her toy train rounded an old track.

***

A jumble of metal and tires, grease stains, goop, the shop looked a big mess. The guts of cars, tools, scattered all over the floor, but he knew where everything was. He'd said to his wife, "I know where it all is, just don't touch anything." His place was like the back of his hand, and he was just as attached to it.

Folks brought their cars and trucks for fixing. Dented, broken down, crashed. The fixer-uppers. The "keep 'em going until I get some money" cars. Junkers. The shit that happened to their riders, to them, these people, their cars, some he knew all his life, accidents waiting to happen.

***

Some guys were satisfied, he saw them in cities, at peace with themselves. Businessmen and their pricey briefcases, proud papas, with IRAs, their babies pressed to their narrow chests. Cocks of the park. Their young women expected everything. His friend told him, years ago, "Oh, she's not for you, buddy. She's too good for you." He didn't believe it, then.

***

Big Joe gave her a ride when she found herself stranded in town. He just appeared, and she figured he had time on his hands. His hands, arms, were covered in tats that disappeared into his skin, darker than hers. She'd arrived from the city, and, after a time, not surprisingly, discovered they were the only Black people around. It happened often enough that the anomaly was really normal.

He'd lived around here all his life, Big Joe told her, except for the time he went to 'Nam. He lived near town, not in it, camping out. "I like it. I don't pay rent. I don't have responsibilities. Except to people I like." Big Joe smiled at her. She said she was glad.

He'd been around, and played pretty good guitar, good enough to work the bar circuit. Maybe he was really lonely, but wouldn't admit it. She was, and she wasn't. She was used to being alone. She couldn't do her work any other way.

He was way too old for her, and they had hardly anything in common. But what's common, she thought. He isn't. She had never met anyone like him. Still, after a while, she knew they'd run out of talk.

Big Joe took her for long drives in landscapes completely new to her, and their growing silences worried her.

***

"No, she's a girl," her mother would say. Or, "I'm a girl," she'd say. Her straggly hair, or that she was lean and tall for her age—just turned eight. "She looks like a boy," they'd say. Well, she wasn't. They seemed disappointed, some of them. She'd be a pretty boy, or maybe she was less pretty for a girl. For a girl. It didn't make any difference to her.

She and her mother camped in fields where trees without names sheltered them from the sun, and a sky of dazzling stars lit up their nights. She did her homework, and then ran around until she fell down, breathing like a racehorse.

They met strangers everywhere, some on their own, or they got to know other families. Some people were friendly, but most kept to themselves.

"A boy or a girl," they'd ask.

***

Bobby's nails and hands were covered in grease, gas and oil embedded in the lines of his palms. He was easy reading for a palmist, his future simple: just a lot more dirt.

Bobby hurled a knife at his kitchen wall, and the pink ceramic vase his mother loved, with tiny yellow flowers, crashed onto the floor, smashed into smithereens.

When she was alive, his mother went for manicures every week, had her hair curled in a place not far from town, and, when he was little, she took him with her. Bobby liked watching his mother get her nails filed, cleaned, fingers dipped into little bowls of warm water, and then painted a color. Red, sometimes pink, one time orange.

She sat under a bonnet to dry her hair, which was wound around little rollers, while Bobby colored animals in his book—red and pink. Sometimes his mother worried that her hair came out too yellow or orange, brassy. The women told her no, they all liked it, and told stories about their lives, and one of them always knew something that the others didn't. He couldn't remember her name, but his mother told him she had a beehive on her head. He didn't understand that.

The beauty parlor was warm in winter, hot in summer, a whir in the air, the space bonnets blowing heat, and the women's voices rose high, unless they were whispering. Sometimes they'd laugh and scream. His mother laughed, too, and he'd laugh along, but he didn't know what was funny.

When his mother was ready to leave, all of the women would give him a kiss goodbye. He'd protest a little. In the car, he'd tell his mother her hair looked beautiful. "Do you really like it?" she'd ask Bobby. "Oh yes, Mama, I do."

"Any of that shit," his father yelled at his mother, "any of that shit comes off on him, it's on you."

***

In the distance, a freight train roared at the foot of white mountains. A young boy, no more than ten, turned to watch it. Where was this one headed, what was it carrying. One time a train had stopped, and he'd run closer to it. He waved at the conductor, who wore a stiff gray hat and had a scarf around his neck. The boy wondered what that job would be like, riding all across the country; he knew one day he'd need a job. The conductor waved back, so that was nice. The boy watched the train until he couldn't see it anymore.

His mother would call his name soon, for lunch, or maybe she'd want him to go into town with her, or maybe they'd decide to pull up stakes, which is how one man in the camp put it. Pulling up stakes. Which people actually did.

His friends at home were jealous, because he did exciting things. He met people who had horses, two or three of them, and they let him ride them. That was a big deal.

He watched his mother write in a book. She kept notes about everything. He knew she had thoughts she didn't tell him. Troubles, too. She explained that she tried to observe what was around her. She told him it was important to remember, and he said he'd remember everything.

But he might forget that woman and her dog, Blackie, in the last place they stayed. Or, the train today in the distance, the shape of the white mountains, how the sun hit them, or that conductor, and how he waved at him.

His mother called his name, and he ran to her.

Stranger Spaces

> You toy with the idea of the human—almost human, not quite human, a little too human. You like to confuse the difference between the two.
> —Sarah Charlesworth

Fiction is art, art is fiction. The word "fiction" comes from the Latin *facere*, to do or to make. Art is making; it's an idea about objects and it is also objects.

Like all fictions, Laurie Simmons's pictures are like-life, life-like, verisimilitudinous. But not life. Her simulations of lived lives are her field of inquiry: She concocts life-like realities and phantasms. A Simmons picture lays the ground for imagining, for stories, and charges "reality" with other, putative realities.

A doll floats in a swimming pool, light bouncing in stripes on the water; she seems suspended in time.

A cut-out, life-like model stands, collaged into a 1950s living room, a piece of the furniture, perhaps, a puppet in an environment that makes her who she is, or rather the other way 'round.

A camera sits on top of a female body, a camera as a head, technology and the body as one, an early representation of AI. How much has the camera made the image of women.

Simmons's work startles with its dissonant visions. There's always a play going on between the illusions people have and what they look for and why. Her work tells us that desires are lived through objects, things, and other people, and that nonhuman substitutes allow us to see ourselves if not better then differently. Our fantasies serve our realities.

Simmons's art conjectures about places and characters. Sometimes the photographs are fantastic, sometimes realistic, sometimes both. Simmons undoes the familiar—impossible eyes get set into too-perfect faces; tiny female bodies stand in toy kitchens; oversized puppet-people overwhelm stages. Her images go with and against received ideas about, say, how a woman should look; how decor imagines or constricts lives; and how interior design, in all senses, can suffocate or encourage imagination.

Simmons's work fools the eye. There's a degree of magic in her images, with their slight shifts, and her work creates distractions from the obvious and ordinary. Her tricky, unexpected images recognize that a viewer's expectations are always there, waiting to complete a picture with her or his own predilections. Simmons subtly counters those, disrupting "should be" with "might be" and "could be."

Art is a distraction from distraction—it can be understood that way, especially now in such a cluttered image world. A Simmons picture arrests viewers because what is imaged juggles perception with wish, curiosity with desire. Stop, focus, look. Look again. It may be that what one sees is always what one gets. But her art proposes differences that toy with "seeing is believing," say.

If art could speak, and it can't, it might say: Can you see outside yourselves?

In Simmons's *Two Boys* series (2013), men, boys, appear as only Laurie Simmons could represent them. They have their own strange spaces, these boys in a changing world—boys displaced, boys unsettled, resigned, and, as much as girls, set in a corner. Call it Gender Corners.

"Boy 1" is in a predicament.

Here I am, flattened, on the surface, an image of a guy, no hero, no name. I'm stuck in a corner, a little Jack Horny. I know, it's too late to become a rolling stone. But I am on my own. I get it. But I'm not that guy. I was a hero once, now I'm down. I fell down, a fallen hero, and I'm down here, checking it out. Clownish, but I don't want your pity. Shit, maybe I do. I'll be quiet, as patient as I can be. I'll wait around, I'm comfortable enough, for now, so I'll just stay here. Somebody will come along, I know it. Somebody will save me. LOL.

Simply Profound

For *Untitled* (1998–2004), Robert Gober specified that a hole must be cut into a wall, have a diameter of 2 ⅛ inches, and sit 53 inches from the floor. Further specifications indicate that its installation is essential, part of the work. That necessity is evident in all of Gober's work. Fixing a piece in place, making it immobile, plays a role in his art. Once installed, it can't be easily moved, not without trouble. It's meant to stay where it is, at least for a while.

This artwork is a whole/hole greater than its parts—gestalt art. Each aspect must be studied for its implications to the whole. Gober's rigor about its placement and installation reflects on art's permanence or temporality, and that universal matter—mortality.

A drain is a homely object, essential to a sink, but otherwise insignificant. Its banality startles, but is mined like gold in Gober's project. Its aesthetic provenance and predecessors include work by Duchamp and Warhol, though, I believe, neither cut a hole in a hole in a wall and stuck an object in it.

All banality is not the same: A drain is different from a urinal and a soup can, though all are human-made products. Banality also denotes unoriginality, which attaches to Gober's service to the everyday, rescuing the ordinary from oblivion.

A wall piece comments on what's not there or expected to be there—a painting, a canvas affixed to a white wall. To come upon *Untitled* is surprising, and requires another kind of attention to apprehend what this thing is.

"It's only a hole in the wall." I can imagine that reaction, because the unexpected in art is regularly dismissed. Or: "Anybody can do that." Reality gives evidence that anybody doesn't. Gober specializes in art that overturns and undermines those self-righteous assumptions.

The brain's chemistry and neural patterns allow humans to focus, by relying on its "attentional networks." To focus on a single object, the brain filters out all other stimuli, or noise, while keeping humans standing upright—constant work for the brain. An artwork requires focus, so the brain guides the body to structure attention. All art depends upon its being awarded attention. In a sense, looking at art requires specific brain work, and the entire body.

Sculptures usually relate to the human body. People stand near a piece, walk around it, if that's possible, and gauge it according to themselves, also physical objects in space. Whether it's Kara Walker's *A Subtlety, or the Marvelous Sugar Baby* (2014) or Rachel Harrison's *Alexander the Great* (2007), or Gober's *Untitled*, spectators respond from their own position and size.

My body is sixty-two inches high, so *Untitled* relates to my eyes, but the majority of Westerners who aren't children will be considerably taller—and it might be level to their shoulders or chests.

A working drain's position is low, mid-waist in a sink or in the ground. Gober's *Deep Basin Sink* (1984) doesn't have a drain, so actually and metaphorically it doesn't allow for egress. Everything stays inside. The basin/sink contains, holds like an unconscious or a cradle, two of many implications of that work.

The sink brings to my mind what the theorist Slavoj Žižek once said in a lecture I attended: "Throw out the baby, keep the bath water."

Later on, maybe Gober thought about the absence of a drain in his basin/sink, though an artist's motivation generally won't have a single desire or reason.

Untitled is a dysfunctional drain. Alone, without a context, it makes its own place fifty-three inches high in a wall. A stark work, nothing else supports it or adds to it.

In art, film, writing, what is left out is as significant as what's there, because, for one thing, leaving out encourages imaginative readings. Then, there is room also for the unconscious to be activated, not just the artist's who makes the object but also and most especially the viewers'. They will see it and give it meaning, if they pay attention. All of Gober's work targets an unknowable and uncanny strangeness, which urges viewers to investigate a humble thing and consider, perhaps, the abjection of certain objects.

A hole in a wall is covered by an X. An illusion of depth is created by the flat black paint required behind the object, an aspect of the work that is like a mask. The drain is made of cast pewter, a soft metal, an alloy of tin and another, harder metal. Its softness also relates to bodies; skin is soft and porous, inhales oxygen, excretes fluids. Looking in, getting close to it, viewers see an illusory inside, depth and space. That illusion is an incitement, viewers want to look inside, just as they may want to look inside their own bodies, say, with a speculum.

This drain fits into a specific hole. Obviously, human bodies come equipped with a number of holes. Eye sockets; crevasses in ears, and, in biological females, a vagina, a urethra, an anus; a biological male has a urethra in his penis and an anus. All vertebrates have anuses. There are various entries and exits in the human body.

History records that Gober first made a drain work after AIDS and HIV had been devastating the gay community for nearly twenty years, when protease inhibitors were just coming onto the market. Many people were still dying, and some couldn't be helped by the drugs. Without access to the drugs, many people still die. "AIDS is not over" around the globe.

In the 1980s, when the epidemic began, the anus was singled out as a site of infection, made into a criminal body part. Gay men themselves were indicted as sites of infection, and as oversexed criminals.

> The pewter ring forms an X over a hole with no entrance, no exit.
> This hole rejects or refuses entry.
> It is a barred or barbed peephole.
> X marks the spot, for danger. X says "Do Not Enter."
> Lived history guides these interpretations and associations.

Now, close to the third decade of the twenty-first century, the work fosters many other interpretations. Someday, I think, no one who lived through the AIDS epidemic will be alive, and this interpretation may be taught as part of art history. And, then, this piece could become a minimalist monument to a long-ago plague.

Untitled proposes an intimate relationship to a body.

From a distance, I could imagine it's a tiny speaker in a wall. Imagining this, I might think it could speak to me, and it's likely that people bend down and place an ear to it, expecting it to talk.

Up close, to peer into it, vision will be occluded by a minimal grid, a pewter X—maybe a coy allusion to the modernist grid. It blocks deeper seeing into something that goes nowhere. At the end of a faux tunnel, nothing is there but an illusion of depth. Now Gober's object trucks in the mystery of blocked wishes.

In writing on art, words reach for other words, phrases, idioms, and through them more images and ideas leap out. I never shy away from the resonance of words and their connotations in an artwork, and words bounce in and off Gober's art.

In it, an abundance of possible metaphors and similes are at play. Gober likes wordplay, and the drain offers it up, to a literal eye or a literary one.

People can be a drain on resources, a drain on their friends. With "drain" as a transitive verb, you can drain a swamp, drain a cyst, and drain a bank account. In the weird and comic TV series *What We Do in the Shadows*, vampires live in Queens, New York, and one of them—he wears a dreary suit—drains the life out of people by boring them almost to death. Boredom inhabits people who lack curiosity about others, about the past and the present, and about life. Nothing given, nothing received, to the incurious.

Untitled plumbs curiosity, and takes time to consider. It is deceptive, plain, understated, and provocative in its seeming simplicity. It doesn't announce its meanings; the uncanny also doesn't. It is ironic, not what it appears to be. Gober's artwork dissembles—literally, hides its intentions—but with attention assembles in the mind.

Playing Both Sides

Guy walks into a bar. Sees a really sexy woman sitting there on a barstool. He sits down beside her, looks over, and says flirtatiously, "Hi, there. Can I buy you a drink?" She turns, smiles sweetly, and says, "Sure!" They drink, they talk, and soon he says, "Hey, wanna get out of here and go somewhere quieter?" She says, "OK! Your place or mine?" He says, "Listen, if it's gonna be a big hassle, let's just forget about it."

> The same tragic themes must exist everywhere.
> —Raymond Pettibon

A homegrown massacre, or all-in-the-family double murder, it's breaking news, whose repetition almost inures me to these horrors, which is the American way, casual, raised on pulp fictions, and besides I have bills to pay.

A little solipsism goes a long, long way: The electrical grid on the East Coast goes down, the lamp beside you must need a new bulb. Anyone and everyone makes that mistake, you are where you are, local not everywhere, narcissism is human, right, which is why there are so many egomaniacs jerking your chain. They think everything happens only to them.

> A monster, however horrible, secretly attracts us, pursues us, haunts us. He represents, enlarged, our advantages and our miseries, he proclaims us, he is our standard-bearer.
> —E. M. Cioran, *The Trouble with Being Born*

Raymond Pettibon's art is charged with flashes from a communal journal of headaches, mistakes, threats, sermons, disasters, in drawings, b/w or color, with headlines, essays, editorials, catchphrases, pull quotes. Everything unfit is fit to print.

Drawings are writing, drawings have many lines. Words can be drawn, pen and ink, gouache, watercolor; they have meanings, and are also shapes. In Pettibon's work, a word or many may sit beside one object or many in unique juxtaposition. His art unsettles, the way other contrarians' work did and does: Bosch, Goya, William Blake, Käthe Kollwitz, Karl Valentin, Claude Cahun, George Grosz, R. Crumb—their visual presentiments, prophesies, jeremiads share a sensibility. A Pettibon drawing of a child's tricycle, with no little kid on it, has a sentence: "Who will finish his odyssey?" The piece has the ugly elegance of an Egon Schiele watercolor.

Pettibon pulls his lines and objects from a virtual or physical file cabinet. On pages in earmarked books, I imagine he's made loads of underlinings. Then he collages or galvanizes these objects, drawing them together from many sources: his extensive allusions and references are to pop, punk, graffiti, comic books, action and superheroes, movies, politics, Christianity, Christ, a favorite action figure, art history, literature, sexuality—the phallus has its own suite of drawings—sexual threat, domestic violence.

Pettibon's art lies in its many, many details—God and the devil are in the details. Visual puns, irony and fervor, oxymorons, collisions, he may see in visual collages. He may think as a collector. In any case, he's his own chief curator and archivist, one who doesn't really want to keep it in his head or files.

> History is for Heavies.
> —Raymond Pettibon

Looking at Pettibon's work, I especially recall two "underground" artists, say, lesser-known ones who blazed a trail on the B-side of art: Antonin Artaud, the French poet and artist, whose dramatic verses, and rants, attacked pretense and propriety; and Samuel Fuller, a brilliant B-movie maker, whose *Shock Corridor*, *The Naked Kiss*, and *White Dog* shredded American niceties, starkly portraying, respectively, mental institutions, sexual perversity, and racism. These two artists' work is stark, with a sense of emergency, a controlled chaos, which compares with Pettibon's, as if the pictures were executed during a time of sleep deprivation. They are not soporific, actually more like action drawings, frantic, direct, electric. Stark. They're anxious drawings, anxious texts: Anxious art creates anxiety about unanticipated and uncanny meanings of the familiar.

Time was, the B movie was an institution, a singular art form unto itself. People who saw every A movie went to B movies, the imperfect side of the Hollywood dream machine; dedicated moviegoers had B movie faves among the features Hollywood produced cheaply. Time was, double features were standard fare in movie theaters, palaces, where a ticket bought cartoons, an opening act, and the headliner/feature, the way bands are programmed now in clubs. The studios needed cheap content; and, in a sense, they made the indies of their day, before experimental film arrived, making its pictures.

Crime was a B movie's compelling subject, weird and dark, perfect for human imperfection done to imperfection. (There was once a B-side of records; now, no sides.) The French New Wave directors of the 1950s and 1960s reveled in Bs, flipped the coin, and took revisionist stands on Alfred Hitchcock's thrillers and Douglas Sirk's melodramas, Todd Haynes's treasure trove.

Preferring a minor work by a so-called major artist is B-side. Weegee is the B-side to Diane Arbus's A-side. Or, the way pop artists did the B, mixing high and low, reducing, or trying to, the gap between them. Obviously, there's Warhol.

Pettibon upholds the B-side, as do, in their different ways, Ryan Trecartin, Nicole Eisenman, Barbara Kruger, Jessica Stockholder, Rodney McMillian, Amy Sillman, John Waters, to name some. In Pettibon's work, the improprieties of that combo are blunt, in your face. He reports all sorts of crimes, committed by religion, politicians, abusers of persons. His visual sorties leave no stone unturned, and under each stone is another, so his work hides in plain sight.

Pettibon plays both sides, A and B. A serious reader, maybe a voracious one, he constructs a visual idiolect of signifiers and signifieds from various languages, including classic and modernist literature. Pettibon's superheroes include Joyce, Ruskin, Faulkner, and Henry James—I don't think there's a more elegant mind or writer of minds. No writer is more A-side or I suppose A-list, though I can't imagine James hanging out at a Hollywood party. If he were ever to go, he would swan past the glittery throng, past the aqua-blue swimming pool, through the garden and out.

> Here is the subject!
> Oh what a subject for a novel, I cried.
> —Raymond Pettibon

Pettibon has referred to James's story "The Figure in the Carpet." In it, James tells a story about a story, a novel whose interpretation, its elusive meaning, becomes the center of three people's lives: George Corvick; the unnamed male protagonist/narrator; and Mrs. Gwendolyn Erme, Corvick's married lover (whom he later marries). The narrator feels great fortune in being asked to write a review of Hugh Vereker's novel for *The Middle*, a prominent literary review, edited by Corvick. Corvick and he are best friends and competitors.

Vereker, the author of the novel within James's story, meets his reviewer at a dinner party, shortly after the review has appeared. Vereker tells the narrator later, after reading his review, "You miss it, dear fellow, with inimitable assurance . . . the particular thing I write my books for." Vereker's novel is also, like the narrator, unnamed.

The narrator, nonplussed, anxiously pursues Vereker: What is it he has missed? Vereker teases and baits him about "the fact of my little secret"; he says, "It's the very string that my pearls . . . are strung on." It's a sexual pun, one that James's younger writer-friend Edith Wharton was given to making, as well.

The narrator just has to know IT, and believes: "It was something I guessed in the primal plan, something like a complex figure in a Persian carpet." The use of "primal" is significant; every word of James's holds its own.

Earlier, the narrator had asked Vereker, "Don't you think you ought—just a trifle—to assist the critic?" Vereker rebukes him: "What else have I done with every stroke of my pen?" Many writers and artists have rebuked critics for such a question, and feel in opposition to being "read" at all. But artists and writers are often expected—the well known, always—to explain their work, why they did it, and sometimes themselves along with it. To explain one's work may be titillating, and may seem gratifying; but ultimately, writers and artists usually recognize it won't necessarily help the work, and discussing their own motivation can be self-defeating.

"The Figure in the Carpet" propels a multitude of readings, from the meaning of meaning, hermeneutics, to Vereker's "secret"—sexuality itself. The story may be a paean to homosexuality, to which heterosexuality can't compete. The triangular arrangement of Erme, Corvick, and the narrator—their relationships are embedded in their own "Persian carpet"—encourages that interpretation. For example, the narrator wonders, "Was the figure in the carpet only traceable and describable for husbands and wives—for lovers united?" His question shadows the story, especially because, the novelist Vereker says: "A woman will never find out." He proclaims this to the narrator, casting doubt on women's capacity in themselves and as wives to help their husbands, intellectually and emotionally—incapable of being men's equals.

Whatever James's position, his intentions for this story, there can be no subtler cheerleader. "Figure" is one of his most perplexing, enduringly fascinating stories, full of possible readings, and great because of it. James understood, as well as any writer ever has, the dimensionality of subtlety. And, this most subtle of stories has long captivated James's readers and critics, because of its finely wrought narrative, its sexual innuendos and inferences, its obsessive, embroiling quest, and especially its commentary on criticism, on interpretation. But an artist's intention matters little in the bigger scheme of things—an idea solidly embedded, I believe, in Henry James's story.

> The author has a fund of reminiscences.
> —Raymond Pettibon

An artwork becomes meaningful when its reader/viewer associates to it—that's when a cigar is really not a cigar.

In "The Figure in the Carpet," the characters are consumed with finding out how to read Vereker's oeuvre the right way, what is his meaning, his intention for it. Their lives become lived only to analyze what the author meant: They don't "read" themselves in his work. The narrator lives to see everyone die: Vereker, Erme, Corvick, sometime after he has married Erme, and, through everything, he wants to know. He glimpsed it, when Erme told him, "It's my Life!" and won't say more. But her response doesn't set him on another course—toward himself, say—and, he is crushed. He will never know.

Curiously, he muses on Erme's being independent of Vereker, not needing, when the author died, to see him again: "She had gotten what she wanted without that." Still, he returns to his loss.

Three people entrapped in an author's puzzle seems weird, far-fetched, exaggerated, but each time I read the story, that sensation drops away. I begin to feel I might be caught in a riddle, seeking an answer to a question I don't know I have asked, or didn't yet, but want to, and shouldn't.

> The pages which contain truth are blank.
> —Raymond Pettibon

A critic, a commentator has been cautioned by Pettibon. He won't tell you, and it doesn't matter, anyway, if he did. That's not the point, right. And getting it wrong isn't the worst thing in the world.

Pettibon on war: There's a drawing of a male soldier and a female civilian embracing, with the words "One of the best things about war is LOVE." The picture presents a visual oxymoron, a flipped take on war: It is a way to love or is love. And, "men being men," men as heroic figures, is war's bounty. The id will be let loose on the battlefield. Men will fight and die not only for territory and gold, oil, but also to possess and dominate women. They also are trophies, and "to the victor go the spoils."

Pettibon on literature: There's a drawing of a crying baby's face, mouth open. He's a little crybaby, whose face has turned pink. Pettibon's drawn the sentence: "For a Long Time I Used to Go to Bed Early." Many will think of Proust. Once upon a time I did go to bed early, everyone did, infants and young children do, if they have childhoods in our contemporary sense of it. Then, along with that sense, I thought: The sentence itself is an image of childhood. "Going to bed early" is in effect a return to childhood. So, two languages, two ways of presenting images.

And, my two readings, reactions, associations, to and about these works—not the end of the story.

> You can't tell the whole story. Sometimes the more you go on, the more ambiguity there is.
> —Raymond Pettibon

At the end of "The Figure in the Carpet," the narrator tells the story of the search for Vereker's truth to Erme's third and last husband. He knew nothing of it. She has died, never telling him. After his initial shock, that his wife kept it from him, the husband listens to the narrator's tale with "waves of wonder and curiosity." Now "Figure" becomes a story within a story within a story.

In these waves, stories go on and on and on, and, with them, the desire to know and the oh-so-human wish for a life of meaning, to believe that life has purpose.

Note
All material or quotes from Raymond Pettibon are from his work, a published text he's written, or an interview.

Death Drive

> How far is instinct from a thing like belief? Not far,
> apparently. At what point is believing so close
> to knowing, that any difference between the two isn't
> worth the fuss, finally?
> —Carl Phillips, "Dirt Being Dirt"

I once asked the sadist of an S&M performance team why she didn't mind hurting her masochist partner. She said, "It's not my body." A more noxious response, "This hurts me more than it hurts you," sustains the corny "I'll be your mirror" metaphor. No disrespect meant, Nico's 1966 rendition was great.

As much as any person who ever lived, Sigmund Freud wanted to understand human behavior: why people couldn't be rational, control themselves, caused pain to others, wished to dominate and destroy. Destructive impulses include self-destructive urges: A murderer may be committing suicide. Mildly weird behavior emerges from a lower-pay-grade neurotic, whose failures demonstrate an incapacity to apply Occam's razor. The neurotic instead chooses, but also doesn't, a labyrinth of complicated operations that prevent achievement.

Inhibitions and sublimations check the eternal wish to be "His Majesty, the baby." But lust simmers, and panting arousal burns a hole in psychic walls. The neurotic, tempted, goes toward the opening. But it is closing. Or the thrill wasn't worth it, and he wants a do-over. Stuck again, with no satisfaction. Anxiety hammers, a clotted, cyclic energy pushing toward stagnation. But there are excellent drugs now to dull anguish, so it's a good time to live. Still, the brevity of human life, once upon a time, has its appeal to all kinds of chronic sufferers.

Neurotics watch the borderline and worse characters—grandiose, amoral, indifferent—forge ahead. They plot their schemes, giving others the big "Fuck you." Everyone may have been presented with a ticket for the show but few get the great seats, near the stage. The super-egoical—who politely check their coats so as not to take up too much room, trying not to impose—later can't get them back, even with a ticket. Most people sit in the back of the theater, very much in the dark.

In Wallace Shawn's play *Evening at the Talk House* (produced in London in 2015; premiered in the US in 2017), the characters come together at the eponymous club. Under the guise of a tenth anniversary party for the production of a play, in which all were involved, they're having a party. Since that play closed, they lament, theater has died, and its death makes the party a wake. As the banter, jokes, and talk go on, one after another, all tell what they've been up to. A mysterious past is alluded to, and a mordant creepiness creeps along.

Surprise comes in blurts. Suddenly, a woman tells the group, sitting on couches, lounging with a drink in hand, that she's been killing people who are not quite right. The line is lobbed like a grenade; it doesn't explode completely, but might later. The particular "bad" acts that result in a person's being killed are not specified. It's kind of acknowledged that the person was, well, deserving. A few characters look shocked, but then the facade, or true face, wears off. Nothing caused it, but a decision was made by higher-ups for the execution.

In the New Group's New York production of the play, the director Scott Elliott conducts the party convo adroitly, subtly; he keeps it casual, which ramps up the chill. People come and go, à la T. S. Eliot, talking of acceptable barbarism, while the group's unsettled scores pile on. With each revelation of a murder, as each character exposes him- or herself, Shawn builds his play, an architect for the new normal. This comedy kills.

Everyone is following, or supporting, the dictates of a vicious social and political order. It's the near future. Recognizable, and recognizably off, and, for a pessimist, not so far from today—the best kind of sci-fi. Polluted values are like carbon monoxide, no one sees or smells it. Society has been or is adapting so as not to notice.

People want to live, mostly they do. Some can't adapt and die. Primo Levi eloquently, without peer, described his survival in Auschwitz. He knew what he was adapting to and, for the rest of his life, questioned his capacity for having that ability. Forever, Levi stood with those who couldn't. Nowadays, and this is cynical, they'd be called "losers."

Life would be simple if money were the root of all evil. Wanting to survive is not evil, though it comes with stipulations or caveats. Usually how one behaves is called "character." But survival has many primitive, irrational parents. *Evening at the Talk House* sharply ponders, through its guileless and guileful characters, how people are adapting now, and, most urgent of all, to what.

Correspondences

I shuddered. I seemed. I wanted. I tried. I loved. I proposed. I discovered. I knew. I studied. I dug. I needed. I imitated. I believed. I was. I realized. I wanted. I had. I became. I initiated. I gushed. I declared. I recorded. I recognized.

I shuffled the deck. It was given to me, but I colored the cards. I dealt a hand. I threw the cards in the air. They fell on the floor. I picked them up in no special order. Failure hung around, pale, shapeless, ready.

I fox fate, it's a daily routine.

The wind's crazy. People walk, their umbrellas collapse. I can't fight the elements. I'm alone, watching. Another ugly brown shoe was lying at the back door this morning. It matches the one that dropped there last week in the middle of a wet, dark, wild night. I wasn't waiting for the other shoe to drop, then it did. My expectations are my own, sometimes I share them. Sometimes I'm disappointed or surprised. Expectations are secrets. I play with mine, them. It's a tricky business.

Fourteen ugly brown shoes could be sitting at the back door tomorrow. Maybe there was a party. Everyone took off their shoes. The shoes fell from the roof and landed at the back door. If fourteen bodies were lying there, dead, I'd need other explanations. A séance on the roof; they left their bodies behind. Or a mass suicide. I'd want to scream Murder, call the cops, if death was skulking at my door.

The shiny bags of garbage scattered in the backyard shimmer in the occasional sunlight. They sometimes look like a novel form of aboveground burial. The wind blows the bags everywhere. They've always been there. No one removes them, and I'm not going to touch them. I hate garbage, full of morbid ideas, crap.

Now a thin, tall guy is walking down the street, bent by the wind. He has to go to the post office and stand on line, negotiate with people who hate their jobs. The way he sees it, it makes him a kind of human retrospective—writing letters, walking to the post office, being willing to stand and wait patiently.

I engage with things as much as people. But I usually don't have fantasies about them. That probably isn't true. I watch television, I talk to it, it's not only talking to me. I'm not a sieve. It isn't, either. Something else could be there but that doesn't mean what's there isn't conclusive, in its way. Inconclusive, too.

This tall, thin guy liked envelopes. Envelopes enveloped, and usually words were incommensurate. He folded the letter into three equal parts, the way nothing ever is, with definite edges, and stuffed it perfectly into the envelope. He sealed it up. He didn't hate licking glue. It reminded him he had a tongue like other animals who use it more. Letters usually reach their destination and, unseen by others, are read in private. Often the recipient doesn't really get the message. He knew that. It was a more controlled exchange even with the interference of the post office. If it's not the post office, it's the telephone company. He couldn't control that.

I don't come to any conclusions alone, even when I'm held in my own silly, irrelevant isolation. I think my isolation isn't solitary, it's a concoction—you're in it, so is he, she, they are too. You might have other ideas. You and I can appear to be interchangeable, easy to substitute. Like pronouns, just as deceptive. I can believe, pretend I'm volunteering. I renew myself, things. If I tremble, it's a disease. Nostalgia for the new.

The thin guy wrote his longtime fiancée, "We share heaven and hell. Hell's being right and wrong. You think I betray you by my indecision. It's how you think. What can I say. I'm vanishing imperceptibly."

A cranky magic act. The guy in the post office often disappeared behind the horizon between himself and others. He couldn't tell where the edge was for somebody else. For her. He pushed at her limits regularly. Cunning, silent, he demolished raw feelings which arrived from a purple nothing, a needy nonplace. They rushed out in clumps and wanted something to hang on to. Finders, keepers, weepers, his words were held responsible.

Now he was almost at the head of the line, worried about how he'd written her. He knew there was trouble ahead. He inevitably thought that, a record stuck in its own, ancient groove.

Your cover songs and mine could be danceable, fast, slow, permeable, intransigent, opaque, accessible, beautiful, reluctant, funny, tough, different from what's in store. I want to go far and still stay in touch, on line. I don't have a dog, but I could walk one mentally if I decided to. No one would know I was just walking the dog. I can more easily do the laundry dramatically. In the laundromat, MTV's on, I see other people's clothes, I watch their eyes, mouths, how they fold their shirts, they notice me or don't, smile, don't. Music caresses, pounds, a rhythm for everything. We're doing laundry in the same time, even if we're in different cycles. It's intimate and alien. Underpants flop around in dryers. That's anonymity. Signs hang on walls and doors. I always forgot which dispenser is for the bleach. I approach the attendant, a woman with sweat on her lip, annoyance on her tongue, acid in her stomach. I smile, tame her fury temporarily, find out, pour in the bleach, go home, come back.

He thought hard about what to say, how to put it, what shapes and colors to use when he tried to draw it out for her, even how to sign the letter. His effort exposed him. When Dorothy Parker was restless, or lonely, she hung a one-word sign on her office door: MEN. Men walked in, thought it was the men's room. She laughed probably, enlivened. He had never thought of that—WOMEN. On his door. And he wouldn't, ever. He was surprised by what was immediate to him, but wasn't to other people. Same way around, them to him, her to him. His jaw ached sometimes, explaining, and he hated the sound of his own voice, repeating himself in different settings. All the words in his universe taunted him, pictures multiplied forever in a series of mirrors. Even his reasoning was an image of itself, feeding back. He was often, he was now, frightened for no reason. Outside the wind blew indifferently.

I change, don't, can't, have habits, am a habit, want to make everything flip into another register, can't find the register. Someone

I knew once worked at the reception desk at Claridge's. A man called up and said, "There's a bomb in the hotel," and my friend opened the hotel register and looked for the name and answered, "I'm sorry, there's no Mr. Ahbomb in the hotel." Then he hung up. Later he realized it was a bomb threat.

You try to reach me, with reflections and illuminations, and I might not find what's evident to you. It's scary, this strangled distance between us, worrying about agreeing to agree even about the terms of agreement. Something may be avoided in the contract. It may be implicit, elusive, but necessary.

Sometimes I think that's all I can do—leave room. I build a room. I paint it, wallpaper it, furnish it, sleep in it, leave it, return to it, hope the room's still there. There's litter in it. I don't mean to return to garbage, but there's a lot of waste in my life.

The guy was staring at a man in the post office who had twenty packages to mail and was holding up the line. A robber stealing time. At least he was next. He wondered if his letter was to her or for her, or for someone else. Or for no one. He glanced back at the long snake of people with envelopes in their hands. Their vulnerability was on display. In that instant, he understood that a letter stands for something which has many letters in it. He wasn't sure if he was standing for himself and others, or not.

In the nineteenth century a French performer named Le Pétomane farted for the public. He set his farts on fire, too, to give the audience a good show, an olfactory night on the town. I have a picture of Le Pétomane, ass sticking out, long unlit wooden match in his hand. There must be a slit or opening in his trousers so he won't get burned. Hell of an entertainer. I wonder how he got the idea to go public.

The guy listened to his stomach growl. At home he let his body go, heard it compose a soundtrack—groans, sighs, moans, farts. He took painful, heavy breaths. He belched, chomped, chewed, slurped, smacked. No one compared slurps, belches, and groans, the beauty of life's secret, disgusting moments. His turn finally came. The postal worker he liked whispered, "Did you hear about the crash? Everyone was killed."

If weirdness was usual, expected, I'd be forced to think on my feet and sitting down. Make things up on the spot—dialogue, ways to walk, look, relationships. Nothing would correspond to anything for long. In a private arena, I'd have my own agenda. I wouldn't hurt anyone. See, I'm walking to the point, along the edge, where a fantasy of doing whatever I like and a drive to be liked compete. I'm not unique, so I don't have to worry. But in the present, I can't decide how many people I should speak to.

The guy shook his head, just grunted to the postal worker who had whispered about the devastating crash. Strangers share the grotesque. A shadow crossed over the envelope, it was the postal worker's hand. But the guy felt darkness, a gap, in the middle of his brain. She could've been killed on that flight. It was possible. Maybe he wanted her to die. He enjoyed the fantasy and tasted the sensation, bittersweet loss. Anguish and relief played a wistful song in him.

He mailed the letter. He wouldn't know how beautiful flesh was, he realized, until he couldn't touch hers anymore. He couldn't know how beautiful flesh was. He recorded all of this and more, and he wrote her again and again, "I can't. I won't." He invented a virtual reality game—a funeral home and cemetery for love. He stole and was stolen from, he deceived and was deceived. Don't try to contact me, she wrote back. Ever. She thought he was crazy.

I listen to Archbishop Desmond Tutu on the radio. He admits, sheepishly, "I love to be loved." I'm amazed by how many ways there are to go and how many dead ends. I can't try everything. I want to. I'm improvising, everything's provisional.

By now the thin guy was such a wreck, his gums were bleeding. He finished work at the insurance company. He locked the doors, turned on the burglar alarm, looked down the street, and glanced warily at some other men who stared vacantly at him. He turned his back. He saw the ocean, sullen and green. The gray sky was perpetually monotonous. Then the ocean roared. A huge flock of birds, thousands of black marks, dark ideas, streaked across the sky. He watched them swirl and dart. They flew in unison. They broke away from each other. They swelled and dropped and swooned. They rushed, scrambled, and took their shape again. Then they abandoned it and separated. They went on and on. He wondered why they did that. Things never total up. They never stay still.

Yesterday morning a man with a red nose and face cut from too many close shaves removed the shiny garbage bags from the backyard. He had to climb through a window to get outside because the door wouldn't open. It wasn't locked, but it was stuck. When he couldn't get the door open, he cursed it. Then he turned and shot me a creepy, even sinister, half smile. He said, "I don't know what you're doing. But you've jinxed the place." I didn't say a word. If that's what he wants to think, let him. There are a million other explanations, but he must like the idea, be invested in it. It's not my bank, but I could begin to appreciate, investigate, his characterization, throw a party for it—a bad recognition is better than none at all, distorted mirrors still reflect an image. I have my illusions, he has his. I would stop celebrating loss, if I could figure out what replaces it.

The plumber has just left. He said he told the man with the red nose months ago that the door was stuck, the faucet needed to be fixed, the toilet seat was broken. I didn't jinx the place. It was already jinxed. I arrived, saw the damage, demanded repairs, got them. There are promises and mistakes everywhere. It's hard to tell them apart. I keep going.

Generation Gap

I was thirteen, beginning to read stories by and histories of artists and writers, memoirs and essays. Oh the Americans in Paris at the turn of the twentieth century, how wild they seemed, bohemians they were called. After college, in a middle-class tradition, I was offered a trip to Europe and grabbed it. Once there I would transform into the writer I was destined to become since the age of eight. Whoever I was, I was riven with images from books, delectable visions, say, of Parisians, their antics, streets, and cafés.

Then I was in Paris. I walked from the Left Bank to the Right, and back, sat in cafés, slowly drank café au lait, watched people. I was told that in Paris people watch people, and I saw it happen: Heads popped up when anyone strolled by or took a seat, which aroused my potent paranoia. I was too shy to do it.

I saw women in dresses or pant suits with little silk scarves tied neatly around their necks, men in suits and ties, rarely jeans, no T-shirts, and felt disappointed. Parisians were conventional.

I lived in Europe for a long time, a determined expat. A friend asked me to interview Meret Oppenheim, who lived in Paris. I had never interviewed anyone, never thought I might meet a famous surrealist artist, and knew almost nothing about Meret O. other than what most people knew: her fur teacup and saucer. I read about her, studied up, but still didn't know what questions were intelligent to ask a great artist.

Meret O. welcomed me into her studio. She was in black shirt, pants, lithe, and lively. She answered whatever I asked. At some point, and I don't recall when, a moment now swallowed in embarrassment, I asked a question only a young person might ask an older one, someone of a different generation. She had lived in Paris in the 1930s, the period about which I'd read so much; she could tell me about it. I wondered, What was it like then, what did it feel like then?

Meret, what was it like being alive then?

She heard my idiotic question and didn't laugh.

It was just like it is now, she said. I am friends with artists and writers. I do my work.

With her answer, I realized the idiocy of my question, realized that my imagination was silly, as if Paris was only what I read about. That people did then, were then, the same as what they do and are now, that life is life whenever you live it.

Meret O. was born in Switzerland, to a well-off family, and could have lived a different way. We are the same, and we are different. Another person wouldn't be like her. As Gertrude Stein wrote in "Composition as Explanation," "There is singularly nothing that makes a difference a difference in beginning and in the middle and in ending except that each generation has something different at which they are all looking." Looking at laptops, or ironing boards, billboards, or texts makes a generation. Warhol claimed he was the same "as rockets and television." What we look at makes a generation, and what we think like makes an identity.

I kept in touch with Meret O., and overcame my anxiety, and sent her my first book, a novella called *Weird Fucks*. In exchange she sent me a drawing, which thrilled me, and when she came to New York for a show, I think it was 1987, I went to the opening. Next, we had coffee in her hotel room. I took many pictures, including one with a coffee cup to her lips, but only one shot was good, even beautiful—a portrait of Meret O. standing in front of her room's window, resolute, the light mellow behind her. So I saw her again, extraordinarily happy to be in her presence and to know her even a little.

A number of my books were published in the 1990s, and since then, I have been interviewed often.

One interviewer asked: What was it like to be alive in the 1970s?

I said something, I don't remember what. Maybe I quoted Meret O. The past can be magical if you haven't lived it.

On Influence

I'm almost certain Kiki Smith introduced me to David Wojnarowicz. I knew about him, his Rimbaud pictures were pasted on walls and stenciled on sidewalks in the East Village. In my mind's eye, we're on a sidewalk, maybe on Houston Street; it's windy, late fall or early winter, and Wojnarowicz is standing behind Kiki.

Consciousness superimposes scenes from the present onto the past, or mixes one distant moment with another; memory has forever been Photoshopped. The technology replicates a natural, involuntary default position in the brain, or a human inclination to fuse events. Photoshopping can deliberately distort or corrupt historical events; human memory is distorted, first, by subjectivity or point of view, then by the passage of time. Was it a dream, a photograph, did I hear the story, did it actually happen?

The clock marks seconds, minutes, hours; the calendar, days, months, and years—these human productions divide now from then, and from the future. The unconscious doesn't obey time, which also confuses memory, and can make days feel endless or too short. Maybe that's why people invented what Shakespeare, in *Richard II*, called time's "numb'ring clock."

I picture Wojnarowicz with his head down; he was tall, I'm short, which would influence how I saw him, and he me. He might have been looking sideways, and appeared shy or elusive. He had a long face, uneven features, and a smoker's raspy voice. Other adjectives pop up: gangly, rawboned, intense, weirdly funny, restless, sad, sensitive, vulnerable. But this isn't a portrait of the artist as a young man. Wojnarowicz's portrait was, in a profound sense, shot by his time.

Wojnarowicz knew he was homosexual before the word "gay" took its place; he came of age with Stonewall and the movement it incited—gay liberation. Then, an individual's "coming out" was a revolution of great and intimate proportions, a public and private declaration of startling consequence. Wojnarowicz's art and writing were born and nurtured before, but fomented in and exploded during, the AIDS crisis.

Artists and writers are often very different from their work. They work with and against their education, fear, anxiety, hope, angst, values, to build characters, find words or concepts, build structures or images that defeat or deny these things their power, or sometimes to venerate them. The gap between person and artist can be inexplicable, but people, including artists, often conflate the two. Art historians and critics might merge them, judging the work by the person or the person by the work. But history judges what history also produces.

What is now called "history" was Wojnarowicz's lifetime, his present, which insidiously produced what mattered to him. His best talents were made furious use of during the 1980s until his death in 1992. His impassioned writing became a powerful voice of the AIDS epidemic, his blunt-force-trauma art a singular and passionate face. Wojnarowicz's work, I believe, even without the exigent circumstances, or influence, of AIDS, would have been knife-sharp and arresting. Without the consequences of AIDS, though, there would have been time for him to mature as a person and an artist, to have a future.

Consequence and influence share territory. They can't be predicted or entirely comprehended, since the two radiate from a myriad of sources and will settle without foreknowledge and, usually, without acknowledgment. Mostly, people don't get to choose an influence, unless they're conscious adults, and by then the wish to be influenced—to absorb—means that a person has been, in a sense, prepared. The preparation for influence develops independently of consciousness, while simultaneously creating it. In the 1980s, being infected by HIV and developing AIDS was an unchosen, horrific fate, fatal. People were very frightened, and felt hopeless. Not every artist or writer responded as Wojnarowicz did. His responses were unique, thoroughly felt, and driven by an urgent necessity. In his time, his work was extraordinarily moving—it stunned. It will never be experienced again as it was then, in that very dark moment. Contemporary artists sympathetic to Wojnarowicz's work, who say his work influenced them, find meanings in it that have been profoundly useful to them. They are a diverse group, their work dissimilar in appearance from his, and from each other's. Some of the artists might say: "His work gave me courage." Or "Wojnarowicz was a courageous artist." Courage in an artist or writer is different from the courage of firefighters, who rescue people and risk their own lives. Artistic courage might be conceptualized as an internal drama about overcoming rules or inhibitions, dicta of all kinds, the art a manifestation or result of a multitude of processes.

Art won't save people from burning buildings, but not all risks are the same or equal, and they shouldn't be measured by one ruler. During his time, Wojnarowicz's work might have sprung from rage, fear, and compassion or been inspired by them, his approach or sense of form enabled by and called to address them. An abiding necessity to save himself and others arose.

A cruel disease had suddenly and quickly made helpless victims of an already stigmatized group. The tragic waste of the disease, and also the injustice of stigma, probably urged Wojnarowicz toward a kind of overcoming. To have his life be meaningful, he would keep living by doing his work. He would rage on.

Artists are not mythical beings or romantic heroes. In their chosen fields and in a certain time, they make aesthetic, intellectual, conceptual decisions; they may react variously to social and political questions and to concerns central to their mediums and practices. As artists, they evolve from and are influenced by not just other artists, but also their own psychology, religion, race, economic background, and more. Influence is everywhere, and they take chances, too. Everyone who lives sometimes does, everyone sometimes has to. That curious notion of character also comes into play: Existentially, artists and writers become who they are, and make what they do, in the moment they act.

Sometimes an artist's work opens up a space. I'll call it a "mental space," a space for themselves and others, where random thoughts, images, ideas germinate and occur—these might have consequence. When that happens, when an artist's choices do that, an artist might be called courageous. Something that was broken got metaphorically fixed; something that was blocked breaks through. A solution arrives to a problem no one ever mentioned. Some will notice that in the work, and it helps them.

Shannon Ebner, Wade Guyton, Henrik Olesen, Adam Putnam, Emily Roysdon, Zoe Strauss, and Wolfgang Tillmans, among many other artists who mention Wojnarowicz's influence on them, probably recognized, reacted to, or internalized something they gleaned in his work; usually they mediate it so thoroughly, a viewer wouldn't spy it. Or, because it was an idea for them, an idea, say, without materiality, it never materializes in their work.

Harold Bloom theorized that influence produced anxiety and troubled poets who turned to writing poetry after reading other poets. Bloom studied the romantics, but wrote *The Anxiety of Influence* under the sign of modernism. Ezra Pound's call was "make it new" (though Dante shaped his poetics). Influence from that purview was a staining or tainting, an inhibiting or retarding, of an artist's originality.

To rejig the concept of influence as an actor-agent in the work of artists and writers, to make influence newer, the computer must be restarted with another program. Influence occurs, in this register, because an artist perceives in another's work a space, or opening. Maybe it's whimsical, inchoate, wishful, a fragment of a fragment. Rarely a direct taking, more like the flow of information. Rarely "stealing," as Picasso said great artists do rather than borrowing. Instead, something is shown, intimated or associated, noticed, and it feels true or right or necessary. A diffusion is transmitted and received. Influence reconceived would be a heuristic device, an emboldening or an encouragement.

One artist can and often does encourage another. One artist's courage in making, or what another perceives as such, becomes another's space to take up. "Courage" and "encourage" have a similar root: In Latin, *cor* means heart. To have a heart is to give heart. To give heart is to embrace and charge others with a kind of love.

The Last Words Are Andy Warhol

I'm going to speculate about some of the issues raised and some of the ideas I found compelling and daunting in *a: a novel* (1968). *A: a novel* is a narrative based on twenty-four audiotaped hours in the life of Warhol superstar Ondine, an articulate, funny, volatile man. When Pope Ondine acted in *Chelsea Girls* (1966), his performance exceeded, crossed—even violated—the supposed boundary between life and art, a line Warhol wanted crossed. The line was blurred, if not effaced, in his only novel, *a*.

I've written this essay as a list, a shopping list in paragraphs. Warhol liked to shop. I don't, but I like lists.

1. "A" is for Art, Andy, and Amphetamine—Ondine lived on speed, and the story is speed driven.

2. Reading *a: a novel*, I sometimes felt like one of its participants: "Nine more hours to go," says the Sugar Plum Fairy. Time is of the essence—actually it's the essential element in the book. There are just so many tapes to fill, hours to stay awake, and so time's on everyone's mind. The tape recorder's going; a book is being made. The Book is being made. In fact, the last words in the novel, spoken by Billy Name, are: "Out of the garbage, into The Book." Warhol, through Name, is claiming garbage—the minutiae and tedium of daily life, the unedited flow—for literature.

3. *A: a novel* is a project of—and an exercise in—consciousness and self-consciousness. Ondine and most of the others recorded are not unwitting characters or subjects. They're self-conscious even when they're nearly unconscious.

4. Ondine, the protagonist, sometimes fought against the chains of the tape recorder, a new master, asking Warhol many times to stop it. But Ondine continued to let himself be recorded, as did all the others who questioned Drella's demands in making this novel-book. Maybe they knew they were participating in something new, or interesting, maybe even worthwhile, simply because it was Warhol. Though they struggled with him, they complied. Others may now be horrified by this compliance, believe that everyone in the Factory was manipulated, taken advantage of. They used and were used, perhaps, in every possible sense. But another view is that, given the problems in their lives at the time and their insecurities, which *a* documents, Warhol offered them something—work or a feeling of significance for that moment or a way to fill time. The tape recorder is on. You are being recorded. Your voice is being heard, and this is history.

5. What about authorship in *a: a novel*? In part two, there's talk about the typists who are transcribing the tapes, and who, in a way, through errors, mishearings, and incorrect spellings, contribute to or create the book with the speakers. It's the typists' book. It's the tape recorder's book: *A* could not exist without the tape recorder, just as the novel could not have been born without Gutenberg's press. Or it's Ondine's book: He's the author of himself, and the protagonist; it's his twenty-four hours. Or it's Warhol's artwork, a conceptual and experimental book. Part of Warhol's work was to regularly produce a blur around authorship.

6. Warhol dropped the mirror, let it crack into pieces, and instead held a tape recorder up to life. He saw a god in the machine and

used as many machines as he could—*a* notes the arrival of video, a new toy, to the Factory—and he didn't fear the loss of authorship to machines, when his hand, literally, wasn't in or on it. He constructed another kind of artist, one who directs machines and people, who uses technology, whose imprint was virtual.

7. *A* reveals realism as a form of writing, a type of fiction, a genre, not an unmediated, exact replica of life, not a mirror image. Books are not mirrors, and life doesn't go onto the page like life but like writing. Warhol's novel is closer to life, reality, than a realist novel. It's mediated by the elements I just mentioned—the apparatus, the speakers, the typists, and Warhol's idea for it—and by the continuous twenty-four-hour frame he wanted to use.

But Warhol was flummoxed by Ondine, who became exhausted or bored after just twelve, so the book does not go twenty-four hours straight. At the end of those twelve hours, Warhol asked Ondine for his last words, and he said, "My last words are Andy Warhol." A lot of reality is in that—and self-consciousness and consciousness. In *a*, reality is gotten at differently, without any of the codes of realism.

8. If Warhol had recorded a continuous twenty-four hours, *a: a novel* would have adhered to the classical idea of unity necessary for tragedy, and might have compared with Joyce's *Ulysses*, which may have been on his mind because it stands as the twentieth century's representative or exemplary modernist novel. (Bob Colacello says Truman Capote's singular, brilliant novel *In Cold Blood* was on Warhol's mind.)[1]

The second half of *a*, instead of being continuous time, is a series of fragments, more out of joint, more out of time—more timeless or against time—than Warhol originally planned. What started as a modernist novel became a postmodernist one. Warhol taped Ondine's life, whenever he could get it, in all its discontinuous and disjointed glory, or gory, as the wit Dorothy Dean—DoDo in the book—might have put it. He abandoned his original idea, *a*'s purity. But the words "pure" and "purity" appear often.

9. One of the typists was said to have said of the book, "It's worse than Henry Miller." Dirtier, she meant. It's certainly more complex and difficult to read in all senses than Miller. *A* sometimes falls into unintelligibility, into illegibility. When Warhol held a tape recorder up to life, the result was streams of consciousness, many narratives intruding upon and interrupting one another: phrases and anecdotes, wordplay (there's none in Miller), incoherence, coherence, poetry, puns, witticisms (I love Ondine's remark that "charity begins alone"), documentary, bits of all of these. It's not an easy read. None of his work is.

10. *A* challenges reading. How do you read it? Sometimes I heard it, sometimes I thought it was radio, not TV or movies—I didn't see it. Though I checked Victor Bockris's geographical notes at the back of the book, I couldn't find "place." I tried to stay with Ondine, but when he became very high, what happened to me, the reader? It was a relentlessly strange reading event. *A* felt cerebral and became claustrophobic, airless. It's a book with no space and in which space is a context, an area of contest, in which space is psychological territory that's fought over. The space at the Factory, for instance, was fraught: There were territorial skirmishes, fights for primacy—over

whom Ondine wanted in or out, what the Factory rules were and should be—all of this is discussed in *a*. In one part, so many voices appear in one taxi at one time and with so many interruptions that I began to think about the book as music, as a score. When I did that, I relaxed some, and reading *a* became less stressful.

11. *A: a novel* challenges writers because Warhol's idea of what should be on the page allows for the chaos that writers are meant to control, to turn into art. *A* underlines how unlifelike most written dialogue and conversation is. The novel's most peculiar challenge is to the writerly conceit that writing just pours out of us, from our guts or our heads, without an enormous number of de facto decisions made even before what we're writing comes to consciousness or to desire. In other words, we receive language for the page, because other pages have been written. *A: a novel* wasn't written or conceived for the page in that sense.

The novel follows its protagonist and in its way, and within Ondine's limits, remains faithful to its structural idea: time. Time's a constitutive element of narrative; it's material. Novelists use time the way filmmakers use cuts, or long shots, close-ups, and so on. In *a*, the reader is in real time, whatever that is, and every moment is precious or boring. Time and art in a sense are collapsed: Moments are precious or boring both to the reader and the story. Ondine could ask himself, What am I looking for tonight? (and he does), What do I want? Where do I want to go? (all narratives are journeys). The reader could ask, What am I reading for? What do I want to find?

Boredom tells us something about life's relentless movement toward entropy and death. (It's said the psychoanalyst D. W. Winnicott once commented that he knew when to take someone into therapy—when they bored him.)

12. Warhol wanted Ondine to say everything, to keep talking, to say whatever came into his mind. It's a psychoanalytic idea, and if that's the case, Warhol's the analyst, Ondine the analysand. Robert Polito suggested to me that it could be priest, confessor, and the talking, confessing.[2] Confession mixes with the psychoanalytic, and one reads *a* expecting revelation, which is common to both forms of talking. I read expecting or hoping for discoveries—and found some. Warhol reveals a few secrets, Ondine many, and all kinds of vulnerabilities and fears are displayed—eventually. Writers would have headed toward this material more quickly and edited away most of the other material. But the other material is not cut out in *a*; it is *a*. The unedited relates powerfully to confession, to psychoanalysis, to not leaving anything out, to wanting to hear, to say, to listen to everything. To me, Warhol's lust for the unedited is the most resonant and mysterious aspect of his work.

13. In another way of looking at *a*, along the lines of Stevens's "Thirteen Ways of Looking at a Blackbird," Warhol's the queer-listening priest, Ondine the queer-talking pope. An unexpected, moving moment occurs when Ondine says to the Sugar Plum Fairy, Joe Campbell, "You may think I'm not searching, and He—Drella—may think I'm not searching, but I'm searching. Which one of us, who isn't searching, for God?" Joe Campbell was a formidable interlocutor—no wonder Dorothy Dean was in love with him—and induced Warhol and Ondine to make some of their most revelatory statements.

Pope Ondine was searching for God. With this revelation his desire to get high suddenly shifted into a different gear. In *a*, he speaks over and over again about beauty and the beautiful, and so, in a way, his quest, his journey, was for the illusory sublime—some kind of state of grace. Taking drugs and listening to opera—especially to Maria Callas—were his tickets to God.

14. Reason is retrospective, so it makes sense that reading *a* as a score, as music, loosened me to its idiosyncratic rhythms. Opera is the soundtrack, the background music, to this book. The opera might be *Tosca*, because of its aria, "Vissi d'arte." "I lived for art, I lived for love," Callas sings. *A: a novel* is a record of a life living for art, being recorded for the love of art.

15. Superstars like Edie or Ondine transformed themselves into what they thought was sublime. They were antiheroes performing a mostly unscripted high-wire act. Warhol believed in them, as self-creations, believed in their fictiveness. His belief acknowledged their desires and the power of fiction itself, the reality of fantasy and illusion—and also contradiction, one of fiction's difficult truths.

Another is verisimilitude, likelihood, a similarity to reality. A likely story resembles reality. It may use make-believe to arrive there. His superstars are likely stories, resemblances close enough or odd enough to question stars and stardom, actors and acting. They live inside a narrative that doesn't stop when the film does. Serial, cinematic images, they perform their antiheroics again and again. Their will-to-be matters, their will-to-be there matters, and on Warhol's screen their psychic realities matter most.

16a. In a Warholian world, authenticity is ironic, even a joke, and essences are funnier. Actual histories, biographies, and sometimes bodies were left behind and new ones manufactured in the Factory. Warhol's superstars could march in a parade for those who want to be switched at birth.

16b. The authority or authenticity of any fiction resides in the ability to make others suspend disbelief.

17. Warhol's art questioned what art was, what was expected to hang on a wall, and the same is true of *a: a novel*. It asks: What do we expect in novels, how should they be written, why do we expect them to conform to certain rules? Whose rules? Factory rules? Recently back in print, *a: a novel* may be responded to, albeit less vehemently now, the way everything Warhol did in the 1960s was responded to—as garbage or genius. Or it will be ignored and its perplexing, vital questions never considered seriously. This novel—and Warhol's work generally—doesn't provide a walkway down the middle. It's unorthodox, a walk on the wild side.

18. "The last words are Andy Warhol." He was the last word, maybe, on the twentieth century. Though think what he would have done on the internet. (Is *a: a novel* the precursor to the internet novel?)

But are words important to Warhol? I don't know. Talk was. Is talk cheap? He was both a spendthrift and thrifty, even cheap. He surrounded himself with articulate, talkative people—with wits like Fred Hughes, Ondine, Viva—but he was stingy with his words.

He often pretended to do a dumb show and often had others speak for him.

19. The last words are Andy Warhol unedited. Warhol started *Interview* magazine and insisted on publishing unedited transcripts. He wrote an unedited novel. He didn't want to edit his films in the usual sense. Unedited versions came closer to what he wanted, but I'm not sure what that was. He wanted to keep his hands off, or to hide behind the density, opaqueness, of the material, or to let the idea do its work. He wanted to be inclusive, democratic. (After all, he wanted to name pop art "Common Art.") He wanted something he could never imagine to happen, something he couldn't fathom to occur, and he wanted to be there when it did, to see it or hear it.

Or he wanted the unedited in the way—sort of the inverse way—that John Cage wanted silence. How do we know what to pay attention to? How do we know for ourselves what's important? How do we choose? How do we know if it's art? How do we decide what to see and to read? How can we tell unless everything is there to see and to read?

Notes

1 Bob Colacello, speaking on a panel about *a: a novel* at The New School in April 1998, on the occasion of its reprinting by Grove Press.

2 Robert Polito, director of the writing program at The New School, comment made to the author after the panel on *a: a novel*.

Imagined Places

> I'm not sure how I got to these places, but I realized they were pictures about summerness, fullness—deep, complicated spaces.
> —James Welling

I'm traveling mentally, the way I usually do, from a lush marsh, to a secluded road, to a chain-link fence, to a tower and abandoned railroad tracks. In the hush of these intensely static photographs, I concoct associations that bridge the four disparate, ordered views. Order breeds narrative, but I stop myself. Pictures don't tell stories, people do, and every interpretation is an exposure.

Uneven black borders, part of what's pictured, threaten to spill, like ink, over the putative views. Their reality could be obliterated. "The black border is the shadow of the film holder," Welling told me, "the reality as opposed to the illusion. It's about materiality, which is a kind of valueless death, the thingness of film."

These photographs are part of a larger project Welling began in his home state, Connecticut, in 1997. "It's still evolving and hasn't been exhibited," he says. "But it relates to my most recent work, the *New Abstractions*, representing a parallel if very different track." Appearance and illusion, the reality of the camera and darkroom, perception and a world external to us, what we see or think we see, have been at play in Welling's elegant photographs since the 1970s. His subject matter shifts from abstraction to documentation: crumpled aluminum foil; drapes; shadows; light sources; trains, tracks; trees; industrial sites; views outside his studio. His work questions any assumed differences between abstraction and representation, between modes of presentation.

Studying Welling's variety and range is a curious experience; the more you look, Yogi Berra might have said, the more you see. Welling's photographs are objects in themselves, beautiful compositions that also gloss and comprise a history of photographic practices. Almost every idea its apparatus offers has been noted, somewhere. "From the beginning," Welling observes, "there was a dichotomy: the shadow of the object and the representation of the object, the two great historical poles that are photography's foundation." He tells the medium's Manichaean history, ingeniously enlarging it with work that loves and ironizes both sides of the argument. Take this portfolio: Each photograph documents a real place and presents a view (Welling thought of Edward Weston when he took up the eight-by-ten view camera to do these); but the image—and its conventions—is draped in mourning black. In effect, Welling lavishes us with illusion and shatters it, too, simultaneously dispensing a shot of contemporary ambivalence to the mighty image.

I oscillate within the dissonance, but proceed, longingly, into imaginary spaces. There's room for stories, memory. A tiny body of water in Salt Marsh provides a start. From there, I wander into the woods and vanish. I find Route 81, where Cindy Sherman's Hitchhiker might have waited. Walk on until New Haven. Fenced out or in, I peer through the bars, spying a picture within a picture. But I'm blocked, so reaching the tracks, Devon Tower, is a relief. Escape. But does the train still stop here? Am I traveling into lostness? Where did everyone go?

Early Years of the New Museum: An Intellectual Reminiscence or Pieces from a Consciousness

If I were writing a history of the New Museum, and I'm not, the first sentences would include Marcia Tucker's name. Tucker was the unique, essential element, the sine qua non, of its birth and existence. Her vision for a new museum evolved during a time when the institution of the museum was undergoing serious criticism. Did it shape art and how we see it? How do politics, of all kinds, inflect canon-building; how do important galleries and collectors affect museum collections and exhibitions? Who is excluded?

Not surprisingly, this investigation occurred in the same breath that many American institutions underwent rigorous scrutiny. From the 1950s on, in America's postwar decades, the denial of almost any right, and any minority its rights, the denial of any group's inclusion, was fought. Exuberance and optimism after winning the war in Europe, whose emphasis was freedom and democracy, turned into disillusionment at home. A clamorous, human surge for justice, for civil and human rights, resulted, convulsing and transforming American society and culture.

Since World War II, civil and cultural wars have been constant. And inclusion has been central to them. Inclusion in a museum, also.

I'm not sure when I first visited the New Museum in SoHo. I'm not sure which show I first saw. What I remember striking me, first, was its large picture window onto Broadway. The museum seemed instantly less grand and more like a place to drop by and browse, like a retail store. That may not be a great way to describe a museum, but window-shopping has its glories, as Walter Benjamin wrote. The museum's designers made the space feel familiar, and approachable, which encouraged me. Over the years, the picture window was used differently by artists and groups. Anyone on the street might get a sense of what was happening in the museum, and also catch a glimpse of contemporary art and its conversations. The New Museum became one of "my museums," just as St. Mark's Bookshop in the East Village was one of "my bookstores." Some of the museum guards were there for years, and we always said hello and talked, and that made it homey.

History/histories are made by individuals inside larger historical movements, and written about by individuals. Marcia Tucker acted as an individual, and she also acted in concert with others who supported her goals and recognized the same inequities and discriminations. They sought inclusion for "underserved" artists. So, the New Museum was both an effect of and an agent of change in the politics of representation.

The New Museum staked a claim in the "new." The adjective may even be definitive, since its mandate would be to present new art, to address the contemporary quickly. But presenting the contemporary could mean that what was exhibited might be only of "temporary" interest, something most museums avoided. The museum took risks.

My two intelligent older sisters, considerably older when we were all younger, schooled my feminism. I called myself a feminist when I was eight. My mother was not quite a good-enough mother, but I didn't doubt her intelligence. So I never bought the canards—women weren't as smart as men—never bought the vague and explicit dismissals of a class called women. I knew they were wrong, but the prejudices affected me, first, psychologically. Sexual prejudice affects the ways that my writing, say, is received or read: "written by a woman." Or, by a gay writer, Black artist, woman artist, Black woman artist, Black male writer, et al. An adjective works to limit the noun, which belongs to "the majority," and little headway has been made to break this down. In my book, I am a writer, first. Qualifiers follow.

The impact and import of feminism, sexuality, and gender on and for artists and art-making were urgent to the New Museum founder Marcia Tucker. Mounting exhibitions under those categories and their vicissitudes, the museum would distinguish itself with its thematic shows—*Classified: Big Pages from the Heresies Collective* (1983), *Difference: On Representation and Sexuality* (1984), *HOMO VIDEO: Where We Are Now* (1986), *Girls Night Out (Femininity as Masquerade)* (1988), *Bad Girls* (1994), *Picturing the Modern Amazon* (2000)—and major solo shows by Carolee Schneemann, Mary Kelly, Rosemarie Trockel, Ana Mendieta, and David Wojnarowicz, among others.[1]

By the mid- to late 1970s, the discourse around so-called feminist art was divided, roughly, between two addresses: essentialism versus anti-essentialism, which included the Great Mother, Goddess, or spiritual feminism, and the theoretical and/or politics of representation feminism. Within these divisions, another: pro-sex and anti-pornography feminists. The New Museum played a role in exhibiting or staging their differences.

Again, roughly, the exhibitions *Girls Night Out (Femininity as Masquerade)* and *Difference: On Representation and Sexuality* represented work that was feminist in intention, might obliquely refer to "women," used appropriated or mediated images, and engaged with other art forms, for example, conceptualism. The art recognized nonessentialist differences between men and women, proposing theoretical, especially psychoanalytical and deconstructive, approaches to imaging women, to gender generally.

The *Bad Girls* and *Picturing the Modern Amazon* exhibitions displayed art with a focus on the body, often actual bodies, and physically powerful female ones; some of the art encouraged a contemporary identification with prehistorical and mythical female figures and imagery. *Bad Girls* did not necessarily show work made by declared feminists, because, as Marcia Tucker wrote, and I paraphrase, there wasn't agreement as to what that meant. The art was in your face, sometimes tongue in cheek, and allowed, Tucker suggested, the anarchic and comedic into those questions.[2]

The title *Bad Girls* was meant to embrace and, by doing so, defang a term of opprobrium. But a pejorative, even used "positively" about minorities, almost never depletes its sting. Instead, it can reinstate it.

The burden of slippery language is heavy, and any descriptions, my descriptions, of these arguments and exhibitions won't be definitive or adequate; instead, they serve as briefs for further elaboration. In writing a ten-page essay referring to "history" or "histories," brevity is a requirement, ironically, even when discussing the need for inclusion.

Framing the past for the present, without reducing its complexities, is fraught: All interpretations get shaded by the predilections of their authors. That is, the subjectivity of the language user. Words have associations and carry attitudes, and words connote more than they denote.

Memory is the single most unreliable narrator. You might remember a panel discussion differently from me, and who is right, if "right" is the right word? Can this be adjudicated? More, what will count in the historical record? I read versions of events I attended twenty years ago that I don't recognize. It's weird.

Looking back, as the New Museum asked me to do, I face another irony: Many of the debates during the period were predicated as binaries, which reiterated a Western mind/body dualism that poststructuralist thinkers on "both sides" hoped to efface. Debates about pornography, pro and con; actual women versus mediated images; what was or wasn't feminist art: They were invigorating, intense, frustrating, confusing, and sometimes confused.

Still, one would not be discussing intersectionality (an ungainly new word that Virginia Woolf wouldn't entertain), wrestling with what hadn't been a dominant factor in those debates, if those earlier dialogues hadn't happened.

I was mostly a viewer/spectator at the New Museum, but my work was included in two exhibitions.

The feature film I wrote and codirected and coproduced with Sheila McLaughlin, *Committed* (1984), was among the films shown in the *Difference* exhibition. *Committed* was based on Frances Farmer's life (a 1930s movie star; a defiant, free-thinking woman; a Communist; an alcoholic, whose mother committed her to a mental institution). It wasn't a biography, but a narrative of "fact" and fiction, an imagined and interpretive work, treating historical conditions—attitudes toward mental health, defiant women, Communism, etc.—through the vector of a forgotten woman.

Committed is considered a feminist film, one of a wave of independent and artist films of the early 1970s into the mid-1990s, I'd ascertain, whose new narratives spoke to those who had been excluded, marginalized, or designated unimportant to history. Filmmakers tried, in various ways, to create cinematic treatments that would align with (form and content) "difference," about gender, sexual orientation, sexuality. People worked "against" the classic Hollywood film or used it differently, and Laura Mulvey's now familiar concept, "woman as object of the gaze," was seminal.

I wrote "Madame Realism's Imitation of Life" because the curator William Olander asked me to write a Madame Realism story for the catalogue to his exhibition *Fake: A Meditation on Authenticity* (1987).

My fictional character Madame Realism reports (thinks):

> One of the women [at an opening, in the ladies' room] said, "This isn't a good mirror," and Madame Realism relaxed a little, the idea of a perfect mirror terrifying, anyway, and besides she didn't like the way she looked just then. Still, she thought, if there is no inner life or self, and I'm not being conduited, this physical presence, this facade, might be all one really did have.

The subtitle *Femininity as Masquerade* for *Girls Night Out* drew on the psychoanalytic theorist Joan Riviere's 1929 essay "Womanliness as Masquerade," whose notions about a self as a pose, a presentation, gender as performance, were of extreme importance to this story and my thinking at the time.

Among the subjects in the various aesthetic and cultural debates of the 1980s and the 1990s, "authenticity" reared its head. The idea, to some an ideal, confused many already confusing issues, especially around identity politics. It was a variation on essentialism.

The authenticity of an art object, in a sense its sincerity, even that of its artist, was scrutinized: It became, and still is, a difficult, critical subject. Fake or fakery is the other side of authenticity; if one is not "authentic," whatever that is, if one's art is not, then one is fraudulent. These are ongoing, persistent questions: Who has the right to do or say this, to write or make art about this; who can name themselves what; who has the right to speak, and for whom?

The art historian and critic Craig Owens, who died of AIDS in 1990, suggested that "we" do not speak for others but to them.

An authentic self? Even a self . . . Identifications and behaviors vary so much from people's supposed "essences" and "roots." Whatever their origins, human beings are generated by highly combustible fantasy engines. (How else, in 2016, could a preponderance of white American women have voted for Donald Trump?)

I follow Kafka, who wrote, and I paraphrase: My people, if I have one.

Andy Warhol wrote: "I don't know where the artificial stops and the real starts." Some or more of the world might consider Warhol a fake, inauthentic. I don't. For one, performing gender fits his succinct statement perfectly.

Installing the art of its time, the New Museum mounted exhibitions that were almost like exposés, foregrounding art that reflected on prejudices and stereotypes about women, races, ethnicities, nationalities, and sexual orientations. That was fundamental to its stake as a truly new institution. Its curatorial program demonstrated an institutional awareness that art can be a form of consciousness, of consciousness in process.

Some shows were better, more coherent than others. That was my sense of them, my experience. But even if I took exception to some, I usually appreciated the organizing principle, the curatorial project, because, for one thing, consciousness is always partial, which means that knowing what good art is, and how to install it, especially in its moment, can only be partial, too, in both senses of the word.

Mistakes. Wrong moves. How does learning occur? As a species, Homo sapiens' greatest faults: the wishes to appear faultless, to be right, and to win. Those wishes obscure doing wrong, being wrong. Most people hate being wrong, and won't admit it. Pointless arguments follow. (If nothing else, googling a question of fact—what year was that movie?—settles dinner-table arguments fast.)

The overarching tragedy of the 1980s into the mid-1990s was AIDS. The disease was a constant terrorism. New York City was mined with the disease.

The curator William Olander died of AIDS, and many, many artists, editors, writers, filmmakers, actors, directors, designers, and on and on. And an entire audience for art, dance, music, theater, and film was decimated, as the writer Fran Lebowitz noted. Those who lived through those years will probably never forget how, one day, daily life changed into daily death.

The New Museum was like a first responder in art; there was an urgency to its exhibitions, such as *Let the Record Show . . .* (1987), *Until That Last Breath: Women with AIDS* (1989), and *Love for Sale . . . Free Condoms Inside* (1991). The ferociousness of the disease produced an extraordinary activist movement in which, for one thing, lesbians and gay men acted together, in common cause. A grave purpose effected greater solidarity, many members of various groups have reported over the years.

What does it take to bring about common cause, I often wonder. Only the fear of death?

Shifts and modulations in attitudes and positions have emerged by making, doing, thinking, unthinking, and by working through, that is, by working toward an understanding of motives, say, by compassion, through trial and error. There are always mistakes, often damaging ones.

Artists know how much they learn by accident and through mistakes. A museum does that, and presents their "mistakes," also.

When I walked into the lobby of the new New Museum on the Bowery, and entered a huge elevator, I had to adjust to a very different place, to its many floors, and much more space. It's taken me time to get used to it. But, fortunately, two of the guards were the same.

Notes

1 I chose to cite only a few names of curators, artists, participants on panels, and writers in catalogues. I have mentioned some group and solo shows from the New Museum's earlier years to indicate its program's direction and engagement with feminism, sexuality, and gender. I have had to leave out many more names than I could cite. So I'm erring on the other side, and I urge intrigued readers to use a search engine.

2 Marcia Tucker, "Introduction and Acknowledgements," in *Bad Girls*. Exh. cat. (New York: New Museum; Cambridge, MA: The MIT Press, 1994), p. 4.

The Experience of Time

> And the earth was without form, and void; and darkness was upon the face of the deep. And the Spirit of God moved upon the face of the waters. And God said, Let there be light: and there was light. And God saw the light, that it was good: and God divided the light from the darkness.
>
> —Genesis 1:2–1:4

If the Bible were a theoretical text, the writers of Genesis would have been describing how they understood the unprecedented. There were no scientific explanations for Life, Nature, existence: They wrote from knowledge they had gleaned, experience they had had, and stories from their elders passed down over time. The Bible was written to explain inexplicable events and behavior.

Early Homo sapiens lived in light and darkness, and found ways to survive. Time didn't exist, and nothing was regular or irregular. Bolts of thunder, flashes of lightning, rain, hurricanes—births and death—great forces destroyed or nurtured. Well before the Bible, people fostered explanations, gods of all kinds. With time passing and language—at first grunts, visceral words—people must have begged sapient elders for ways to comprehend, say, a round ball aglow and then gone, in its absence a vast darkness. Even the Hebrew God was famously capricious.

Before naming, there was no separation—no forms, as Genesis says—except light and dark. Beginning in the third century CE and into the seventh, Manichaeism was a major religion, whose teachings promoted the dichotomy of light and dark, as if a war existed between the good, "a spiritual world of light," and the bad, or evil, "a material world of darkness."

Darkness was called evil, I might theorize, because things could happen unseen, anything might happen in the dark unchecked, and it could not be legislated. In Shakespeare, those great asides would have been spoken in total darkness, so that others nearby would be unaware of who spoke. The word "obscene" might apply to those asides, as it describes what happens offstage.

By the fourteenth century, Manichaeism fell out of favor. Though its idea that darkness is evil has had pernicious consequences well beyond religious belief.

"Let there be light." What an amazing, tremendous, monumental command.

In his last paintings, Ad Reinhardt eliminated abstract shapes. A single color dominated, though each was more than just one color. Light didn't emanate from his canvases, he didn't paint for light, and he didn't forsake illusion. His monochromatic works are not what they appear to be.

The discussion about a lack of attention and listening worries contemporary society—how impatient people are, how social media demands instant responses, and how thoughtlessness prevails. Media has changed people's capacity to concentrate and focus, while life is lived in sound bites and a blur of images. So, expectations have changed, also about culture and what is produced. Films are edited for speed—no time for Antonioni's slow *L'Avventura*—because people can't slow down. Over the last decades, artists have responded to distracted viewers, say, by enlarging work, blowing it up. Bigger may not be better, but it takes longer to see or apprehend, supposedly. Time is always a question in art.

James Turrell's engagement with Reinhardt might seem contradictory, but their work sits on two sides of the same coin: Art's coin of the realm is perception, in which light and dark play their necessary roles.[1] In Reinhardt, Turrell might have recognized another artist's resolve to apply the brain's sensorium as if it were paint. That is, the sensations of the viewer, impulses produced by stimuli, would affect the work as if applying another layer to it. Turrell also relies on these impulses as he shape-shifts light to make sculptures that emerge because of perception. The function of visual phenomena is essential to both men's art.

The Reinhardt gallery is quiet. His paintings appear to be set into the walls, not on them. Each of the larger paintings is enclosed by half walls, creating a corridor to it, an approach to it; viewers must walk down the corridor to see the work more closely. The walls turn the spaces into side chapels, like small rooms in a great church. The installation's effect is reverential.

For the center of the gallery, Turrell designed a flat, round, white sculpture for sitting, and viewers can see all the paintings from it. There are also white benches in front of several paintings but at a distance. Perception changes, subject to proximity, and is also affected by a person's subjectivity.

To look is different from to see, observing is not exactly watching. The brain does the anatomical work of seeing, but watching, observing, noticing, focusing—these qualities are human decisions.

To see Reinhardt's paintings properly, fully, Turrell constructed a serene space, for patient and long viewing. The viewer is invited to sit down and take her time. And as you look, stare, gaze at one of Reinhardt's works, things change right before your eyes, as it's said, and suddenly areas of the painting appear to light up, browns and blues emerge from black, and soon the surface is moving, swirling, dancing. Looking for a long time, I felt I might be hallucinating, seeing what wasn't there. Or maybe it was.

In Ad Reinhardt's last years, it's hard not to wonder if what he wanted to do was slow down the reading of his paintings. Perhaps with aging, slowing down himself, new insights occurred to him. Reinhardt was known to be philosophical, and these paintings are works for contemplation. They reveal themselves only if attention is paid, time is given. There's a recognition here that all there is is time.

Note

1 James Turrell curated an exhibition of Ad Reinhardt's work, titled *Color Out of Darkness*, at Pace Gallery, New York, in 2022.

On Clint Eastwood's *Unforgiven*

In 1992, Bill Clinton was elected US president, and Clint Eastwood directed and released *Unforgiven*. *Unforgiven* was anomalous that year: The classic American Western of the filmmaker John Ford had been parodied by the Italian Western and "killing Injuns" was understood, finally, to be genocide. The Western that heroized pioneers unsettling the West was moribund. *Unforgiven*, an anti-Western Western, buried it.

William Munny, "a killer out of Kansas" played by Eastwood, had stopped drinking and killing, and lived with his wife and two children in Big Whiskey, Wyoming, raising hogs. It's 1878, Munny's wife has been dead for three years, and the hogs are sick. Munny needs money (pun intended). He rides out to visit his friend, Ned (Morgan Freeman), a retired killer like him. Along the way, he meets a young man, named the Schofield Kid after his gun (the Schofield is a type of revolver produced by Smith & Wesson), who brags he's killed five men. The Kid tells Munny about a $1,000 bounty on the heads of two men who "cut a whore."

Munny tells Ned about the bounty: "[But] I am not like that anymore. . . . Cured by my wife." Still, he is desperate. Reluctantly, Ned agrees—"I guess they have it coming"—while Ned's wife, a Native American, glowers at Munny. They set off to right a wrong and collect the money, the holy grail at the end of the trail.

Munny, Ned, and the Kid reach town, tell the women they're going to kill the slashers. Eastwood has installed in this town the usual suspects, characters bigger than life, and each a cipher in the battle of good versus evil, Western-style. They play their roles—sheriff, barkeep, whore, drunk—and all congregate in the saloon, the clubhouse for Westerns. A brilliant addition to the crew is an

Eastern writer, a "historian of the West." The writer is following the gunslinger English Bob (Richard Harris) to record his story. He gobbles up the "romance" of English Bob's murderous missions, intending these boasts for his book. The metafictional writer delineates how untruths about the West were inscribed in histories, in films, functioning, in part, to validate Manifest Destiny, the bloody nineteenth-century political project that argued the US had a right to expand across North America.

Eastwood's morality tale turns dark and nasty fast. The trio finds one of the men, and Ned has him in his sights, but can't pull the trigger. Munny does. The man dies in agony, and Ned, shaken, can't take it, and heads home. The Kid, who actually had never killed, kills for the first time—the other slasher. He's unarmed, sitting on the can in an outhouse. The Kid feels disgust and remorse. Munny tells him: "It's a hell of a thing, killing a man." The Kid gives Munny his gun and rides away.

One of the women rides out to give Munny the bounty; he learns that Ned has been murdered by the sheriff and his posse. Enraged, Munny mutates into the assassin he once was, the man who has seen "the angel of death." He takes a drink, finishes the bottle. His eyes dead, he rides to town.

Munny sees Ned's body in an open coffin, set upright, outside the saloon. First, Munny kills the saloon keeper, then kills as many people as he can in the saloon. (The writer hides beneath a table.) In the scene's climax, Munny confronts Sheriff Bill (Gene Hackman). Bill has been building his house. Now, in the saloon, shot in his gut, lying on his back, Munny standing over him, Bill tells Munny: "You can't kill me. I'm building my house. I don't deserve to die."

Unforgiven's last shot is the same as its first—on Munny's property, unpeopled, where just a single tree, the tree of life, stands, when the film turns from color into black and white, the image with which it began. *Unforgiven* is as stark as Ingmar Bergman's *The Seventh Seal* (1957). Stylistically, with Eastwood's direction, nothing is depicted or said that isn't relevant to Munny's deadly journey, when killing makes the killer a monster. Eastwood's Munny is very different from his infamous *Dirty Harry* (1971), who spit out: "Make my day."

In *Unforgiven*, the "whore who's been cut" offers sex to Munny, because he revenged her. Munny refuses. She asks if her scars make her ugly. No, he says, "You've got scars like me." His identification testifies to male vulnerability, anathema for classic Westerns. In Eastwood's oeuvre, the films he acted in, directed, or both, men attack women or protect women from men. Both are variations of men's attempts to control women. But what doesn't occur in Eastwood's own films, except in *Tightrope* (1984), is men trying to change how they relate to women. Eastwood doesn't attack the binary that heterosexuality has mandated as "masculine behavior."

Context ineluctably renders interpretations and meanings. We live inside our time; and, more, it lives in us. Now, the Me Too movement shines a light on *Unforgiven*, especially that paradoxical masculinity: If men didn't violate women, they wouldn't have to protect them.

Art of His Time

> It may have been wrong to say that after Auschwitz you could no longer write poems. But it is not wrong to raise the less cultural question whether after Auschwitz you can go on living.
> —Theodor Adorno, *Negative Dialectics*

> Once is enough for tragedy, I think, not to repeat it.
> —Agnes Martin, *With My Back to the World*

In August 1945, the atomic bomb was dropped on Hiroshima and Nagasaki. Earlier that year, in January, Auschwitz was liberated, and the Nazi genocide was exposed to the world. During the war, between fifty and seventy million people were killed, murdered, starved, or tortured to death. What had not been living and killed had been destroyed—cities, streets, schools, parks, churches, stores, houses, roads, and fields. Also demolished: the warring nations' sacred notions about their civilizations. The foundations on which Europe and Japan based their societies and cultures lay in ruins. Humanity was found to be barbaric.

Postwar artists confronted a new world, in shock.

***

On Kawara was born on December 24, 1932.[1] Two days before his birth, the Japanese fascist party Kokumin Dōmei was founded. That year, Werner Heisenberg was awarded the Nobel Prize in Physics, John Galsworthy in Literature. That year, the Nobel Committee did not award a Peace Prize. Albert Einstein was granted a visa into the US: He had first been refused because of "Communist associations."

By the 1950s, Kawara was an active artist in Tokyo. His work was exhibited, he was well known, he participated on panels and wrote art criticism. Then, in 1959, he left Japan for Mexico. From there he traveled to New York City, and widely in Europe, but ultimately decided to reside in Manhattan, where he would live the rest of his life.

On Kawara stopped giving interviews; his last was in 1965. He chose not to explain his work, he didn't write art criticism. He didn't attend openings, he wasn't photographed, and people didn't know what he looked like, unless they were his friends. Mostly, he absented himself from the art world and also did not attend public events, including funerals, weddings, and graduations.

In the years between 1959 and 1965, I imagine Kawara contemplating his reasons for being an artist and making art, and what he specifically could make and contribute, a newer aesthetics: to discharge some of the past—not to forget it—and find his way to working in, and even for, the present. Ultimately, Kawara resisted or refused various artistic tropes, truisms, like the old chestnut that art is a way for an artist to express himself. He eliminated self-expression or "personality" from his work. He dedicated himself to a single, lifelong project, the Today series, in which he strove to emphasize the most ordinary and fundamental fact of life—having it.

The Date Paintings

The notation of the Date Paintings can be tricky, though the simplest answer is that collectively all of the paintings

> form the single series known as Today, 1966–2013. Each painting is generally recorded with its individual title and its reference to the overarching series. For example, the Date Painting in Glenstone's collection from January 1967 would read: *JAN. 24, 1967*, from Today series (1966–2013).
> —Anne Reeve, email message to author

Kawara painted all Date Paintings within twenty-four hours. For each one, he handmade a cardboard box to hold, say, a clipping from that day's *New York Times* or a newspaper from whatever city he was visiting.[2] The plain cardboard boxes, when opened, are not Pandora's boxes. They don't reveal the untoward, they don't shock. They accompany the paintings, a visual pas de deux. And each box is an interior for each painting that, like unspoken speech, intimates the painting's thoughts. The contents of the boxes exist unseen, until opened and studied like the unconscious.

Seeing one, looking at its contents, affects the reading of a Date Painting. For instance, *JULY 6, 1980*: The box holds a double-page spread from *The New York Times*, a page of news, a page of wedding and engagement announcements, one of the weird juxtapositions that collide in newspapers. What else happened on that day . . . ?

Trillions of events—a house on fire, a diary purchased, job lost, laundry hung on clotheslines—so much occurs in a day. Relatively little becomes history. Little is saved or collected. The seemingly unimportant pieces in the cardboard boxes represent the multitudes neglected, overlooked, or lost, profound reminders of how much has disappeared. If paintings have inner lives, these are the Date Paintings'.

Kawara's most strict rule was to finish a Date Painting within twenty-four hours; but, within his chosen constraints, he varied the dimensions of his canvases: He allowed eight different sizes, from eight by ten inches to sixty-one by eighty-nine inches. He also varied the hues of his paintings, whose colors ranged "from muted gray to blue to bright red."[3] The letters and numbers, punctuation, though, had to be white; everything had to be centered. Kawara didn't use a stencil; he painted by hand, then ultimately erased the evidence. He was precise, so it's as if his hand had never been there. There but not visible, like a palimpsest.

Looking at *JAN. 24, 1967* on a white wall, viewers might see or read significance into the day or night, even if, for them, there had been none, none they could remember. The more they look, standing quietly in front of *JAN. 24, 1967*, the more they might reflect, and the more they might feel time weighing on them.

No one can quantify that sense of time, the experience of an hour or twenty-four when some speed along or drag, when some days feel short, others never-ending. But where does time go?

Time and Space

On Kawara's decision not to set spaces between letters, numerals, and punctuation struck me. The usual way would be: JAN. 24, 1967. He sets the characters contiguously, almost touching: JAN.24,1967. That may be because of his sense of the best use of the canvas's space.

Or, maybe he preferred the visual effect of a block of type. I reckoned with Kawara's compression of space, and read into it.

Time and space are relative, Einstein discovered, bending into each other. How much time does one have; how much space does one have? These concepts are relative, and also not. Space registers, in this theory, not as physical space, though there is actual space on the canvas, but rather as the space given to a life. An absence of space is also metaphorical: a life restricted, full; free, empty; healthy, sick: a life with or without good fortune.

It's said that Kawara chose to make a Date Painting randomly. The date was random. But what is randomness for a meticulous, exacting artist? True randomness, scientists say, is extremely rare. Random numbers in a row eventually form a pattern. Scientists claim the most random event is traffic, where patterns are unpredictable. No one can predict all of the accidents and delays that will occur; no one can account for the millions of personalities in millions of drivers' seats, their moods, who is sleepy, drunk, angry, weeping. No one can predict when two, four, or six of these cars driven by people in very different moods might crash. Or, when a bridge might collapse. Traffic is random, and no system has yet been devised to change that.

I imagine: Kawara has awakened. Then what? He decides he is going to make a painting. Is the decision random? What happened the day before? What conversation might have stirred, inspired, or worried him? And, from what dream did he awaken in which those matters fluttered, disguised, but if analyzed might bring forth memories of his childhood—his own kind of turbulence, perhaps? These are my inferences; the artist has not betrayed his thoughts.

A random choice or selection can be or seem unmotivated, though Kawara's art, I would propose, was anything but unmotivated.

Kawara might have liked or wanted randomness—there's the enticement of possibility, excitement of chance. In a sense, he, like John Cage and the abstract expressionists, desired a kind of fate produced by movements and events outside subjectivity or individuality. The fate of the roll of the die; the fate of a composition comprising irregular street noises; the fate of paint dripping onto a canvas—that kind of fate: accidents.

Moon Landing

Kawara's *Moon Landing* Date Paintings were not accidents. He had decided, in advance, to mark this highly anticipated launch, which was well planned and scheduled. A worldwide event, people everywhere who had access to any media would have watched or listened. Bars would have their TVs on; screens lit up in big railroad stations, in large store windows, in homes.

The first of these Date Paintings from Kawara's *Moon Landing* set is *JULY 16, 1969*. Its subtitle cites all of the astronauts: NEIL A. ARMSTRONG, EDWIN E. ALDRIN JR., MICHAEL COLLINS. The cardboard boxes for two *Moon Landing* paintings hold the entire first sections of *The New York Times* for July 16 and July 20; and, for July 21, Kawara put six copies of the *Times* in two different boxes. These were the dates when liftoff, landing, and walking on the moon occurred.

"Space" emerges again, in a different register. I once read a study in which women were asked to draw their ideal homes. Many drew houses off the ground, on stilts, up in the sky like satellite-homes, or way under the ground. When I read the study, I thought this was evidence of women imagining places they could exist without the usual demands on them.

I have no way of knowing if Kawara believed that outer space offered new freedoms, or that exploring space could provide constructive alternatives and possibilities for generations to come. I don't know, but I think his *Moon Landing* paintings might be considered homages to unknowable and unpredictable fates, but especially to the most extreme kind of exteriority—"outer space events."

> Where life ends, where art begins, I am the poet of my life.
> —Friedrich Nietzsche, *The Gay Science*

Histories are written, first, by participants, witnesses, survivors, and onlookers, who record first-person accounts and provide primary information and material. Future historians borrow or appropriate their accounts to build arguments about why and how things happened. Others produce representations in fiction, essays, poetry, movies, and plays.

To do primary research, I visited Kawara's studio and discussed his work with his wife, Hiroko Kawahara, and their son-in-law, Yoshito Yoshioka. It was a privilege to be in his studio, and a genuinely strange one. I tried to think it wouldn't be so dissimilar from visiting Jane Austen's house in Bath, England, which I did one summer years ago, but it was, quite. For one, Kawara had not been dead very long. And, I didn't feel I knew him through his work, as I had felt, rightly or wrongly, about Jane Austen—Kawara's work discourages that feeling. He seems to have wanted to extinguish the illusion of knowing the artist, to offer, instead, a more general or common intimacy, oxymoronic as it might sound.

In the studio, which I visited twice, I asked Hiroko and Yoshito many questions. Still later, by phone, I asked about the *Moon Landing* paintings, because I kept wondering why Kawara chose to paint them. I had already noticed that, in his *Journal* (which included subtitles for the majority of the Today paintings), for February and March 1966 he cited these space events: "The soft landing on the Moon"; "Luna 9 is electrically dead"; "Soviet ship lands on Venus"; "Gemini-8"; "Numerous sightings of unidentified flying objects since March 16, in Michigan, U.S.A."[4]

When Kawara learned the moon landing would be broadcast over twenty-four hours, he decided to watch as much of it as he could. Staying awake for twenty-four hours allowed him the opportunity to do a larger-scale work. He would complete the largest canvas he had yet made for the Today series. The three paintings designated as the *Moon Landing* triptych were not intended to be a set when he painted them. That happened later.

During my two visits, I saw the desk where he worked, a modest, modernist piece of furniture. I saw the wall-length bookshelves behind his desk, built so that the books and files inside weren't always visible. I was encouraged to sit in his chair, at the desk. I looked at what he had looked at while he worked—the wall where he hung his finished pieces. I sensed his rigorousness and desire for perfection. Or, a purpose and purposefulness—there was nothing that would distract him from his work. The simplicity and openness of the space reflected his art. Like it, I thought, anything other than a stripped-down statement might be an exaggeration, even decoration, and might lack integrity.

Kawara was fascinated by outer space, science, astronomy, and was a reader of science fiction. He liked to discuss philosophy and politics, all kinds of ideas, with his friends, and liked to joke. Later, I thought about his postcards and telegrams as serial, existential jokes. I tried but couldn't really assemble an image of a man I didn't know, an artist sometimes called a minimalist or conceptualist. He was engaged in reality, or realities, but Kawara was not a realist. Artists and writers propose other realities, in their work.

Duchamp troubled conceptions of art by signing a urinal R. MUTT and submitting it for an exhibition. He divorced the object from its ordinary use and value, so that context, installation in a gallery, would determine its status. Kawara's paintings had no other or original use (though the news clippings he put in the cardboard boxes once had). But context was essential to Kawara as to Duchamp. A date is a common thing, not a physical object but a familiar, probably universal thing. When that painting of a common thing is hung on a gallery wall, it is art. His postcards and telegrams, sent through the regular mail, from wherever he was, were also art.

Kawara's art wasn't a modernist retort or manifesto in the sense that Duchamp's R. MUTT was. Rather, Kawara's work evinces a wish to veer away from, dismiss from view, questionable or restrictive ideologies. His aesthetics, I would theorize, formed in opposition to war and to ideologies of all kinds.[5] Could he escape them, these forces, entirely? No, no one can. But looking at his art makes a space for time away from them.

Postcards and Writing

In 1968, as an extension of the Date Paintings, On Kawara started mailing a postcard series called I Got Up (1968–1979). Mail art had been produced by artists in Japan since the mid-1950s.[6] In 1960 in New York, George Maciunas formed Fluxus, whose many members were American, European, and Asian, and also made correspondence art. Kawara didn't join Fluxus, or other groups; but doubtless he knew artists who did.

On every postcard, he stamped in black ink: I GOT UP AT . . . He also designated a specific time; say, 12:24 p.m. From February through July 1970, he mailed 131 postcards to the artist Dan Graham, each with a picture of the Statue of Liberty on its island site. Later, he mailed I Got Up postcards to the artist John Baldessari, among others. "In 1973 On Kawara sent postcards from twenty-eight different cities."[7] I Got Up was the first of several declarative art statements.

In 1970, the poet and painter Joe Brainard published his now classic book *I Remember*, all of whose sentences start "I remember." Like Brainard, Kawara used "I" in his postcards and telegrams. The pronoun is a shifter into which any he, she, we, or I can sit. "I" is common and also specific—I is I. But "I" can be you, reader, or anyone.

Just a pronoun and verb, I Got Up sets in place a quizzical narrative, which provokes or prompts curiosity, a hope for embellishment, or more story. But it doesn't require a response. Postcards are, anyway, usually one-way communiqués. Kawara sent a message and didn't expect a response.

Telegrams and Writing

I AM STILL ALIVE, Kawara declared in telegrams mailed inside envelopes to various people between the years 1970 and 2000. The telegram is history now, another remnant of the past. It has been superseded by the internet, social media sites, and texts; but it existed before the telephone. In the mid-nineteenth century, telegrams were close to instant communication. They were usually a surprise, often carrying great or terrible news—in American World War II movies, mothers, especially, are depicted receiving telegrams about their sons' deaths in battle.

Kawara wrote I AM STILL ALIVE. Not I AM ALIVE, which, syntactically, would have matched I GOT UP. With the addition of the adverb "still," the message is transformed: It seems more serious, even worrisome, and also more mysterious, a declaration harder to parse. "Still" puts in play ambiguities and questions: Was there an expectation this might not be the case? What has the sender experienced that makes "still" necessary? Was his life in danger? Kawara's text is printed by Western Union, and the only one of his messages not made by his hand. I AM STILL ALIVE, it says, and its recipients should realize that the situation is not dire. But still . . .

Daily events in an "ordinary" person's life are rarely recounted, but since the eighteenth century, novels have been a place for them.

In *Mrs. Dalloway*, Virginia Woolf portrayed a day in the life of a middle-class woman, as she prepared for her party that night. Woolf's novel and all novels, a product of the Gutenberg press that could print multiple copies quickly, were also inventions of a new bourgeoisie, who wished to tell their stories, ordinary or not.

With words and pictures, Kawara launched a cryptic art-novel comprising a calendar of common, random dates; simple sentences about his awakenings; boxes of interiors; and maps showing his comings and goings (his I Went series, 1968–1979). He represented one life among the billions. A life that could have disappeared without notice.

I AM STILL ALIVE, On Kawara wrote, again and again, and sent a telegram. It is a shocking, unexpected message. But more than the shock, or just after it, comes a certain poignancy. Its affect is bittersweet. Still alive. With this, Kawara marks the temporality of the present, and life's staggering temporariness.

Time and Art

Time regulates human life. It was developed by people for that, and we all have it in common, though some have more of it than others. Anyone's reality can seem provisional, improvisational, and invented, like art, but all people are born into circumstances beyond their control. Then unwelcome death arrives at everyone's door. In that sense, life is a time-based medium. How does an artist speak or respond to that, to make time count, to make time matter, and turn the mattering into material?

A person, an artist, might ask herself, Why am I alive? What should I do today? (If I had asked myself, when I awoke today, Why am I alive? I could have answered: To write this essay.) Kawara created work that does not waste time and recognizes not only life's brevity and fragility, but also art's.

> The artist produces nothing until the onlooker has said, "You have produced something marvelous." The onlooker has the last word in it.
> —Marcel Duchamp, *The Afternoon Interviews*

On Kawara was exceptional. He was an extreme nonconformist in art and life. He took "life-time" as his subject, devoting his work to an aesthetics of dailiness. He created a body of impressive, demanding, important, curious, and unique art. He avoided hyperbole and drama to attend to life's little moments, to the passage of time, to everyday presence and loss.

Over time, Kawara's great oeuvre and its meanings will be interpreted, and reinterpreted, determined by its viewers in changing contexts and in different eras. Indeed, the Today series interrogates existence and confronts existence itself. Doing that, it also poses complex questions about its own—and art's—existence.

The Today series will make its own way through its viewers. The series creates its own morphology, its own vital, novel form, and here, it seems to say, the living can contemplate their lives. And, here, being alive is everything.

Notes

1 On Kawara's registered birthday, in Japan, is January 2, 1933. His actual birthday is December 24, 1932. In the traditional Japanese calendar, individual birthdays are not celebrated; instead, a year is added to a person's age every New Year's Day. This different method of ascertaining age is no longer used in Japan, but accounts for some confusion around Kawara's birth date.

2 Kawara made the Date Paintings in eight sizes, which he designated "A–H." The boxes made to correspond with painting sizes A–E could hold the painting as well as any other material Kawara placed inside, if he did, usually a news clipping. The boxes for F–H are smaller than their respective paintings; therefore, they may only contain a news clipping or the entire newspaper.

3 Jeffrey Weiss, ed., *On Kawara—Silence*. Exh. cat. (New York: Solomon R. Guggenheim Foundation, 2015), p. 75.

4 The dates for the subtitles given are, in order, February 3, February 7, March 1, March 8, and March 25.

5 The German artists Gerhard Richter and Peter Dreher were born in 1932; in 1931, Roman Opalka was born in France (he died in 2011). They would become artists well known for their rejection of aesthetic norms, for their antagonism or indifference to, or negotiation of, ideologies. Richter refused allegiance to a single style or painting program; Dreher rejected abstraction, painting a plain water glass in his project *Tag um Tag ist Guter Tag* (1974–2014; translated by the artist as "Day by Day, Every Day Is Good"). Opalka's number paintings were simple arithmetic numbers, marking and representing time, direct and abstract, too.

6 John Held Jr., "Japanese Mail Art, 1956–2014: Mail an Octopus with Stamps on Its Head," *San Francisco Arts Quarterly* (August–October 2014), p. 58.

7 Held, "Japanese Mail Art," p. 58. Though according to Kawara's estate, there are thirty-seven locations from which he sent postcards.

Courtly Love

In film, no long shot is more iconic, precise in its intention, disturbing, and startling than Alfred Hitchcock's of a tennis match in *Strangers on a Train*. The camera looks at the crowd looking intently at a game in action; the crowd mirrors the audience watching the film (the meta Hitchcock loves). In a full grandstand, multiple heads move left, right, left, right, back again, synchronized, following the ball like cats do a swinging object. But only one head, among so many, remains absolutely still, staring straight ahead at the camera. It is that of the malicious mastermind, played by Robert Walker, one of two conspirators to murder, looking across, lethally, at his coconspirator on the other side of the court. Each man had sworn to murder a person not known to him but to the other. There would be no reason, no motivation—the perfect crime. Walker already did his murder, but the other man wants to back out of the deal.

I have been fascinated by a tennis ball's being hit over the net (and Hitchcock's movies) since I was a child. My mother played, and I would accompany her to the courts. In summer camp I played every day if I could (in competitions, I would lose when applause for me started). I played a lot, especially as a teenager, and fantasized I could go pro with the right coach. Ridiculous. Then I loved watching tennis as much as baseball, horse racing, and human racing.

My first tennis hero was Pancho Gonzales. One day, when I was six, walking up Fifth Avenue with my mother or father beside me, I saw a man coming toward us. I thought I knew him and ran up to him—Pancho Gonzales! Oh heart! He smiled his gorgeous smile, amused, maybe delighted. Now, my heart thumps for Federer, Serena, Djokovic, and newer players coming up. It also cycles way down for players like Donald Young, a fast-rising US star as a junior, who hasn't reached his potential.

Watching matches, I sense how a player begins to defeat herself, how a certain twist in a match, a mis-hit, sends a player spiraling into more losses. Regularly, I make analogies to writing, how a writer can beat herself, how in writing there is no best, but in tennis there is, for a moment in time. (Tennis players are much better at applauding the other's game.) The fierce, highly visible competition in tennis makes it painful, say, to watch Serena and Venus battle against each other. Or an injured player going on with the match.

The romance of tennis, if you love the game and follow it, depends on knowing the players, having favorites and dream players, rooting for underdogs, wanting champions to keep winning—the elegant Federer—seeing on their faces hopes, wounds, the vicissitudes. Then, to you, each match is a heroic endeavor, in which psychology is as much in play as skill. I am fully conscious that this heroism I perceive may seem very strange to others, because it's "just a game." But also, "*la vida es sueño.*"

Rowan Ricardo Phillips's *The Circuit: A Tennis Odyssey* (2018) is a tennis romance, and unique. Phillips knows the love. He is a sportswriter and poet, and remarkably, because tennis love isn't easy to explain, he has found the right supple, sometimes tactile, and tender language for it. "Because tennis can offer what Robert Frost said poetry provides: a momentary stay against confusion."

Phillips writes as if he's near the players, calling accurate play-by-plays and doing color. I could see the ball speed over the net, drop over, or go into it on courts that are blue, green, and red—clay, grass, and hard. I could see the players racing for the ball, nearly doing a split. "But tennis is a game of undulating rhythms that exist in four concentric circles—the rhythm of a point, the rhythm of a service game, the rhythm of a return game, the rhythm of a set—that are interrelated but don't necessarily touch."

Phillips decided to follow all of the ATP tournaments of 2017. Miraculously, he did. It is the kind of promise I would want to make, that I would daydream about making, and know I'd never keep. He followed sometimes in person, other times on the screen, waking at crazy hours to watch matches all over the world. "It's January, and 2017 has a vise grip on the mind. And here I am, groggy as hell, keeping up with news about tennis from sixteen hours in the future." He didn't just cover the majors—Australian, Roland-Garros, Wimbledon, US Open—but all of it.

Phillips might call me a Grand Slam fan. "The extremely public spectacle of Grand Slams . . . tends to bring out the tennis fan in all of us, even if only temporarily—[and] reaches its peak with the final one of the year." That's the US Open. (As it happens I'm watching the 2018 Open while reading Phillips's book, and have to put it down, reluctantly, to watch the players he's talking about.) To the slams, I'm pretty faithful, a fan not a fanatic, attending the US Open only three times. But I watch every game I can on TV. Everything else can go to hell.

Phillips is the complete tennis lover, knowledgeable and a player, amateur but serious. Reading his book, I learned more about the intricacies of the game, court tactics and when they're employed, who serves which type of serve to whom and why, and how Federer recently altered his backhand to hit flatter. Tennis is cerebral and physical human chess, the players figuring it out as they go along, if they can, mind and body changing. The greater the players, the more flexible they are, the better able to alter their plan of attack. (Phillips has also provided a glossary of terms. See "inside-out forehand.")

As if writing a mystery, Phillips keeps his tour story suspenseful. He develops each player as a character in the greater game—that is, their lives—and, through the narrative, also tracks their hopes, travails, luck, failures, their tennis magic. He knows and assesses the players very well, gleaning, to my mind, their tennis souls. Since he was very young, Phillips has felt tennis love and grown up along with the players and the game. "When you're in your teens, words like 'resilience,' 'endurance,' and 'perspective' aren't real."

The narrative was determined by the 2017 ATP tour's chronology, from the start of the season until its end. Phillips augmented its drama with stories about previous matches and player anecdotes. He never loses the book's propulsion; I kept up with it and him, relishing it to the end, but "to be honest," as Dave Chappelle says when he's going in for the kill, Phillips's minute explanation of how a player is seeded drove me a little crazy. I couldn't focus on it, so didn't learn how it worked. I did, though, learn its importance: The draw, based on the seed, can make or break a tournament. "A draw exists to keep the presumed two best players in a tournament as far away from each other and out of each other's way until the presumed showdown at the end." The two best players in the world should not be on the same side of the draw, because the order of contests must lead to that denouement: the two best players against each other. If not, it would be like finding out that the butler did it before the murder.

You may never have played tennis or watched it, but Phillips beautifully describes the experience of loving it. His exegesis might stand in for any fan's love of any sport. Which can be strange for a nonbeliever. (I am dumbfounded by ice hockey.) So, I often ask myself about this strange phenomenon—grown people watching a ball putted into a hole; or slam-dunked into a basket; or hit into the upper decks at Citi Field.

Let's think about what a sport is—an activity that engages the body and mind. Loving an endeavor, developing a skill, pursuing a goal. To me, practicing a serve hour after hour, a backhand slice, and the obsession to get it right—this is akin to the practice of writing, but practice never makes perfect, for writers. Not perfect the way Djokovic smashes a forehand right down the line. Writing doesn't allow for that, really. But people have a need for a goal, and hope to succeed. All of these activities and attributes, or symptoms, entail existential questions. Sports are a microcosm of life—it's how you play the game. I mean, what do you do with the time you have, and what is your approach to the trouble of being alive.

It's not surprising that many writers and artists love tennis. There are definite winners and losers. With exceptions. There are chances at coming back. Some love to play (me, once). Some also love to watch (me, now), to feel on edge, to be in amazement at rallies that appear endless, heartbeat accelerating, when, say, that white or yellow ball skims over the net and remarkably lands in the ad corner, back of the court, right on the line.

These shots are to die for. Or to live for. You feel that in players, that they live for it. You, fan or fanatic, see their passion and exist in that moment with them. They play to win, but there is no murder, there's ferocity, losing faith, regaining it, overcoming, going on; there's the pleasure of a win and the acceptance of a loss. "Everyone dreams of the Grand Slams, and for that reason they are for everyone; they are as much the fan's dream as the player's." It's just a game. What a game.

Warhol, Existentially

> What's great about this country is that America started the tradition where the richest consumers buy essentially the same things as the poorest. You can be watching TV and see Coca-Cola, and you can know that the President drinks Coke, Liz Taylor drinks Coke, and just think, you can drink Coke, too. A Coke is a Coke and no amount of money can get you a better Coke than the one the bum on the corner is drinking. All the Cokes are the same and all the Cokes are good. Liz Taylor knows it, the President knows it, the bum knows it, and you know it.
> —Andy Warhol, *The Philosophy of Andy Warhol (From A to B and Back Again)*

> Any reality is an opinion.
> —Timothy Leary

In reality, whatever your opinion of it, life has no do-overs, there's just one take. There can be makeovers, like cosmetic surgery and status climbing: The most blatant standard-bearers are the nouveau riche.

In Warhol's *Before and After* works from the early 1960s, an advertisement for a nose job might appear simple, except that it comments on one of the melting pot's required ingredients for climbing: assimilation. You can't redo or undo the past, but you can fix your nose. You can't be young again; you can have Botox or a facelift. Or, as in his fright wig self-portraits, men can hide baldness and appear to have more than they do, in more than one sense.

Artists can decide what to make, remake, do, undo—there is probably more choice in making art than in most jobs. Still, artists are limited also, by their predilections, assumptions, tastes, sensibilities, habits that were formed, in large part, with their first objects and surroundings, unconsciously and involuntarily absorbed. Even rebellion against imbibed, unwanted values maintains some of their sway.

Artifice Is a Reality

As a fashion illustrator, Warhol learned how to sell a product by creating a fantasy about it. He could make a product look appealing by embodying it with "personality." Sociologists claim that personality exists only when people relate to one another. An individual alone in a room doesn't have a personality. The theory seems right to me, although I wonder about comedians: They're constantly imagining how they can get a laugh from other people, even when alone in a room. That is, they are always on, always performing.

Personality is a performance, the way gender is.

A can of Campbell's soup might have personality to an individual who grew up eating it. Just seeing it on a shelf in a grocery store, among rows and rows of Campbell's soup cans, might arouse memories, good and bad. You didn't like the taste, associating it with school lunches in dreary cafeterias, or nasty family fights around the dining table, so you feel disgust just looking at it. The image or thought of Campbell's soup has affect.

For I. Miller advertising campaigns in the mid-1950s, Warhol drew high-heeled shoes. His delicate lines made the shoes look not only appealing, though not necessarily comfortable, but also lots of fun, playful. The lines flow gaily, letting potential buyers fantasize that they, too, could go with the flow. Shoes are common yet can be special, utilitarian for the office, frivolous and fun for a party. Shoes can be very inexpensive and very expensive. But everyone wears them, and everyone drinks the same Coke.

Warhol's 1950s drawings of shoes, male nudes, a sewing machine, and self-portraits all have graceful, fluid lines. Some of his subjects were offbeat and daring: a man shooting up, a cock with a ribbon around it, various body parts, and, by the early 1960s, front pages of newspapers with freaky headlines. Eventually, though never entirely, Warhol stopped using his elegant hand, putting that skill aside as if tying his hands behind his back. Conventional beauty was not his object, or he needed to produce what was beautiful to him, differently. Or, he was surrounded and compelled by a multiplicity of manufactured objects, a kind of democracy of objecthood. Or, the handmade was just not his thing.

Products Produce Attachments and Vice Versa

People are "products of their environments." Whatever their class and first environment, everyone is a product, everyone is, in that schema, produced. And each of us is an object to others. In Freudian and object relations theory, objects are, first, actual people who become internalized as images. The transference may have little to do with the original objects, but it acts like a transcription of the original into another form that resides in the psyche.

Warhol's art relies on the reality of objects: attachments to them, and fantasies—transferences—about them. He used objects, including people, differently; he personified commodities as if making portraits of people. He pictured a can as if it were looking at him, while he looked at it. He stacked Brillo boxes as though cardboard boxes could amount to bodies of some distinction.

Metaphorically, and actually, things people environments. They did his; they do anyone's.

Over Warhol's career, he silkscreened many portraits, and made self-portraits and photo-booth portraits. It is said that when he began painting the wealthy and celebrated in the 1970s, he did it only for the money. But he must have liked to look at people, especially famous people, observing the faces of success—human glitter. Warhol liked silver, gold, brilliance of all types. He painted criminals silver and Marilyn gold, like religious icons.

A bottle of Coke is a thing of celebrity, depending upon how you look at it, and no one can buy a better Brillo pad. Though, recently, Balenciaga designed a faux Ikea bag; the original at Ikea sells for ninety-nine cents. Looking exactly the same, but made in "blue, wrinkled leather," the Balenciaga bag sells for $2,700, probably the most perverse knockoff in fashion history. If he were alive, Warhol might have bought it and kept it in its shopping bag, unopened, a shopping bag inside a shopping bag, along with his massive collection of unused, unwrapped objects.

Made and Unmade in America

Warhol responded mostly to products made in America and to American obsessions, from celebrities, the "most wanted" criminals, political campaigns, and Dick Tracy comics to ordinary commodities.

In the 1960s he appropriated images of car crashes, electric chairs, the police and so-called race riots, Jackie Kennedy, Marilyn Monroe, and, later, Elvis. In each case someone's luck has run out. For the people in the cars, for those who will be killed in the electric chair, there are absolutely no more chances, while Jackie didn't stop Jack from flying to Dallas, and Marilyn's psychoanalyst couldn't keep her from killing herself. Warhol's *Race Riots* (1963–1964) show police violence against Black Americans, whose chances and choices are limited by white racism and systemic racial prejudice.

Pictures of end points, pictures of endings, bad endings, again and again, the images, stopped in time and in their many iterations, don't change radically. They vary in color, say, or hue, with small differences from each other, but they are always apposite, metaphorically, to the idea of "no other outcomes." By serializing them, creating duration with still images, Warhol offered time and space to reflect on the inviolability of causes and effects.

The most somber, single image, to my mind, was his electric chair, an American invention credited to Dr. Alfred P. Southwick, a dentist from Buffalo, New York.

The word "electrocution" first appeared in 1887, in a newspaper article reporting on Thomas Edison. Edison was competing with the Serbian American inventor Nikola Tesla, who preferred alternating current (AC) to Edison's direct current (DC), both methods of electricity distribution. Edison publicly demonstrated the killing of stray dogs and cats with AC current to prove his way was better. In 1903, Edison electrocuted an elephant at Coney Island, and filmed it, even though Tesla had won the AC/DC battle.

The electric chair was first used in 1890 in Auburn Prison in upstate New York. Here was this new thing, electricity, and, like all new things, it had to be used in every way possible. Its inventor thought it a more humane way of killing. That first time, though, it took eight minutes to kill the man, whose skin peeled off his body. The stench was disgusting.

Inventions have dark sides—examples mount daily—even one formulated to produce artificial light.

Warhol's race riots, like his electric chair, picture a cruel, violent postwar America. No optimistic views, these images, especially those of police brutality against Black Americans. They were not what white Americans wanted to see or acknowledge.

Warhol hung ugly realities on gallery walls.

The Factory: Real and Artificial

> I don't know where the artificial stops and the real starts.
> —Andy Warhol, *East Village Other*

Warhol called his studio the Factory, with the word's many implications, and he was its artist-boss. His un-workers—often called his entourage—could hang out, maybe help Warhol, cavort at Max's Kansas City, or at Factory parties (how many there actually were is disputed by Factory people). Warhol worked in the back of his studio, and had one assistant helping him silkscreen.

By the early to mid-1960s, his studio had become a film studio. Before and during this period, Warhol frequented the Film-Makers' Cinematheque, where he watched experimental films. Jonas Mekas, its founder, recognized Warhol's talent, and was an early supporter. Warhol saw Jack Smith's work there; Smith was an important influence. Teenaged Stephen Shore met Warhol at the Cinematheque in 1965, and soon began photographing in the Factory, documenting Warhol behind the camera, for one thing.

Warhol directed hundreds of films, one after another. He shot people who hung around the Factory, or were just visiting. One day, Marcel Duchamp showed up, and Warhol filmed him. For a time, he seems to have shot daily, sometimes with a plan, sometimes impromptu. Warhol "made" stars, superstars, of various characters around the Factory, like Edie Sedgwick. The stars made scenes, and they were the starry scene for a brief moment. Some of them imploded or exploded; Warhol was regularly blamed. His impact on others is still contested.[1] But like any object, a person is capable of being used, loved, misused, cared for, abandoned, and also of using, misusing, abandoning. Humans are casually cruel to one another; worse, deliberately cruel.

It's impossible to divide completely what artists make or imagine from who they are, psychoanalytically.

Warhol might have recognized himself as a product of his environment, a creature of his time. He once said he was "like rockets and television," part, not ahead, of his time. And he did try to make himself appealing—a nose job—and noticeably different and weird—with crazy wigs. He was aware of the market, in people and art. He once sent another man, Allen Midgette, to Utah and Oregon to lecture in his name. Midgette bleached his hair, and people were fooled. If you had never seen Warhol, except in pictures, anyone could be him.

One thing is agreed upon: Warhol was always working, observing a Catholic's Protestant work ethic. He gave Factory habitués roles in his films. He told the Velvet Underground they didn't work hard enough. Warhol may have wanted to make something out of his entourage's habitual presence. He took the opportunity and in that way he was an opportunist.

Andy Warhol—artificial or real?

Really Artificial, Artificially Real

Warhol wasn't the "compleat Fordist." He had no regimented assembly line, but repetition and seriality were elemental to his art. Rather than perfection on his line, he permitted small differences, aesthetic mistakes, and the perfectly imperfect iteration. Warhol's films reveled in imperfection, the imperfect was reality and an aesthetic. Perfectly imperfect performances, perfectly imperfect characters, one-of-a-kind scenes, the impossibility of retakes—would Pope Ondine ever say the same thing twice?

One take only. No do-overs. Warhol's verisimilitude.

Each of the *Screen Tests* (1964–1966) was a "still-film" portrait three minutes long, the length of a 16 mm roll of film. Each was a unique sitting, transcribed in film, allowing for movement but wanting none. Some sitters looked at the camera, as Lucinda Childs did, unwavering in her pose. Some couldn't hold the pose, like John Cale, who was scolded on camera. Some looked away, blinking a lot, like Lou Reed. Freddy Herko was a reluctant sitter and kept dropping the pose, his head falling out of the frame until his face was barely in it. Warhol, from behind the camera, directed him to return. Herko lifted his slumped head and moved it into the frame.

Holding the pose or dropping it is like maintaining a personality or not, keeping up the performance of self, or gender, or not. Warhol's sitters were highly conscious, sometimes very self-conscious—the curator Henry Geldzahler was—that he was watching them; some tried harder than others to relate to the camera. From behind it, Warhol could observe people being themselves, or trying to be, or "acting" in an unusual situation. His desire to look was indulged by being a filmmaker and a portraitist.

In *The Life of Juanita Castro* (1965), its screenwriter Ronald Tavel plays the on-screen director. Tavel based his scenario on the August 28, 1964, *Life* magazine article "My Brother Is a Tyrant and He Must Go," written by Fidel Castro's sister, Juanita. She described Fidel's involvement with Communism, their family, and the Cuban Revolution. Warhol shot *The Life of Juanita Castro* three years after the Cuban missile crisis, a dire event and no laughing matter. The film is a weirdly funny fiction.

The cast sits on chairs like an audience for a film or play. None of them looks at the camera unless directed, suggesting that the cast may be watching the movie in which they are acting, are unaware they are being filmed or indifferent, or are looking at or watching something else. Tavel feeds them their lines, which they repeat like wedding vows.

Fidel (Mercedes Ospina), Che Guevara (Aniram Anipso), Raúl Castro (Elektrah), and Juanita Castro, played by the filmmaker Marie Menken, are arguing with one another, their arguments more personal than political. Fidel, though, delivers a long monologue about Cuba and the revolution in Spanish with no subtitles.

Formally, Warhol is doing a turn on the concept of an audience, and on the differences between watching and looking. It's an aesthetic joke, some would say Brechtian. The audience is watching the actors; the actors are being watched but are also seemingly watching something else, or just looking elsewhere. Watching is a matter of engagement, an activity; looking can be merely directional.

We never know what others are seeing, which is another aspect of vision whose difference Warhol cinematically postulates.

Figuratively, Warhol is shooting expectations; he shoots for them and portrays them. The cast doesn't know what to expect, and waits for direction and lines. The audience also doesn't know, and manages—or doesn't—its frustrated expectations. There's no action in the usual sense. The audience becomes absorbed, bored, or falls into a kind of suspense or sustained anxiety. Viewers can watch the blank faces of the actors, while the actors can't entirely efface their body language. They appear uncomfortable or discomforted, even as they hold their poses, some failing.

Camp (1965) is unscripted, and directions are shouted from off-screen. Warhol is instructing his actors, people gathered in the Factory, to do something—directing them to move or speak. When one man takes the mic, and begins to tell a story, he can't be heard. The soundman runs onto the set, and adjusts the mic. This becomes part of the film. In *Camp*, what should happen off-screen—literally, the obscene—happens on-screen. Camp, as a stance and attitude, also entails these reversals.

A lack of action, then furtive movement; chaotic lighting, then everyone's in the dark until more light is brought onto the set. Mics are moved from person to person—it's all spontaneous, accidental, haphazard, even chaotic, and all for the camera. None of the actors appears to know what to do. When called upon to act, they must perform themselves on the spot—spotlit, however dimly. In *Camp* awkwardness is a style.

Suddenly, the filmmaker, artist, performer Jack Smith appears. When the camera finds him in the chaos of the set, he takes charge. Smith is riveting. Warhol's camera loves him. Smith has sharp features, a pronounced aquiline nose, and he knows how to look for the camera. He knows how to be a drama, to be and also not to be, so to speak.

Finally, Smith speaks: "Should I open the closet now, Andy?" I hear laughter on the soundtrack. Maybe Warhol's?

A double entendre, a camp line. Smith, a cinematic object, filmmaker, and performer, wanders around the set, an internal drama playing on his striking face. Warhol doesn't want to lose track of him—that face; the camera stays with him. Smith walks, or creeps, toward the rear of the space, in and out of the light, to a cabinet or closet. He will eventually open it, as if it were an ancient crypt. This is pure Smith, his face as compelling as Greta Garbo's, his mind unlike anyone else's. Smith makes *Camp* work.

The artifice of filmmaking is crucial to *Camp*, exposing the microphone, lighting, the mistakes. Hollywood film is supposed to appear "real," or about reality, though constructed with artifice, a product like all others. To make a film appear seamless, natural or real, a filmmaker uses tricks. That's the reality of "reality cinema"—it is magic, it is make-believe. But that's cinema verité, Warhol style. He undoes the illusion by exposing it, and, showing it, he also embraces and embodies it.

Reality Is an Oxymoron

Where does the artificial begin or end? Where does the real start? These perturbing questions contest and collide with each other in all of Warhol's films. They worry the idea of cinematic truth. What is an audience really watching?

Consider *Empire* (1964). The camera doesn't move, and, of course, neither does its object, the Empire State Building. *Empire* is a structural film: Its structure mimics the actuality, or reality, of a fixed object. Watching it, a viewer will notice the movement in the celluloid, its grain, and, in the distance, will see the iconic building. Warhol is shooting stasis; there's movement without visible movement. *Empire* is a cinematic oxymoron. Viewers watch for however long, maybe waiting for something to happen or change. When will it seem like a real movie?

The Empire State Building is a real thing, it exists, and it is also artificial, constructed, and, in a film, can only be a representation. The "action" of Warhol's movies is, in a sense, the conflict created for the viewer between artificiality and so-called reality or realities.

Warhol's dilemma—his not knowing where one begins or ends—is central to his body of work. His project, or this trope, makes, unmakes, and revisits meanings that surge with relevance, since his dilemma is ours. It is contemporary, ubiquitous, and endemic in a postmodernist world, with its multiplying conundrums, its presumed progress, the technologies of AI, cyberspace, virtual realities. There is an epidemic of uncertainty and insecurity at all borders, whether on the internet, between nations, or among computers. And always between the artificial and the real.

Reality Is Fantasy, and Everything Else

Andy Warhola was the youngest son of immigrant, working-class Slovak Americans. His mother adored and doted on her sickly child, and his brothers recognized the baby as special and different. In the 1940s, he would be the first of them to go to college. He graduated from the Carnegie Institute of Technology, and entered the labor force in the ebullient postwar period.

Warhol's provenance doesn't align with his image, which was, anyway, discordant with that of an "artist." Warhol was said to be a lover of money, celebrity, shopping, fame, etc. In his way, he injected the American dream with significant differences. An artist lionized, despised, and famous for the intense ambivalence he aroused, Warhol was considered a joke by many, and still is.

An artist's reputation is a curious thing. The further one gets from the time in which artists lived and worked, the closer one might come to seeing their art, stripped of context, much of it informative and important. It will also be stripped of rumor, gossip, personal animus. The art will, in a sense, stand on its own two feet, or fall down. Get up and fall again, or disappear forever.

During his lifetime, Warhol was so celebrated he appeared on America's most democratic institution, TV, on *The Love Boat*, playing himself. The pianist and wit Oscar Levant played himself in 1940s Hollywood movies, a rarity on the big screen then; he once quipped, "I was miscast." When Warhol did it, it still wasn't ordinary, but today anybody can appear on YouTube, etc. Or can play real make-believe on reality TV, whose modus operandi scripts a "one size fits all" image: "ordinary" people doing anything for fame and attention.

Shaming is alive and well in Puritan America, where the elect are known to God by their worldly success, or for just getting likes on Instagram. Anything to be known.

I think Warhol would have watched reality TV. The Kardashians. *The Biggest Loser*. *Hoarders*. He probably would have appreciated a genre that produces the same product, when it is the human spectacle, the human comedy.

Judging the Judges

Warhol's *Rorschach*s (1984) are paintings of projective tests, the most popular psychological test. They are used to judge subjective, individual reactions to abstract images "objectively," according to guidelines developed by psychologists for measuring and interpreting a subject's reactions.

Projections are a reality with which artists contend: Others project into their images not only what they hope to see—what they expect to see—but also what they can't help but see—their states of mind, associations, internalizations. Far-reaching assumptions are produced about what a work means and is, and about the artist's character.

Painting Rorschachs, Warhol appropriated the theory that looking at an image and interpreting it can reveal a person's psychological state. In effect, with his Rorschachs, he pictured the problem of interpretation. That is, he made pictures of it. No artist could make the problem plainer: Whatever art one makes, viewers project into it. Artists may acknowledge that their intentions don't matter, but when interpretations stray into the ozone, they might ask—artists do—what are these people seeing?

Warhol's Rorschachs are clever, smart, but they are much more than that: They are formidable conceptual works that perform serious commentary on subjectivity, objectivity, meaning, and the status of an art object. Art criticism once laid claim to objectivity, as most disciplines did and some still do. But if a critic were to analyze or interpret one of his Rorschachs, even formally, the critic would necessarily reveal herself. So, the critic—myself—escapes that by interpreting the fact of Warhol's having painted them and asking what they do.

These paintings ask questions.

Warhol was querying—or queering—interpretation, the heart of aesthetics. In queering objectivity and truths in interpretation, he built a space for the criticism of criticism, criticism's version of historiography.

In the same period that he painted Rorschachs, Warhol used camouflage design in various works. Soldiers wear camouflage uniforms to hide from the enemy, so it may be too heavy a metaphor—was Warhol in hiding and what was he hiding, etc.? Still, I can't ignore camouflage as "material" for Warhol.

The design emerged with and accompanied modern warfare—with the invention of the rifle. In both world wars, modernist art, such as cubism, played a role in developing camouflage. The dazzle ships of World War I bear its influence.

During World War II, László Moholy-Nagy was teaching in Chicago. In 1941, he was appointed to the mayor's personal staff . . . charged with helping conceal Chicago in the case of an attack . . . "To absorb views of the city under diverse weather conditions . . . [Moholy-Nagy took many flights and] pondered how to conceal the vastness of Lake Michigan with a simulated shore line and floating islands."[2]

Imagine trying to conceal Lake Michigan.

So, Warhol's adoption of camouflage was not outside the province of art. But art is meant to be visible, at least perceived or apprehended, "seen" in some sense. With camouflage, Warhol construed an art object as a thing hidden in plain sight. Going further, metaphorically, that thing can never be seen fully; it will always be hidden. While his camouflage self-portrait portrays him, it also reveals, without revealing, that he is incapable of being known by a picture. Or, on the contrary, that he is and remains an image only.

His camouflaged Last Supper represents a world-famous painting whose greatness—let's say, its spirit—will be hidden. Those who don't appreciate its truths, who don't believe in Christ, his having been betrayed at that supper, his dying on the cross for their sins, those without faith will not be capable of seeing Leonardo's masterpiece in its glory, in its reality. Without faith, it's just a picture.

Without faith in art, its cultural, political, and social significance, what is a painting, a photograph, a dance, a film?

After the End

> All the Cokes are the same and all the Cokes are good. Liz Taylor knows it, the President knows it, the bum knows it, and you know it.
> —Andy Warhol

Warhol's philosophy bears repeating: He liked repetition and objects when they could be reproduced and the same for everyone. Nobody gets a better product, no one gets a better Coke. It's a simple definition of democracy.

It's also a retort to the grandiosity and high ideals of earlier generations of artists who proposed art as transcendent. Not Warhol. "All the Cokes are the same" reveres not only sameness, unoriginality, but also commonness. He wanted to call what he and others did "Common Art," not pop art. Coke is good and tastes the same. And another reason he was hated: He debunked taste, leveling the field on which art is played.

> People come and go, talking of Michelangelo.

How Warhol's art, his smudging the borders between high and low, his "bad" reputation, will be received years and years from now is impossible to predict. "In the future everyone will be famous for fifteen minutes," Warhol's most famous statement, is repeated often and speaks to an American's desire for fame. Fleeting as fame is, it may be enough just to be seen even very briefly. A Puritan can hope God watches reality TV.

But I wonder if Warhol's statement isn't also a wish.

If everyone is famous for fifteen minutes, if fame is evenly distributed as if it were wealth, if everyone gets attention and everyone is known, then everyone is special, and then being special isn't special, because everyone is.

Imagine if everyone were special.

Imagine if there had been no Warhol.

Notes

1 It is argued that Warhol exploited people. Some Factory people say yes, some say no, but only the work exists now. Will his putative behavior forever taint his work? How do we look at it now, and through what frame? If "reality is an opinion," whose version of the story does one trust, and why?

2 Kelsey Campbell-Dollaghan, "The Forgotten History of How Modern Art Helped Win World War II," Gizmodo (August 2, 2013), accessed online.

Drawing from a Translation Artist

I

In recent years I have been characterized as a translation artist, grouped with others who have similar concerns, tendencies, or affinities. I'm slippery categorically, the way words are, since they are my medium, my art; but I can accept, after a fashion, my association with the group (some call it a movement; I don't), because I believe every object or person is a translation from something or someone else. I consider how history ranges and settles, seamlessly or roughly, in the present; how writing can be accurate even with the inherent obliquities of words, and how naming is usually renaming. Basically, all my written transmissions are, in these senses, translations. Nothing is denied by me as an effect or influence. (Uninvited memories spring up; forgetfulness occupies its own omniscient realm.)

Things get lost, turn up, go missing again, but in an intimate way an object isn't lost if it was never known to exist: Imagine, as I might, a day in the third century for a man in the Far East who might have been a relation. I see him in a loose brown robe, in a field, wearing a wide-brimmed straw hat against the sun. (Is my consciousness anything like his?) Yet about the day and the man, I feel no sense of loss. But I lose my favorite jacket—maybe it was stolen. I only know it's gone because I once had it and now want to wear it. I need it, search for it, nervously tossing clothes out of the closet. Head bursting, I retrace my steps, mentally or actually. If I hadn't noticed or needed it, it wouldn't be lost to me. (Someone else has found it.) A lost tree in a lost forest. (Entire histories get lost.) This is similar to the diminution of a friend's or lover's affections, which lack is not immediately noticeable; but when love is needed, it's not available. "I can't see you, haven't you noticed, you lost me, I'm gone."

Disappointments and private disasters can provoke self-persecutions or reenactments of scenes meant to ascertain the exact moment when a mistake occurred or a bad turn was taken. I avoid such endeavors; yet, as a translation artist, I am not of the "what's done is done" variety. I am, rather, of the "done, undone, redone, done over, done more differently" breed. (I may be a neoclassicist.)

The days and nights of the 1960s or 1980s are images now—words and pictures—and schoolchildren may skip over the assassinations of JFK and Malcolm, or the Iran-Contra scandal, like cracks in a sidewalk. A translation artist might want to reclaim the cracks or ruptures those sinister events caused and acquaint viewers with their stealthy after-effects and after-images—enigmatic historical figures or periods as regenerations, not memories. (Steven Spielberg's *Jaws* is the work of a translation artist: The killer shark is a remake of *Moby-Dick*, a presentiment of American disease and fear, which is why Spielberg's translation can be viewed again and again and still evoke horror.)

World or national tragedies differ in scale from intimate or personal loss, though they translate into it too. Also, the need to retrieve history's artifacts and narratives veers off from the need to remember them. For recovery or retrieval from the past, another want, curiosity, or engagement is required. A translation artist draws on and from previous conditions and renditions—a painting, news photo, snapshot, text; the actual event existed primarily in representation.

The often painful act of recuperation is performed typically to produce jolts to the system, neurological, aesthetic, cultural, political. (I may intend to activate my translated object like a bomb or, less hyperbolically, software.) There's a kind of skeptical idealism involved. On the one hand, the past can't be recaptured or relived; on the other, as a translation artist, one doesn't expect to capture the past but to interfere with settled notions about it, which is in some sense idealistic.

In 1985 the lost *Titanic* was found, the result of a secret CIA mission to find two missing nuclear submarines. The *Titanic* and its sunken treasure lay at the bottom of the deep blue sea. Pieces eerily intact were brought to the surface, but they have not been translated into the present. They only haunt it as specters of a tragedy in history, because the remnants of the *Titanic* have not been recuperated (I doubt they ever will be). The tragic-historical aura of the porcelain and crystal glass is shatterproof.

II

I accept change in forward, backward, and neutral gears. Art offers me a meta-place where idiosyncratic gestures and odd alignments get tested. Ideas about form, scale, discipline, practice (studio; no studio) are shattered regularly, and the resultant mess on the floor, or foundation, can be swept away or utilized in a piece. Let's say that I, a writer who translates from realities and unrealities onto the page or into cyberspace, find it insufficient to evoke objects for memorialization only—no monuments to mark disasters or fallen heroes or innocent victims. No. (Physics insists that matter returns, that it doesn't die. I might claim matter as a zombie. Others wouldn't.)

As a translation artist, I resist sentimentality and nostalgia. Looking back, for me, must be a cool operation; so I remain detached, whatever my first attachment was. I hold some occasions close, some people, dates, like John Lennon's death, and who told me he'd been shot. (Those few with "superior autobiographical memory" remember every single day of their lives.) One can be overwhelmed with the ennui of time passing, the "where did it all go-ness." But people can't know where things have gone or how the past will be stacked in memory or what will return later when thinking or in reverie, awake or asleep.

When I turned thirty, I thought, not atypically, I'm an adult, there's no going back (though in some ways I have and do), assume your responsibilities; at forty, I thought, I'm a middle-aged man, "in the middle of my life"—a difficult realization, especially since maturing forces involuntary translations (caring for sick parents; uninvited deaths; hair loss) and is often incomplete. Time keeps slanting my perceptions and shaping my interpretations. I wonder, as I write a story and draw portraits in it, or claim recollections of a dead day, what is beyond recognition. (Are there ideas and times that can't be brought forward?) Artists for re-creation monitor present-day comprehension through new iterations. Things don't mean the same thing forever. Most things disappear.

III

Some things don't disappear. Kafka writes in my fictional life, where his hunger artist invests in translation art-making and vice versa. And, if I write the words, "In recent years," as I did, I hear the echo of his first sentence from "A Hunger Artist" (1922). "In recent years . . ." The words recur in translation, since I don't read German.

There's a play by Eugène Ionesco called *The Lesson* (1951). I saw it when I was a teenager. The play rotated my thinking 180 degrees, and eventually turned me toward translation art. In his play, a teenaged student wants to learn Spanish. The teacher tells her to say, "The pen is on the table," in Spanish. She protests that she can't, she doesn't know Spanish. He says she can, she knows it. Just say it, he says. He insists. Haltingly, she speaks, in English: "The . . . pen . . . is . . . on . . . the . . . table." There, he says, that's right, that's Spanish. It's the same thing.

There's the story "Pierre Menard, the Author of Don Quixote" (1939), in which Jorge Luis Borges tells the tale of Pierre Menard. To understand Cervantes's great novel, Menard immersed himself in it and rewrote it in seventeenth-century Spanish. Since he wrote it again, but in the present context, Menard contends it is a better work than the original. Crudely, one might believe Menard is copying Cervantes, but Borges's assertion, through Menard, is a radical concept, at the heart of postmodernism, upsetting dearly held beliefs and truths about creativity, originality, and authorship. For one thing, making and remaking can't be separated, like writing, rewriting, revising can't be; and also, which came first is not the right question. (The original may be an atavism.) In any case, Cervantes never left Borges for long, and vice versa.

IV

Gertrude Stein drew inspiration from cubism, especially from Picasso's and Braque's paintings; a kind of borrowing occurred, because through them she found delight and an object to translate into writing. The object wasn't simple: a broken picture plane. How could she break syntax as they did a flat, painted surface. So, Stein unmoored words and created uneasy repetitions to write prose like a cubist work. Also a painting could be apprehended in the present, which fanned Stein's desire for reading and writing in the present tense. Whether her language experiments succeed or fail, they are never futile. Stein can never fail a translation artist.

I (and you) start somewhere, lean on or draw from art and life, draw meaning from others' lives and work. Where a story takes off is invariably in medias res and enmeshed in other stories. Inspiration may be a reprobate, but I have to get myself going, that's all. I might ask you: Tell me a story. I listen. I hear where and how it begins. But it was hard for you to begin it. You said, Let's see, let's see, where should I begin? I say, Begin anywhere. I read Virginia Woolf's diaries and swoon and fall into her great mind. "Bartleby, the Scrivener" goes to work with me. I look at a map drawn of America that marks the towns and cities where soldiers who died in war once lived, people I had no idea about.

I can draw something from all of this, I think. It takes time. Drawing, writing, eating up time; it can be slow work, often it's meticulous work. (All things can be done fast, too.) I imagine artists drawing with their heads down, bent in concentration (a hoary image). I see a hand moving on paper, erasing a line, doing it again. It's so human. Maybe it's intimacy, the sense of a presence, and willfulness or agency that confront and content me. In the second decade of the twenty-first century, I want to assert, slowness is fine, though I like my fast Lenovo, wirelessness, tiny, light things that make big sounds and carry masses of information. (Still, objects, like people, can crowd me.)

At the beginning of the twentieth century, speed and machines were everything.

Walter Benjamin wrote in his seminal essay, "The Work of Art in the Age of Mechanical Reproduction":

> For the first time in the process of pictorial reproduction, photography freed the hand of the most important artistic functions which henceforth devolved only upon the eye looking into a lens. Since the eye perceives more swiftly than the hand can draw, the process of pictorial reproduction was accelerated so enormously that it could keep pace with speech.

Benjamin, before Borges, assaulted the primacy of the original and proclaimed photography—its reproducibility essential—the century's most salient art form, one that would in its course eliminate or supersede others. It would also rid art-making of the hand.

I like the shapes of hands, watching hands pick up a fork and noting which hand is used, or scratching a head, an arm, or caressing a cheek. On a cloudy day not long ago, I pondered the many negative associations to the hand—like manual labor: being a grimy worker, with filthy nails. Hands instantly show your station in life. (Probably why there are so many nail salons in New York City.) In art, the hand became a fetish—the artist's hand, even its griminess was artful. But the hand raised craft over idea. And it wasn't a machine of the future, it wasn't modern, or modernist, it didn't break with the past. It couldn't. It was attached to the human body, and necessarily to human development and history.

The camera, Benjamin hoped, could make art democratic, because anyone's hand could press a button. Also, everyone has eyes which operate anatomically in the same way. Yet the eye isn't neutral, my eye is not like yours, yours not like your sister's. Seeing is a craft too, since it can be taught. And, subjectivity prejudices how and what we see, so vision isn't divorced from undemocratic causes.

Less abstractly, the hand that ties people to their animal bodies doesn't allow for the distance technology offers as a demonstration of progress, which, in the twentieth century, was a matter of belief in Europe and America—society was absolutely moving forward, getting better.

Now the fast thumb is a marvel, the twenty-first-century digit, speed in the hand.

V

There's no way around beginnings, middles, and ends, which ghoulishly stroll the streets like zombies.

I'm visiting a cathedral in Santiago de Compostela, in northern Spain, which was consecrated in 1211, and breathing its musty, incense-scented air. The capacious stone cathedral draws thousands to it every year, Christian pilgrims following the same trails as ancient pilgrims and feeling tethered to those first travelers. They are inspired to walk the true path with them. The pilgrims end their walk at this ancient site where Saint James once preached the gospel. Arriving, entering the church, they experience transformation perhaps, or bliss. (I can't know this.) They all stand in line at a column, and when they reach the front of the line, they bend forward and place a hand on the column, where Saint James's hand once was, and by now so many centuries of hands have touched the column, a handprint is grooved into it. Outside bagpipers play and welcome more pilgrims.

The Celts invaded Galicia about 450 BC and stayed until the Roman conquest. Incongruously, the bagpipe took hold and is the region's national instrument.

Cervantes must have heard bagpipe music when he visited the ancient town, if he did, and looked with curiosity at the pilgrims. Maybe the author, who centuries later led Borges, like a pilgrim, to make authorship mysterious, noticed a pilgrim there, a picaresque creature leaning on a gnarled cane, who, having once caught Cervantes's eye, one day returned in his imagination. The pilgrim was transformed into a character he named Don Quixote.

All About the Writing, All About the Writing

In this writer's dream, deadlines don't exist, just desire; unexpected words slip onto pages, sudden word-miracles and foreign associations incriminate received ideas.

And then there is Gertrude Stein, whose writerly goal was to leave nothing the same.

Stein wrote *Dix Portraits* (1930) to parody, imitate, or "be" cubist paintings, the prose equivalent to work by Braque or Picasso. The ten portraits in the book are extreme examples of how Stein eradicated much that is expected in prose, in a sentence or in descriptions.

Stein was extreme in most ways, how she thought and lived. She divorced herself from America, and Paris became her "hometown," though she knew many Americans in Paris. She loved women, not their minds, brilliant minds were men's, mostly. She broke definitively with her brother, Leo, a great mind though lacking in her accomplishments; they once believed themselves "genius twins," but then she never saw him again after 1920. She cut herself off from what blinkered or hurt her, and also from others about whom she didn't care much. France was overrun by Hitler's army and the Gestapo, and she, a Jewish woman, moved to the French countryside, protected by a French Fascist who had attended her salon.

But she was not thoroughly extreme; in some ways, she was a bourgeois. She had a domestic life and a wife, Alice B. Toklas, who cooked and arranged their social engagements.

This is mostly a negative portrait of her, isn't it. I do make separations, I do admire her writing, its unique intelligence, insouciance, and humor. Stein makes fun of the way it is, things are, so I read her also as a humorist.

Anyone can say anything about Stein, and it might be accurate. She is a loose canon.

Stein may not be read as much as she once was but is a mainstay on syllabi for courses in modernist literature. Literary critics and scholars and poets read her. Her books certainly never again had the popularity of *The Autobiography of Alice B. Toklas*, a bestseller in the United States in the mid-1930s. She figures as a spectral presence in contemporary American literature. "A rose is a rose is a rose is a rose" still pricks, baring the randomness of naming and its incommensurability with the actual, the Real.

But there is no denying, whatever you make of her writing, its originality and its influence. Hemingway was a friend and learned a lot from her; then they broke, but her hand can be felt in, for example, "A Clean, Well-Lighted Place":

> It was all a nothing and a man was nothing too. It was only that and light was all it needed and a certain cleanness and order. Some lived in it and never felt it but he knew it all was nada y pues nada y nada y pues nada. Our nada who art in nada, nada be thy name thy kingdom nada thy will be nada in nada as it is in nada. Give us this nada our daily nada and nada us our nada as we nada our nadas and nada us not into nada but deliver us from nada; pues nada. Hail nothing full of nothing, nothing is with thee.

In her day, visual art was revolutionary, sprung majestically to the forefront of the avant-garde—in Paris, Moscow, Weimar. Less immediate, great changes in writing. Think of Woolf, Pound, and Eliot, H.D., Proust, Jean Rhys, Joyce, Katherine Mansfield, Hemingway, that grand cluster, and others. Probably Stein dismissed their accomplishments or ignored them; besides, they might be giants, rivals for the throne. And, she might have thought, compared with painting, "there is no there there."

Also, she believed she and Picasso were the only geniuses.

I wondered if Stein had liked crossword puzzles. But no:

> I never was interested in crossword puzzles or any kind of puzzles but I do like detective stories. I never try to guess who has done the crime and if I did I would be sure to guess wrong but I like somebody being dead and how it moves along and Dashiell Hammett was all that and more.[1]

Stein designed her own whodunits for literary detectives, devising a version of word games by inventing a genre all her own in which they dominated, and one in which everyone knew whodunit—shedunit. There were no simple solutions for her linguistic crimes.

Necessarily, language couldn't be stuck with intended meanings; she had to erase denotations to question complacent meanings. With linguistic theorists, Stein divorced the signified from the signifier—repetition could achieve that—and through strange combinations, she unglues even associative thinking. The early futurists might have been influences, but Stein never wrote straight manifestos. To write a cubist painting, she chopped at syntax with an axe. But did she succeed.

Is intention irrelevant, or if it has some slight importance, in what way? In other words, Stein's putative intention was to make portraits of people: Did she? But can I, a supposed critic, describe her art without interpretation? I suppose that's formalism. The ten portraits by Stein, ekphrastic texts, construct a major problem: how to describe description. If they are really descriptions.

To describe Stein's portraits, to put other words to them, describes her poetics.

A portrait is a resemblance, usually considered a visual form, or it is a poesie, like Titian's six paintings derived from Ovid's *Metamorphoses*. Titian turned Ovid's writing into what were called "painted poems."

Stein traded her poesies for the artists' portraits, which artists do, trade with each other. But when Man Ray wanted to be paid for his portrait, Stein ended their friendship. He must have been very hard up to ask.

Was Stein tightfisted or a purist who stood, or fell, on principle? She left nothing in her will for Alice. But Alice did keep some great paintings from Stein's collection, and could sell them. She lived a very long time. The money didn't last, and I bet she never complained. But still, another discomforting portrait of Stein.

A portrait is supposed to be like the person, similar in some sense—Picasso believed Stein would mature into his portrait of her. Stein made unlikely work, didn't write likely stories, circled around and around her subject—which was always also about writing—and repeated and repeated. Some recognizable points of reference serve as descriptions, one could say, though she immediately cloaked putative meanings with contradictions, doing a dance with seven veils.

Picasso's portrait—Stein characterizes him by comparison:

"Would he like it would Napoleon would Napoleon would Napoleon would would he like it."

Napoleon was short, everyone knows, and maybe a bullish man like Picasso, maybe impetuous, impulsive, fearless, definitely romantic and mad about his Josephine. Picasso romanced many, his devotion more transient.

Napoleon was an emperor for a while, a commander with a commanding presence; Picasso led a corps of modern painters, maybe bossily, very occasionally sharing the throne. Picasso must have liked the comparison with Napoleon, but did Stein write to please him?

Picasso's self-portrait, a simple line drawing, depicts two versions of himself, one the face of a thoughtful man in profile, or a dreamer, hand under his chin; he's gazing somewhere into space. The other is a cartoonish figure with a funny face and a little body that could have been drawn by an eight-year-old. Was he kidding, giving this to Stein?

"I judge judge," she writes. Their relationship was likely based on judgments. Who is right about art, who can be the Judge of it? Their arguments might have been fascinating, and they never split, I believe, though she split with many friends.

Picasso lived much longer than she—Stein died in 1946, he in 1973, at ninety-one. Leo, the brother she stopped speaking to, died of cancer, as she did, a year after her, in 1947. The genius twins shared some lethal DNA.

Her shortest poesie describes, if it does, "Tonny by Tonny." Kristians Tonny was Dutch, considered a surrealist, a child prodigy who first exhibited at the age of twelve. Stein and Tonny were close until he wanted to marry a woman Stein didn't like, and their friendship ended. Curious that, the judge and the judgment.

Tonny's paintings are not looked at much now, maybe not for quite a while. I knew of him by reading Charles Henri Ford's diary, *Water from a Bucket*, and by way of Stein. Tonny's surrealist work lost its place or colloquially went out of fashion, a discomforting word applied to art but also accurate. Tonny's self-portrait, unusually, is not a solitary figure, but a potpourri of delicately drawn objects: a woman with her back to the viewer; a standing figure, probably male, in the center; paintbrushes in a canister; small animals and other whimsical creatures. The drawing buzzes with life. This was done in 1930, when Tonny's career was high, and so it seems was he.

The four lines that Stein chose for Tonny are dominated by "hope," "handles," and "rose." The last line:

"It, it is usual to add rose which is four rows. It is usual to add it."

Rose and rows, a funny rhyme, but "usual to add it" pertains, as most of these portraits do, to her writing. She attaches "hope" to him: Does he lack it, has he had it and lost it, does he need it now—maybe she sees his star falling. "Handles" has several connotations, none of which I read as particularly flattering to Tonny. Handles and handlers—Stein might be implying that he needs her handling, and can't handle himself. Marrying the wrong woman, she thought, for instance.

These descriptions are descriptive, but I am not sure what a description requires to be one. About Tonny, Stein's poesie fashions an invisible object—a psychological issue. But making sense of it may not be valid. Stein operates against sense, not to make nonsense but as sense is embedded in the words we use, how we use them, and in what order and context—ordinary sentences, phrases, and their ordinary thoughts need disrupting. To be understandable is sensible. Stein didn't accept the sensible, her sensibility was to undo it, and common sense would be anathema to her.

Eugene (Genia) Berman, along with his brother, Leonid, was a Russian émigré. They exhibited in Paris in the 1920s and, like some artists of *Dix Portraits*, were grouped as neoromantics. Their art was very different from the work of Picasso, much more fantasy-driven, and it's curious Stein favored them.

"Berman by Berman." In his self-portrait, a pen-and-ink drawing, half his face and all of his neck are darkened. The eye in the light side—his face is in chiaroscuro—looks like a glowing marble; the other, deep and black. His torso is enclosed in a loose, white shirt, which might be similar to a peasant blouse. Both hands are visible, one holding a brush or pen, crab-like, perhaps representing him as he draws his portrait. He appears melancholy, prosaically telling of his Russian soul. His self-portrait renders a personality or character.

Stein's taste, predilections, or aesthetic might have been changing when she wrote about Berman. I believe it is the subject of her portrait "More Grammar Genia Berman." And a strange title to associate with Berman, who was not a native English speaker. Grammar is an abstract idea here, certainly. Knowing little about Berman, I read Stein's concerns.

Her poesie emphasizes paragraphs and sentences.

> A last sentence is not interesting neither at first. After a while he may be mistaken.
>
> To do not follow. Blue by blue.

Stein uses the word "blue" again and again. It could be linked to having the blues, but she dwells on blue, plainly, I think, in reference to Picasso.

> He had painted blue. He did this when he was young and it was known as his period. . . . It is a funny story. I will tell it again. He painted blue. It was blue. It was a beautiful blue it was in a blue. As blue. He painted blue. Thank you. . . . Before I knew him he had painted in blue. . . .

Later, Stein writes, "I was mistaken," a declaration about herself that is, I believe, unusual. It might also be about Berman, about his art, or about her judgment of his paintings. Then Stein returns to writing qua writing intriguingly:

> A hue is a blue.
>
> Think of that as a paragraph. That a hue is a blue. That a hue is a blue. A paragraph.
>
> Simply misunderstood. They simply misunderstood.
>
> None of these sentences are other than paragraphs. Think of a blue. That too is a paragraph. Not to think of a blue as a hue. That is not a paragraph. Thank you.

Her blatant or coy contradictions can be meant to re-create the angles and superimpositions cubists employed so as not to represent so-called reality as an understandable object but one that can't be assembled into a picture, whose traditional visual grammar can't hold. It can't make a simple pictorial sentence where everything is where it should be.

Stein can't, either. Any reality is complicated, subjective, fraught, mysterious, as much directed by the unconscious mind as the conscious one. The eye that looks at a cubist painting will be split, cut the way an eye was in *Un chien andalou*. Stein wanted her writing to do that, split the I into pieces.

Art that causes disbelief, even momentarily, is preferable to one that sustains settled values. In an unsettled time, it can't settle. Physicists aver that the universe wants stability, but to achieve it, it needs to find its balance continually, and will be unsettled seeking it. And, what people make—culture—won't achieve a consensus; in art, for example, not immediately if ever, because there is no longer one critical voice or judge or single aesthetic.

But like Picasso's portrait of Gertrude Stein, the new might become understood later, then recognized as a classic, as Stein wrote in "Composition as Explanation," and the cycle will begin again.

Gertrude Stein wanted her writing to be read modernly. She wanted her prose to ally with art, to be its accomplice. Dismiss her writing if you want, it often is, but it is great. It has marked American English. It is great in its ambitions, disturbs language in its status quo, which can be called political, though I believe Stein herself was apolitical. Great also because it teeters on a great failure, as she attempts the impossible, and fails. Great because she fails and fails better.

Language disrupted on the page will fly home to its usual bed. But it can be argued, since Stein was interested primarily in the "continuous present," even a brief efficacy in her experiment must be called a success.

Note

1 Nathan Ward, "The Night Gertrude Stein Met Dashiell Hammett," CrimeReads (August 22, 2018), accessed online.

Decade-ism

In work and love, people get boxed in, edged out, ruined; others find acceptance, win prizes, and are vied for. A few are venerated, even adulated. True meritocracies are rare. Talent aside, whatever it is, human beings, like other animals, favor their own, cautiously adopting outsiders, especially those who will keep treasure close. A sociologist once told me that the only outcome your college statistically and reliably predicts is your marriage partner.

Our aggressive species has its survival methods, which usually relate to competition. Class, race, ethnicity, religion, sex: These categories for exclusion and inclusion were long ago transformed into naturalized or so-called civilized mechanisms. Snobbery persists based on these dubious categories. Self-described snobs, necessarily deluded, sit on top of this survivalist heap, priding themselves on their taste. "Taste," in this instance, connotes "good" but everyone has taste or preferences. "I prefer not to," declared Bartleby. He had no taste for copying anymore.

Calvin Tomkins's new book, *Marcel Duchamp: The Afternoon Interviews* (2013), is my latest friend. Tomkins met Duchamp in 1959 to interview him for *Newsweek* magazine; over time, the art critic and artist became friends. Of Tomkins's many books, two earlier publications are on Duchamp: *The Bride and The Bachelors* (1965) and *Duchamp: A Biography* (1996).

Duchamp talked to Tomkins about taste: "Taste is an experience that I try not to let into my life. Bad, good or indifferent, it doesn't come in. I'm so against interior decorators. . . . You don't have to be happy or unhappy about it, you see? . . . Taste can't help you understand what art can be."

Taste is a five-letter word no one discusses. Mentioning it, I notice friends and colleagues look at their menus or their nails. Mumbling begins, then silence. I'm not kidding, completely. People like to believe their sensibilities, approaches, or attitudes have been educated, nurtured, or expanded beyond mere taste, "bad, good or indifferent." It is also a matter of taste not to appreciate taste.

Duchamp distinguishes between the "onlooker" and the artist. "The priority of the connoisseur or whatever you call him isn't to speak the same language as the artist. . . . But don't say the artist is a great thinker because he produces it. The artist produces nothing until the onlooker has said, 'You have produced something marvelous.' The onlooker has the last word on it." Duchamp holds that these formations—artist and onlooker—perceive the same object differently, having very different aims. But the onlooker will determine the worth and fate of the art(ist).

Conversations among artists and writers about work often center on "how to make it work." Craft, materials, and considerations of space regularly come into discussion—work talk. Periodontists see diseased gums, wherever they are, just as musicians and composers hear with other ears.

I regularly question my preferences. Why I like or dislike writing, a photograph. I don't trust experience, even if it has shaped me; I don't fervently trust what I think or believe, while I believe it still. A pox on absolutes! I could trace a genealogy of what I think and like, which is, to some extent, what I was exposed to, taught, made conscious of, and decided not to be or accept. Tendrils of difference and objections sprouting rebellions and self-discoveries—I could list them. But I couldn't create an order for my character, and hold it/me to a neat line. (When I learned to write, I wrote fast, not on the lines, only below or above.)

My preferences change and change again. Once I believed, doing studio painting with Ron Gorchov and Doug Ohlson, that the figure would never return. Once, involved in showing and making experimental films, I believed Hollywood movies were uninteresting. One night, at a screening of a structuralist-materialist black-and-white film, I asked myself: "Why am I watching this?" Like Bartleby, I preferred not to, anymore. Whatever I've "renounced" resides somewhere, pinging and ponging, because ideas live on, more or less alive in different moments. Being for or against something now is less interesting to me than understanding what it does, how it does it, and why it's being done.

Which brings me to the art world's obsession with decade-ism. The so-called literary world stores much less faith on periods of emergence. The new is treasured more in visual art than in writing; the literary world is backward in so many ways, and I will not count them. But a first book comes out in 1991, say, and the year stops being of interest, with the next book, whenever it comes out, which counts more, and then the next. A writer is thought to mature, even to write better and know more. The actual age of the writer matters today as a form of "branding," but the brand becomes old, just as the writer will.

Artists get pinned to a decade. It's as if time had stopped, the artist suspended in it. Artists think in and through their work, during all the decades after the one in which they debuted. If humans weren't perverse, in postmodernity the "post" would become valuable.

People now live so long, many past one hundred. Extended middle and old age pushes youth further and further back in time, making being young really a thing of the past. Something interesting could emerge from that.

The Hardest Thing

It's Independence Day, the Fourth of July, and America is 236 years old. I've been pondering the tortuous coupling, "art and politics." Each partner resists easy definition, especially "art" ("Is it art?" and "What is art?" are jokes); I can't imagine Ludwig Wittgenstein countenancing their murky conjunction. It's hard to avoid the couple's traps.

Art is not usually measured by its utility (the school of "relational aesthetics" attempts to call that hand), while politics is. What usefulness is believed to be is also a matter of contestation. In 1972, in Amsterdam, with the artist Jos Schoffelen, I ran a cinema with an eclectic program, the first in the Netherlands to feature double-headers and to screen an Andy Warhol movie, *Bike Boy* (1967). A rogue film collector approached us with a 16 mm print of *Tarzan Escapes* (1936). He screened it for us: Its white supremacy and brutal racism were shockingly casual. Black African men fell off steep cliffs, while their white British masters exclaimed about the loss of precious equipment.

Jos and I wanted to pair it with a documentary about the Black Panthers. Amsterdam's Communist Film Club distributed it, but wouldn't rent it unless we organized a protest march. "Why do we have to organize a march?" "Because it's a political film," they said. I said, "If people want to march afterward, they can." Juxtaposing the two was art and politics; "Art could be a dialogue," we said, "which is political activity." "No way," they said.

The cinema wasn't considered "serious" because of its emphasis on art; soon their club vetoed the cinema getting funding from Amsterdam City Council. Maybe this is too strident or absurd an example of conflict between, and in, art and politics. Generally, I proffer the idea that all art is political, though I'm not satisfied by it. It seems subtle, yet too broad, and because of this not convincing. But I may be trapped in it, not having a better argument.

Writing novels and stories, I've become convinced that narratives concern themselves with justice or adjudication. Writing fiction, I might be able to avoid mental traps, habits of mind. I try to be vigilant about how I write—style, form—to trample complacency of all types; in concert with a writer's lacks, it generates truisms and stereotypical characters.

I often recall other artists' choices. Ad Reinhardt drew political cartoons and made nonreferential paintings. The American poet George Oppen stopped writing poetry for thirty years, after he became a member of the Communist Party in the 1930s, because he wouldn't write Party poems. When he started again, he produced an exceptional poetics.

In a performance I once saw, the artist Bob Flanagan hammered a nail into his penis. I put my head in my hands, covering my eyes (one man fainted); but I wouldn't think of stopping him. It was his penis. Was this a political act? Flanagan was born with cystic fibrosis and was told he'd die at twenty. He'd been a cystic fibrosis poster boy at thirteen. His art fought his genetic identity, and what the disease didn't cruelly claim, he tormented. For his exhibition *Visiting Hours* at the New Museum, New York, in 1994, Flanagan built a hospital room and lay on a hospital bed, attached to an oxygen tank.

Viewing Flanagan installed as a piece in a museum, knowing him since the 1980s, I felt disorientated—installed momentarily in his hell. "Voyeuristic" pales as a description of my looking. Was his métier disorientation? Flanagan's conflation of art, body, and disease bewildered me, rebelling against any modifier, such as progressive or regressive, which might characterize the politics of an art practice.

Some say artists should make work for an audience, that anything else is indulgent; art should be "accessible." To whom is never clear. Recently, in various newspapers and literary magazines, a debate about so-called difficult books has been unfolding. Writers should remember their readers, one side insisted, by making books enjoyable. For one thing, "difficulty" and "pleasure" are relative terms; without foundation, the argument lacked cogency and drifted into nowheresville.

The filmmaker Trinh T. Minh-ha reckoned with the concept of audience differently. Minh-ha was present at the New York premiere of *Naked Spaces: Living Is Round* (1985), at The Museum of Modern Art. The film pictured women working, walking, socializing. No narrator explained the women or the spaces they inhabited. Instead, words shaped and suggested more impressions, ways of seeing.

The first question to Minh-ha came from a man, who asked, vehemently: "Who is this film for? Who's the audience for this film?" Minh-ha took a moment, then said: "I make films for sensitive people." Her audience fell silent, maybe stunned by her tactic, which leaped over patterned responses. Minh-ha allowed for the contemplation of positions, by escaping the usual discursive traps. It's the hardest thing to do, and in art and politics the most imaginative and stimulating.

The Life and Deaths of Jane Bowles (or, Reputation)

Jane Bowles was born on February 22, 1917, a short, usually harsh month—it seems right for her. Bowles's unique writing and life were cut short, derailed by neuroses, alcoholism, physical illness. Her friends remember her sharp wit, agile mind, gaiety, humor, outrageousness. While she lived, stories about wild Jane Bowles circulated in Tangier where she resided from 1948. Back then she was a living legend, but the flux of reputation—here today, gone tomorrow—sends her body of work into and out of print (OP).

Among certain contemporary writers, including Lydia Davis, Deborah Eisenberg, Michael Cunningham, Jane Bowles is celebrated and revered for her work, notably her sole, singular novel *Two Serious Ladies* (1943). It has also been praised exuberantly by Tennessee Williams, Truman Capote, and John Ashbery. Bowles finished six stories, and a play, *In the Summer House*, which ran on Broadway in 1954, with incidental music by Paul Bowles.

Jane Bowles didn't subscribe to what life held in store for her, an upper-middle-class Jewish American girl from Woodmere, Long Island, New York. Willfully, it seems, she undid her putative future; the unexpected—accidents of fate—also changed it: the death of her adored father, when she was thirteen, and, then, as an adolescent, she developed tuberculosis in her knee. The teenager recovered in a Swiss hospital, her leg in traction for months, when, it is said, she discovered her love of reading and literature. Ever after, she walked with a limp. Paul Bowles's hated, anti-Semitic father called her "that crippled kike."

Out of her mother's house, according to Millicent Dillon in her definitive biography, *A Little Original Sin* (1998), Bowles rebelled hard and fast. She led a super-fueled young adulthood, hanging out with writers and artists, barhopping in Greenwich Village, pursuing love and sex with other women. She was adamant in her desire for thrill, a Bohemian when the term meant something. The composer Paul Bowles and she met in 1937, and, surprising everyone, they married in 1938.

Bowles rejected comfort and complacency; she disdained middle-class values. Ease never befriended her: She questioned everything. "I had met nervous girls before," Tennessee Williams wrote in his preface to *Feminine Wiles*, "but her quicksilver animation, her continual cries to me and herself: 'Shall we do this or that? What shall we do?' showed such an extreme kind of excited indecision."[1]

Reading her work, I can feel that anxiety in slight shifts of tone, in her unusual juxtapositions, both jarring and productive. I read her phrases again and again, adjectives abutting nouns in unlikely relationships, an innovativeness with language that she shared with Jean Rhys. I might become melancholy, reading her, though her writing also makes me laugh out loud, the way Kafka's does. But Kafka's work is cooler. He's observing his writing and himself writing it. His work, in a sense, depends on distance—between psyche and society. He writes about and with detachment. Bowles is not detached, not in any way; her irony might even have boomeranged on her.

The way she lived differed starkly from her middle-class beginnings, but more the way she wrote veered from conventional literary modernisms. In writing, she didn't pursue a self; I can't imagine she believed one existed. She didn't write to discover an identity. She denied identifications and worked toward disidentifications. While a sense of the fragmented underlay her order of things, she didn't strive for it. Her métier was seams and fissures.

A Jane Bowles character, like its author, will have trouble making up her or his mind. I take "making up one's mind" literally: Minds are made, not born. Bowles was exceedingly conscious of this and stymied by it. She was kept in doubt, undone by right and wrong, by what she didn't know, and what could be in her mind without her wanting it. Bowles's characters play in this absurdity, having choice and no choice simultaneously. Irrationality ineluctably figures into action and inaction, causing contradictions, and sometimes paralysis.

Any sentence from *Two Serious Ladies* displays Jane Bowles's disorienting, elegant style—in fact, any sentence from all of her writing:

> Arnold had just taken quite a large bite of his sandwich so that he was unable to answer her [Miss Gamelon]. But he did roll his eyes in her direction. It was impossible to tell with his cheeks so full whether or not he was angry. Miss Gamelon was terribly annoyed at this, but Miss Goering sat smiling at them because she was glad to have them both with her again.

The movement from Arnold's cheeks, to Miss Gamelon's reaction to him, to Miss Goering's feelings about them, makes a sketch of each—I want to say, they're line drawings. Arnold's full cheeks can't be read as angry or not, which annoys Miss Gamelon, while Miss Goering smiles, happy to be with them. A reader can see the composition at the table, these three curious beings.

(I wonder: What troubled Jane Bowles when she wrote those sentences, which words worried her, what made her anxious.)

All choice—in life, writing—pained her. Making a choice, which writing allows and supposedly encourages—be as free as you can be!—created perpetual havoc. Working on the exceptional short story "Camp Cataract" (1949), Jane got stuck. She told Paul Bowles that she couldn't name a kind of bridge, cantilevered, unless she knew exactly how it was built. She made no assumptions even about her mother tongue, and said no to the first thing that came to mind. Her mind saw fit to unmake even plain words and phrases, to unveil home truths' hidden messages. Writing turned into a representation of her intensity and fierce integrity, she wanted honesty in language and syntax.

Like everyone else, Jane Bowles's volition was regularly compromised, and she moved to dictates she couldn't know. Psychoanalytically, home is always where you go, and, though Jane Bowles left hers to be herself, let's say, or to figure out her own way of life, or to write, she appears to have been unsatisfied, always restless. She and Paul Bowles, dedicated to difference, to being strangers in a strange land, chose their new home, but no place was home, I think, for her, and she didn't find it in her writing, either.

Paul Bowles found an odd comfort in estrangement; it suited his disposition, his dry humor. His story "You Are Not I" (1948) is a tale of psychological horror, of a young girl's "madness," and sent proverbial chills down this reader's spine. Jane Bowles's stories weren't horrifying or cold-blooded. Nothing she wrote is like Paul's "Pages from Cold Point" (1949), a father/son incest story in which the son is the predator. The kind of horror she understood seeped into ordinary events and daily obligations that had to be faced, couldn't ever be avoided, and where deception lay in wait.

Jane Bowles portrayed all societies as unforgiving and alienating. Her writing oxymoronically sustains a condition of permanent disorientation.

The short story "Everything Is Nice" (1951) begins:

> The highest street in the blue Moslem town skirted the edge of a cliff. She walked over to the thick protecting wall and looked down. The tide was out, and the flat dirty rocks below were swarming with skinny boys. A Moslem woman came up to the blue wall and stood next to her, grazing her hip with the basket she was carrying.

In this "blue Moslem town," everything is nice and strange, for Jeanie. The Muslim woman, Zodelia, calls her a Nazarene.

> "Where is your mother?" Zodelia said at length.
>
> "My mother is in the country in her own house," she said automatically; she had answered the question a hundred times.
>
> "Why don't you write her a letter and tell her to come here?"

To Zodelia, Jeanie's mother living so far away is weird, maybe unthinkable, certainly not nice. Later, Zodelia pointedly inquires about Jeanie's aunt: "Where *is* your aunt?" (The italic "is" is Bowles's.)

Her fictional characters often track homeward. Bowles's own sense of exclusion, of being on the outside, was powerful. She wanted to belong, somewhere, and "home" is a problem and question in most of her work.

But home or away, life was very strange, and it was also frightening. That is ever present in Bowles's writing. She seems to say, "This is how it goes." Life is incomprehensible, existence is bizarre, unaccountable, mean. There may be beauty or joy, momentary as a parting glance, so her characters will hope for even momentary happiness, as does Jeanie—genie—when she rushes out into the unknown to feel it before it goes.

Two Serious Ladies's protagonists, Miss Goering and Mrs. Copperfield, leave home, bearing opposite psychologies: Miss Goering strikes out, wanting bold adventures, while Mrs. Copperfield trails after her husband, an unwilling traveler/tourist, full of fear. At the end of this seminal, tragicomic, picaresque novel, they both return home, something their author never did.

Jane Bowles died, in a Spanish hospital, Clinica de Reposa de Los Angeles, run by Catholic nuns, not knowing her name. She lived there—existed—for over five years. The year she died, 1973, the copyright for *Two Serious Ladies* should have been renewed: The law then was to renew copyright twenty-eight years after the date of first copyright. But it wasn't. Jane Bowles died, and the same year her only novel, forgotten by its publisher, was sent into the public domain.

Tennessee Williams proclaimed, "I consider her the most important writer of prose fiction in modern American letters." This most important writer's body of work summarily disappeared, and, ironically, sadly, absurdly, her corpse did, too. Upon her death, Paul Bowles had her body interred in a cemetery in San Miguel, Málaga, but leased the plot for only ten years, then let it lapse. The location of her grave became a mystery, and, without a renewed lease, "because no one had claimed Jane's remains in response to official notification, her body would [have been] thrown into a common grave."[2] Let's say, the public domain for corpses.

Paul Bowles built his own shrine to Jane Bowles in his apartment in Tangier. He dedicated a wooden shelf to her books in all their editions and translations. (I visited his home in 1987.) Ultimately, though he had no truck with graves or an afterlife, he permitted a young student, enamored of Jane Bowles, to move her body to another cemetery (the cemetery where JB had been buried might itself be buried under a highway). The young woman was rebuffed by Málaga officials, who suddenly decided Jane Bowles's grave was important to the city's cultural history.

Bowles's skull and bones have a very peculiar trajectory, if I can call it that, and to say her corpse has been homeless is too cute. It's a long, complicated saga about which both Millicent Dillon and Jon Carlson have given full accounts.[3] To cut to the quick, Bowles's final resting place has depended upon what Tennessee Williams called "the kindness of strangers."

Searching for her grave, Jon Carlson found a kindly priest, maybe saintly, called Padre José. He had become the keeper of Jane Bowles's flame.

> Padre José said that Jane's new grave, established through the efforts of the municipality of Málaga and the Association of Friends of San Miguel Cemetery, had been unveiled mid-October, 1999. Afterwards, he added

> secretively, "But in the evening she moves all over the cemetery, and I am here to watch over her."

Mentioning her work in conversations, assigning her novel and stories to students, and writing about her, those who treasure Jane Bowles's body of work try to watch over it. Though I'm not completely pessimistic, I regularly observe the literary drift, the burials and unearthings of writers' reputations. They come and go, "talking of Michelangelo," T. S. Eliot put it, and Eliot also, like Chaucer for two hundred years after his death, will likely come and go. Here today, gone tomorrow.

Any writer who believes in her or his literary immortality is delusional. Writers, especially females—Clarice Lispector, for example, who is enjoying a rebirth of interest—writers whose work is mordant, elegant, even grim, their books will disappear. And maybe they'll return from the OP cemetery, rise from the dead, but only if a living person or two feels a great debt to that great writer. And, if that writer's books are reissued, smartly repackaged, it will have resulted only from vigilance, devotion, and love.

Notes

1 *Feminine Wiles* is a collection of Bowles's unfinished stories published in 1976.

2 Millicent Dillon, "Keeper of the Flame," *The New Yorker* (January 27, 1997), accessed online.

3 Jon Carlson, "The Gathering Spirit of Jane Bowles," *Rain Taxi* (Summer 2022), accessed online.

Remember You Are a Body

Just Back from Los Angeles: A Portrait of Yvonne Rainer (2016–2017)

Just Back from Los Angeles: A Portrait of Yvonne Rainer was Adam Pendleton's second film portrait. It opens on a street scene, people walking back and forth, to the sound of Charles Trenet's "La Mer," a romantic, dreamy tune, light and sweet.

Inside, Yvonne Rainer is sitting in a booth in a brightly lit diner, ordering a turkey burger. Pendleton is across from her. In black and white, the two stand out from the diner's bland decor.

"We're rolling, we're going," Pendleton says.

"Where?" Rainer asks.

"We don't know yet," he says. "But we know where we are . . ." Rainer tells Pendleton that this Manhattan diner is her office away from home.

Rolling is the movement of the conversation between the two, fifty years apart in age, sitting across from each other; like any conversation, where it will lead is not known. Their conversation, an exploration.

Yvonne Rainer is a singularly important choreographer and filmmaker, whose dances, starting in the mid-twentieth century, radically changed dance. Her films, employing text, dance, voice, and image, strongly influenced feminist and other filmmakers and directors. She is a postmodern icon, who wouldn't like that designation, and continues to make dances. She is also straightforward, sometimes blunt, and often funny.

So, where are they going?

The camera settles on her gesturing hands, as she talks about her background, where she's performed lately.

Pendleton hands her a text to read, a collage of writers' words including those from Stokely Carmichael, Malcolm X, and her own from *Feelings Are Facts: A Life.*

During Rainer's readings, film of her performance of her signature dance *Trio A* (1966) is intercut. The film moves from words to dance and back again:

> Things are very wrong with this illusion of democracy and equality in this country . . . Many people ask . . . why do we want to criticize the liberals . . . he promises the oppressed that he will be able to alleviate their suffering. (Carmichael)

Trio A, a joyful dance, is juxtaposed to the stasis of racism. It doesn't move.

She reads the dancer Barbara Dilley's recollection of being in Rainer's dances: "The breathlessness of the lifting section . . . the opening bars of the Chambers Brothers and doing *Trio A* . . ."

Rainer seems to be reliving the past.

Reading Keeanga-Yamahtta Taylor's painful litany of recent murders of Black men and women by the police, one after the other, Rainer pauses as if shocked, taking in what she's reading, absorbing these massive assaults on Black people.

There's a leap, both are standing: Rainer and Pendleton are balancing the weight of their forearms in each other's. It must be an exercise, something like a warm-up she did with other dancers. It's about holding, not dropping the other's arms, it's about balancing, trusting the other, and not letting the other person down, metaphorically. When they touch, they look at each other. This doesn't occur in any of Pendleton's other films. It's a very private moment happening in public.

Bodies are foremost in all of these portraits, voice too, action and activity predominate, a distinct contrast to Warhol's *Screen Tests*. Warhol wanted still bodies, no movement, heads in paralysis for the camera. Adam Pendleton looks for the body's freedom.

Ishmael in the Garden: A Portrait of Ishmael Houston-Jones (2018)

In life and art, context and frame set the limits within and by which people understand, interpret, see; POV starts in contexts. Pendleton's film of Ishmael Houston-Jones begins with a long pan, from the side of a building to a park, trees, sounds of the neighborhood, and lightly picked guitar music. A man's voice is heard over the urban landscape. He first tells Pendleton his mother's name, not his, which is unusual, then he says his, which at birth was Charles, but at twenty-one he changed it to Ishmael, in the Bible "a troublemaker, a bastard child." Ishmael is an only child, his parents dead, no partner, no children, so "It's just me," he says.

His approach to himself is felt, very personal, his telling about himself allows for great intimacy, which continues throughout the film. He seems shy in one way, Ishmael pausing before he speaks, and also bold, as one thought opens easily to another. His honesty makes him a wonderful subject, but it is not easy for him to speak about himself, so he takes his time to frame his thoughts. He wants to get it right.

Ishmael has been fascinated with death and dying since he was a child. The 1980s and 1990s AIDS epidemic in New York City profoundly affected him.

Like Pendleton's film on Rainer, Ishmael's hands are shown gesturing, but in very different ways from hers. He cups the air, seems to form parentheses around what he says. In contrast to Pendleton's brightly lit portrait of Rainer, shadow and darkness encircle Ishmael, when he, also a choreographer, dances.

Pendleton has asked him, "Do you want to dance?" Ishmael says he doesn't know. But then he is preparing to practice, taking off his shirt. The camera stays close to his face and body, following his every movement. He limbers up, recites a diaristic text, each sentence beginning "I remember," and recalls joyful moments. He remembers dancing and sweating and loving that; teaching soldiers how to dance in Nicaragua, and sad moments, seeing his father in his coffin. Pendleton doesn't intervene during this litany and long scene. When Ishmael speaks again, the scene shifts into color, and he is among the trees in the garden near his house.

When Ishmael dances, he's in the near dark, and the mood is somber; his dance is sober and exacting until his body turns into an emotive field of energy. I don't know which words specify what his dance means to him, but he is thoroughly in it. I am watching an experience. His sweat catches the light on parts of his body as if a spotlight is glossing him.

Practice over, leaving the space—the main hall of St. Mark's Church—now seated, the camera on his face, Ishmael remembers a tryst with a prostitute, who smokes in his apartment, "He's so cold-blooded." He stares ahead, defiantly, then tenderly kisses his own hands, with some humor.

Ishmael slides into and out of moods—benevolent, ambivalent, dubious, a mind always complicated. Watching him, and listening, I recognize how much remains hidden; he's cautious and also bold, a curious combination. He's saying and not saying, pausing, thinking, resistant. The unsaid must be what I witnessed in his dance, the inchoate, the body speaking what the mind refuses.

In the beginning, he talked about both parents being dead, watching a friend die, and toward the end, Ishmael reads a poem from *Dead* (1981):

> My mother, my father / John Bernd / Deryl Mackie /
> Martin Luther King / Two or three popes, I
> can't remember / Keith Haring / Trayvon Martin /
> My cousin Jackie / Every cat I've ever owned /
> Tamir Rice . . .

The political and the personal are entwined in him.

At the beginning of his portrait, Ishmael revisited his beginnings and spoke lovingly about his parents. He said he and they were "like a three-person unit." And now he's one, but everyone he loved, and loves, lives with him.

What Is Your Name? Kyle Abraham: A Portrait (2018–2019)

The screen is black. Pendleton speaks in voice-over:

"What is your name?"

"Kyle Abraham."

Abraham will be questioned differently from Rainer and Houston-Jones. In this dialogue, Pendleton poses direct and existential questions to Abraham: "How did you end up here? Can you feel it? Does it hurt? Is it too soft? Do you like it? Do you like this? Is it all right? Is he there? Does it weigh much? Do you have to carry it far? Can dance take your body apart?"

Abraham says, "It takes my body apart every day."

Suddenly, an image appears, a figure is moving, wearing black pants with fringes, and the hips swing, sway, move from side to side. The fringes dance around his lower body.

The camera moves to his back, his head, shot from behind him—until there is a full view of him, Kyle Abraham. Unusually, the image is never full-screen. The screen is divided vertically into three equal parts; the image of Abraham is always in or at the center. The rest remains black, a mode very different from that of Pendleton's other film portraits. The screen's look is an image in itself—the film will be as much about Blackness as about one Black man.

Pendleton continues asking questions of Abraham; many of them he has asked before, but now Abraham is in motion, and the context disrupts or inflects Abraham's meanings. Also, in light of the order in which the questions and answers come, there is change, which brings up Gertrude Stein, her repetitions and disturbances to the usual order, the "normal" sentence, words out of place and indifferent to their prescribed definitions. Abraham is dancing, the voice-over dialogue goes on, and he moves to, against, or along with it.

Sometimes, Abraham appears to be battling with the space in front of him, like a Don Quixote and windmills. His arms constantly encircle themselves, rotate in front of his chest. And, oh, it's hard not to feel that some of Pendleton's questions arouse questions in Abraham that disturb him, that some questions address elements he faces in life that twist his thinking, make his mind go round in circles.

"Is it hard? Does it weigh much?"

Abraham screws up his face, tightens his body, his stomach turns concave as if punched. The weight of everything on him rises in his dance.

"Can we talk about Black dance?"

"Yes." Abraham agrees with the artist/choreographer Ralph Lemon, who claims that a Black dance maker is always a representation of Black dance. A strong assertion, because choreographers, whether Balanchine or Robbins or Rainer, will demand dancers to adhere to their script *à la lettre.*

Lemon and Abraham imply—I think this is what they imply—a Black body is never absent and can't be; Blackness is a marker, signifier and signified. Is this essentialism, exceptionalism, or a position enforced by racist ideology? The word "race" scarcely covers the vast meanings and effects the category produces, and how it functions, in society and culture.

Abraham embraces being a Black dancer who makes Black dance.

New questions, and the screen again is black:

"Can we talk about Black music?"

"Yes," Abraham says. To him, everything is Black music.

"Once you find a monetary value to our music, it becomes American music."

"What's your name? How did you get here? Can you feel it? Does it hurt?"

Abraham appears, the camera focusing on his arms and hands. He reaches up, as if beseeching the heavens or rising from a troubled place. He clasps his hands, then swings his arms to his back, where his hands touch and clasp again. Maybe it's comforting when the body holds its own hands.

The psychoanalyst D. W. Winnicott wrote about, and theorized, the "holding environment," which begins very early, from the way babies are touched and held by mothers (now parents, one hopes); this early care affects the child's development, allowing it to feel safe or secure later in the world. It is a more complicated theory than this brief explanation, but this is one of the analyst's central ideas.

To extrapolate: Abraham touches his body, his face, he sometimes holds himself, and, in this way, creates a sense of safety, a safe environment for himself.

Abraham's answers augment the shape of his film portrait. He moves and speaks, and Pendleton finds imagery that responds, like call-and-response in a church. Bodies represent, and Pendleton presents dance as a medium through which feelings manifest. Dance refuses inhibitions, dance urges the body to tell its truths, joys, pain.

Abraham: "Dance gives me a different sense of articulation."

Readings of bodies are interpretative, just as dance is. Mine might differ, say, from Pendleton's, but I wonder: Are words about our states of mind and emotions more clear, really more definitive? Because bodies blush, sneeze, cough, gasp in surprise, get hives, scream in fear, have orgasms, and some can be "acted," some not. What can be trusted when trust is so hard to attain or feel? (I remember that Rainer and Pendleton enacted a trust exercise.) Does the body lie? And if it does, how would it?

The screen returns to black. Pendleton's voice is heard over a screen divided into three parts. In the bottom third of the central panel, Abraham's legs. Another third, his torso. The other third, his head and shoulders. He's dancing in all three spaces, a body divided into parts—sometimes they appear to mesh, mostly there is a disjointed dancer, a man of many parts:

"Does dance take your body apart?"

"Dance does take my body apart, and in some way it's the same as maybe society is doing . . ."

The screen mimics an exquisite corpse; the design renders a living body in pieces, coming together, drawn apart, still and whirling.

Pendleton recites a list of infinitives, of motions:

"To divide by; to stand up; to sit down; to divide by; to assemble; to yearn; to protest . . ."

From another angle, high above, the camera watches Abraham dance upon a light-gray floor. As he whirls, he places his hands on his head, caresses his body, and leaps. The floor seems to disappear. Finally, Abraham is in motion, dancing, flying, as free as he can be.

So We Moved: A Portrait of Jack Halberstam (2021)

Pendleton's film uses a complex cinematic register, from wide, long, and medium shots to very tight close-ups, with interior and exterior locations. In black and white, the film's effect is as stark as that of the Rainer portrait.

Halberstam is sitting in profile. An unseen Pendleton says:

"This is such a strange process. Do you accept it?"

"Not really. I'm not made for this. I guess I accept it, but I struggle with it."

Sometimes acceptance can be resignation, and ambivalence is common to love.

Halberstam might feel uncomfortable being the object of Pendleton's gaze but has committed to this "strange process." He will be investigated by another's eye, sometimes merciless, unflattering maybe, but he allows Pendleton full access. It's a first intimation of Halberstam's character—no halfway measures, commitments are fully lived. Also, Halberstam would rebuke a camera that glamorized him.

Halberstam is a queer theorist, an author, a professor, and he is a walker, bike rider, and swimmer. These last activities—avocations—characterize him also. Throughout the film, he is either teaching, biking, swimming, walking, talking, and a sense comes: Here is a body that doesn't want to stay still, a mind that doesn't stay still.

"I strongly believe in a kind of anarchist sensibility where we have to unmake the world we're in, in order to find something else."

That state of mind, those ideas, must be held gingerly to find and inhabit a changed world. This intellectual fully embraces and embodies Antonio Gramsci's dictum: Optimism of the will, pessimism of the intellect.

Wearing a black bathing suit, a towel around his neck and shoulders, Halberstam is walking up a staircase; then the camera moves outside to sunlit trees and sky, JH in a park, biking in the city. When walking his bike, he moves with a dense crowd of people waiting for a traffic light to change. The mass surrounds

Jack who disappears, then reappears. No other Pendleton portrait captures city life this way, crowds of people, shots of the court, parks, and a monument—statue of a man on a horse (about which we find out more, later).

Another intimation: Jack Halberstam often exists in the public eye, out there in many senses, and very much with others, engaged with them, in his work. A healthy skepticism is subdued by a spirit that needs the world to clean up its act.

A very tight close-up of his face fills the screen. From a crowd of faces to a single face is startling. His bare face looks exposed, with no shadows.

"I'm Jack Halberstam, I research gender and sexuality, I grew up in England . . . I have been living in the US for the last several decades."

Pendleton asks him a question that is muffled, to which Halberstam says, "Give me more," the only one of the portrayed who makes this specific demand. The camera pulls back.

Halberstam is demanding, and demanding of himself.

"I believe that we live in a pretty shitty world . . ."

Pendleton focuses on Halberstam's face and body, and on spoken and written words, with more text here than in the first three. A poem by T. S. Eliot is its very first image, in fact, and later in the film Halberstam recites it:

> So we moved, and they, in a formal pattern,
> Along the empty alley, into the box circle,
> To look down into the drained pool.
> Dry the pool, dry concrete, brown edged,
> And the pool was filled with water out of sunlight,

And the lotos rose, quietly, quietly,
The surface glittered out of heart of light,
And they were behind us, reflected in the pool.
Then a cloud passed, and the pool was empty.

Eliot's imagery—drained pool . . . water out of sunlight—the surface glittered . . . a cloud passed—is visualized. The images are tropes, and make the film's imagery poetry.

A young Black man strides on a path in a park, trees around, his bare, toned back to the camera. Halberstam recites a string of words, maybe freely associating: "Stone. Liquid. Not. Scream. Cut. Take. Monster. Wild. Shock. Don't. Control. Mess. Chaos. Time. It. Off. Tree. Mushy. Institution. Insanity. Clever. Obscurity. Mayhem. Collapse. Unnatural. Devious. Variant. Unsupportable. Pedagogy. Make. Media. Stop. Watching."

Halberstam has changed himself, his body, radically, by having top surgery.

"I was given the name Judith at birth. This is the name of my paternal grandmother, which is quite meaningful to me, but I needed not to have a female name, and so I gave myself the name Jack, but my sisters call me Jude."

He says, "I needed not to have a woman's name," not "I needed to have a man's name." Halberstam doesn't accept binaries, man/woman, for one, and, besides, removing breasts doesn't make a man, either, but a person without breasts. What a man or woman is, is a received idea. But now, more than ever, it is a question.

A body swims and dives, pool water roils with the impact of Halberstam's body; a river is flowing, water is flowing is like film moving is like day moving into night.

The sound of a body diving into water, those splendid splashes, creates another music.

Underwater cinematography takes us beneath, in water, looking at a body in novel ways. Sometimes a swimming arm lashes the water, a head lifts, a breath is taken, or two legs kick, propelling the body forward.

Being in water, Halberstam says, "disconnects you from the air . . . you're alone. . . . There's a kind of womb-like space, because the water actually holds you, you can float, but then under certain circumstances you can't . . . you can also sink, it's that tension between floating and sinking."

Overhead shots of an Olympic-size pool, empty of water, appear several times. From above, the black lines dividing the pool into lanes seem to be a minimalist painting. The empty pool is also juxtaposed to the flow and flux of city traffic. Emptiness haunts days and nights. But it can also be, I want to write, a space to be filled differently. A space of change, but then that may be to fill it with a political agenda or will.

The longest scene in the film occurs when Halberstam walks into and around the pool's changing room. The room looks like a prison, institutional and somber. Men to one side, women to the other, a segregation of the sexes. Halberstam refers to his "bodily ambiguity," which isn't "liked in the changing room."

Halberstam led us viewers, me, around the space, marking its peculiarities, its dictates, inclusions and exclusions. His comments challenged this discrimination by sex or gender. Why and when do the sexes "need" to be separated? What now will be the new logic around privacy?

That statue of a man on a horse, seen several times, is Robert E. Lee. Pendleton filmed it in Richmond, Virginia, where he was born and lived as a child. Not that long after the shoot, the statue of Lee came down, a change Halberstam might appreciate, even though a symbolic not systemic change. Maybe Pendleton saw its relevance to Halberstam's discourse in and on the changing room, and to Halberstam's theory of trans* in his book, *Trans** (2018). Halberstam set an asterisk next to the word to broaden its purview, to encourage trans-formations, movements across and beyond, to recognize that beings mutate. He wants the idea of trans to be inclusive not exclusionary. In other words, Halberstam resists turning trans into another essentialist identity.

> And the pool was filled with water out of sunlight,
> And the lotos rose, quietly, quietly,
> The surface glittered out of heart of light.

Let there be light . . .

Ruby Nell Sales (2020–2022)

Pendleton's most recent portrait transmutes or translates a woman named Ruby Nell Sales into film. Sales is an almost excessively brilliant orator, a great intellectual and spiritual leader, a profoundly moving mind, a civil rights activist, feminist avatar, a messenger of love but no saint. Ruby Nell Sales is an inspired and inspiring truth-teller.

Sales's life has been long and full, and this is Pendleton's longest film to date. Sales understands what she has lived and what she is living in. She tells us how she did it, and speaks to the camera, the viewer, with an almost brazen intimacy:

> My name is Ruby Nell Sales, I grew up hating that name . . . I lived in a community where everyone knew my name . . . and went away to Tuskegee and read James Baldwin's essay "Nobody Knows My Name," and I didn't know how to deal with that as a Black person, as a Black girl who had grown up in the South . . . Being known always was about having a place in the world, having a context.

This is a very different portrait film. In each, Pendleton cinematically assesses his subjects, frames the character of the character, and shows how that character lives. The camera moves with and follows the character's lead. In the case of Ruby Nell Sales, whose person and work overflow a life's frame, Pendleton's film concerns itself with speech, language, with orality. It is a collage, a Venn diagram, an intersection of, and crossing from, Sales's words and thoughts, as she speaks, to a meeting with her writer friends, and old pictures, home movies, and documents that spill across the screen. Some of it is related directly to her, some of it is evidence of other people's lives and histories.

Ruby Nell Sales is shot primarily in lustrous black and white and also in color. While many directors use black and white for the past, Pendleton colors the present with Blackness. It is this present moment that concerns Pendleton, and how history has shaped it and been carried into it.

Sales embodies it. Hers is a singular life, and extraordinary life, but it has not only been lived by her. *Ruby Nell Sales* is about an individual who recognizes herself as a product of history and an agent in it. As she says, she grew up in a context. She is most often pictured seated in a chair, in a private setting, where it is quiet, and telling viewers about her life and how she sees things now. The solemnity of what she speaks is foregrounded by the quiet around her. The focus is usually on her face in a tight close-up, but most especially on her mouth as she speaks and it moves. The focus is also there when she doesn't speak. Silence is important as a frame for what this eloquent woman offers to the world.

The speech that emanates from her mouth bursts with a sense of a magnificent life, thoughts on her early life in the South, being queer, community, race and racism, spirituality and love. The breadth of the film expands with every image and primarily develops through what Ruby Nell Sales has to say about experience, her philosophy, her loves. Through her spoken thoughts, her words call up images.

In a sense, *Ruby Nell Sales* is a text-driven film. In none of Pendleton's other films is the mouth the center of movement. Here is an excerpt from one monologue:

> I was greatly loved and greatly motivated by my community. And even when I did audacious things, to be

> audacious for a Black girl was considered something good and positive . . . I was taught to talk back to the world, not to be passive before the world. I didn't know abandonment. I knew cultivation. I knew love. I knew security. And not only that, I knew what it was to be loved, to belong, and to be claimed, not only by my parents but by my teacher, by my Sunday school, by my community, and by people who even lived outside of the community who knew my name. And my mother was part of a generation of African American women who sat tall and walked tall in a world that conspired to render them small.

Sales's upbringing, she says, helped her be the outspoken and loving person she is today. She compares her nourishing upbringing with that of Black children who are coming up today:

> I've thought a lot about the generational continuity, which was essential to the development of Black young people when I grew up. And I think, today, how that is so missing. I think that this generation, the generation since the 1970s of Black young people, are an abandoned generation. They did not have the Black adult support or connections that my generation had. I think that desegregation decimated the physical space in the Black community, as well as relationships. And I think that young people today do not have the grounding, the frame of reference that I had, to even understand what it meant, to have the words, to understand.

In *Ruby Nell Sales*, talk animates the film as much as the images of trains that glide on tracks, as much as her car traveling on a road. Her words create movement, dancing from idea to idea, her propulsive thoughts generate more in a viewer's mind. Nothing stops or stays the same for Ruby Nell Sales. And nothing does in this eponymous film. It lifts viewers into dimensions and spaces of light and love through the presence of a unique and great woman.

Pendleton wants his films to BE as alive as his subjects, even to be them. He comes as close to his subjects as he can. He impresses their lives onto the film's skin, which may sound strange. Metaphorically, celluloid becomes skin, a surface, the largest organ in the body; skin is a current vibrating in all of his films: skin as a color, a racial category, a false one but a lived and vicious reality, skin as tone, soft, hard, bright or dim, images lit or in shadow. Each film wonders about how people live in their skins.

By not adopting a single cinematic approach, his films follow, shadow, look at his subjects to see them as they are, to the extent possible. His characters make their work, love what they do, wrangle with themselves about it, and go on. They need to do it. Pendleton leads with indirect and direct questions, follows up their answers with words and also visually, and depends upon abstract imagery for mood, for ambiguities, for celebration. He uses the dynamism of silence and the power of watching and listening: He becomes a viewer also. He lets his characters lead him, metaphysically and physically, where they want to go.

These portraits represent modes of being, not role models, which exist constructively with and by their imaginations, variously claiming or disclaiming identities. In movement, say, in swimming, identity becomes immaterial, and all identities are at least provisional.

As Jack Halberstam put it:

> But then under certain circumstances you can't [float] . . . you can also sink, it's that tension between floating and sinking.

Those existential moments—that tension—describe the human, and sadly inhuman, condition.

Soft Pink Light

Kaitlin Maxwell is daughter and granddaughter to the two women in this photo series. Maxwell appears with them in some pictures, imitating or mimicking their poses, wearing the same costumes. She shoots them alone, shoots herself alone, she poses them against different backgrounds, mostly domestic spaces, but not only. Maxwell's images represent an intense curiosity about them, the women who raised her, about who they are, apart from her, and who she is because of them. Maxwell wants to know if she looks like them.

Nine and six years younger than my two sisters, I watched them as I grew up. They fascinated me. From my bed, I watched my middle sister put on her bra on a freezing winter morning, and felt sorry for her—I wore an undershirt, but a bra wouldn't keep her warm. They were my brilliant sisters, my heroes, until they were not.

My mother, the first female, was a "prude." Our female bodies were not talked about, they were our secrets; what happened to them, and what we did with them, was secret. We didn't walk around naked. My father's body was also kept under wraps. When my breasts started growing, I thought the small mounds, or lumps, might be a disease.

Maxwell's images are revelatory to me, unusual: She looks at her close female relatives as characters in their bodies, with bodies. Daughter and granddaughter, she seeks ways of seeing them, and to perceive femininity, sensuality, sexuality, and "sexiness" in them and her, and also as coded images. That is, she depicts all of this as "just pictures" of women. Her mother and grandmother are shown as sensual, voluptuous, while the archetypical "Mother" is not. Good-looking, fit women, they pose, and don't; they reveal their bodies, and don't.

The poses and postures of "femininity" and "womanhood" supply part of Maxwell's material. Simone de Beauvoir famously wrote, women aren't born, they are made. (I love Aretha, but don't believe there's a "natural-born woman.") And, the concept of "natural" changes over time, indicating that so-called natural behaviors also change, or that nothing is natural. Females will be inculcated, educated, indoctrinated with how to look; how to get looked at; how to behave, and what they can expect of life "as women."

In photography, the knowledge that pictures are constructed, that they are in some sense always fictional—that is, made up—has troubled and wounded the medium. A photograph can't assert itself as a fact or document. Because like the humans who invented the medium, photographs can dissemble and shape-shift. It is this understanding among photographers that presents a great dilemma: They assemble or frame or construct an image that already is an image, and already seen.

When I was seven, I saw Marilyn Monroe in the movie *Niagara*. I don't know who took me. In one scene, Marilyn appeared in a tight-fitting, low-cut fuchsia dress. I had never seen anyone like her. She was sexy. I sent away to her Hollywood studio for an autographed picture. It was the only time I ever did that. It was a little black-and-white picture of her in a bathing suit. She was smiling, posed high on her toes, standing in profile, and looked cute and friendly, I thought.

Monroe became an object of fascination to me, a baby feminist. Her performance of sexuality startled me. Was I supposed to be like that or only admire images of women like that. In the early 1980s, I tried to write her autobiography, to write as Marilyn Monroe, tell her story intimately, but after reading what had been published about her, I became too depressed to write it—her early life was miserable—and, in the 1990s I turned what I had written into "Dead Talk," a short story about Marilyn.

Animals flirt, give off signals for mating; male birds do elaborate dances, their colors brighten and shimmer; some males fight to the death for a female, and sometimes an animal merely rubs against a tree or sprays leaves to lay down its scent. Marilyn Monroe's flamboyant dress, her exaggerated stroll, her ass in perpetual movement modeled one version of the female of my species using vivid, revealing costumes to catch a mate.

In this Western world, it's a toss-up. Sometimes it's the job of females to attract partners; perfume can be used as scent. Men often appear not to need prompts; they were bred to play the aggressor. (They have image problems, also.) Too passive, they may not get what they want. Too aggressive, they might frighten their target. Some are predatory.

In several of Maxwell's photographs, the women strike poses that might be considered sexy or provocative. These replications are studies in sexiness.

In the first image of the series, Maxwell faces the camera, its remote device on her lap, and shoots from there. She is sitting on a stool in jeans and a black bra, beside a yellow stove. Her legs open into a V and mimic the V of the corner behind her back. The kitchen's yellow wallpaper, the background, denotes its era, the 1950s or 1960s.

(My immediate association to seeing the yellow wallpaper was a story, "The Yellow Wallpaper," by Charlotte Perkins Gilman in 1892. A woman is suffering a terrible, postpartum depression, and kept in a room—a cage, a prison—with yellow wallpaper.)

Maxwell shows herself in a homely, dated environment. The photographer makes herself a target, boldly central in the frame. She is also to be investigated. Later, as the series progresses, Maxwell will contrast this homeliness to her mother's and grandmother's versions of domesticity and the feminine.

Voluptuous bodies wear casual or revealing clothes. The women appear not to mind being shot; Maxwell herself seems more tense or, as the photographer, less comfortable in front of the camera. Maybe the women were uncomfortable, they just know how to perform. A viewer can't tell. Poses are performances, and Maxwell's photographs are not didactic, yet one could decide that, through her photographs, she is depicting a girl's education of learned "womanliness," and how to do it. "Strike a pose."

She uses bright light, natural light, shadow, or low light to build moods, feelings—openness, secrecy, obscurity, ambiguity. She mostly foregrounds her subjects, while the background embraces them—the women appear to have a place, in a place. But Maxwell frames her subjects as if an actual border were surrounding them. She uses color subtly, often pastels.

Her pictures mostly work with a few elements, and not extraneous information. There's overhead light in a bathroom scene, where her grandmother applies lipstick. Maxwell has shot her from an angle. We see her in profile, and also, her full face in a mirror, one side of which is bright, the other dim. The mirror she looks into is divided.

In Maxwell's images, women mirror each other. Maxwell lies in bed, part of her body under covers, while her grandmother lies, curled on the floor in a shift dress. In two other shots, similar poses are struck by Maxwell with her mother, and with her grandmother.

In the first, Maxwell and her mother stand side by side in a backyard, an old wood fence behind them. The mother's head leans toward her daughter's, and both are wearing black pants, casual tops. They look at the camera, they look "ordinary."

In the other, Maxwell and her grandmother stand in front of a white garage door, next to each other but not touching. Her grandmother is wearing a low-cut black sleeveless dress that reveals her large breasts. Maxwell wears a see-through top, her smaller breasts peeking through the interstices of the netting. Both women have angled their legs, as models do to present a slimmer image.

Dueling images, let's say, juxtapositions within juxtapositions, facing each other.

Apart from her formal concerns, Maxwell's content—femininity, gender, sexuality, women as constructions, representations and self-representation, mothers, daughters—are compound(ed) subjects, not separable in her pictures. To represent females and their bodies is a thorny job. Any one issue engages others. "Motherhood" is a construction, and its representations of maternity shape ideas about how a mother should look and act. A mother is also an image—but whose.

Women look at women, men look at women, straight, queer, nonbinary individuals look at women—looking is complex.

I'm recalling Laura Mulvey's seminal essay on classic cinema's "look" and "gaze" at women, a function of patriarchy, control by men of women, particularly in a narrative, which breeds in women an internalized male gaze. (Recently, Mulvey has said she understands her seminal essay as a manifesto, as polemical.)

A woman is looking at other women, she gazes at them, and herself, she makes pictures of all. Viewers look through her lens, her eye. So, as a viewer, I can only project, which is what I am doing. My responses or interpretations, my seeing, get filtered through my psychology, my associations. My curiosity stems from a desire to apprehend the psychological moment in them, and how and why Maxwell's work produces or promotes certain stories.

I don't know if I can see, separate from my gender, the ideas I have unconsciously absorbed. I don't think I'm a woman. Consciousness awakens one to inherited or educated biases. That is my hope. I might be able to see as a queer woman or straight man, say. Or, I might be caged in my own room of yellow wallpaper. I can't claim a clean sweep of that room's indoctrinations, my early education, can't say it's been done thoroughly or completely. Making formal analyses helps me, I think, see other ways than subjectively to see, but still . . .

I suppose I want to find a coherent narrative, and know I will not. Questions have been around for a long while: If female bodies are represented by women, are they any different from those shot or painted by men? Maxwell's photographs dive into these muddy waters in visual monologues and dialogues.

Photography's virtue is its vice: A seeming, immediate clarity—what you see is what you get—hides its truer illegibility.

One day, while writing this, I turned on the radio for background noise, which fills in for something, maybe an absence of ideas. It's a woman's voice. "My husband thinks I'm obsessed with my breasts." She's written a book about women's breasts, the American obsession with breasts since World War II. I can guess what she's going to say, and turn off the radio to wrestle with how to write about breasts in Maxwell's pictures; they figure prominently, under clothes or partly unclothed. I might be looking at their breasts the way a man would.

Maxwell seems to be comparing and contrasting her body and their bodies. In one photograph, she wears the same costume as her grandmother. Their breasts are exposed in the same way, just above the midriff of their lingerie.

The first time my mother mentioned breasts to me, I was five and with her at a beach club my family had joined. An elderly woman in a bathing suit passed by; she had extremely large breasts that hung down almost to her waist. My mother, who was not "busty," said: "It's good to have small breasts so that doesn't happen when you're old. And then your back won't hurt." She never said anything like that again.

Toward the end of the series, Maxwell presents two suggestive, ambiguous, and puzzling works, disconcerting in ways her other photographs or scenes are not, and they are of herself—self-portraits.

She is sitting at the edge of a bed, fairly close up, and wearing a red plaid shirt. Blood is dripping from her nose; a hand is raised almost shoulder level, one finger also bloody. Her face seems naked, surprised, upset, shocked. She appears to have been crying.

It took me a while to recognize her bloody nose. (I think it is a bloody nose, I have had bloody noses.) This pose, and why she is showing us it, suggests many responses, and I find myself associating wildly. First, blood and women, menstruation and other bodily functions. But the blood forms a straight line from her nose down to her chin, then across her upper lip, forming a cross; the way she is holding her hand up and cupped, with two fingers raised more than the others—this, I think, mines religious imagery. Stigmata, stigma, a sign of disgrace.

The photograph's ambiguity allows, encourages, sensitive or harsh readings—for one, women's shame about their bodies. Not all women, not in all societies, not all at all. This shame is mostly a hidden terrain, and contemporary women are supposed to be over it. If only.

A woman can feel shame about her vagina. Vagina dentata! She might be embarrassed about having her period, or the "curse." (My mother never used that term; she also never told me about periods, I sent away for pamphlets.) Come menopause, this woman will be told she's no longer attractive, here's room on the shelf. Controlling weight, that fixation to be skinny, functions as a way to submerge these other feelings, to control the body. It's an illusion, but an all too common one. Her body is trouble. The stigma is to be a woman.

Maxwell has set her final scene—a self-portrait—in a pink bathroom, with pink tiles, in soft pink light, pink towels on a rack. The background is in soft focus. Maxwell wears a delicate pink bra and pink half slip, and is seated on top of a toilet seat. Her hair is pulled up neatly in a bun; she is looking at the camera at an angle, not facing it, the remote again in her lap.

Maxwell's look at the camera, at the viewer, seems significant, and different from the other self-portraits. She might be peeking at us, exposing herself. Setting it in a bathroom, she has invaded a private realm. The photograph acknowledges she is doing this, exposing herself and her mother and grandmother. Maxwell has taken liberties, and recognizes that she is invading their privacy with her pictures of intimate relationships. She also reminds viewers of their/our common bodily functions.

This picture is beautiful, I think, though its setting might read as unglamorous. It's a compelling picture, for one, because of Maxwell's gaze, a question rests in it, and also defiance, and yet a sense of serenity. Maybe a feeling of completion for her.

This final picture cannily returns us to the beginning, to her first photograph, another self-portrait. Maxwell is in a kitchen, sitting next to a yellow stove. She starts the sequence with yellow and ends it with pink. It's a soft landing.

Fighting Talk

Max Weber defined the state simply: It was legitimated to kill, and no other entity was. This singular right separated it from every other institution.

Separations are rarely so neat. A nation is regularly anthropomorphized: A nation has a face, it can feel "shame" or lose its "honor." President Barack Obama's threat to Syria about "crossing a red line" (new meme for grievous verbal misstep) forced the president's hand. Obama would lose "face," i.e., the US would be "embarrassed" if he/it did not "punish" Syria for its use of chemical weapons against its own people.

The language people have invented and employ for nations creates problems, because words act in us—they carry emotion, say, as fighting words or loving ones. Obviously, nations don't have faces or feel humiliated. Only the humans who lead them do, and maybe their citizens or subjects. Those who represent a nation might go to war out of pride. For instance, George W. Bush started a preemptive war in Iraq, not just for oil but also to avenge his father, the first Prez Bush. Shakespeare's history plays and tragedies regale readers with tales of just such ambitions: kings' and queens' dubious personal reasons for war and murder, desire for revenge, power. Lust and greed. To go to war is a tragedy; to go to war for a nation's face, pride, and honor is delusional.

Weber brought "charisma" into the political playbook. Theorizing it, he analyzed people's fascination with leaders, how certain personalities' fantastic charms could cause others to follow them blindly. Weber didn't anthropomorphize nations, but he did sometimes use metaphors. At the end of *The Protestant Ethic and the Spirit of Capitalism* (1905), he tendered the striking image of "the iron cage" that capitalism—spirited by "Puritan worldly asceticism," its idea of "labour as calling," and the drive for "the acquisition of worldly goods"—had built for its believers. (Studying Weber with Joseph Bensman, a noted scholar, I learned that, as a young man, Weber lay in bed with depression for five years, during which time, I thought, he might have begun to rationalize the irrational. Weber instantly became a very sympathetic character.)

Obama has eulogized victims of "massacres" often since his presidency. He speaks for the US, he says. Commentators chew up the TV screen discussing "gang violence" in Chicago, "a lone gunman" at a Washington, DC, naval base. "America grieves," Obama might say. "School shootings" is a familiar term. A "massacre" provokes shock as well as truisms, words badly used, duly applied, sapped of vitality. "Massacre" smothers unique beings under a mass of anonymous, dead bodies. The word itself steals what humans call "humanity."

Terms for brutal chaotic acts specify unusual occurrences, while also normalizing them; meanwhile, these "exceptions" happen week after week. A "lone gunman" and "gang violence" have many precedents. A "homegrown terrorist" is applied only to US-born or naturalized citizens who murder with political or religious motives. For assaults aroused by virulent prejudices, the term is "bias" or "hate crime." Statutes and laws against this type of crime were introduced in the US in the late 1980s.

Some might call this seemingly boundless violence a domestic war. I don't know what to name it. To call it "war" might not be accurate or helpful. Sigmund Freud wrote that "civilization began the first time an angry person cast a word instead of a rock." Certainly, this society is less civilized than it should be, even uncivilized. But then Freud would not say "uncivilized" (though expecting the American experiment to fail), because he comprehended what most people find most perplexing—contradiction, especially the unrelenting power of the irrational: the drive for life, libido, and also for death, the death drive.

I was a writer in residence at the University of Sussex, Brighton, when Quentin Tarantino's *Pulp Fiction* opened in 1994. The English/American Department hadn't had an American writer in residence for twenty years. I was a curiosity. When American literature, art, politics were discussed, the Americanists turned to me, sometimes sullenly. I was meant to be the real thing. Now, "authenticity" is troubling as an idea or ideal. I don't buy into it. But holding a US passport, I was the American, though not Edith Wharton's or Henry James's edition. "Let's go to see *Pulp Fiction*," I said to my grad writing workshop.

I'd been out of the country nearly three months, and laughed at Tarantino's wry, dissonant dialogue between hit men (played by Samuel L. Jackson and John Travolta), who compared French Big Macs to the American original (talk about authenticity), before "eliminating" another man. Smart talk, nihilism, and the movie's casual violence, weirdly and sorrily, brought me back home. Home, where, in the Constitution's second amendment, citizens have the right to bear arms and form militias, because the state alone should not have the right to kill.

My English students and I walked outside, onto Brighton's boardwalk, when I remembered where I was, and who, supposedly.

Modernism and photography developed alongside, and in relation to, each other. But at its mid-nineteenth-century start, the field of photography split, one side documenting so-called reality, courting humanism, emphasizing the centrality of human beings, and the other courting spirits. Spirit photographers documented women whose recently dead husbands' faces "emerged" from their bodies. Ironically, the same chemicals that produced logical results also produced ghosts.

The imagery of Susan Hiller's *Rough Seas* (1982–2018) originally came from tourist postcards. Hiller discovered them in seaside shops all over the United Kingdom and began collecting them in 1972. In 1976, she exhibited the postcards, at the Gardner Arts Centre, in Brighton, as part of *Dedicated to the Unknown Artists* (1972–1976).

Hiller wondered at people's fascination with the imagery in its many iterations. Wondered at the commonality of the images, their significance, and the spirit animating them. Destruction threatens, horrifies, but with that comes excitement and beauty, the very definition of the sublime.

Rough Seas could be spirit photographs.

The images are dreamy, and encourage dreams, and embolden ghosts of time past. With them, Hiller asserted the commonality of dreams and dreaming. Dreams connect people. "In dreams," Delmore Schwartz wrote, "begin responsibilities."

Hiller once did a performance-based event, *Dream Mapping* (1974), not for an audience but with and for the participants. They were asked to sleep near each other and, upon awakening, to write down their dreams. Hiller was curious if, during sleep and with proximity, the participants might transmit messages, or find that their dreams interacted with another's, that their unconscious spirits might find each other.

Hiller engaged the unconscious in unique ways. *Rough Seas* beckons to it, to unwanted thoughts and unacted desires, hidden below consciousness. The relentlessness of waves also mimics the restlessness and pulsing of sexual desire. The rising and cresting of the waves imitate the body arching toward orgasm.

A great wave threatens at the end of a pier. It rises, higher and higher, widens as several waves unite with it and crest, white foam spitting and sputtering. Unfurling, the massive wave is about to destroy the pier and drown anyone in its wake. In a grid of nine, "rough seas" vibrate in lurid, fantastic purples, electric reds, and deep-sea greens, ready to destroy anything nearby, and to overwhelm the grid itself.

Versions of *Rough Seas* abide within a grid, whose history represents adherence to logic and order, but these images implicitly question or disenfranchise it. Great, harsh waves will erase boundaries, and these images represent the uncontainable. The darkness and mystery of rough seas, or emotions, or sexuality, were not so welcome within the modernist canon, which promulgated light, open, and clean spaces.

Through their infinite stasis, absolute stillness, the images speak to the permanence of the irrational and of nature's uncontrollable forces.

There are no people in these photographs, but one can conjure them, waiting with terror for the crash, the end. Invisible as people, invisible as the deep, are the unwritten stories that accompany these pictures. They might produce associations to childhoods and provoke long-buried angers and sorrows. They might make viewers feel small, when nature's will, beyond human control, drowns this species' narcissism.

Rough Seas represents the inevitability, also, of random occurrences at their most extreme: Waves may hypnotize with calm and steady movements, but suddenly they turn into monsters. The sea, awakened and aroused, is transformed and attacks mercilessly. Its own hidden world is as unknowable as the unconscious. *Rough Seas* is Eros but also Thanatos, and, in these images, love and death fuse, but Thanatos's deadly mission is checked, fate denied but not obliterated.

Hiller, who died on January 28, 2019, focused her exceptional, beautiful mind and mind's eye on the undocumentable, unknowable, unbelievable, incredible, unfamiliar—"uncanny" only begins to describe her unique body of great art. She doubted the ways in which people were trained to think and see, the categories by which people understood and interpreted their world. She let the implausible surface and believed in the truths of others' visions. What might not be actual or visible might still be true.

Over and against certainty and category, Hiller recognized and advocated for the power of the imagination. She believed in the spirit of people and in their imaginations that reside in *Rough Seas*.

Beyond Good and Evil

Nan Goldin's *Memory Lost* opens with Super 8 film of beautiful, young people dancing, having fun, while Eartha Kitt sings about "unspoiled gender" and "being pure . . . not wanting to be chased." No, Kitt sings, "I want to go to the devil; I want to be evil."

In the 1980s in New York, heroin and coke fueled parties, clubs, minds. Fashion photographs of the 1990s portrayed stoned models in images called "heroin chic." Fun didn't last long: too many overdoses, and the AIDS epidemic's onslaught of death.

In Goldin's first major work, *The Ballad of Sexual Dependency* (1982–2022), she declared her commitment to an unabashedly autobiographical project, culling images from her life. Goldin would add more photographs to the series, and, with fame, new interiors, hotel rooms, landscapes, yet always many of the same faces, reliable, often troubled friends who are, in the worst of times, her lifelines.

Memory Lost (2019–2021) recalls the all-night parties of *The Ballad of Sexual Dependency*; Goldin's addiction; rehabs; friends' anguish and deaths. It moves from pristine shot to blurred image, every frame a memory. Goldin may not remember as much as she once did, but the photographs do.

Memory Lost's visual pleasures abound, though sadness permeates the film. Its superb soundtrack tenderly heightens every passage of time and place.

Sporadically, there are recorded voices, old phone messages. A dealer says, "I am here. I've got all you wanted." A friend says, "I hope I get better." Goldin asks, in a tortured voice, "Why am I in a hospital?" A friend tells her she was found unconscious on a sidewalk.

The film ends at the beginning, when everyone is young and healthy, Goldin's paradise lost. Maybe they all wanted to be evil, but they weren't. They were just fucked up. That ongoing Judeo-Christian fiction, good and evil, shows no compassion for our flawed species. If "evil" existed, Goldin recognized, in the 2000s it was legal, prescription drugs, and she organized Prescription Addiction Intervention Now (P.A.I.N.) to denounce the profiteering dealers of those deadly opioids.

Nan Goldin survived her addictions and cherishes the memory of her friends who didn't. *Memory Lost* is her testament: The grand drama of life is surviving it.

It's So American

Nate Lowman pictures how Americans live now—what fascinates them, what hurts them, and what they love, which might be the same as what hurts them. Like him, an American, I grew up watching Westerns on TV and in movie theaters, where fierce-looking "red Indians" were demonized. I saw war films in which only the other side, the enemy, killed prisoners of war. I thought I knew who the bad guys were.

As Franz Kafka wrote, "My education has done me great harm in some respects."[1]

In 1994, I was writer in residence at the University of Sussex in Brighton, England. The PhD students were usually poor and drank a pint of Guinness for their dinner. I took my workshop to see *Pulp Fiction*, a kind of treat, I thought.

I laughed at the assassins' ironic Big Mac conversation and was amused by the famous John Travolta/Uma Thurman dance scene. But the students told me they were disturbed by the casual violence to which I had been indifferent. On the old Brighton boardwalk, I heard them, and remembered thinking, whimsically, I am so American. Even now, I know I have been desensitized to violence.

Yes, many white Europeans sought freedom from religious persecution, but in the so-called New World they stole land and freedom from Native Americans and used enslaved African labor. Historical aberrations live in a nation's DNA, its psyche, society, politics, and culture. Diverse and contradictory histories are written about any period in the past; there's never one story about events and people. Historiographies detail the ways that historians have performed their jobs—accurately, or with small or great distortions, with purposeful, fact-based revisions, with prejudice or lies, to recover truths, to damn or exculpate actors and actions. American history is under severe and serious examination, of its untruths about its beginnings, the myths, and ignored realities.

Looking at Nate Lowman's oeuvre, I see his response to this indifference. I perceive an "American family" art album. It's all here: national headlines, trivia, kitsch, military weapons, guns, mass murders, and domestic and foreign terrorism. Events can be sources, backgrounds, and subtexts in his work. The love of guns, Americans' desire to possess and use them, figures in his paintings of bedrooms, where all kinds of weapons lie on beds waiting to be taken up and used.

> My great-grandmother was a crazy quilter, and I have most of the quilts that got left behind. I'm sure that's where I got the idea to use all these errant scraps.
> —Nate Lowman

The errant scraps come from drop cloths Lowman saved over the years, after having used them to protect the floors as he painted. He cuts them up and collages pieces into multicolored paintings of maps of the United States. From a distance, the maps are beautiful—they might be water lilies or funny Hans Hofmanns.

Moving in closer and seeing the accidental and random drips and blobs, I think about the paintings' homely origin: Each map is made from a crazy quilt, and now it represents these disunited states. Each state is distinct, and, like abstract art, there are swaths of color without figures. Abstraction beckons interpretation and projection, and I will see what I think about America now. The surface may be beautiful, but it's not a pretty picture.

In Lowman's painting *Drone* (2021), a military drone is in midair, in the center of the canvas, a massive whitish-gray machine against a background of blue-gray hills or mountains. The ground is sand-colored, and may be sand. The drone is flying low.

Pilotless, drones fly missions to "eliminate" enemies without endangering Americans. They are meant to hit their targets "without collateral damage"—without civilians being hurt or killed. These unassuming, stealthy warplanes commit tragic errors; unintended deaths do happen. But these are "clean kills," metaphorically bloodless, not as dangerous as combat.

Here, the drone (Lowman has painted four, one of which is on paper) is undramatic, calm as drones are lethal. In a way, the work could be called "Portrait of a Drone." This way you have to face it.

One of America's horrific national tragedies especially captured Lowman's attention and led to a series based on an actual event:

> On October 1, 2017, Stephen Paddock, a 64-year-old man from Mesquite, Nevada, opened fire on the crowd attending the Route 91 Harvest music festival on the Las Vegas Strip in Nevada. From his 32nd-floor suites in the Mandalay Bay hotel, he fired more than 1,000 bullets, killing 60 people and wounding at least 413. . . . About an hour later, he was found dead in his room from a self-inflicted gunshot wound. . . . The incident is the deadliest

> mass shooting committed by an individual in United States history.[2]

The "deadliest mass shooting committed by an individual in United States history" hit home, figuratively and literally. Lowman was born in Las Vegas, a city whose image is indelibly linked with gambling and taking chances; its motto, "What happens in Vegas stays in Vegas," boasts of a Wild West for its hotel guests. But Vegas's wildness has been greatly overshadowed and overwhelmed by an irrational act much more "scandalous" and "shameful" than what happens in Vegas.

> This was the first mass murder I dealt with directly [in my work]. Six months after it, the Las Vegas Police Department released nearly thirty images from the crime scene. The images were provocative, because the event was; but [their] forensics' A-team wasn't documenting the shooting. I used oil paint to match the colors in the photos as accurately as possible, then painted a layer of black dots on top of the colors, like a black-and-white photocopy layered on top of a color picture, all done by hand, and blurring the lines. The rooms appear ordinary, not a place where such violence could have originated, where a homicidal man chose to destroy as many lives as he could. The clumsiness and badly lit dramatics of many of the photos seemed to tell an analogous story about the ways we will and will not understand this event for years to come.
> —Nate Lowman

The mass murder may have affected Lowman viscerally and psychologically—the killings happened in his hometown, also attacking his childhood and early memories. Whatever his initial motivations, Lowman responded with art.

The Vegas series is somber, bizarrely quiet, the antithesis of the noise, in all senses, of its subject matter. The deliberateness rests in the subdued and rather bland rooms, and his blurring the lines, I think instantly, between sanity and insanity.

Lowman's approach emphasizes the incident's ordinariness, there have been many massacres here. The grays, he told me, represent fogginess. The grays, and even the blurs, in a descriptive stretch, did bring to mind the fog of this ongoing domestic war, in which Americans kill each other every day.

What interrupts the calm and quiet are the "scribbles," which is how Lowman refers to the hand-painted, random-seeming streaks on the paintings' surfaces. They create a pictorial tension or dynamic, like a sudden turbulence in the room. Mark-making is a kind of writing, and in this horror chamber, it is writing on the wall, portending more chaos. And insinuating uncertainty.

Uncertainty is a facet in some of Lowman's work. That is, uncertainty in the way that Ludwig Wittgenstein argued about it in the use of the verb "to know." What does it mean to say, "I know." Where is doubt? And what do you know when you look at these pictures, the rooms from which a mass murderer shot off a thousand rounds of ammo. What does anyone know about these bullet holes. What meaning is to be ascribed to these objects other than, I propose, that they represent slices of American life, portraits of the contemporary moment and its attributes and accessories.

Mass shootings are, supposedly, unnatural. People don't "naturally" turn into mass killers, or they do. Early humans were predators; predation exists, usually in other forms than mass killings—rape, kidnappings, domestic violence, and other forms of abuse and brutality. The scale and enormity of violence here seems "inhuman," even if human behavior includes every kind of good and grotesque act.

Lowman's paintings mark various meanings of a natural order. There is human-made aggression, such as mass killings, which might now be second nature. While the hurricanes, storms, fires, and floods he depicts, usually considered natural events—that is, beyond human control—have become more uncontrollable and devastating because of people's mismanagement and corruption of the earth's resources.

> I dread hurricane season.
> —Nate Lowman

Recently, Lowman painted the eyes of various hurricanes. Their fury and rage have beaten down and extinguished cities and homes, bridges and seawalls, causing huge floods. The canvases are large and dramatic: Each eye stuns with ferocity. The storms are painted with especially garish colors that, Lowman explains, do not exist in reality (they are from meteorologists' graphics). The paintings are unique, each based on a specific hurricane's shape, and are named for that hurricane: Andrew (1992), Katrina (2005), Irene (2011), Sandy (2012), Harvey (2017), Irma (2017), Maria (2017), Florence (2018), Ida (2021).

Unlikely and "unnatural" colors match these hurricanes' increasingly unnatural state, that is, the storms have become more destructive and more numerous than ever before recorded. Human interference has caused the worsening climate. The concepts of nature and natural, since people are part of nature, will need new descriptions.

In response to Hurricane Ida, which had flooded his studio, Lowman executed *Yonkers Sept. 1, 2021* (2022).[3] *Yonkers* foregrounds two cars floating in water, submerged by Ida's massive flood. The stormwater, which is the painting's ground, is murky, mauve, a purply gray, a fusion of colors. The effect reminded me of how, when mixing paint, the resulting color becomes so diffuse it is hard to define.

A flood drags and carries everything in its wake, the water filthy with bacteria, poisons, muck, unhealthy even to the touch. The flood transforms water into a dangerous killer, a "natural" terminator.

I am drawn to this particular painting, it is beautiful and deadly. It feels intimate, and for readers to understand my attraction better, here is a closer description of it:

In the bottom left foreground, a car is submerged, immobilized. A second car is also; it is also toward the left of the work, but veers toward the center of the canvas, and is nearer to the top of the painting. Both cars are silver or silvery white—they are different models, lined up, as if drowned together at the same time. Their headlights reflect on the murky water, and bursts of red light, like small fires, appear in front of both cars.

In this context—against the murky purplish-gray background—the hand-painted slashes seem like unformed words, they might be about struggling. It's a stretch, I know, to suggest this interpretation, but I can imagine it here, some sort of intimacy. Now Lowman's mark-making is about human gestures, and so represents human loss. Where are the drivers and the passengers?

It is a particularly tender work, heartbreaking and curiously romantic. Maybe because of the cars. Because Americans love their cars, or because driving can make people feel free. They can escape, or just get away, ZOOM. But not here.

Cars let people move from place to place, that's a freedom, or just as likely a necessity, a lost job, a need to find work elsewhere. For people without a place to live, cars can become their home. While abandoned or junked cars look sad, they were once attached to people. Cars are attachments. People love their cars, are identified, even judged by them. People identify with them. Cars 'r' us.

In *Yonkers* cars are metonymic, they are lost or dead people. They can't move. They have lost the freedom they promise, and to Americans, freedom is about being able to move, just as flight to the futurists meant freedom and progress into the future.

> At age 18, an American can expect to move another 9.1 times in their remaining lifetime, but by age 45, the expected number of moves is only 2.7.[4]

In comparison:

> Recent research indicates that, on average, Britons move once every 23 years.[5]

Movement also is in the American DNA. Early settlers pushed west, leaving one place for a better one, they hoped. But they stole land and decimated Native American tribes. In Frederick Turner's frontier thesis, which has been thoroughly discredited, he proposed that, when Americans traveled west to the Pacific, the arduous crossing separated them from Europe and transformed them into a new people and nation. They would have left their past behind.

That myth of the making of Americans valorized movement as progress; it was an American virtue and was used to excuse genocide. Still, the idea was sutured into the American imagination, where the invention of cars encouraged that idea of movement being an American's essential liberty. It's why advertisements for SUVs show huge cars gliding up mountains and traveling on rough roads—this is the American way of life—while actually SUVs mostly clog highways and city streets.

Lowman's work represents a troubled, contentious, and contradictory America. It wonders how come guns and AR-15s have been assimilated here, how come military-grade weapons wind up on beds, how come so many schoolchildren are dying in school shootings—how did this happen. His art is not didactic and doesn't tell anyone what to think. He sometimes renders offbeat, funny objects, like painted air fresheners, and regularly depicts disturbing scenes and difficult events. Then the work stands on its own, confounding a viewer who wants to know what it all means.

To many of us Americans, this country is perplexing and vexing, and its future seems very uncertain. America becomes more disturbing with every bullet shot. An inescapable and essential aspect of Nate Lowman's work is an engagement with this America. He challenges himself to render unwanted realities as he challenges viewers to see them with their eyes wide open.

Notes

All quotes from Nate Lowman are from a conversation with the author.

1 Franz Kafka, *The Diaries of Franz Kafka, 1910–1923*, ed. Max Brod (New York: Schocken Books, 1976), p. 15.

2 "2017 Las Vegas Shooting," Wikipedia, accessed online.

3 The painting exists in two sizes. The smaller version is *Yonkers Sept. 1, 2021 (Second Version)*.

4 "Calculating Migration Expectancy Using ACS Data," United States Census Bureau (last revised December 3, 2021), accessed online.

5 "How Often Do Brits Move in Their Lifetime?" Open Access Government (March 13, 2019), accessed online.

Screen Presence

New York City, 1977: A private screening of *Jeanne Dielman, 23, quai du Commerce, 1080 Bruxelles* (1975) drew filmmakers, critics, feminist film theorists, and writers. *Jeanne Dielman* began. Three and a half hours later, it ended, but something else had begun: the emphatic influence of a young, brilliant director: Chantal Akerman.

Akerman's suicide, on October 5, 2015, felt personal to many; her movies like friends who never disappointed. In the auteur tradition, Akerman's unique cinematic sensibility impressed itself on each of her films.

I looked in my files for an essay I'd started in 1981 and never finished. I wanted to return to my first responses to *Jeanne Dielman*. Nothing had prepared me, or I believe anyone, for it, and its lasting influence.

Jeanne Dielman takes place over three days. Akerman's meticulous direction, her use of real time, attention to detail, and emphasis on repeated gestures, built her protagonist's character. Delphine Seyrig played Jeanne, her beautiful, placid face an enigmatic screen within a screen.

Jeanne is a middle-class woman, mother, housewife, widow, prostitute. Each day, she follows a routine: cleaning up, washing dishes, turning on and off lights; she has one client a day. Akerman makes the viewer notice every gesture. By the second day, her fastidious routine is off, she and it have shifted, and by the third, everything has changed, dramatically.

The film was eerily quiet, not silent. Where were the words? Scant dialogue occurred, and it was between Jeanne and her adolescent son. Their conversations, striking as Akerman's direction, commented upon and augmented the visual narrative. At dinner the first night, the son asks Jeanne: "How did you meet my father? Why did you marry him?" She implies that she didn't love his father, but it was the thing to do. The son says, "If I were a woman, I couldn't make love with someone I didn't love." Jeanne answers, "But you are not a woman."

On the second day, when Jeanne shows her day's client to the door, her hair is mussed. Maybe she's had an unwanted orgasm. That night, she puts her teenaged son to bed. He asks her about real women and orgasms. The son appears to have noticed, like the viewer, her unusual appearance. (In my 1981 notes, he mentions her mussed hair, her housecoat's top button undone.) He tells her that, as a child, he worried his father hurt her when the two made love. She cuts him off, saying that making love is just a detail.

On the third day, in bed with a client—Akerman now lets the viewer into the bedroom—Jeanne grabs a pair of scissors off the dressing table and plunges it into him, killing him. A long, last shot of Jeanne sitting at her dining room table, staring at the camera, ends the film.

From 1968 on, Akerman approached narrative boldly. Her work engaged female subversion in film, writing, art. It participated in debates about film theory and feminism, from subjectivity, classic cinema, the gaze, to new readings of the canon, etc. *News from Home* (1977) pitched the sound of her voice, reading her mother's letters, over scenes, or the visual news, of New York. In *Les rendez-vous d'Anna* (1978), Akerman depicted an intimate mother-daughter relationship, one inseparable from the devastation of the Holocaust. The daughter, a filmmaker on tour, listens to survivors' testimonies wherever she travels.

No Home Movie (2015) was screened at the New York Film Festival, days after her death. *No Home Movie* is a punning title for Akerman's film of her mother's last year—no home anywhere, anymore, a movie about no home. It's a love story, narrated not only in images, private views, but also by conversations at the kitchen table and on Skype.

Her mother's kitchen reminded me of Jeanne Dielman's. I recognized it, with somber surprise. A special effect of Akerman's work is the production of shocks of recognition. Another scene startled me: Her mother is very close to death. In long shot, Akerman shows her lying on a lounger, her face obscured by distance, an inert shape that could have been any sick, dying mother's body. That could be my mother, I thought. Akerman's cinematic genius allowed for an emotional identification and, also, simultaneously, represented death's ubiquitous process, dying's indifference to person.

Akerman appears in *No Home Movie*, but mostly keeps herself out of the frame, sometimes running away, avoiding the camera. I could speculate: She opened a space for a viewer to impose herself. But, more, Akerman's determination not to be present on-screen signaled her wish to be absent from it forever.

Once, I believed writers must be innately curious. But some are interested only in their stories, which might be culled from anyone. Anyone is material.

People do go on—"total strangers" we call them, the odd partner at a dinner party—but through them I've learned about the manufacture of paper clips, the discovery of the glue for Post-its, and fears I never had; losing my fingers in a garbage disposal unit, for instance.

Incuriosity is curious. Humans are highly selective about what they want to find out, as if knowing what they need to know. So, a total stranger probably can't tell them anything. Lack of curiosity protects people from strangeness. To protect themselves also, humans build comfy nests, settle into routines, and, if they have them, cocoon with mates. To be safe, couples—married, unmarried, queer, straight—walk in symbiotic lockstep.

Sure, some surprises are awful. The news of death is a grave shock. But, unconsciously, people inure themselves to it by creating situations—war, for example—that depend on it. War, Sigmund Freud explained, placates the death drive.

"Only in novels does one change condition or become better," wrote Albert Camus. When morose and pessimistic about life, I believe Camus was right (though would add "uninteresting novels"). "Legal" brutality rampages here; in small and large US cities, police are killing young Black men while, of racism and police criminality, many whites speak in platitudes, empty phrases. Platitudes stifle even dim possibilities for change, since change requires, first, self-reflection. Platitudes in novels, shows, and movies offer readers and viewers small satisfactions and no surprises. But work that incites doubt, or that is ambiguous, provokes uncertainty and psychic disturbance.

With smart uncertainties, all manner of art stays with me. Joseph Roth's last novel, *The Emperor's Tomb* (1938), follows the only surviving member of the Trotta family from his earlier novel, *The Radetzky March* (1932), who arrives home in Vienna after fighting in the Great War, during the fall of the Austro-Hungarian Empire. Home is an enigma, a city surviving bitter defeat in an incoherent present. Roth relates the disintegration of the nation as a process of loss of identity and power through its distraught fictional characters, who are, as the author himself put it, "homesick for the Kaiser."

Two recent works linger in my mind: Amie Siegel's *Provenance* (2013) and Bennett Miller's movie *Foxcatcher* (2014). *Provenance* is an installation comprising two films and one framed wall piece, recently exhibited at The Metropolitan Museum of Art, New York. Using pans, tracking shots, and ambient sound, Siegel filmed "the flow" of commodities between India and the West. She looked at Le Corbusier's Chandigarh, the model city he was commissioned to design by the Indian government in the 1950s, and its furniture, specially designed by Pierre Jeanneret. In the West, the furniture—especially the chairs, which, in the film, signify the human body—is extremely valuable. The viewer's realization of how the furniture "sits" or functions in Chandigarh is part of the work, the experience one of the film's uncertainties. Siegel put this film up for auction at Christie's, in London, and recorded the raw exchange—the other film in the installation.

Value and values are lived by people, who every day engage with and relate to objects. Siegel's work is an ethnography of specific objects, for one, by registering their contextual differences. Also, no voice-over tells viewers how to comprehend the flow. Instead, the installation represents the wiliness of value and culture, the ambiguity inside which we make work and exist.

Silence hangs heavy in *Foxcatcher*. Scant dialogue and long pauses build its hushed track, the sound of repression. This movie, a strange ménage à trois, is based on the life of John E. du Pont, progeny of one of America's wealthiest families, and his relationship to two brothers, wrestlers. Du Pont wanted the US to win a gold medal in wrestling at the 1988 Seoul Olympics and "bought" his wrestling team, bringing them to his great house, Foxcatcher, to train.

This brotherhood does not result in Hollywood bromance. Class and masculinity are at play, with hierarchies resting on wealth and physical strength, power in both senses. The wrestling poses make a choreography, men dancing dominance and submission. Sexuality feels like a stealthy panther about to pounce, insinuating itself, while physicality and violence are simultaneously acted out and suppressed, as sport. Libidinal desire takes a turn for the worst.

Miller directed *Foxcatcher* with immense curiosity about the story and the men, the camera closely studying the obliquity of their motivations. I was watching, waiting, held in suspense, even though I knew the ending. That seems paradoxical, but memorable art often is.

Parts of Some Sextets in Parts or as Yvonne Calls It: Mattress Monster

Preface to the Dance

One afternoon at the Rhinecliff train station in upstate New York, Yvonne Rainer and I were talking about abstraction. Both of us were teaching in Bard College's MFA arts program, where, every night, there were critiques of student work from three of the disciplines. The paintings were usually abstract. Every night, we faculty were required to speak in front of a group of one hundred people, students and faculty.

> Yvonne: I don't get abstract art.
> Lynne: But dance is abstract. Your dances are abstract.
> Yvonne (adamant): No, it's the body. It's always about the body.

Not the first time Yvonne Rainer has shifted my thinking 180 degrees.

On *Parts of Some Sextets* in Parts

The stage is bare except for a stack of eleven mattresses (stage right), and a single mattress (stage left). For nearly seventeen minutes, the audience sees the mattresses while hearing a recording of Rainer reading from the diary of Reverend William Bentley, an Episcopal minister born in the latter half of the eighteenth century. Then three dancers appear onstage, but disappear behind the high stack of mattresses. Soon they will be onstage again, joined by the rest of the company who have been hidden behind the stacks. Suddenly, dramatically, the entire company runs onto the stage. Dance erupts everywhere. Foreground and background churn with activity. The dancers in the foreground execute intricate steps in various groupings, while in the background, other dancers are lifting, carrying, and dropping stacks of mattresses in different configurations.

Staring at the mattresses, I wondered about Rainer's use of them, and their origins.

> We learn that the Elephant exhibited as a Curiosity in this town lately, was shot in open day by a villain at Alfred, Maine. . . . We believe our manners very correct generally, but we have Savages still.
> —William Bentley, July 29, 1816

The first use of "civilization" in English is attributed to Adam Ferguson, who in his 1767 "Essay on the History of Civil Society" wrote: "Not only the individual advances from infancy to manhood but the species itself from rudeness to civilization." A society is rude, or it is civilized. "Rude" is so very English. Rude is rough; rude, here, means primitive. That a civilization must have good manners serves Enlightenment ideals of order and reason.

Pondering what's embedded (forgive the pun) in the concept of "civilization," I wondered if the development of bedding and mattresses coincided with it. I mean, in various societies over millennia, a better mattress probably indicated a more flourishing culture or greater individual or social wealth. More need for comfort impels invention, too, when there is more leisure to enjoy it. Comfort usually comes to those who can afford it, though kings and queens sat on very uncomfortable thrones.

In "The Princess and the Pea," a princess's "authority" was judged by her lying upon many mattresses, troubled by one pea under the pile. The upper classes and aristocracy were meant to be "sensitive." The history of royalty, for one, is anything but. Our civilization, which Ferguson signified, has learned something about its past: It used slave labor to create it; plundered in war and raped in war and peace; invented cruel and expedient forms of torture; was ruled by impetuous kings, queens, with divine right, and dictators; condoned horrific behavior by the mighty; and much more.

> [James Joyce] said to me that history was like that parlor game where someone whispers something to the person next to him, who repeats it not very distinctly to the next person, and so on until, by the time the last person hears it, it comes out completely transformed.
> —Sylvia Beach, *Shakespeare and Company*

Diaries are like Joyce's theory of history, subjectively experienced (seen and heard) micro-histories. A writer—a Virginia Woolf or a William Bentley—notes the day's happenings, who said what, did what, and describes their feelings about incidents and events, like a war beginning or a gruesome death.

> [A blacksmith] declined at last into intemperance, dishonesty, & derangement & died of a cancer which took away all his face, & made him as ghastly to behold as he was terrible to hear.
> —William Bentley, December 23, 1800

Yvonne Rainer's choreography is mostly based on what healthy, well-trained—and some untrained—people can do: walk and run, swing their arms, turn, climb, lift, and drop. (The untrained won't have a dancer's muscle memory, and will undoubtedly work harder to memorize sequences.) Her world-famous *Trio A* (1966), composed of a string of disparate movements, distilled this concept into a four-and-a-half-minute piece. It's not easy to learn—"ordinary" movements are made extraordinary by the dance's composition—but around the world people learn it and teach it to others.

I would compare a diary with choreography that works with everyday movements. For *Parts of Some Sextets, 1965/2019*, Rainer gathered eleven performers and twelve mattresses, and extracted sections from Bentley's late eighteenth-century diary. There are thirty-one variations, each lasting thirty seconds. All of the dancers lift and carry mattresses, crawl on top of them, lie in between and on top of them, leap on and off them, and more. The changes coincide with specific words from Bentley's diary to coordinate the movements of the dancers, but do not illustrate Bentley's thoughts.

Parts of Some Sextets is a revival with differences. For one, Rainer collaborated with the dancer and dance historian Emily Coates to re-create it.

As in the original 1965 version, the cast includes a mix of visual artists and trained dancers. In one case, a dancer, David Thomson, performs tasks formerly assigned to Robert Rauschenberg. For the most part, everyone engages with mattress manipulations, while the "dancers"

> execute movement combinations commensurate with
> their training.
> —Yvonne Rainer

The past is present not only in Bentley's sentiments, but also in the recordings of Rainer's voice from the piece's first presentation and for this new iteration. The changes in her voice mark time's passing.

The collision of different voices from the past, Bentley's and Rainer's, along with hers now, occurs in the present: I watch dancers in the foreground, singly and in groups of varying sizes. The dancers move constantly, change groups, run or walk from one place to another. Maybe they are communing with each other, doing errands, speaking about the day's events, having sex.

In the background, the mattresses are in constant movement also, carried by the dancers who stack them, one on top of the other in the same direction, then tear them down, build them up again. They weigh enough that two people usually carry one, though sometimes one strong person does. (Suddenly I hear a wolf howling. And it chills me. A wolf is at the door, I think.)

The mattress must be essential to our species' well-being, and probably something akin to it is a universal artifact. Since early on, human beings fashioned some kind of bedding to sleep and rest on. And like most everything in culture, except what is deemed a treasure, mattresses are used and discarded; they change in design and materials in relation to their place of birth, technology, and manufacture.

I imagine the dancers as inhabitants of an imaginary town, and the mattresses as building blocks of this community in formation. The dancers and mattresses transform into metaphors for "civilizations," people engaged in doing many things, while nations, societies, and cultures rise and fall, razed, buried, defeated in war or by natural forces until something arises and covers the debris from the past. Repeat is on repeat. Histories record failures and successes, but much is left out. Diaries address what is usually elided—daily life.

The dance goes on, Yvonne's voice, younger and older, reads from one man's diary, seemingly narrating the dance. But she's not. Bentley's story recalls the minutiae of his daily life, and what he found important to write down. His diary exists among immeasurable numbers of human stories, millennia of stories, written and unwritten, people walking, thinking, farming, running, sad, happy, writing, hunting, opening stores, starting businesses, studying, reflecting, building, dying, their perceptions and beliefs produced in a time and in a place.

Words say; dancers do, and Rainer uses both. Spectators draw, or don't, relationships and meanings from the linkages. No one's interpretations can be absolute; and meanings can be many, even indeterminate, which is one of art's licenses—to embrace complexity and ambiguity. Rainer's intent is not Delphic, even if she sometimes appears to be an oracle.

In her choreography, typically Rainer connects the dancers to each other, as people are in society, on their own, in couples, in groups, and she also attaches them to objects, such as chairs and pillows. People have many attachments and arrangements in a lifetime.

Viewers imagine ways of understanding what is happening in front of them.

First, I think, there is a long silence—let's say, before the Big

Bang—then life erupts and activities happen at the same time in the same space, different levels, planes. There is a simultaneity of movement and jarring juxtapositions, and there is a dissonance between watching and listening.

With time, not only do voices change, but language also. Reading passages from Bentley's diary, I was struck by its language and attitudes. He describes people and events the way "civilized" people thought then:

> Upon our return, I had the great pleasure of seeing Calvin, a dwarf child from Bridgewater, which has lately been exhibited at Boston. . . . They have taught it only the childish amusements of ball, play at marbles, & with a whip. . . . The reason offered for so little attention to its mind, are its impatience, & obstinacy, & the design of exhibiting him continually to the public.
> —William Bentley, July 26, 1797

Kafka wrote about such exhibitions in his short story "A Hunger Artist" (1922). A man starves himself in a cage as an amusement for the public, much like the fat lady at a carnival. That wouldn't happen now, you might think, except early in the twentieth century, Coney Island opened its gates with a display of a family of midgets who lived in a model house for all to see. And in this moment, what are the TV shows *My 600-lb. Life* and *The Biggest Loser* but spectacles of obesity and starvation?

The optimism about progress with which the twentieth century began was disabused by its second half. Antibiotics were discovered around the same time as the discovery of the death camps.

Civilizations foster great feats and despicable ones in a terrible simultaneity.

Parts of Some Sextets relies on coordination, timing, and also chance—no one can jump exactly the same height repeatedly, no mattress will fall precisely where it did before. Sometimes Rainer's choreography seems to happen on a Cagean roll of the dice, yet it is all planned and rehearsed vigilantly. The juxtaposition of differences on the stage, the dissonances, might produce new meanings or test the possibility of meaning. And, can something physical be primarily conceptual? Because, as Yvonne told me years ago, it's the body, it's always the body.

And there is the body of the text, and the eleven dancers who form a body, together and apart, in sync and not. Yvonne Rainer's work always entails an idea of democracy, which depends upon responsibility. The dancers do their parts. Their movements can't be predicted, but the dance is not anarchic. They have autonomy, and also need each other, help each other. They fall into one another's arms, carry mattresses, they work together. To what end, if there is one, I wonder.

What is achieved may be ridiculous or profound, but it's also the way people live, isn't it, with plans and uncertainty, not knowing if what they make will be worth it, and any choice they have, when they have choices, might be good or bad, right or wrong. The paradox is to expect the unexpected, and let the mattresses fall where they may.

Presence

Pat Steir's paintings resonate with visual spectacle, with broad sophistication, with an artist's philosophical resoluteness about art's significance and place. They present an existential experience. Being with them, relating to Steir's timely and time-free art, which, on its own terms, offers new ways of seeing and thinking, one discovers novel spaces for contemplation and challenge.

Steir's steady vision and knowledge of philosophy, art, literature, and art history supersede and inform her art practice; they undergird it. Her appreciation of poetics and aesthetics thrums in her work. The idea of mind and mindfulness inhabits her undivided attention to her medium, and figures into her oeuvre. In a sense, Steir's most demanding content might be attention and consciousness.

Of her contemporaries, the poets Steir especially admires are Anne Waldman and Mei-mei Berssenbrugge. Their approaches, syntax, subjects, are very different, but like Steir the poets have been influenced by Buddhism, other Eastern philosophies, Asian and other art, all articulated and embedded in their poems.

These stanzas, these lines from their poems—sharp, sensuous, self-aware—remind me of Steir's numinous paintings:

From "Hello, the Roses" by Mei-mei Berssenbrugge

When you see her, you feel the impact of what visual
  can mean.
Invisibility comes through of deep pink or a color I see
  clairvoyantly.
This felt sense at seeing the rose extends, because light in
  the DNA of my cells
receives light frequencies of the flower as a hologram.

From "Cabin" by Anne Waldman

I want to sit high want simple phalanx
  of power independent of everything but free will
    & one long hymn in praise of the cabin!

it is a confession in me impenetrably walled in
   like aesthetics like cosmos an organ of
     metaphysics and O this book gives me a headache

It seems to me when you put down a line, there is a line. How could that line be abstract? Whatever else it represents it is always still a line.
—Pat Steir, quoted in Anne Waldman, "Pat Steir"

Many of Steir's recent paintings have a line down the middle; it's not straight-edged or uniform, but a streak of colors that bifurcates the painted plane. Looking at her paintings is similar, then, to reading a word-free book, two pages open on a wall, a form of writing—mark-making—that eludes specific meanings, signifiers without the signified. That freedom encourages interpretation, movements away from fixed points of view.

Similarly, the line down the center is not about building binaries, but about suggesting ways of reflecting on shades of difference. What strikes me particularly about Steir's line is that it is unruled, its edges irregular. Irregularity seems to me at the core of her art: There's nothing regular to be found in it. A line might be rubbed, sanded, more paint applied, but it will be uneven, like life.

> The painting tells me what to do.
> —Pat Steir

I once watched Steir work. She stood at the top of a very tall ladder, and poured paint down a section of a massive canvas. That pouring is often contrasted to Pollock's drip, an art-historical gesture, pregnant with difference. There's a sense of flow, and some of her work is compared with water, and, yes, the paint falls or travels down the canvas. Like water, it performs itself, finding its own course, not controlled, principally, by the artist but by gravity and its own composition, viscosity, and the texture of the canvas. The canvas has been prepared to receive it, but it makes its own way. And will become part of the whole, the larger, developing composition.

To rely on chance or to trust chance operations seems oxymoronic. And it is. Flow is chancy, creating effects a writer can't achieve. I can write "sky" or "river," I can write "flow," but none of the words *is* that. The words don't substitute or fulfill a painted flow, which is an actuality and also already a metaphor. Steir's pouring technique produces irregular viscosities, shows texture, and tactility, all indifferent to language, really, in the territory of the sublime.

> What first attracted me to Pat Steir's work was that very few painters use the properties of paint. She uses the fluidity of it. She makes an action that is the first stage in a process, and then the paint takes over. Then she responds to that. So it's always a collaboration between the natural elements and her.
> —Kiki Smith

The painting tells Steir what to do. That's akin to reading the unwritten, seeing some kind of secret visual commentary no one else does—not yet, anyway. Maybe only when the painting is finished. Maybe it can never be explicated.

Physicality gives Steir's paintings an objecthood, which shows process, but also, and always, a finished work, the artist's mind in its chosen surface, colors, marks. Steir pays attention to and affects all of these, allowing chance to surprise her and it. Her work embodies taking chances but also forging an awareness, in the viewer, of actions taken, and of her being an agent of change.

> There is no such thing as silence. Something is always happening that makes a sound. No one can have an idea once he starts really listening.
> —John Cage, *SILENCE*

Chance is unruled, unruly, as in a John Cage composition. Cage notably paid attention to sound, and wanted listeners to hear music in the ordinary, the sounds of dailiness: an environment, the rattle of boiling water in a teakettle, the noise of traffic, which of all things in life is most patternless. When scientists look for randomness, they can find it only in traffic. Because of accidents, because of human beings, it is unpredictable.

John Cage and Pat Steir see possibility, or beauty, in accidents. Part of Steir's operations gain from unpredictability, which comes, for one, from the flow of paint, inconsistent like the flow of traffic.

I keep musing about and pondering Steir's predilection for randomness, for risk-taking. She has told me that, in the studio, when a painting is giving her trouble, she will keep at it, not allowing herself to be stopped by obstacles. Her persistence in making art is total. I read into it a commitment to "being," which obtains in all of her paintings.

> Everything is happening all at once.
> —Pat Steir

Looking at random-seeming and deliberate marks, small areas of color, in every painting there's a sense of life's not always being available to reason, and a rejection of Western values privileging science over spirit. I see in the process a refusal to favor conscious decisions over unconscious motives; though Steir's paintings require consciousness, a mind to "see" them. Her project suggests that believing oneself always in control ignores the reality of the world, and that to accept one's inability to determine every outcome might offer solace.

In the way Steir makes a painting, she accepts what she can't entirely determine. Curiously, she pursues what might obstruct her will, because of another reality, limits. She handles limits when they arise, and, when they obscure solutions and novelty, she works within those limits and against them, and fixes things.

Any meaningful practice pushes an artist's limits—writing does mine. So, working through, formally, psychologically, conceptually, practically, is necessary to realize an idea, to complete a work.

> I used to feel that the more out painting was, the more I was attached to it, to being anonymous, slipping through,

> being my own thing. Now I feel that everyone should have a little beauty in their life.
> —Pat Steir

Looking at Steir's work, viewers move within the parameters and inside the ambiguities of nonreferentiality. They must make a visual rambling with their projections in tow. In other words, to use their imaginations.

In front of *Red and Red* (2014), I never know where my attention will land or for how long. There is no vanishing point, and, even if there is a line down the center, that is a marker of difference, not a place to stay. I might try to apprehend the entirety of the painting but can't, not wholly, because my eye is roving. And, each area has its own world. Is it possible to comprehend the whole? I don't know.

Her art is also about the serenity in not always knowing, and in the pleasure of just looking.

Up close to *Red and Red*, I notice the subtle changes in the eponymous color, two variants, and, within each variation, many variables: surfaces, paint thickness, undercoatings and layers emerging, the blending of these.

I move back, farther back, the markings merge on the surface, the reds pulsate, the line dissolves. The colors make their own distinctions, and where do my associations go? I think about pairings, resemblances, and, of course, differences. How one image or a word next to another creates new meanings. I recall Derek Jarman's meditative film *Blue*, only a blue screen, and Antonioni's *Red Desert*, that red concrete wall. Color supplies moods, areas for reflection. I conjure paintings by Josef Albers and Mark Rothko, their work on the walls next to *Red and Red*. I think about what happens when the hand is applied and apparent, or not applied or entirely erased. Or, when the hand is steady, as in Agnes Martin's drawings, or looser as in Kiki Smith's. I consider different uses of color, shape, juxtaposition, and approach, returning me to Berssenbrugge's and Waldman's poetics, their different line lengths, language, imagery.

Writing about Steir's paintings is curious, because her work confounds words. Words are literal—denotative; but they also connote, suggestively, associatively. They slide and slip into their synonyms, with minute shifts that move meaning a millimeter to the right or left.

> If you love something, it's beautiful.
> —Pat Steir

Steir's approach to painting encourages insight and second sight, not literalism; it encourages various kinds of recognition. As she told me, "I feel that everyone should have a little beauty in their life." Her art evidences that feeling. And proposes that one go deeper, inward, where a different kind of beauty might exist and where the unconscious resides.

Interiority is not a physical reality, neither is the unconscious. The mind isn't physical, though the brain is. How does the brain set about allowing human beings to believe they have a mind? What enables them to imagine at all?

Paradoxes—the brain can make a mind—thrive in her paintings' rich, colorful fields of inquiry. At once, any of her paintings is an object, physical, there it is; but also hers is a nonobjective art, which draws from being alive, but is not representational. More, it is not just what is painted, because the paintings create phenomena that affect a viewer's senses—for instance, the sense of having an inner life. Human beings have conjured interiority for themselves, and it comes from a belief, I speculate, in their potential, in what might be in them that isn't apparent, not yet anyway, but that has the possibility of becoming.

These paintings, like all serious, important art, send diffuse messages, and many ways of receiving them. But, as Jacques Lacan wrote, a letter always reaches its destination. Steir's paintings will be completed by their viewers, sensationally—that is, through bodies and minds. Her paintings are events, activated by the pleasure of thinking and looking. By experience. In a sense, Pat Steir's paintings, with their great immediacy, are holding places of and for the present.

Note

Unless otherwise noted, all quotes from Pat Steir, and the quote from Kiki Smith, are from a conversation with the author.

Homage to Homage

Peter Gay's tome *Modernism* appeared in 2008, and, under "blacks," its index cited three entries, all brief. Twelve years later, in the light of this day, the idea that so few Black artists and writers are listed in a study of modernism seems implausible. Affected by prejudice, special interests, and ignorance, the accuracy of histories must be questioned. When a group dominates, other groups and individuals go unrecognized or are silenced, and achievements uncounted, denied their pages and place in the past.

In the last twenty years at least, Black artists and writers have been receiving greater attention, acknowledgment in various histories, and credit for their achievements. It is progress hard-gained, but whatever progress is, which is always a question, it is unfailingly uneven, and indifferent to equity and equality, and happens in a time and context. It has been won, let's say, after challenges to the prevailing order. But the effects of one time on another are unpredictable, so how progress will hold up is questionable, because the contemporary is always temporary.

Modernism was presented and promoted as European—white, Western, and primarily male. Its practitioners borrowed without compunction from various African, Japanese, Chinese, and other cultures. Early modernists appropriated freely, suggesting a droit du seigneur, a grandiosity inherited from their nations' imperialist and colonial dominations. Pablo Picasso: "Good artists copy, great artists steal."

Histories are barbed with ironies and contradictions. When, in the 1960s and after, minority artists—Black, Brown, women, queer—surfaced in greater numbers, the after-effects of political liberation movements, they landed in a theoretical paradox. In high modernism, the figure and narrative were done and dusted, but for some newly recognized artists and writers, the modes were still consequential. New narratives, new stories were felt necessary, new bodies and faces called for their representation. Differences made differences in art.

It's always said, histories are written by the victors, but reality, whoever names it, has millions of writers who go unread. Any reality comprises the external and internal worlds of individuals: Each subject perceives it through herself, from a world external to her—the one she didn't make. Any reality is experiential, subjective, not measurable, not necessarily logical or rational.

> The very serious function of racism . . . is distraction. It keeps you from doing your work. It keeps you explaining, over and over again, your reason for being. Somebody says you have no language and so you spend twenty years proving that you do. Somebody says your head isn't shaped properly so you have scientists working on the fact that it is. Somebody says that you have no art so you dredge that up. Somebody says that you have no kingdoms and so you dredge that up. None of that is necessary.[1]

Minorities are provoked and prodded to defend themselves against stereotypes and bias, as Toni Morrison says. From the mid-1970s on, the politics of representation, alongside identity politics, emerged to counter prevailing canons and pieties, by reading and making art and literature through other angles of vision. A powerful idea for some was to encourage and produce positive role models and imagery.

The production of positive images and roles hopes to "defend" minorities, by replacing ugly images with "good" ones that challenge prejudices, while emboldening the oppressed. In the 1970s, artists who were feminists divided around this notion, some making art in support of the idea, as Black artists did also. Some feminists and Black artists produced conceptual and appropriation work, and aligned their art with modernism, its aesthetic theories and practices, and later postmodernism.

According to Darby English in his book *1971: A Year in the Life of Color*, for Black artists to work with abstraction drew sharp criticism. English focuses on two major exhibitions of that year. Both featured abstract work by Black artists: One showed only Black artists, *Contemporary Black Artists in America* (Whitney Museum of American Art), the other, *The De Luxe Show*, in Houston (supported by the de Menils), exhibited abstract work by both Black artists and others. Abstraction, some felt, was antithetical to Black culture and Black art, even a renunciation of it or inimical to it, not supportive of Black people's lives. And, the exhibitions were highly controversial.

In supporting abstraction as a mode for Black artists, English argues, "In fact, modernism opens an interval of reflection that disrupts and expands our purview of 'black culture,' precisely by breaking it up, making it harder to survey in general terms."[2] English's positions are themselves controversial.

An "interval of reflection" is a spacious phrase that itself demands reflection. With it, English is suggesting that all cultures are matters in negotiation and need space to grow. That curiosity creates "intervals," perhaps. Living cultures morph and shift, embrace and reject perennially. And, like languages, unless cultures move and transform, they will die.

Theodor Adorno's essay "What Does Coming to Terms with the Past Mean?" argues against "positive images," though he never uses that term. He might well have. Bringing together German Jews and German Christians, after the Holocaust, to create friendship and positive feelings, he wrote, would not eradicate anti-Semitism. The problem, he assessed, was not in Jews, or who they are, because anti-Semitism was not based on Jews. That hatred was based in the anti-Semite.

To extrapolate from Adorno's thesis, any image positively extolling Black people, or women, or any minority, will be viewed by a racist without sympathy. Or, if that did occur, if it is felt, racists can always find an exception to their bias. T. S. Eliot, for instance, was anti-Semitic, but displayed a photograph of Groucho Marx in his home. Groucho, presumably, wasn't one of those "bad Jews."

With appropriation art, artists grab images from deep inside the proverbial glut but take a left turn on recontextualization. The move might empty images, say, of their "reality" or so-called truths. The stolen images will be discomforted, out of their usual contexts, to expose their saturation in the depths of society. These images propagate models for life that seem to be "natural," naturally occurring, not construed by people. And, only people can unmask their artificiality.

In the sociologist Erving Goffman's seminal work *Gender Advertisements*, he annotated pictorial advertisements using men and women to sell products. In the ads, the women were shot in positions inferior to the men. They were lower down in the image, they were looking up at the men. A man's hand might rest masterfully on an adoring woman's shoulder. These images depict female subservience, and, literally, represent women as a lower order of being.[3]

Isaiah Berlin designated two poles of freedom—"freedom to" and "freedom from." Let's suppose that abstraction and conceptualism represent a freedom to mark a worldview with its own and other realities. It also can mean freedom from the necessity to defend a subject position, gender, race, or sexuality.

The modernist Josef Albers found freedom in abstraction. I would fit "interval of reflection" inside that sense of freedom. When people reflect on a problem or on the natural world, say, they don't know, necessarily, where their thoughts will take them. Solving a problem in any field demands abandoning long-held beliefs, and trials by many errors, failures, and strange combinations of objects, materials, not employed before.

In John Milton's poem "Lycidas," he used the word "gray" as it had never been before in English literature. "While the still morn went out with sandals gray . . ." "Gray" modifies "sandals," linking the "still morn," an inert morning, to death and mourning. Milton felt free to make use of "gray" differently. Infamously, Sylvia Plath invoked the word "Holocaust" in relationship to her feelings about her father. It was scandalous in the early 1960s, but wouldn't be now, because she, for one, changed the language, which means that poem affected social meaning and thinking.

Language is abstract, the signifier and the signified are illogical partners. Or, a rose is a rose is a rose is a rose. A rose could have been so many other words, and is in other languages.

In Josef Albers's 1935 lecture "Abstract Art," he discussed how abstraction is an everyday matter, and in everything. A woman choosing a hat, he writes, "stud[ies] its form, seeking relationship to her face, eyes, mouth, dress—well, she is a judger of abstract art." He talks about the other arts—for one, musical composition—and asks: "Why should we painters not have the same right to combine, like the musician, our medium—form, colors, proportions, and so on?"

"Freedom from" does not imply irresponsibility, but another kind of responsibility. Delmore Schwartz imaginatively put it like this: "In dreams begin responsibilities." Though abstract artists work with unpredictability, "rules" inhere through the process, in the making. Their art is inductive, not deductive, and does not usually elucidate a specific idea, explanation, or reason. But their ideas, associations, psyches, and everything an artist knows and feels direct their art—and no one can definitively claim an absence of all autobiography, or politics, for that matter, in their art.

> It is obviously insufficient to repeat empty slogans: the author has disappeared; God and man died a common death. Rather, we should reexamine the empty space left by the author's disappearance.
> —Michel Foucault, "What Is an Author?"

> There is no one left to blame.
> —Steve Locke, 2014 exhibition at the Museum of Contemporary Art Detroit

For ten years, Steve Locke painted male faces and distinguished them with the same, odd expression. Each man is open-mouthed, his pinkish tongue hangs down, covering the bottom lip. The faces must contort to adjust to their hanging tongues. Hangdog, one might say. They could be dogs, not men. They are portraits of men whose masculinity is disturbed, loose tongues causing doubt. Or maybe they haven't zipped their metaphorical flies. Adrift in space or set against a grid, with loosened tongues exhausted from explaining.

A man is aghast, resigned, appalled, panting.

Men without bodies, can they defend themselves. Are they men, then? Locke's way of addressing masculinity relies on a discernible figure, a recognizable object, but as he has reckoned with it, separating a face/head from a body, he fuses it with an idea, making it a conceptual work. An incarnation of isolation.

Art historians might refer to the many disembodied heads in art history, such as Artemisia Gentileschi's *Judith Slaying (or Beheading) Holofernes* (c. 1620). Locke's faces are painted flat on a background, without dimensionality. These faces have been stripped from absent heads and can suggest mutilation, skin flayed from bodies.

Locke asks if these men have no one to blame but themselves. Maybe. In a conversation with him, Locke explained that all the faces are based on his. It's a puzzling assertion: An artist, a man, a gay or queer man, a Black man—all of these are faces are his. If they are, they are unlikely self-portraits, but then Locke must know himself in many guises, and I suppose he has himself to blame for that, if blame is to be assigned.

> The more "honestly" you put yourself into the story, the more that story will concern others as well.
> —Rainer Werner Fassbinder

Locke looks back to history, making work for, in, and of the present. He appreciates modernists and is a postmodernist, working all the angles available to him, lifting, combining, juxtaposing.

In 2018, Locke was commissioned to produce a public artwork to appear on a wall of the Isabella Stewart Gardner Museum in Boston. Not long before, Freddie Gray had been murdered by the police in Baltimore. Locke decided to pay tribute to him, a Black man killed by the cops.

His work, *Three Deliberate Grays for Freddie (A Memorial for Freddie Gray)* (2018–2019), consisted of three broad horizontal swaths of different tones of gray. It was like a flag. It was a modernist painting, half a grid, Mondrian-like. Or a sky, a heaven of gray. It was an abstract work, and his choice of abstraction was critical. No figures, no scenes, just colors.

Looking at the three-toned gray wall, I remembered Claude Lanzmann's film *Shoah*, his monumental and minimal documentary about the Holocaust. Lanzmann's momentous decision was not to show images of the terrible massacre of Jews especially, but also of homosexuals, Roma, Communists, people with severe infirmities. Lanzmann theorized that no image could represent it, and questioned what can be represented.

An unspeakable horror cannot be reduced to pictures or shown, he proposed. Showing corpses, mounds of teeth, starved people lying almost dead on bunk beds, one on top of each other was more degradation, more dehumanization. Acts of murder and torture cannot reside in pictures, but in the insidious mentality of the perpetrators of horror. A mentality cannot be pictured. The obscene can't be. It is why Oedipus tears out his eyes offstage, which is the meaning of obscenity, out of sight.

Instead, Lanzmann filmed railroad tracks that led to places of extermination. Instead, he talked to people who lived near those sadistic houses of murder who said they didn't know what was going on.

Images will form in minds, memories awakened when people speak, and seeing railroad tracks that will end at concentration camps. The film records silences, which also speak, and sounds from rooms, and breezes, the occurrence of the everyday that travels along with the horrors in any day.

Locke followed Lanzmann's route to paint Freddie Gray's portrait, to picture his absence—his "empty space"—and only in tones of gray. It was, after all, because Freddie Gray's color was black that he was murdered.

When the Author is gone, what will be authored.

Modernism and modernity affiliate with ideas about invention, new technologies, and progress. Modernism in art emerged or started, though definitive beginnings and endings of great movements and periods are usually murky, in the mid-nineteenth century. Historians cite different beginnings of modernity, some say the late Middle Ages, and some cite the seventeenth century into the eighteenth century and the Enlightenment, some say the change from agrarian life into cities. There are many theories.

In the beginning of the seventeenth century, the buying and selling of human beings came to the New World. The first slaves who landed in America—"land" is a terrible euphemism—had been captured in Angola. The captives arrived in Jamestown, Virginia, in 1619, four hundred and two years ago. People forced into slavery helped America prosper, which is part of modernity's trajectory. Wars always contribute to progress through scientific and medical discoveries and new technologies. Progress often progresses because of social and political violence.

This essay has largely concerned itself with modernism, abstraction, appropriation, and freedom. Broadly, the weight and gravity of nationality, race, ethnicity, sexuality, and gender influence and shape behavior, rights, and possibilities—the futures for bodies. No one's art, writing, ideas, sentiments, or beliefs—no one's life—can be completely separate from conscious and unconscious burdens, from ideologies, from past and present indignities and oppressions.

Urgent questions about unjust governance and regulatory structures, which restrict bodies, plague the work of various contemporary artists. A necessity to gloss these histories, judgments, and concepts emerged from my paying attention to how so many of these issues arose in Locke's latest project. Or, that Locke's art arose by his paying attention to and operating within these ideas and histories.

> For a very long time everybody refuses and then almost without a pause almost everybody accepts. In the history of the refused in the arts and literature the rapidity of the change is always startling. Now the only difficulty with the *volte-face* concerning the arts is this. When the acceptance comes, by that acceptance the thing created becomes a classic.
> —Gertrude Stein, "Composition as Explanation"

Locke has moved from making portraits of an abstract kind, to an abstract and conceptual project, *Homage to the Auction Block* (2019–

ongoing). His series appropriates Josef Albers's *Homage to the Square*. Conceptually, Locke incorporates one history inside another, by inserting an auction block into the center of Albers's square.

Locke does not repudiate Albers's work, or modernism; he uses it, in part as an homage to Albers. His project, though, reflects on the relative absence of Black creators in modernism's canon. It considers how various and different forms might figure into abstraction; and how difference itself can be one of its subjects. By inserting a historical and tragic marker into white modernism, Locke designates a puzzle about progress, a paradox. He fashions a dialectical relationship between it and an ignored history, or let's say he foregrounds a residue of history.

Many differences stand between Locke's and Albers's paintings. Locke uses colors Albers didn't, in combinations Albers didn't. Locke's stripes are sometimes straight-edged, sometimes bleeding, a bit blurred. At the center, Locke paints an auction block, a form Locke created for it. Sometimes the auction block is highly visible, and large; sometimes small, and sometimes it blends into the background of the square it sits inside.

Turbulence upsets the stability a square promises, and this dissonance might unsettle viewers familiar with Albers's brilliant series. Like Hamlet's father's ghost visiting Hamlet, demanding his son avenge his murder, the violence of slavery haunts the square, and demands recognition. Something rotten sits inside modernism's narrative of progress.

Locke's gesture is analogous to Rauschenberg's erasing, in 1953, a de Kooning drawing. De Kooning ambivalently consented to giving him the work, Rauschenberg has said, because he understood why

Rauschenberg needed to "erase" him, the Master, for Rauschenberg to move on and do his own work. De Kooning's allowance understood artistic freedom, and the exigencies of being the Father to the son. Though he may have hated what Rauschenberg did, de Kooning chose to be a permissive parent.

Steve Locke was born after modernism's heyday. Along with other contemporary artists, he acknowledges and appreciates it, and uses it. *Homage to the Auction Block* doesn't repudiate its aesthetics. But aesthetics shift, since political, social, and economic conditions do, and whatever is designed—design in its broadest sense, or deigned—is inseparable from its time. That art is meant to break unwritten rules, annoy traditions, and commit sacrileges is a truism—much too simple. If modernism was heretical, as Peter Gay proposes, its heresies, as Stein explains, were time-bound. And, "art for art's sake," a fantasy of pure individuality.

Artists everywhere labor in a global environment, in cohort with others in their part of the world, and also connected to others faraway. All cultures embody specific meanings and differences, which affect artists unequally, that is, differently among them. But these differences can or will be recognized as art; whose will figure into art that gets brought to market; whose will be seen and written about; and whose will be called "important"—no answers for unknown futures. Questions prompt thinking and doing and letting go of the old, and, in a new time, with dissent, with and without wars, changes will be compelled.

Steve Locke's *Homage to the Auction Block* is arousing, invested, irascible, and irreverent art. Like mine, like yours, his future is unsettled. Let's see what he does next.

Notes

1 Toni Morrison, "A Humanist View," a speech delivered as part of the series *Public Dialogues on the American Dream Theme*, Portland State University, Oregon, May 30, 1975.

2 English explains that he has borrowed the phrase "interval of reflection" from Jacqueline Rose's *The Last Resistance*. Rose, in turn, had borrowed it from Simone Weil in her essay on the *Iliad*.

3 Goffman was the first to do this type of analysis of gender.

Please Let Empathy Change the World

There was a man who loved his dog. The dog was as loyal as the day was long. But the man had a hard life. The only good thing in it was his dog. So he threw himself off the lower level of the Queensboro Bridge, into the East River. He held his dog in his arms. The dog was discovered in the river, tugging at the man's body. He was trying to carry his master to shore. But the man was dead, and the dog was placed in a shelter.

Your Image of Imperfection

There was a little girl. She wanted to be a movie star. She plotted and worked hard. She became a star, universally adored. But she was insecure, and as the years went by, she became more and more afraid of the public who loved her. She labored for hours to achieve the right look, but as she got older it took more and more time. Finally she spent all her time preparing her face. She never left the house. Her fans forgot her, and she committed suicide.

Mean Spirit

There was a violent man. He bludgeoned, skinned, and butchered a neighbor's pit bull–collie mutt. Then he barbecued the meat on a home gas grill. The dog's head was found on a fence outside the neighbor's house. The violent man was sent to jail. The lawyer said of his client, "When he gets to state prison, and he's the only one there on an offense like this one, I don't think it's going to do him a bit of good."

Get Lost

There was an unfriendly old woman. She worked all her life and then she retired. She never said hello to anyone. When she stopped leaving her house, and her neighbors never saw her at all, they mowed her unruly lawn and collected her mail. Then, one day, when her house was falling apart and the stink became unbearable, the neighbors called the cops. They discovered that the unfriendly old woman has been dead for four years. The telephone was near her rotting body. A neighbor said, "No one's to blame. She never said hello to anyone."

Don't Threaten Me with Love

There was a man whose wife left him. They had four children. He didn't want a divorce, but she did. He tried to get her back and pleaded, but she said no, never. And she expected him to help support their kids. He became more and more enraged and frustrated. So he phoned her one day and arranged to take the whole family for a drive. He planted a bomb in his car and picked them up. The bomb exploded. He killed them and himself with one blast. "HE WAS EVIL," a headline screamed. "Love rage drove dad to blow up his family."

What Is Hell Like?

There was an unhappy husband. He watched TV all night. His wife was bored with him and complained. He just wanted to be left alone and dreamed about running away or murdering her. But he couldn't do it. His wife wanted to divorce him, but she couldn't do it. She hated her job, too. Her boss yelled at her, and she yelled at her husband. They were stuck with each other. He sulked in front of the TV every night. She drank. At fifty-five he died of a heart attack. He left all his money to charity. His wife couldn't break his will and had to take another job to support herself. She couldn't control her temper and lost both jobs. She ended her life on welfare and blamed him for everything.

Not Skinny Enough

There was a woman who wanted to be skinny. She ate no fat or starch. She kept no food in her house. Her eyes grew big in her head. She stared hungrily at friends as they ate their food. One day she disappeared. It's said she wasted away.

Is There a Perfect Mate for Everyone?

There was a happy couple. They couldn't live without each other. They were never apart. They were everything to each other. If you were friends with one, you were friends with the other. If you saw one, you saw the other. You made a date with one, there was the other. At dinner they ordered for each other. Occasionally one of them would complain about the other. But that was rare and unimportant. They were everything to each other. They were never apart. They couldn't live without each other. They died on the same day.

Your Power Trips

There was a determined wife who stayed home and took care of the children. But her husband was cheap. He didn't give her enough household money. She argued with him and grew to hate him. One day she met a young man and fell in love. For a while she was furtively happy. Then she and her lover went to a hit man and arranged to have her husband murdered, for $10,000. She saved her meager household allowance. Her husband also fell in love with someone else and went to the same hit man to murder his wife. Both plots failed, and the miserable pair went to jail.

The Illustration of a Pathetic Stereotype

There was a woman whose only wish was to be beautiful. But when she looked into the mirror, she saw only flaws. Her friends told her she was crazy, so she didn't trust her friends. The truth was her mirror. She went to a plastic surgeon. He changed every feature on her face. Then one day she found fault with her new face. She moved to another part of the country, had more surgery, and made other friends. She wasn't satisfied, though, and kept having surgery. Eventually her nose was smaller than her lips, and she couldn't breathe. So she expired.

Your Acrid Alignments

There was a woman who wanted a child. The man she was with didn't know if he did. He said he loved her so much, he wanted her all to himself. She waited a long time for him to agree. And when he finally did, she hated him. So she left him and never had a child.

Your Taste Is in Your Mouth

There was a young woman who liked to drink blood. She met a man who had advertised his "wish to become a donor to a female vampire." It was love at first bite. Now they nibble and suck each other's necks, happily. They trust each other to be forever free of disease and think they're ageless. "Drinking blood's very intimate," the young woman says. "Also I like pain to a certain degree."

Busy Wanting

There was a woman whose lover was unhappy. He always wanted to commit suicide. But she loved him very much, and, no matter what, she wanted his baby. Every time he failed to kill himself, she'd accompany him the day after to a sperm bank where he'd make a deposit. Finally he succeeded; and his suicide note read: "I would rather take my own life now than be ground into a mediocre existence by my enemies." He left behind fifteen vials of sperm, which he bequeathed to the woman. But his former spouse and their children objected to the woman having artificial insemination after his suicide. So the battle raged in court, which lately sided with the woman and decreed that sperm was property and could be passed on. The decision's being appealed. Meanwhile, the woman visits the cryobank and speaks to the vials. "Hang on there," she says to the sperm, "you'll be here soon."

Big-Shot Careers

There was a young woman who worked her way up the ladder. Many people in her company envied her, but she had her boss's approval. Then one day her boss died, and she was fired.

Don't Tell Me to Relax

There was a married couple who were very much in love. But one day the man saw his beloved talking to the mailman. He became enraged and slapped his wife. He told her not to leave the house or talk to anyone. The woman was afraid and stayed home. But finally one day the terrified woman ran away. She left the house and him for good. But her husband followed her and menaced her. The wife went to court to obtain a protection order against him. So the husband murdered her in the courthouse.

Picture This

There were two brothers. They had a strict mother. She was religious and made them study hard. The older brother hated her. He wanted to kill her. He asked his younger brother to help him. He was going to use a crossbow and arrow. The brothers argued. The younger one refused to do it. So the older brother shot him with the crossbow and arrow. The arrow lodged in his neck, but he survived. "He did get seriously injured," said a detective, "but he had God with him." Their forgiving mother expressed no vengeful feelings toward her older son. The mother was just "trying to cope with the tragedy of having one son in the hospital and the other in custody," the police said.

Please Read Between the Lines

There was an ordinary woman. The woman had a dream. In it, someone wrote a book about her. The ordinary woman read the book and exclaimed, "There's nobody like me."

Your Ritual Scoldings

There was a sweet little girl. When her mother loved her, she thought her daughter was good enough to eat. When her mother hated her, she thought her daughter was the devil. One day, at the school cafeteria where she worked, the mother placed the little girl in the oven. She set the temperature to 425 degrees. School employees quickly removed the girl. But the girl went to the hospital with second-degree burns all over her body.

Not Cool Enough

There was a man who loved cookies. He couldn't control himself around them. He was an overweight bumbler and hapless burglar. His wife left him after he was released from his second stint in the slammer. He became very depressed. He broke into a restaurant. He wanted to steal the safe, but he tripped the burglar alarm. He grabbed four chocolate chip cookies and fled. He was caught, cookie-handed. It was his third felony, a third strike for him under the new three-strikes-and-you're-out California law. So he was sentenced to twenty-six years in jail. "That's six and a half years per cookie," said his public defender.

Your Ridiculous Lack of Irony

There was a German tourist in Florida. He was on a plane back to Germany. It was about to take off, but he had to piss very badly. He didn't speak much English. He called the attendant over and used German slang, which he translated into English. He said, "Then the roof flies." They thought he was a terrorist, and was threatening to bomb the plane, so they put him in jail for nine months. At his hearing the judge said, "Do you see anything that happened that couldn't have been remedied by letting this man go to the bathroom?"

Please Live and Let Live

There was a moderately autistic boy. He was lost for four days in a snake-filled swamp. Somehow he survived. When asked about his time alone in the dark and cold, he said, "I see fish, lots of fish." His mother had always encouraged him to enjoy a life as close to normal as possible. The boy had learned to swim, and he swam like a dolphin. It was probably how he endured a desperate situation that four Rangers hadn't—they all died of hypothermia. The boy's mother, Mrs. Touchstone, thought lightning might've "penetrated his shell" and kept her son swimming, moving. "Do you really think," Mrs. Touchstone asked, "God would strike him dead with lightning? Wouldn't that be redundant?"

Note
All titles for the stories are taken from texts in Barbara Kruger's artworks.

Potter Agonistes was settled in place, in the midst of it. Potter had been alone and preferred that. Now, others surrounded Potter, and occasionally it was encouraging—to feel part of a group—but their facelessness bothered Potter, who worried about a loss of identity.

Informed citizens, unique bodies, the unaware, just things, volunteers, captured innocents, outlets, various shapes and objects . . .

They pretended to be something, busied themselves, stood or sat, and mostly temporized or were waiting for something; maybe they would be transformed and set into motion, eventually. A few appeared rushed—they must have believed they were late for an appointment. Some appeared to know their reality.

Potter wasn't all-seeing and omniscient, just in charge. The others may have been done or doing nothing; it was difficult to tell. Figures, things, caught in the miasma of a kind of existence, mute about it all. Potter Agonistes couldn't discern what they thought or hoped, or if they were mindful at all. Usually she didn't care, occupied by the mound, in need of constant attention, and, as long as they didn't bother her as Potter enhanced it, sometimes automatically or fiercely, Potter went on and on.

The mound's marks were reminders of every day and night, time spent and passed, and also survival. Potter's survival was measured by her progress; yet, though attending to the mound every day, she couldn't tell if it made progress, and sometimes worry overcame this sober magus.

Occasionally glimpsing the others' good impression of Potter, her dedication to the amorphous mound, she felt almost proud. They didn't doubt her, or they were not aware of her. The incurious reign, sadly, yet lately Potter fought her need to know the why of it and felt assaulted by doubts and questions about their ontological status.

The others—curious objects with no possibility to reproduce themselves or create something of value—looked raw, rough, at the ready to argue, collapse, or cry. Some stood, some lay, some reached to the ceiling, one crawled on the floor, some gained height by sitting on plinths. Some looked cut out of a larger entity, some were flat as a board, and some were made of board.

Usually she didn't look up, her head to the grindstone.

I mean, Potter thought, I have to keep it spinning, otherwise everything will stop, our world, it's on me. I have to goad and remind and praise all of them. And all of this, Potter Agonistes had to do by her good example, because she also had no words.

A trying endeavor, spinning the wheel, slapping clay, bits sticking, bits falling off. Potter attempted to create a pleasing form while piles and piles of muck dropped to the floor around her. Potter looked askance at the unused chunks, they might be rebukes.

Outside, at the perimeter of the formation, human creatures circled and ringed them, staring without embarrassment and often for a long time. They walked from one group to another, then back around, delighted, skeptical, disappointed, amused. Some bent down low, others—of these people, as they were known—stretched high up on their toes for, Potter guessed, a better view. People had advantages, the ability to move, speak, build, but with such attributes, nothing special ever changed in them, they stayed the same.

If Potter could, she would remake the world as she did her mound.

Potter perhaps vaingloriously decided they recognized her force and centrality. She noticed their expressions, their faces or facades, and gleaned from them that they were reflecting what they saw. Some were what they saw.

Potter's work was not simple.

They stared at her, and she disguised her dismay at being a thing to be looked at, she and her mound. She wouldn't say she was like Sisyphus—that would be overreaching, which she physically couldn't do. But she wouldn't say she wasn't.

Some onlookers hid their chagrin at her odd form, certainly different from theirs. The less sophisticated pulled faces. What was wrong with them?

It hadn't always been this way. Once feral, Potter was an idea without substance. She had come into existence slowly, and made to be immovable for a reason, Potter supposed. Recognizing her impossibility of becoming something other, she grew into her pose, knowing her significance derived from their imaginations, by pleasing these people-creatures who walked in, around, and out.

Some ignored her, some gazed at her too long. Potter was available. She was stable. Consistent. Permanent. She'd like to think her permanence gave her value. Those who strolled around and peered at her could never achieve what she had.

Potter Agonistes felt almost jubilant: Her fate would be to outlive anyone who came to see her. Then she added a bit of clay and patted the mound tenderly.

Soon an onlooker spoke loudly to another:

"I'm so pissed. She dumped me. I feel like kicking this dumb . . ."

"Don't. Don't make a scene," the other said.

Jubilation fled.

And then a wayward idea entered Potter Agonistes's hard head. She could be kicked, mauled, she could be broken. She had to be valued, she needed more and more value in order to . . .

Potter kept working, kept her head down, and tried not to think about what her future might be.

Psychologically, a reenactment occurs when people unknowingly repeat or imitate relationships and behaviors from the past. A historical reenactment is a form of mimesis, a planned imitation.

The photographer An-My Lê's project *Small Wars* (1999–2002) pictures Americans repeating skirmishes and battles from the Vietnam War. Lê was born in Hanoi in 1960, and grew up during the war, hearing bombs dropping, gunfire. After Ho Chi Minh City (then Saigon) fell to North Vietnamese forces in April 1975, she and her family were airlifted to the US on a military transport plane.

Through the repetition of traumatic events in these reenactments, the war's history is engaged, and its psychological effects reactivated. Former soldiers and civilians plan maneuvers and clashes, restaging actual battles. The soldiers act their parts; Lê photographs them, but also performs in some scenes, dressed as a North Vietnamese soldier, enemy of South Vietnam and the US.

She "documents" a war and acts of violence she never witnessed but might have imagined. Through her lens, scenes based in fact turn phantasmatic and address not only her imaginary but also history's. The past to the present can only ever be a fictional narrative, more or less accurate.

The photograph *Small Wars (Lesson)* is an intricate, formal composition: A landscape of tall, flowering trees frames two relatively small figures in the middle distance. Lê, in uniform, sits on a log close to a US Special Ops soldier. His rifle is at rest as they are. Lê seems to be taking notes. They may be strategizing. She could be a "Kit Carson," a North Vietnamese soldier who turned to the American side. In the foreground, a packed rucksack resembles a slumped-over or sleeping body. The two soldiers, posed against the base of a tall tree, construct the photograph's vanishing point. The moment is very still, belying aggression and violence.

Curiously, although war is the norm and always somewhere, it's said to "break out." But peace is what breaks in. The natural setting in *Small Wars (Lesson)* is not what it appears to be, unless nature includes human nature. Lê's photograph upends, even subverts, a landscape and makes peace anomalous.

Try Again

Recently I gave a fiction reading with the poet Matthea Harvey at New York University's Lillian Vernon House, which lodges its creative writing program. At the end, we took questions. The last to me was: "What would you tell younger writers is the most important lesson you've learned so far in your writing life?" The next night I dined with a friend who's an artist. He and I discussed how—and whether—to answer questions about our work: "I've said I believe in something, an idea or cause," he said, "then someone in the audience says, 'But I don't see that in your work.'"

No one strong-arms you into becoming an artist or writer—most often you're dissuaded—and volunteers who bemoan their chosen gig seem disingenuous. Visual artists are often called to account for their choices and asked to defend their positions. Few occupations other than finance, politics, and crime entail this reckoning. Writers and artists may ask themselves why they make art or write, and many feel the pointlessness of their self-chosen jobs, but all rebuttals and answers to their existential questions rest on faith in Art or Literature. Faith itself will be tested.

Art and literary projects regularly fail, but the announcement of mistakes or failures is rare. There's no written history of these failures, unless artists record them. In art, mistakes can be happy, revelatory surprises. Failures are also intriguingly resisted, by people who keep on trying. My dermatologist has researched a cure for cancer for forty years. At eighty-two, he appears undaunted, but then he is one of many scientists engaged in cancer research. This commonality of purpose and group effort doesn't pertain in the arts. The field primarily supports individual achievement at the cost of a general goal, like a cure for cancer. But pursuing a common goal for art would be misguided.

A comic gets rid of bad jokes, or is a bad comic, though failures might make it into the act, since they're at the heart of funny. Comedy wouldn't exist without failure, especially that of other people. Writers may publish idiocies and artists make dull objects, and some of this work may be celebrated as good writing or art. Some write more and more books, hoping to get it right, often digging a deeper hole to fall into. Success itself can be a rut, since, it's said, it breeds success, so might condemn an artist to doing the same thing forever.

To the question about my best lesson for younger writers, I answered: "Don't expect that being published will make you happy." I didn't mention the inevitability of rejection, luck, money, nepotism, etc. Before my first novel appeared, I'd naively believed that being published would compensate for every bad thing. In those prepublication days, my writing was for me, I was its only reader, and I could believe it was without sin.

At dinner with my artist friend, I told him I didn't know if artists owed anyone an answer or what a writer's responsibility to readers was, if there was one. The ethics of these peculiar relationships remain conundrums. Notions of service to the field may not matter, if the proof isn't in the pudding. Anyway, writers and artists are not voted in or out by an electorate, though institutions—including collectors, gallerists, publishers, art magazines, critics—do vote but not in a transparent manner, not democratically. It's insisted there is a public for art, but those who remark on it generally presume themselves separate from it.

Working with words and pictures engages artists and writers in a world they didn't make, to which they may or may not contribute. I often think about Samuel Beckett and his agonistic relationship to writing and living. Beckett wrote novels, he wrote in two languages, he wrote plays. Beckett talked with actors, had intentions about how his plays should be performed, specified the props he wanted onstage, in service of communicating the incommunicable. A play is such an earnest art form, as it is written for, acted by, and presented in front of living people. Its earnestness also resides in its ephemerality, the precariousness of every performance, tethering the genre to life's temporariness. That Beckett wrote is a thrilling paradox. "Try again. Fail again. Fail better."

Societies find cunning solutions for communicating even the incommunicable. Which brings me to the time I lived in London. I didn't understand the British use of "I don't mind" to mean "yes," "no," "maybe." The phrase seemed to allow for ineffable negotiations between people, though. "I don't mind," I saw, opened a conversational door through which either party could leave, without embarrassment. But it was hard for a foreigner to use, because it's part of a British dance whose subtle moves are learned from childhood. The British also sometimes avoided answering direct questions. I loved that, it was so un-American, and now I sometimes do it in New York, where people expect answers. I change the subject or pretend I haven't heard the question, and watch surprise or chagrin appear on faces. It's a liberation from others' nosiness, a freedom I never expected. I recommend it, with reservations that will be different for each person, discerned only through trial and error.

A Woman I Once Knew

> I made the nude self-portraits at times when I was feeling vulnerable. I never planned to publish them. At a certain point I asked myself, Why not?
> —Rosalind Fox Solomon

Rosalind Fox Solomon's nudes portray a particular woman, and her experience of her body. These self-portraits stun with their unexpected compositions—a body posed in unlovely and awkward postures. Idiosyncratic images collide with historical and traditional representations of female nudes.

Fox Solomon's self-portraits work toward upending the seminal critique that, in cinema, "woman [is the] object of the male gaze," Laura Mulvey's theory that appeared in her essay "Visual Pleasure and Narrative Cinema." Mulvey proposed that on-screen women were subjected and subjugated to the male eye, objectified to satisfy his desire. Yet, an audience of others—gay men and women, straight women—see with their own eyes.

Fox Solomon took up a camera when she was forty, studied with Lisette Model, and found an abiding interest and pleasure in making photographs. From the start, she contemplated and investigated the problems that come with directing a camera at people of various backgrounds and points of view. She brought to photography her previous and prevailing interests—family and other relationships, social and cultural differences, and, in a sense, turned into an artist of ethnographic persuasion.

Photography revolutionized how she lived. Drawn to picturing other lives, she pursued projects in Peru, Mexico, South Africa, and in New York City and the American South; she sought permission in photographing people, in proposing a kind of collaboration by asking her subjects to choose how they wanted to be seen. Behind her camera, Fox Solomon, who was a shy person, now engaged with strangers, new and different kinds of people.

In photographing her nude self, Fox Solomon is no stranger to controversial subjects. With the advent of the AIDS epidemic in the US, experienced first in NYC, people—generations who had seen polio cured and relied on penicillin—were overwhelmed and horrified, while gay men and women with AIDS were further stigmatized. PrEP has eliminated the fear of getting AIDS, for those who have access to it, but has not cured it.

During the scourge, Fox Solomon photographed people with AIDS, spending time with them, often becoming friends. Her 1987–1988 exhibition, *Portraits in the Time of AIDS*, at NYU's Grey Art Gallery, was revelatory and controversial: photographs of men, mostly, their bodies scarred, a face covered by Kaposi sarcoma, a wasting body lying in a hospital bed, a friend or family member at the bedside. The love and affection shown in those photographs rebuked those who would not even touch people with AIDS.

Some reviewers and the public objected to the display of these troubling images—infected bodies. But showing humanity is primary for Fox Solomon.

Fox Solomon shot the photographs in *A Woman I Once Knew* (2024) over fifty years. In this book, she declares her independence as a woman, and as a photographer. The first photograph here shows her seated on a stool, her legs spread out—woman-splaining, I could say now. Her hands lie on her knees, but not in a restful manner—one hand forms a fist. She wears plain black pants and top, and running shoes. It is night, and behind her a black sky and large, screened windows frame her. Not looking at the camera, her face is turned slightly; she might be thinking or looking off into space, her white hair creating another frame inside that of the night sky.

The composition of the space is plain, unadorned, a few objects in it. Her figure is somewhat off-center, one of her knees bent toward the door, perhaps. The running shoe is angled, intimating that this woman may want to run away, out of the picture. The self-portrait is far from still, and far from the usual representations of women: She is uneasy, restless, not making up a face for the camera.

Several nudes—in fact all of them—object to the familiar approaches. Fox Solomon is lying on her side on a wooden floor. Her left hip, in the forefront, seems to guard the body from complete vision. Her raised left arm partially covers one breast, her hand fully covers one eye. Much of her body lies in shadow.

A covered eye incites several interpretations. You can look at me, but not see me completely, since looking is not seeing. Another: You can't see me, and anyway I am hiding from myself. The covered eye is a pun.

In another, Fox Solomon is seated, perhaps in an imperfect yoga pose. Her legs are crossed awkwardly, one knee up, the other under it, while she grasps the foot of the raised leg. Her head juts forward, her dark eyes hooded, against playing with sight. Her nude body is effectively not available, her breasts, her genitals covered. The pose depicts ambivalence, especially to "performing" nudity.

A photograph of hands is an artistic trope, the hands that create work, Michelangelo's finger reaching for God. Fox Solomon's version does not aggrandize hers; instead, they seem *unheimlich*.

The index finger of one points to the other hand, where four fingers are visible. A curious image, the four long fingers stretched out and flat. I spot a wound on that index finger, a detail mostly absent from pictures unless depicting the hands of workers. Behind her, a crosshatched wall imitates the position of the crossed hands.

Her pose in another picture resembles an odalisque, but her look disarms the spectator. Her body is foreshortened, legs cut off after the thighs. Not fully supine on what seems like a bed, her body is angled, only one breast visible.

Her eyes look out of the frame and disrupt the viewer's gaze. Her face is accentuated by the V of one arm, which mimes the shape of her chin, emphasizing it. Eyes will find her eyes and, with her enigmatic, grave expression, lips closed, she frustrates satisfaction—for whose pleasure has she shot this? Her look claims her body for herself.

Fox Solomon hides as she exposes: Her photographs insist that exposing is not revealing. The self-portraits demonstrate interiority, an effect in a photograph or movie that is particularly elusive. A subject's demeanor and visage can suggest thoughtfulness, melancholia, contentment, and so on. There may be nothing behind their expression.

Harry Mathews once commented, "The writer is their own first reader." Here, Fox Solomon is her own life model. But no artist who is a woman can escape the criticism that photographing herself is narcissistic. Men who do it—for example, John Coplans—won't be. Oh, that silly double standard. Fox Solomon says that she shot the nudes "when she was feeling vulnerable." It seems counterintuitive to bring herself forward, then, unless you understand it as resistance, an act against retreating from the world, forcing herself to face the world even then.

Her intent is different. The sculptural aspect of her nudes makes her body appear solid. Those unusual poses, hands and legs, focus attention on her physicality. These are not gentle, passive female bodies. They are strong women who strike poses that show aggression. And in the very last image of this photo-essay, Fox Solomon wears a black bra and high black socks, she is crouched over, her hands in fists. Her determination to exist is powerful.

An Afternoon with Stanley Whitney

Some friends have dressed in black, almost exclusively, since the 1980s. I did for a long while then, with the naughts, opened my palette to colors, especially in spring and summer when flowers bloom—when wearing only black made me a curiosity to myself and, especially under a strong sun, a misguided statement.

I like most colors, strong and faded, reds, oranges, blues, rosy pink and lavender pink, shades of gray, the noncolor white. I like bold and lemon yellows, though I never wear yellow. Black is all colors, it's elegant, it's night, fathomless, steadfast. Black is outer space, and down here on the street, black goes with everything—that little black dress. Color is the heterogeneity of the world.

Which brings me to Stanley Whitney's color-filled paintings. I first saw some in the late 1990s. Relatively small pieces, they formed a geometry of colors, shapes with soft edges, maybe bleeding ones. He and I were teaching at Bard College's low-residency MFA program, two overheated months in summer. Stanley never pressed me to look at his work, which impressed me.

Stanley Whitney's *Afternoon Paintings* happen after he finishes working on large paintings, ones that are, say, ninety-six by ninety-six inches. Whitney takes the leftover paint and makes smaller, faster paintings. I think, comically, "the remains of the day," then consider more seriously how an artist finds a necessity from which to make work, from what remains or hasn't been used. It's not recycling, it's not wanting to waste. I rarely discard any writing I've done, even a scrap may be useful later and I add it to my scraps file.

Whitney tells me after working carefully crafting big pieces, he likes to paint smaller ones, because, at the end of the day, "I'm more relaxed, more loose, more carefree, and I'm kind of tired, too." Seriously, I had never heard an artist say he works when he's tired. I ask why, when tired: "Because after working so hard and being serious, after struggling with 'is it right or is it wrong,' I feel I open up, then I can see what happens, not putting pressure on myself."

Also, he explains, the shifts in size allow him "to think differently. And to move differently." I think about how in writing size shapes it too—a long work compared with a short one, duration and concision. These different exigencies do make artists think differently. Scale must always be considered, it makes its own demands.

In his studio, surrounded by a carnival of colors—reds, oranges, blues, purples, grays—Whitney says, "I don't take color for granted." The world is in color, and people do—I do—forget. A majority see in color, so when presented with black and white, Franz Kline's paintings, say, or a black-and-white photograph by Rosalind Fox Solomon, color's absence is obvious, palpable, and no longer taken for granted. In these *Afternoon Paintings*, there's usually one black square or rectangle settled into the composition, on a row at the top or at the bottom or to the side, usually not in the middle. Whitney tells me he sees the darker colors as creating more weight, a kind of gravity.

> I don't worry about what the color does.
> If it feels right, if it sits right . . .
> To me, it's all about how things feel.
> I never know what the colors are going to be . . .
> I'm trying to open up space, for people to wander.
> —Stanley Whitney

Discussing color entails abstraction; any color represents much more than its literal color, and the discussion is abstract especially when the paintings aren't representational.

The language for color is not very helpful to me, it's abstraction about what is both actual and abstract. Let's say, color presents the possibility of visual experiences for which words are mostly unsatisfying. But the effects of color call up many responses: visceral, physical, neurological, instinctive, impulsive, adjectives that require others to satisfy or elucidate usage. I can say: The eye communicates with the brain, so that we see. The brain receives signals and creates, constructs, or pieces together an image. It's involuntary activity, as are sensations, which have no organic basis.

William James theorized that the body acts or feels before characterization of the action, before ideas about or words for it. Words denote the sensation only after it occurs: Without the body reacting to a stimulus by trembling, there is no "trembling with fear." James's idea helps to consider the manifold, inchoate effects of color to perception, since a person reacts to color before she can, if ever, comprehend why. And only by associating to it, as in psychoanalysis, might one discover the source of those reactions.

"I don't know what color does," Whitney tells me, and says he doesn't have a theory of color. His art engages with and is about that question, actively playing and working with perception, involuntary responses as well as voluntary ones. Knowing something about painting will usually charge a viewer's relationship to a painting, and bring other meanings to it.

Whitney talked about his movements as he works—painting in relationship to his body. "I'm a very physical painter. The big ones are more about the body." He likes his work big so as "to move with it." The smaller ones, like the *Afternoon Paintings*, "are more like jewelry, easel size."

He says, a little later in the afternoon, "Bigness lets a lot of things happen in a painting."

Hearing that, I realize how my eye rarely settles for long in any one area of his larger paintings. I keep changing where I look. There's no vanishing point to follow to an end, no bringing my eye to rest. The invention of the vanishing point allowed for an end point, for a kind of solution and logic. A mystery solved, say, a way to find God, or maybe peace. Whitney's paintings don't enable that, they keep the eye moving. "There's no beginning and no end to it, there's a good rhythm to it. I want clarity to the painting." With his *Afternoon Paintings*, my eye doesn't exactly settle, but I believe I can, maybe do, apprehend the entire painting, see it all at once.

Speed charges the globe, not everywhere in the same time and way; but the speed of exchanges and transmission of information dazzles and bewilders. Working through ideas requires the patience of an artist and a viewer. Patience takes time, that's what it is, and who has the time, who takes things slowly? Some hope to slow down reading on the internet, but the challenges to speed are not victories over it. Instant judgments rule the airwaves as if the past had no importance on the present.

"My paintings," Stanley says, "change very slowly . . . I always liked the way Mondrian changed," he goes on, "step by step by step. So, they do change, but they change very slowly." The viewer also undergoes change through a painting's speed and openness. It's a question of reception to, not the essence of, the painting. Also, Whitney's work, as he goes on, makes its own history, in its own time.

I walk around his studio, checking out what surrounds him. Every artist's studio has its own attitude, stance—I'm not sure what to call it. But each is remarkably different, and usually surprising. Every studio visit I make, I am struck by what an artist—in this case, Whitney—feels good having around. Whitney's work surrounds him. What he has done is also an aide-mémoire for future thoughts and projects. On various tables and shelves, there are many poetry and art books, some fiction, art catalogues and histories, and in the front of the studio, on walls and tables, some work by friends or artists he admires, and some of his own drawings and sketches—these arc in the front of the large space, where he doesn't paint.

I'm drawn to his worktable where many aluminum bowls or plates of paint have been set, with all the colors he has used that day. They are lined up in four neat rows (especially when I compare it with the papers strewn on my desk). I count: five shades of green; one red; two orange; one lemon; one bright yellow; one black; four blues; two lavender pink, one rosy pink. His many paintbrushes are also lined up, neatly.

The studio itself is an institution in the history of art, and part of the history and practice of painting. I often think of Velázquez's *Las Meninas*, which is, whatever else it is—in my view, everything—a painting of a studio and an artist at work.

Many artists know the history of their fields well and refer to it, use it, similarly and differently from the way Whitney does. The history of art, especially of sculpture and painting, is long, and studying it, one can teach oneself about art. Then, one might find how a color in a Matisse painting enters a painting of Whitney's. Maybe as a kind of homage, a gesture, but it is definitely a form of intertextuality, a quotation that expands and deepens an artwork, just as it does a piece of music. A musician quotes another musician's line in a solo, say, and by doing that the compositions layer each other. The musical form develops composition by composition, and that historical development gets built into the new work. All art in some way develops like that, by incorporation. Whitney's work refers to itself, its own development, but also to other work. It happens through his use of colors and forms.

Looking at the paintings, I'm struck with what a catholic artist Whitney is, how broad his interests are, and how he brings so much into his work, so many different kinds of influences and loves. I tell him I'm feeling that. Experiencing other paintings and painters on and under the surfaces of his work—metaphorical palimpsests, I think later. He appears to enjoy that idea. Anyway, I hope he did.

He looks at me with a wry expression.

"Morandi, Van Gogh, Mondrian, a great de Kooning, Joan Mitchell—I want it all," he says.

So I consider his paintings all over again.

Note

All quotes from Stanley Whitney are from an interview with the author, which took place in Whitney's Ridgewood studio, in New York, on May 30, 2019.

The Final Plot

Some writers believe they control their fictional worlds, and nothing else; others that they are conduits for a story—words arrive, characters write themselves. (Few believe they have no control at all over what or how they write.) But even if one can imagine dying or being dead, one can't represent it autobiographically. The impressions and scenes that can be imagined will have been nourished by others' deaths—those witnessed, heard, or read about. (Duchamp's tombstone epitaph, "After all, it's always the other one who dies," means it's always the other's story too.) The way being dead actually feels, a lack of all sensation, supposedly, can't be described, depriving human beings certainty about life's afterlife; but, conversely, fomenting, with death's partner sexual curiosity, a drive for knowledge.

Ones who know they are dying, those physiologically at death's door, and also those who pathologically fear death, might want to rush life's conclusion and kill themselves. Suicides, or self-murderers, as the Dutch put it, can select the method, day, and hour, and direct the last narrative, up to a point. Despair, significantly and regularly, overrides choice and strips it of volition. And, how being dead feels will also elude a suicide's capacity to know. (Virginia Woolf wrote in her diary that it was "the one experience I shall not describe.")

When death progresses naturally, which can be slow going, over days or months, unless from a high-impact, head-on car crash, when organs fail fast, depleted of blood and oxygen, there comes a stunning withdrawal: People, like other animals, remove themselves psychically and physically from the known world. A person goes elsewhere, while the body works hard to shut itself down. One is "actively dying," hospice workers say. Death is oxymoronic until it finishes its work.

On ordinary days, a depressive has her funeral to fantasize, an activity that reassures with sad, cozy comfort. When required in actuality, planning it will probably be discomforting. A dying person may type, scrawl, or dictate a list of demands or wishes for a service or memorial, exerting a sort of posthumous control. (The list can also be a preemptive strike against the omissions or excesses of fond others.) A funeral might be plain as a pine coffin or theatrical. One who is dying might have specified songs, musicians, speakers, and kinds and colors of flowers, or, if possessed of minimalist inclinations, wanted no displays or eulogies, just a plaintively beautiful song. (Both may have designated worthy charities.)

For a writer's funeral, words could seem superfluous, though there can never be enough, also. Selecting speakers raises unique problems. Most particularly, eulogizers script themselves. Some will mumble, overcome or shy, while others will improvise on humiliating episodes in the dead person's life. All jokes will be on the dead. (Most people will speak primarily about themselves.) In fantasy, a depressive mourns herself and watches the abstract procession, loving the inconsolation of others; but soon her morbid pleasures are jolted by the awkwardness of social situations, pre- and postdeath. Inclusions, exclusions, who speaks first, last? (Funeral rites survive, and have changed historically, for the living.) Planning an actual funeral might allay worry or generate more.

For writers and nonwriters, other kinds of writing than suicide notes can be left behind. A letter might confess secret loves and hates, with recuperative gestures of remorse and forgiveness. Or, it could be a screed against the living. A death essay could be an *avant-fin* manifesto, raving mad, or setting out rational principles for existence. (A treatise on melancholy risks mawkishness and unoriginality.) The essay could haltingly document one's protracted departure (exquisitely incomplete).

Any of these compositions might supply a reason to live fully while dying, but inciting, for writers, a specific anxiety. The final text could cause a cascade of revisionist views of the individual and the body of work, staining both, and lasting until everyone who knew the writer had died (considered in Buddhism an individual's "second death").

Most likely, one will have scant energy for planning and writing in the final stages of life. (There are exceptions, who prove the rule.) Meeting death, sometimes called "the maker," though really the unmaker, is essentially debilitating, so its specific conditions dominate and alter the living. A dying person may have no ambition or desire to control anything during the process (in itself unburdening). One's death, though, will likely be written about by someone else or, even more likely, no one. Most deaths go unremarked. So-called ordinary people get thousands of hits on YouTube when killed by a usually docile lion on an ecological safari or pushed in front of a train. (The living identify with the pathos and meaninglessness of random, final endings like these.)

An ignominious death recasts an entire life as unintelligent and witless. A relatively healthy person moves an old, huge TV set or a five-drawer steel file cabinet, which, unbalanced, leans, starts falling, its weight unbelievable, gains velocity, collapses, and crushes one beneath it. (Domestic deaths invariably make foolish last impressions.) An ignominious end is beyond prediction. But the great majority of deaths will be common, following a predictable course indicated by one of several illnesses, resulting in complete organ failure. Sherwin Nuland, in his book *How We Die*, refutes the contemporary delusion of living forever by defeating the aging process. He insists, almost too vociferously, that human beings will die sooner or later, because of the wear and tear on the body, also known as old age, which is not a disease. But if one believes people are dying as soon as they are born, then living itself is an illness overcome only by dying.

Near to death, people usually don't speak or have last words, hospice workers say, especially not those profound or pithy final utterances compiled in books.

> *Thomas Carlyle*: "So this is Death—Well!"
> *Aleister Crowley*: "I'm perplexed."
> *Ulysses S. Grant*: "Water!"
> *Emily Dickinson*: "Let us go in. The fog is rising."
> *Goethe*: "More light!"
> *Edgar Allan Poe*: "Lord help my poor soul . . ."
> *Washington Irving*: "Well, I must arrange my pillows for another weary night! When will this end?"
> *Gertrude Stein*: "What is the question?"
> *Ludwig Wittgenstein*: "Tell them I've had a wonderful life."

If a dying person had her wits about her and enough bodily function—swallowing becomes impossible—she might be able to come up with a line or two. But this also can't be plotted. (Spoken and written communications not close to death are technically not deathbed statements.) Withdrawing from life for days or weeks, one is expected to be silent and uncommunicative, or will communicate but be misunderstood. (The writing of Ivan Ilyich's death, hospice workers say, is eerily close to how dying people feel; they wonder at Tolstoy's prescience.)

Since what death feels like is unknowable, most people fear it, and dying, particularly in great pain. In this time, as no other before, unless wishing to suffer mentally and physically, a patient can receive palliative care and medicines that make the "transition," a hospice term, from life to death painless or nearly painless. (Many believe hospice speeds death along, but often it prolongs what life is left.) Against all reason, which death conquers easily, a few want to feel pain, not to remain as lucid as possible and say their goodbyes, but as self-punishment for past bad acts and guilty consciences.

Hardly anyone wishes "to die badly." In the late Middle Ages, when the concept of *artes moriendi* was formulated, the ideal of "a beautiful death" emerged, and it thrived through the nineteenth century. "Dying well" has replaced "dying beautifully" and is rigorously enforced by postmortem judgments. People aren't supposed to struggle at the end, people should be "ready to go" and "accepting," and opprobrium is cast on those who aren't ready and willing, on those who "died badly."

The ultimate indictment glosses and assesses a human being's last trial. (To die smiling makes it easier for the living.) But in the matter of dying and death, mortal judgments, like most received wisdoms concocted of exasperating pieties and galling stupidity, should be eliminated. Only death's uninitiated would espouse these moralisms.

Of death, mortals are absolutely ignorant. The dead, fortunately, are beyond caring.

Point of View

Tennis, with actual winners and losers, contents me and other workers in fields of indeterminacy—artists, musicians, writers—where first prizes declare arguable standing. Choosing sides is often wrong but not in sports. In this year's US Open, Novak Djokovic beat Rafael Nadal as if Nadal were an ordinary mortal. I was torn between them, and miss that action. Fortunately, since art can be long, sports short, I'm absorbed in *Diane Arbus: A Chronology, 1923–1971* (2011), a new book of her beautifully written diary entries, letters, and work notes.

Sides formed early about her enigmatic, brilliant photography. At home, Arbus's photographs upset my father, viscerally. I experienced them, as an adolescent, the way I did Franz Kafka's *The Metamorphosis*—identifying with uncanny strangeness, fascinated by what I didn't understand. Some of what Arbus had imaged—people once referred to as "freaks"—was usually kept from sight. In the 1960s, families still institutionalized their "mentally retarded" or "insane" relatives. Various art critics and civilian viewers over the years have thought Arbus cruelly exploited unsuspecting subjects. Some felt she was slumming.

There are English words whose definitions confound definition. Words such as "exploitative," "ambitious," or "pretentious," when applied to art and writing or their creators, form blurry impressions, subjectivity shaping them. Mindful of Virginia Woolf's dictum, in her 1937 essay "Craftsmanship," that "words don't live in dictionaries, they live in the mind," I know recourse to a dictionary definition won't clarify much that is significant to me. Words live in usage, with connotations.

Lewis Hine, among other documentary photographers, pictured desperate people in desperate conditions. His photographs presumed what I'll call a "benign-looking contract" between viewer and viewed. "We" viewers were expected to feel sympathy for "others" and their stricken lives. Specific assumptions shaped the spectator as well as those imaged. Hine's subjects existed primarily in one dimension, which might indeed overwhelm other aspects of their lives, but it was likely only one way they saw themselves. Still, Hine had a specific purpose in shooting them as he did: to expose terrible poverty, appalling slums. I can't imagine that he was grilled about intentionality then.

Any discomfort I experience looking at a Hine feels simpler to explain than at an Arbus, because her purpose was various, ambiguous, dimensional. Deprivation, lack, or difference in her work, which encompassed many living situations and conditions, is generally psychological, cultural, and physical, often genetic. There is no consensus about—and in looking at—the characters she pictured. No consensus in part because how "normals" perceive "stigmatized" people, and vice versa, is an ever-evolving process. (See Erving Goffman's *Stigma: Notes on the Management of Spoiled Identity*, which Arbus read.) Goffman called these interactions "mixed-contacts." There was also no "social-looking contract"—my term—codifying how viewers should look at her photographs. Still isn't.

"Someone told me it is spring, but everyone today looked remarkable, just like out of August Sander pictures, so absolute and immutable down to the last button . . . all odd and splendid as freaks and nobody able to see himself, all of us victims of the especial shape we come in," wrote Arbus in 1960, in a note to her friend, the artist Marvin Israel. Arbus recognized the precariousness of her interests and knew her terrain was treacherous. Curiosity, identification, fear, discontent with her upper-middle-class origin, and fascination with what she was not, caused her to seek and embrace difference. Her characters aren't posed in shadows. They look directly, baldly, at the camera. Her photographs don't take a recognizable side: She is not moralistic or judgmental. Her most infamous or celebrated images reside in the interstices of ethical positions, since the eye of a wavering beholder is also a judge.

A viewer might be thrown contending with *Identical twins, Roselle, N.J. 1967* (1967), girls who are common or normal and also different. Or, by Arbus's representation of an upper-middle-class white family in their suburban backyard, *A family on their lawn one Sunday in Westchester, N.Y. 1968* (1968), which appears to have landed in *The Twilight Zone*—"nearly like [Harold] Pinter but not quite," she writes in a letter. Or, by *A Jewish giant at home with his parents in the Bronx, N.Y. 1970* (1970): The giant man and parents stand in the living room of a small apartment and compose an unbalanced image, one that also upends the nuclear family and makes it "other," even perverse.

Risking ambiguities, Arbus vigorously subverted the subject/object position, shoving the viewer onto her soft ground. She interrogated looking, aggressively, and made looking itself controversial.

A naked gaze forced the viewer's look to rebound onto itself, which may not make a pleasant picture. Consciously, unconsciously, viewers hold points of view and attitudes about what's pictured. If it is hard to look at or turn away from an Arbus photograph, it may be because viewers experience unwanted or unclear impulses—disgust, loathing, fascination. Arbus's photographs work with and against self-disguise.

Art-conscious characters know that, early in the twentieth century, Marcel Duchamp threw the seminal art screwball, but his work provoked a mostly sectarian response, testing institutional limits and aesthetics. Arbus's photographs ripped up the "benign-looking contract." There is no social contract anymore.

Do "others" see themselves as "other"? No, she or he is not marginal in his or her life. And, whoever "they" are, they probably view and shoot too. Anyone can "exploit" anyone on TV, and many do. So, "willing" or "unwilling" participation begs new ethical definitions. There's power, advantages . . . I'm looking for an elastic dictionary. Fortunately, it's football season in the US. But the concussions suffered in that game . . .

Don't Cry: Work

Thursday, July 12, 1973, 3 p.m.

The downstairs door is open. First sight is her smile at the top of the stairs. I enter Meret Oppenheim's studio and we shake hands. She makes me tea and says there is only bread for me to eat. I say I have already eaten. M.O. (she signs her work using her initials) doesn't want me to use a tape recorder on either visit (I make two) and I am now using my memory recorder which is not perfect of course.

Our first discussion has to do with Meret Oppenheim's refusal to show her work in a women's exhibit to be held in California. Her reason is that she does not want to separate from men but show with them. (Otherwise women act in the same "racist" way that they reproach in men.)

As preparation I had looked through books on surrealism to learn about Meret Oppenheim and her surrealism. I read of two pieces—*Fur Teacup, Saucer, and Spoon [Object]* (1936) and *Woman Served Up as a Sumptuous Banquet [Spring Feast]* (1959). The books say the fur teacup caused a scandal, was considered very shocking. I ask M.O. about this and she says, "People are easily shocked." She indicates that it was a kind of joke, and an expression of her rebellious nature, not really "serious" (so much for background material).

A story, an artwork, a joke, an idea can be interpreted in ways not intended. As for M.O.'s *Woman as Banquet* she stresses that there were three men and two women eating at that banquet held upon a naked woman (the third woman). It was not just men, not a naked woman for men only, but a fertility rite for women and men. A different Easter, M.O. says, With a different Christ, I say. And why a woman? Because, M.O. answers, woman is close to the earth . . . nurturence . . .

The studio is spacious but not vast. Very light. I sit facing Meret O. A small kitchen is behind her. We sit at a worktable. Thinking about the place now, I realize there were no inessentials, nothing to distract my attention.

At some point I take off my glasses, and Meret O. comments, That's much better. I joke, feeling embarrassed and complimented, What if it had been worse? We laugh and then Meret O. says, Yes, you could have hair where your eyes are.

Meret Oppenheim has made decisions in her life that strike me as coming from terrific strength. Not to marry at all or not until late in life, a decision made when she was seventeen. (When she did marry, she was thirty-five.) Not to continue living with someone twenty years older, a good painter, too, who might have "held up her development."

She tells me of a dream she had in 1972 in which she saw a collage by Duchamp. The next day she made it. Was it like a Duchamp, I ask. No, she laughs, he would never have made it.

Meret O. is a positive life force. Her energy. She may be sixty. I had felt tired before meeting M.O., and during our talk, that energy turns me on.

Before turning to the questions Carla Liss had prepared for all the artists in this issue to answer (if they wanted and in the way they wanted), Meret Oppenheim makes an extremely strong statement. It moves right into me. Yes, there are problems for women, she says, and uses her hands to underline, but we must work and not cry.

Saturday, July 14, 1973, 3 p.m.

It's Bastille Day. I return to Meret Oppenheim's studio and this time the downstairs door is shut. I ring and M.O. comes down. The children: she points.

During the first visit Meret O. had showed me some of her work. *The Secret of Vegetation* (1972) is a painting from a dream she had twenty years ago (normally, she doesn't use her dreams) of a woman friend standing, hidden by leaves. A long rectangle of light with green leaflike shapes and small light-colored rectangles around it (at second glance, I think of money, those small rectangles, and the dollar crisis). Two snakes are on either side of the long rectangle/monolith flowing like electric current, she explains. (Snakes don't have to be interpreted Freud's way, she adds.) I like the painting very much but Meret O. can't find a color photograph of it. It bores her, she says, to keep track of them.

I tell her that I really enjoyed my first visit. I ask her what she thinks of me. She liked it too; you are, she smiles, a young girl.

Meret Oppenheim has made a serial version of her fur teacup and saucer (*Souvenir de déjeuner en fourrure*, 1972). She had been asked "to do it again," and felt annoyed. But then she had the idea to turn it into a souvenir piece and so, satirizes her legend and the past. An edition of 120 fur teacups and saucers under convex glass with small flowers; she used frames she found at a tourist stand in the railroad station of Turin, Italy.

Meret Oppenheim has a way of taking something, turning it around, and finding a unique way of seeing.

She talks of Nietzsche and Schopenhauer. As a young girl she became very angry because of their attitudes toward women. Of course, she emphasizes, these things hurt us all. Nietzsche: When you meet a woman, carry a whip. Rather than continuing to be angry, M.O. thought. Perhaps these men have something to tell women, perhaps they are describing a certain condition that should be changed. Perhaps these kinds of criticisms are symptoms of a change, of the changing picture of what a woman is and what she could be. And while "these men" have "something to tell women," they have just as much need to tell themselves something, because "these men" are just as unconscious of the situation as women are in general. (As M.O. says this I feel, yes, why not turn things around, see something that has hurt in a different way, to move one to a different place rather than absorb it *as is*. Perhaps the interpretation of ideas can come like the interpretation of dreams. Ideas as openings. Even inimical ideas.)

My last question is about the 1930s. Was it so different. Meret O. smiles and says when you are fifty, people will ask you about this period. No, it is not so different. I have always been friends with artists and writers and it is the same, she says.

The last work she shows me is a puppet and four etchings she has made for a deluxe edition of Frank Wedekind's *Mine-HaHa or the Bodily Education of Girls*, written in the 1930s, now being translated from the German into French for Éditions Jean Petithory. *Mine-HaHa* satirizes the classical education for girls: dancing, music, sewing. Some people, M.O. says, don't realize it is satire. The girl-puppet she has made (which will be placed with the book in a box) has a small skirt, and if you pull the stick, her skirt goes up, revealing the pubic hair. On the puppet's belly is written—Ha Ha.

I invite Meret Oppenheim to visit me in Amsterdam. She might come if there is something worthwhile going on. I should send her information she says. I say goodbye and Meret O. says à bientôt.

I see her once again. My last night in Paris, I go to the Coupole and leave at two in the morning. I go for a taxi and there's Meret

Oppenheim getting into a taxi too. We say hello and goodbye again. Our taxis ride in the same direction, stop at the same red light, a man gets out of her taxi, and my taxi turns one way, and hers, another.

Meret Oppenheim has written her answers to the questions; the questions had been sent in advance. In our first meeting she read them to me, explicating them, and promised to make a better copy for publication. We wanted to print it in full.

Topics/Questions/Guidelines
Discuss all, some, one, (none); if relevant to what you want in your piece.

What are your primary concerns as expressed in your work. The mediums you use; why you've chosen them or how they've come to you.
The thing you want to do chooses its way to be done.

How does feedback (from public, critics, friends, lovers) affect your work.
Not at all. Only the artist himself knows (if he wants to!).

How has being a woman helped &/or hindered your career.
One cannot know it, just suppose. Concerning the "career" one has, as a woman, to accept encountering still more external difficulties (from the public). Between artists I never felt "discrimination."

What were your chances of exhibition then/now.
No difference. I never had difficulties in exhibiting.

Has the women's movement changed your work; in content; proliferation.
No difference.

Has being a woman consciously influenced your work.
Being a woman has not influenced my work. But I, too, had to overcome this old mental attitude. It is important to know that the impediment is in our mind. The big change has to go on there. We cannot ask men to change their attitude toward us. We have to change, we have "to think it over." All, in our personal way. Then things will change by themselves. It is much more than only an old prejudice to fight against. It is even not a prejudice at all. We, men and women, must become conscious that we are on the point of leaving a state, the patriarchal, which was very important for humanity to pass through. It does not, of course, treat of a return to the matriarchy, as some naive people say. This new direction of humanity asks as much effort from men as from women. All the intellectual acquisitions the male part of humanity made during some thousand years must be kept. (Women are intellectually on the same height—they have just to become aware of it—that's the work they have to do in the next time.) And then both together have to develop the qualities which had been neglected—to develop intellect—which is intuition, sensibility, and real wisdom.

The first state was matriarchal. And then the old big snake Nature in the Tree of Knowledge told Eve to give an apple to Adam. (She eats too!) The old snake Nature wanted him to take the way of intellectual development. Eve has been damned, and the snake with her—by men. (Men had to leave mother.)

Oblivion

The guys downstairs are smoking weed. It drifts up, powerful stuff. Last time I smoked, I was stoned for three days. Red wine is preferable: a few hours of forgetfulness.

I'm on the phone with a friend, discussing the downfall of our country. What's good for him is good for the country; he's General Motors in his head. A pathological narcissist, it's all him all the time. He's Putin's puppet. Putin tells him: Do as I did. Do good cop, bad cop, dismantle the government, divide and conquer. Trump is all ears, scant hair and eats it up, because Putin is the richest man in the world and wields power with smug indifference. My friend says: "Soon we won't be able to talk on the phone like this." Months ago, I would have rejected that as extreme. Now, I swallow the idea whole.

It's beautiful out, clear and cold. I have errands, walk toward the post office, and see six elderly men, Muslims, in front of the mosque around the corner. They're dragging big, heavy suitcases to a taxi, filling the trunk with them. I wonder: Are they fleeing America?

After November 8, 2016, it was dead quiet for days. Just like after 9/11. I get to the post office, send some mail, try not to picture the usual chaos in the hidden recesses of our notorious branch, "the worst in the US." Then go to my local little jewelry store, where the owner, born in Ecuador, a citizen for thirty years, asks his daughter to help me. The store's named after her, Kathy, and she tells me not to be sad, that good always conquers bad. I make a joke, she hugs me and exhorts: "We have to love, love, love." I smile wanly.

In the new year, I'll keep signing petitions. Don't know about love. Maybe drink less. Maybe drink more. Notably, I recently saw Andy Warhol's *Drunk aka Drink* (1965) in a digitally restored version, which hasn't ever been shown publicly. Warhol was great friends with the filmmaker Emile de Antonio, who died in 1989. In 1965, De, as he was called, agreed to be in one of Warhol's first films. He said he would drink an entire quart of scotch; Warhol could shoot that.

Warhol set the camera up high, at a stark angle to his subject. The camera looks down on De, the frame never changes, though the subject does, and Warhol must've known what would happen. De Antonio was a fierce drinker from a wealthy family. Warhol, from a poor family, did speed. Both were Pennsylvanians. Eight years older, De mentored Warhol. Warhol must have often seen De stupid drunk.

De is a larger-than-life figure, whose head, in the second half of the sixty-minute film, will fall out of the frame. But as Marilyn Monroe told the studio, when they didn't want to use a shot where the top of her head was cut off: "We've already established I have a head."

At first De plays to the camera, kind of winking at it, and at Warhol behind it, with beautiful, clever eyes, opening the bottle with a flourish. He's dramatic, acting for the camera. He pours the scotch, some club soda, tosses an ice cube into it, swirls it all with his index finger. More Scotch, he laughs at his own jokes and talks to Warhol, who walks off, himself laughing. "Self-conscious," De says to himself several times, as if surprised. Drunker, he crosses himself and prays in Latin. Midway into the bottle, De says how really smart Warhol is. Suddenly, it's a relationship film. De's giving Warhol a gift, exposing himself at his best and worst for the camera. Voluntarily exploiting himself, perhaps, for friendship, art. He believes in Warhol's unique talent. They are artists in a dialogue.

By the second half, De has become insensible. He collapses onto the ground, only his torso visible, his words stutters and clutters of moans. His torso turns into a face, his chest rising and falling; he is a body in a dark Andrea Mantegna painting. He is a spectacle. Disturbing, profound, *Drunk aka Drink*'s meanings are uncategorizable. A brilliant figure is an everyman, a lump of flesh, and the flesh is weak.

Days after it was shot, de Antonio told Warhol it could never be shown.

Art, even great art, can't save people from themselves or each other, but it can offer temporary consolation, an experience that speaks to the possibilities, the better parts of our species.

A Fictional Past

The inevitability of death doesn't make death less surprising, but rebukes the living for their gullibility. "He can't be dead," I thought about Stuart Hall, who died in February. Sigmund Freud wrote that nothing dies in the unconscious. And dead friends speak in dreams as they did in life. Humans are creatures constructed by time. Some individuals shift concepts and perceptions, remaking time-bound ideas. Death ended Hall's life, but like resonant endings in novels, it will bequeath other endings: The future holds new books about Stuart Hall, lectures, and conversations.

Conversation can be paradoxical and contradictory. Some can't find words. Writers notably complain, "Words fail me"—especially in consideration of the grim reaper. But, I muse: Words make us, how can they fail us?

There is an abundant misuse of language; then wrong meanings enter the language—for example, "impact" as a verb. "Between you and I" is the worst grammatical error around. When I hear it, I hold my tongue, mostly. Yet I'd want to know if I made a mistake, just as I'd want to know if a bit of lettuce was stuck to my cheek. Mentioned with feeling, of course.

David Hofstra, a bass player and my partner, once explained why a musician's movements were weird, awkward. "He's trying to feel the music," David said. The world of writing divides, from my POV, between those who feel it and those who don't. "I feel you" is a blessed idiom.

Many writers and readers are tone-deaf; and cultural discussions can be airless and flat. In the US, most book reviews don't ponder how a story has been written, or its reason for being. Instead, entire plots get recounted, so most reviews read like school term reports.

Here, supposed "hot topics" are: Is being difficult a bad thing (the self-named "challenging" writer as brat)? Can a woman write the Great American Novel? Is the GAN dead? (Yes, there is an acronym.)

The discussion of the GAN is significant only because it reflects the contemporary American condition: Questions about it refer to loss of empire, not literature. When Britain lost its empire, its sense of humor finally came to its aid. British self-deprecation and irony seem built into the nation's psyche. OK, I was raised an Anglophile, a religion whose god is subtlety and wit. "Taking the piss out" is surgery by British cleverness. (Some of their "best" novelists choke on their own vomit, or cleverness.)

Here in the US, the best political journalists are comedians, and the literary buzz comes DOA. So I come not to praise the Great American Novel but to bury it: The GAN was a war novel, conceived in war, a cultural by-product of America's new role as a dominant world power. The GAN shared cultural importance with abstract expressionism, both appearing toward the end of the war, partaking in the force of America's newfound prosperity, might, mission—to lead the Free World. (See Serge Guilbaut's 1983 book *How New York Stole the Idea of Modern Art*.)

The GAN was written by men who fought in World War II: James Jones (*From Here to Eternity*, 1951), Norman Mailer (*The Naked and the Dead*, 1948), Saul Bellow (*Dangling Man*, 1944). It was gendered, which was constitutive of the genre; this means a woman could write it, but then it wouldn't be the GAN. Here's Mailer: "I can only say that the sniffs I get from the ink of the women are always fey, old-hat, Quaintsy Goysy, tiny, too dykily psychotic, crippled, creepish, fashionable, frigid, outer-Baroque, *maquillé* in mannequin's whimsy, or else bright and stillborn. . . . A good novelist can do without everything but the remnant of his balls." The odd thing is that such idiotic ideas mutated into notions like "muscular style."

The Allies won the war, but the men who fought it were devastated, manned and unmanned both. That trauma underlies the GAN. One of many unconscious reasons for the resentment of women manifested in it might be that women didn't fight at the front, but birthed the men who did. (See Dorothy Parker's 1943 short story "The Lovely Leave," which trenchantly comments on the sullen divide between soldier-husband and stay-at-home wife.)

Recall US novels before World War II: Willa Cather, William Faulkner, F. Scott Fitzgerald, Mary McCarthy, Carson McCullers, Flannery O'Connor, John Steinbeck, Edith Wharton, et al. Let's say, in a bold or foolish stroke, that the conflicted, battered psychology of the GAN's protagonists dominate those novels; while earlier US novels focused less on an individual's torment, more on social unrest and discontent, society's effects on individual psychology.

Simply put, the GAN is a dated artifact: It is actually a time stamp. As the twenty-first century returns us to the end of the nineteenth, with empires up for grabs once again, and the twentieth century seems not to have happened, nostalgia wafts here for those good old days when America was top dog. But that version of America, its innocence and moral calling, is a historical fiction or ideal, depending upon one's POV, similar to dated concepts such as American exceptionalism, Manifest Destiny, the frontier thesis, and the American abroad.

"Can a woman . . . ?" and "Is it dead?" are dumb rhetorical questions. The GAN occupied its time and had its place. What Hall taught us is that culture is also political, ideology inherent in the art and writing people create. To moan about the "loss" of the GAN is to cry over spilled milk, and a fictional past. Who has the time?

The simultaneity of thunderstorms, droughts, wildfires, heat waves, the widest tornado on record, and flood after flood could deliver me to the Bible for metaphors. Disaster after disaster, natural like the aforementioned, though often affected by human machinations; and all-too-human, and inhuman, murder, rape, war. Multifarious, intermingled disasters make separating artificial from natural—irrelevant?

These extremes rendered Nik Wallenda's daring, netless, high-wire walk, 450 meters above the Grand Canyon, as ho-hum excitement. On TV, Wallenda looked tiny and strange, the canyon massive and imperturbable in the background. Man on a wire against the elements. It was very windy. He had to use everything he had, he said afterward, to stay up there. There's the death drive, I thought, in living color.

Motivation is fascinating. Being without motivation is also fascinating, but probably not for the unmotivated, since fascination is one aspect of motivation, and the unmotivated wouldn't experience it much. Also, they have a whole life ahead of them, with a lot of time and nothing they really want to do or achieve, which could be frustrating, making the meaninglessness of life more piquant. Or, they might be content lying around on a couch. Human society bends that way, too, with variances and all sorts of adaptations accepted. In a writing class, an eighteen-year-old student told me his interest in life was soccer. Playing? I asked. No, watching, he said. In a stadium? No, on TV, he said. Is that all you're interested in, really? He warily nodded. But that's not a disaster, it's a life.

Disasters are events out of the ordinary, but happening every day they seem more ordinary, too, just a part of life. Get used to it, people in the US say, get over it.

I would never describe a disaster as mediocre. The ordinary is also distinct from a mediocrity. Being mediocre requires an effort not to be ordinary, then failing. When I hear the term "ordinary people," always a mischaracterization, I reach for my remote. One night I did, and with petulant curiosity, turned to *The Voice*, the extraordinary ordinary (or vice versa) singing contest. On this night, it had narrowed to three contenders who each sounded like many famous but common-sounding singers, or mediocrities because they try harder. The three contestants were paid exuberant tribute by the judges and audience. Seeing this, I realized I was watching the "emperor's new clothes" version of a singing contest. People were crazily excited. I figured the winner had to be the smiling blonde girl, still in high school. She had everything, and that right amount of nothing much that made her perfectly ordinary, and perfect for the dream: "If she can do it, I can."

On *The Voice*, she sang for an audience of millions. How at ease, I thought, she looks onstage, which achievement—ease—is meant itself to be a modern-day miracle. The girl started to sing and imitated what hundreds of pop singers have modeled on TV since before her birth. There was no sense, to my eye, of her wanting to make something her own, just to do what everyone else did as well as she could. She had the moves down, handling the mic, doing the familiar gestures, and could add the usual trill and vibrato here and there. The voice was a sweet, unmemorable voice, a voice like so many voices. I didn't watch to the end, the outcome seemed clear, and she won a day or so later.

Franz Kafka's short story "Josephine the Singer, or the Mouse Folk" (1924) begins with these sentences: "Our singer is called

Josephine. Anyone who has not heard her does not know the power of song." Kafka often starts his human mysteries with a declaration, giving readers a reason to believe in the reality of the story to come. The people who worship Josephine's singing "are quite unmusical," but, Kafka continues, her singing is so magnificent "even the most insensitive cannot be deaf to it." A paragraph later, he sets up a barrier to the first statements: "Among intimates we freely admit to one another that Josephine's singing, as singing, is nothing out of the ordinary." A few lines later: "Is it in fact singing at all?" This tale tells so much, is about so much, I wouldn't try to sum it up. Kafka doesn't allow for summation. His contradictions and self-mocking knowingness also deny me the possibility of telling you the story. The story can't be told. Rather, I want to say, hesitantly, that the story, in part, describes the conditions in which a singer, an artist, and her public, or her people, rely, in a profound sense, upon each other for meaning, joy, cohesiveness, all certainty of which is impossible, and standardless. What Josephine "wants," Kafka writes near the end, "is public, unambiguous, permanent recognition of her art, going far beyond any precedent so far known." Kafka understood futility. What a joke. Then he kept writing.

Whatever else it is, and it is many things, "Josephine the Singer, or the Mouse Folk" is one of the greatest works of art criticism ever written. At the least, the most alert and sensitive.

Real Life and Living Memory

The twentieth century turned anxiously into the twenty-first—Y2K doomsday. Computers, it was feared, would implode, and before 2000, feverish nations spent millions to avoid this catastrophe, which didn't happen, but a year into the century, it did—9/11. The Towers came down, so-called ordinary Americans randomly attacked Muslims, and George W. Bush, Dick Cheney, and Donald Rumsfeld launched a preemptive, disastrous war against Iraq, which had nothing to do with 9/11.

While 9/11's detritus blew in the wind, polluting lungs, the photography editor Alice Rose George and others curated a pop-up gallery in SoHo to display 9/11 pictures. Amateur and professional disaster photographs covered the walls. Easily taken, easily deleted, cell phone pictures were instant, and instantly blurred categories. In them, the decade found its avatar.

In 1991, cell phone technology evolved from analog to digital. Photoshop, released a year earlier, would prove subversive, by inciting ex post facto image remakes. Many artists embraced the software's possibilities, though some photographers resisted it. Their arguments emanated from a commitment to or belief in a photograph's inherent integrity. The original image was felt to have an essence, which should be spared manipulation. That same argument has also addressed digital art forms—that is, manipulation itself has been regarded as somewhat sinister.

Facebook launched in 2004, YouTube in 2005, Twitter in 2006, and Instagram in 2010, all still popular today but for how much longer. Platforms and devices enter homes like new animal companions; but every obsolescence or death, unlike that of a pet's, is welcomed. Obsolescence will bring something better.

In the first decade of the twenty-first century, high-def TV replaced most broadcast analog TV, and digital photography took seed and flowered. Working digitally allowed invention during and after. And its seductive immediacy—no need to wait for an image to emerge in its cloudy chemical bath. Most obviously, photography was no longer a modernist endeavor, since light was not needed to develop an image. In addition, a photograph as an entity, as a thing, did not matter, and would not unless photographers made a photograph's ontology their focus. And many did. Digitalization is now studied as an aspect of post-postmodernism or meta-postmodernism. The bases of classical photography were shattered.

Already laboring under the proverbial glut of images, art photographers and artists were confronted by an exponential tsunami of them. In this decade, an ongoing debate was fomented: What is a photograph? What is its status now? Where is the field? (In those heady days, some artists whose work I describe here appeared in *Aperture*'s pages.)

Barbara Kruger, whose "words and pictures," as she describes her practice, keep changing the face of art, began by doing physical pasteups of found images, and now produces her art digitally across many media. Multiscreen videos are assembled on a computer; works sent as files will be manufactured as vast vinyl prints for specific sites, then installed on walls, floors, ceilings, and stairs. The words and pictures will be in perpetual motion, restless as the contemporary moment.

James Welling dove into digital explorations in the summer of 1998. His first series, *Tricolor*, a group of digital color inkjet prints, was scanned from three black-and-white negatives. In 2000, the final images of his second group of *New Abstractions* (1998–2000) were produced digitally and printed on chromogenic paper. Welling keeps materiality, physical presence, alive, by engaging with photography's historical modes, its possibilities, along with its new technologies.

Zoe Leonard is probably best known for her massive ten-year project *Analogue* (1998–2009), which documents a vanishing New York, especially Lower Manhattan's storefront facades and displays. Her timeless project about a lost time also comments on the vanishing of analog photography. Leonard still works primarily with analog processes, but for a recent work, *In the Wake* (2016), she used an iPhone to shoot old family photographs. She says it was "not a replacement for analog but a different way of thinking and making work. . . . It was a way of working that was immediate and physical."

Leslie Hewitt's works in the series *Riffs on Real Time* (2002–2009)—found images of families and those from popular culture—are composited visual narratives. Her art transgresses disciplinary boundaries, sometimes incorporating sculpture, further amplifying the piece's physical presence, like an installation. Hewitt's pictorial narratives breach timelines, representing family and history as layers of images, words, events, the collision of past and present.

LaToya Ruby Frazier's contemporary photographs of her family and neighborhoods under stress might seem taken in a different time. She photographs primarily with black-and-white film and typically uses three medium-format cameras. Frazier is close to her subjects—her friends and family—and aims for intimacy. In her prints, as in those of Roy DeCarava, Black skin and Blackness are tonally complex, like the individuals and scenes she portrays. The color black is never a background for something else.

Color is meant to show real life—real life is in color. In Frazier's photographs, real life is also in black and white and includes living memory. Stories and histories seem imprinted on faces and in gestures; people appear to be remembering something, daydreaming, having unbidden thoughts. Her photographs outwit reality, the way dreams and memory do. Though denoting, in a sense, her mother's and her lived realities, the photographs connote interpretive, psychological spaces.

To outwit photography's historical motive—to show what is there—informs Trevor Paglen's innovative and speculative photography. He portrays the unseen, for instance, secretive military bases—or what is not easily seen. He pictures the impossible microscopic, while photographers generally show the macroscopic—what is visible yet not noticed until framed differently. Taking pictures of spy satellites through a telescope, with the use of repetitions and magnifications, Paglen contests visuality as it is performed by traditional photography. Its information is questionable, he suggests, because what you are shown might hide "realities," not reveal them. What should be in plain sight is not, and what is cannot be trusted.

Technological change brings new choices, and choice can bring consternation. In every art form, the new, usually called an advance, bedevils the old and stirs up new doubts. People, artists, wonder about the loss of materiality, what it will lead to. If it all happens inside a machine, where is touch, tangibility. By sending a text, not phoning, the voice, its variety of tones and subtle meanings, will lose its significance. How will meanings, this novelist worries, be carried, what makes a text's message clear—probably an emoji.

It is no surprise that the term "embodiment" has, in the past fifteen years, invaded art discourse. Where is the body? Is it in a text? Maybe it's why people, often women, regularly expose so much more of their bodies. It's not that ours is a less puritanical society; I'd argue that, with so much pornography on screens, the human species might need to flaunt its physical availability.

Older people shake their heads, no. Young people grow up in the new, which is not new to them, it's normal. Born into it, no one chooses their moment; and it will be natural to them. Aesthetic choices come down to what's available, to ideas, and to feeling, the way musicians feel their instruments. Sometimes it just feels better to photograph with one kind of camera; sometimes an artist adds an element, picks up a different device. But moralistic thinking about aesthetics and technologies appears inevitable.

Is it good for the world, for people? The invention of fire, was it good for people? In the artist Hito Steyerl's 2009 essay "In Defense of the Poor Image," she writes, "The poor image is a rag or a rip. . . . It transforms quality into accessibility, exhibition value into cult value." This thing, this tattered entity, holds something. It's called information, that is, the image isn't important, what it shows is, evidence maybe, a trace maybe. Degraded images have their place. Glossy or tawdry, well made or desiccated, images circulate massively, and will only accumulate. Often I wonder what photographs are for, and why I look at them. A photograph is not a witness or a document, it's unreliable, it's a there, it's a not there, or there's no there there. Still, I seek something in it.

The first decade of the twenty-first century started with a national trauma turned global, and now everyone says these are transitional times, into what no one knows. Intimations are here. Drastic events carry consequences beyond what we can discern. There will be, and is, denial. Inexplicable and unforeseeable events will produce new conditions, technologies, experiences, and incite new art. The bases for judgment and criticism will undergo upheaval, also; standards will, necessarily, have to change.

In the 1930s, Bertolt Brecht wrote plays to instruct his audience about their true condition, reality as it was. His assumption: He knew what reality was, and he knew it better than his audience did. Maybe he did understand the political situation better than most, but it's a perilous position. I can't think of a contemporary self-conscious artist who would think that now. I would hope not.

Feeling Tuymans

> Each painting demands a specific kind of execution, and Luc Tuymans seems to be willing to execute the paintings differently from each other. He's not controlled by one technique.
> —Brice Marden, in *Luc Tuymans: Exhibitions at David Zwirner*[1]

The work in *The Barn*, Luc Tuymans's New York exhibition, hung in three spacious rooms, several paintings in each room. And each work was different and distinctive. To study them required an appreciation and understanding of their possible relationships caused by their contiguity, themes, style. Together, an idiosyncratic family of Tuymans's art produced a remarkable edifice, a house for contemplation about art, artifice, feelings, and ideas.

Viewers impose meanings on what they see, feel drawn to the art or confounded, perplexed or satisfied by it, while unbidden and unexpected emotions drive and overcome simple reasoning, stimulated in a part of the brain called the sensorium: "The supposed seat of sensation, the place to which impressions from the outside world are transmitted and perceived. The sensorium also means the whole sensory apparatus of the body."

Emotions affect perception and can cause bewildering differences in response, an aspect of subjectivity, and, to this viewer, an extremely significant determinant in how people see, love or hate, fear or welcome art. Too often emotions are excised from the process, because they can't be reasonable, and if emotions enter into seeing, they might cloud vision. But in actuality, they are an indelible component of vision, of how people view and make judgments, which are also involuntarily arrived at. Tuymans's work, each individual painting in *The Barn*, is charged with and provokes emotions, and causes looking to be another kind of aesthetic experience, an intimate one, one not easy to articulate. His work is not easy to assimilate.

> I work from a reaction upon images that are already represented because I believe nothing is really original. But then I have to make my take on it—and figuration in that sense becomes rather abstract, because everybody can have different connotations.
> —Luc Tuymans, in "As Far as Luc Tuymans Is Concerned, Nothing Is Original"

Tuymans "works from a reaction" to images, so his emotions must be embodied in his approach to his paintings, and I believe this embodiment can be felt in how he paints them.

As a fiction writer, I appreciate Tuymans's "take" as a refusal to editorialize. In his art, he doesn't underline his meanings, doesn't enunciate his intention or point of view, which might tell a viewer how to react or what to think. His appeal to the viewer is to take a second or third look, which will recharge the painting with a new slant, often one more disturbing than might have first been thought. His painterliness produces beauty and questions beauty: It is about, I think, the surface of art in tension with its possible meanings. Tuymans is not complacent about the history of his medium. He knows it well. His paintings can refer to that long, contentious past.

Let's say Tuymans's paintings take a dive beneath their painted surfaces.

One of Tuymans's subjects in *The Barn* is Bob Ross, a familiar American TV figure who taught people how to make a painting, very simply. He brushed a few dabs of green here or there on a small canvas—look, there's a forest—or dotted dabs of blue and white on it, clouds in a sky.

Ross stands in a diagonal from the viewer, partly obscured by his placement, holding a palette. A purplish-black background envelops him and the other objects, all of which appear to be planted flatly, stuck onto a flat surface: They could be peeled off. Ross might be a cutout from a magazine pasted on pages in a scrapbook. His signature bouffant orange hair is colorful against the darkness, while orange is reiterated behind his easel as indeterminate geometric shapes.

Oddly, or not, I want to liken Bob Ross at his easel to the painter in *Las Meninas*, also at his easel. A large canvas on an easel, its back to the viewer, is in the foreground on the left of *Las Meninas*; a dark-haired, vivacious painter, who may or may not be Velázquez, is in full sight, standing with brush and palette in hand. He might be painting *Las Meninas*, in which case *Las Meninas* is a metapainting. That painting is not visible, but Tuymans allows the viewer to see Ross's canvas: an orange-brown landscape, it seems, abstract at this point, a product of his simple technique.

Tuymans investigates authorship, for one, the infernal question posed by modern and postmodern theorists, such as Walter Benjamin, Roland Barthes, and Michel Foucault, which includes questioning the sanctity of the original. Tuymans's statement "I believe nothing is really original. But then I have to make my take on it" is significant. Bob Ross's program ignores the high-art wish for originality and promotes the notion that anyone can make a "good" painting. Ross's TV practice encouraged amateur paintings, or what Warhol wanted to call his work: Common Art, not pop art. Ross's own paintings have become valuable for their meaning in popular culture: "A painting from the very first episode of Bob Ross's *The Joy of Painting* could be yours, but not for cheap. Titled *A Walk in the Woods*, the piece is listed at $9.85 million and could be the most expensive and historically resonant Ross piece to ever be sold," according to NPR.

So, Tuymans has painted a figure of irony, a wry commentary on high art, and ultimately a take on his own place in art history. In my conversation with Brice Marden, he said he saw Tuymans as "a figural painter who is making a valid contemporary statement, which . . . also has to do with the work's social and political content."

Tuymans's portrait of Condoleezza Rice, *The Secretary of State* (2005), is a strange and powerful picture of a powerful woman. Tuymans's "take"—he did take an original photograph to use for his work—is far from psychological, revealing nothing of her character. She is expressionless or enigmatic—a factotum of the state and as impersonal as her office.

In *The Barn*, a faceless face, *Abe* (2022), just an outline, is a face to be filled in, also a factotum; any face can fit in the space. Haunting, stripped of features, this ghost face could provoke a fear of erasure, of nonbeing. Will I remember him? His face? It's already a blur.

A portrait of absence can stand for everyone and no one: for the forgotten, for anonymous others whose anguish will never be personal, whose life was unimportant to historians. Anonymity relates also to the demise of the Author, since when a viewer/reader creates the text, author, authority, and identity become an even more contested space and, concomitantly, a less significant one.

Anonymity is apt and true to the human experience. Most people will die unknown outside of family and friends, and soon forgotten, gone as if never having existed. Facelessness accompanies death's aftermath, and Tuymans's paintings haunt that reality. Even a very famous artist in his time will be forgotten in another. Who will be remembered is a crapshoot. Of course, I think, Tuymans is musing about immortality: Some artists wonder, they do, especially as they age (and who doesn't), what will happen to their life's work. Tuymans is realistic, he certainly reads history, and seems amused by the question.

Most of Tuymans's paintings rely, in a sense, on recall, what is remembered and what is forgotten and therefore lost. His paintings will bring back "the dead." To remember Bob Ross, a place visited, a barn, a face, or any place—much can't be brought back or is more like a trace or can be imagined. Tuymans's paintings signal to memory's displacements.

Tuymans's titles, his use of single words, shape and reshape his images, shifting meaning—a fascinating, ingenious aspect of his approach.

His portrait of an old-fashioned rotary telephone, *Vilnius* (2023), is curious. It refers, only minimally, to pop art, picturing a common object like a Brillo box. Painted so differently, in feeling and with texture, *Vilnius* romanticizes its subject, protected in the recess of a wall. It feels kind of dreamy, and, if set in, for instance, a hotel room, proffers fantasy: Is a lover on the other line? Is he or she waiting to hear?

The title *Vilnius* associates the telephone to a city and time that is far from romantic, especially to people who remember or read history. They will know that the Nazis occupied Lithuania, whose citizens were "willing executioners" and, with rifles provided by the Germans, shot Jewish citizens hiding in the forest. After the war, Lithuania was occupied by the Soviet Union for forty years. (In fact, Tuymans photographed a telephone—without a dial—that connected those occupiers directly to the Soviet Union.)

I visited Vilnius eight years ago and was struck by how the Lithuanians I spoke with denied the Holocaust and their role in it; they only mentioned their victimization by the Germans and then the Soviets. Tuymans refers, I imagine, to that denial and terrible history. Is my association rational or emotional? I think both. Otherwise, I think, why title the portrait of a by now antique phone *Vilnius*?

The situation in *Bucha* (2023) is the war in Ukraine, and, like the title *Vilnius*, this title changes the image and augments it with a different legibility. Tuymans paints white rectangular shapes in the center, the shape of a man, also white, on the right side of the painting behind a light stand. The whiteness of the shapes is caused by a camera flash or the harsh lighting for film.

Tuymans had taken news footage of the Russian-occupied city, where shallow graves of civilians and prisoners of war were found in 2022, a contemporary atrocity. On the right side of the painting, there's an icon indicating more pictures to come. And, transformed by the name Bucha, the painting now represents ghostly figures, a scene of death and war crimes, the white shapes, corpses and coffins. The person in white, dressed in protective clothing, vulnerable to disease and death.

With a bit of text, Tuymans charges his paintings with his take: This place is haunted, history is replete with ghosts and with terrible crimes. Viewers will "see" it in another perspective, the image like a palimpsest hiding what lurks beneath. Using language, he transforms his paintings into text-and-image works. With such a loaded title, a viewer must, or will, do a retake.

Engaged in history, whether it's a painting of a cultural object or political figure, Tuymans's representation of painful historical events has been controversial: He proposes they are open to interpretation. To return to the horror of an event, I'd suggest, if rendered as horrific as that event was—say, mangled bodies, people hanging from trees in the forest—might engender a single reading. Tuymans's predilection for ambiguity places meaning and specifically affect squarely on a viewer.

Looking at the portrait of Patrice Lumumba, an African nationalist leader and first prime minister of the Democratic Republic of the Congo, could awaken a memory of his assassination soon after independence, in January 1961. Years later, it was documented that his murder was carried out primarily by the CIA; during the Cold War the CIA believed Lumumba was a Communist threat.

Studying any history drags you into muddy waters. A didactic, instantly legible work can be reductive: Representations of the past are not fact or fiction, but some odd interruption of and intervention into both. The past cannot be presented as fact only, since facts require context and interpretation; by itself a fact cannot provide a narrative—why it happened, for one; who caused it—about which historians fiercely debate. Nothing is reliably what it appears to be; in themselves, paintings are unreliable narrators.

Walking around Tuymans's New York exhibition, I came upon a surprising painting, *Smiley* (2022): a partially deflated, small yellow balloon floating on a pastel background. Its string detached from a hand, the balloon slightly off-center.

Strangely, this cartoonish smiley face—two black dots for eyes, a swipe of black paint for a mouth—appeared downcast, sad, to me. It's a pathetic object: Smiley faces really are, since they contradict the possibility of tragedy.

What to make of it? This smiley face, popular culture's vote for happiness and coziness, born in the 1950s, has remained one of the world's most popular ideograms and emoticons.

Tuymans's good-sized painting of the balloon is poised against a beautiful background, with an aura encircling it. This pathetic yellow thing—artifice planted on supposed nature. Artifice, not artificial. The smiley face is cunning and deceptive, akin to the current mawkish, annoying American phrase "It's all good." Smiley faces and that phrase erase common realities: Life is not always happy, and life is not all good. In Tuymans's painting, the yellow balloon may be reaching for the heavens, when hellish war and famines on earth defeat peace of mind. A smiley face is its opposite, a picture of prosaic irony.

Irony is a double-edged commentary, and Tuymans performs these ironic takes on popular culture—pertaining to Bob Ross also—not as dismissals but to illustrate their ambivalent meanings in society. How do we perceive such objects; why has Tuymans painted a deflated balloon?

I think, whimsically, Who hasn't felt deflated?

Thousands of portraits of the well known and well born hang in great museums and collections. Their faces may be compelling, their expressions, their costumes, and their surroundings inform contemporary viewers about the period. How those portraits are painted matters, often not who the people are; who painted them matters. The portraits represent an attitude, a position in life, the moneyed, the aristocracy, important political and artistic figures of the time. Of these mysterious, long-dead beings, I wonder: What did they think about, what were their lives like? I rarely wonder were they happy or content.

These paintings attend to the times in which they appeared, while Tuymans's portraits of a person or a thing complicate that kind of representation. What do they mean—in themselves, perhaps nothing, and there's an inference that nothing in art can be inherently meaningful. Take the portrait of Lumumba: If no one remembers his fight against colonialism, his assassination, his portrait is not meaningful. It is an image with its own affective meanings to a viewer.

The Frame (2023) cannily embraces all these paintings. *The Frame* frames his New York show, a painting about art-making. Brice Marden said of Tuymans that he "doesn't seem to apply technique;

somehow [his work] grows out of the situation." This could refer to *The Frame*, to the situation in which art finds itself now.

The word "frame" has several denotations and connotations and, not to be pedantic, it's a terrifically resonant title. What frames the discourse about art, and whose ideas about art frame how one looks at it. It is, to me, clear that I look at art through a frame based on what I have learned and seen of it.

The sociologist Erving Goffman first used the term broadly, in his revelatory 1974 book *Frame Analysis*, and brought the concept of framing into his field: Framing guides how people interpret or process information. So, what people call reality is actually many realities structured by different frames, intellectual, social, cultural constructs. It is why people "get" something or don't, say, in art.

Tuymans's painting of a frame is a conceptual conundrum. I, or you, might see everything that isn't there. The painting is all angles, the frame appears to jut forward from, on the right side, a dark gray wall, a salmon-pink wall behind it on the left. The silvery-gray frame is perched on a salmon-pink shelf, and looks old; glass to protect the unseeable painting reflects light, sunlight, and makes shapes. The absence inside a frame reminds me of a very witty and insightful retort about art. A naive friend looked at a picture of a Warhol Campbell's soup can, and said, "This is stupid." A wiser friend said, "What you expect to see there is just as stupid."

What do people want from art? To be edified, provoked, have an epiphany, find beauty consoling, be in thrall to the sublime, be distracted, or inspired? Tuymans's work, for one, interrogates art's function and a spectator's expectations, and, of course, this raises existential questions.

> Let us not waste our time in idle discourse! Let us do something, while we have the chance! It is not every day that we are needed. Not indeed that we personally are needed. Others would meet the case equally well, if not better. . . . What are we doing here, *that* is the question. . . . Yes, in this immense confusion one thing alone is clear. We are waiting for Godot to come.
>
> —Vladimir, in Samuel Beckett, *Waiting for Godot*

Things and ideas change about almost everything but existential questions. In the Bible, Job's first question to God was "Wherefore was I born?" (Job 3:11). In *Waiting for Godot*, Vladimir and Estragon exist "in this immense confusion," the human condition, waiting for God/ot to explain their living internment. About our time, it is repeated: We live in a glut of images. The present image miasma turns into the past immediately; the miasma's future will be known and represented, ultimately, in images and words. The glut augments the general contemporary confusion, and Tuymans plucks and pulls from it to situate his work within and about life now.

Tuymans contends with the consequential and the inconsequential, even silly passing objects, that persist in the unconscious mind, cluttered like a hoarder's house. Tuymans's quasi- or semi-figurative, near-abstract paintings beckon the anxiety of ambiguity. With all his paintings' ironies, provocations, ambiguities, Luc Tuymans is not, I believe, jaded or fatalistic. His work, to me, sometimes feels like that of a beleaguered romantic, who is not angry but worried. In its beauty, its lushness, it can be melancholic the way beauty is, because beauty fades.

No mirror to the soul but to existential doubts, Tuymans's contemplative and startling paintings address the world, and what Freud called "ordinary unhappiness." They draw me in, always. To quote Yvonne Rainer, "Feelings are facts," they are not to be disregarded or dismissed. I look at paintings by Luc Tuymans, I don't know how to describe my first sensations, inchoate emotions. I experience them, sometimes thrown by a feeling I can't articulate. I just want to say, I feel them.

Note

1 The full citation for this quotation is Brice Marden, "Brice Marden in Conversation with Lynne Tillman," in *Luc Tuymans: Exhibitions at David Zwirner*. Rev. ed. (Brussels: Ludion, 2013), p. 26. Subsequent quotes from Marden are from this conversation.

Blue Shores

I

These photographs are, ostensibly, different:
a blue, shuttered used-clothing store;
a blue car parked on a street and a bank in the background;
twenty blue Adirondack chairs scattered on a spacious green lawn; and,
a blue-and-white-striped restaurant facade.

In each but the photograph with twenty chairs, windows figure inside the frame. The bank and car have windows; both storefronts do. But none is there to see through, as if transparent, none is what a photograph once was called, a window into the world. Instead, the windows are covered, partially blocked, or opaque.

Looking at the used clothing store, I can imagine a story for it:

A twenty-four-year-old man standing in front of it. He's just walked a few miles into the small city, because he needed food for a week, a new pair of Nikes. Maybe he wanted to see people, though the city looked deserted. Weird. He didn't want to make friends, that would happen, he didn't want to make things happen, because the right thing would come along. Fate. He relied on chance.

An abandoned clothing store sat lonely on a side street, shut down tight and shabby. There was something sad about it. He stood there for a long while. The blue-painted storefront kept everything hidden. No interior life. Funny, he thought. Blue is a sad color. A kitten emerged from a hole in the wall, or from nowhere. And he picked her up. Tiny, she meowed. I'll call her Blue, he thought, and put her on his shoulder. He knocked on the door of the store and then on the window, and waited to hear movement inside. Maybe someone still lived there, and this was her kitten.

This isn't what the photograph represents; still, I could pin the narrative to its surface, like an ornament. There is no inherent story in the photograph, other than its composition.

In a blue 1970s car, the head of a man, on the passenger side, is visible; his right arm sticks out an open window, elbow resting on the car door. The man may be waiting for a friend, or the driver is beside him in the car, stopped at a red light. Will there be a bank robbery?

Man + waiting car + bank = a story.

The blue car is angular, sleek, long, and its metal detailing, which stretches across its sides, is designed to suggest the future ahead. Ahead, the bank, majestic and stony, stands in the background, dwarfing the car, pale-blue sky above.

A blue car in the foreground, a blue sky above and in the background. A monumental bank, a massive shape, a neutral color, contrasts to the blue car; their scale is extremely different, their placement inside the frame exaggerates the bank's dominance. It dwarfs the car. The eye cycles between car and bank, maybe to adjust to their visual dissimilarity. The empty streets create an open space, while the dark telephone poles and black electrical wires, crossing and intersecting, construct more shapes and planes.

This is not a picture of a car and bank, but a picture with them.

On a lush green lawn, the blue Adirondack chairs are welcoming, maybe a guest will appear soon. Each chair is also a common, everyday sculpture. And each chair suggests the presence of an absent individual or represents one.

It feels especially still, this image. The chairs, suspended in time, appear to be waiting to perform their function. The scattering of the color blue on a green background, color on color, creates its own palette.

Stephen Shore's photograph is a picture of quiet, blue resting on green, a serene composition.

The steak restaurant's facade is a pattern of blue, pale blue, and white stripes, blue and white rectangles beneath. Behind the rectangular windows, there is darkness. The windows only barely reflect the exterior, the space in front of the restaurant. The building is box-shaped, its entryway dark, almost ominous. Above its dizzying op art–like facade, a stormy blue-gray sky hangs. A dark-red diagonal across the restaurant's white sign, which juts out from above the entryway, jars the eye. BEER is also in red.

I don't know of another Shore photograph like this one. It relies on the patterns, almost like a Matisse painting of textiles, to make a picture of lines and shapes in movement.

The play of blue and its placement in all of these photographs pulled them together in my mind. Visually, they related to each other. Though Shore's strategy with blue varies significantly—planes of blue; stripes; lines; squares; rectangles, shades of color, and sizes and shapes of blue objects—a color in relationship to other colors, and on its own, shaped the compositions.

II

Along with other "serious" photographers, in the 1960s, when Shore came of age, he shot in black and white. Before the 1970s, color photography was regarded as pedestrian, meant for amateurs and family snapshots. Art photography was in black and white.

Black and white, with which photography began and which was a necessity, over time became its virtue. Life is in color, familiar, expected. People are surrounded by color. Color is what people see, even if they don't notice it: colors of street signs; trees; flowers; faces, eyes, hair. Lawns are green or brown if parched; oceans gray-green, with white, furling waves. White snow blankets mountains or falls on city streets, transforming a city until cars ruin the scene, leaving dirty fumes on the white mounds, or dogs urinate yellow on them.

If color entered the field, photography would be even more like reality, and further from being considered art. Strange now that the presence of color was feared, that it would negate the medium's artfulness.

Throughout its short history, photographers have fought for their medium to be considered an art, not just a visionless recording of what appeared in front of a camera lens. Anyone couldn't take a great picture. A photograph wasn't just about mimesis.

When Stephen Shore and William Eggleston, famously ignoring the art/amateur dilemma, took up color, they demonstrated that a color photographer who paid attention to life, to so-called ordinary scenes, a breakfast plate or a theater marquee, could transform reality. Color could make the familiar unfamiliar, or color would be noticed, recognized, by insisting on its value within a frame. It depended upon the photographer to find the composition and to reorganize how people recognize what they ordinarily see, but don't see, differently. To value it, differently.

In these blue Shores, the apparent, or manifest, content provides objects, identifiable things, to look at, but what shapes the objects into pictures is their composition, framing, and the color blue. Shore's subject matter is primarily the formal elements that determine pictures, that make a photograph into a picture. It's how I, in my nonexpert way, decide when I recognize a work as a work of art.

Maybe I can explain that best, though it isn't an explanation but an association, with an excerpt from Wallace Stevens's poem "The Man with the Blue Guitar":

> The man bent over his guitar,
> A shearsman of sorts. The day was green.
>
> They said, "You have a blue guitar,
> You do not play things as they are."
>
> The man replied, "Things as they are
> Are changed upon the blue guitar."
>
> And they said then, "But play, you must,
> A tune beyond us, yet ourselves,
>
> A tune upon the blue guitar
> Of things exactly as they are."

The poem reminds me of these photographs, and what color is, and how it expresses and is also inexpressible or different from any articulations about it. The poem says something about blue, as Derek Jarman's film *Blue* did also. Maybe it's best for me just to say that a photograph never completely or adequately shows what it is.

Invitation to *The Visitor*

This is the saddest story I have ever heard.

The first sentence of Ford Madox Ford's formidable novel *The Good Soldier* is perhaps hubristic or exaggerated, but his opening gambit is tremendously effective. It has remained in my mind since I read it. "The saddest story."

Reading *The Visitor* (c. 1940s), I kept recalling that phrase. This may be one of the saddest I have ever read. In Maeve Brennan's stark novel, there is no forgetting, no forgiving.

The prodigal daughter, Anastasia, comes home, and Brennan's depiction of a homecoming trounces plots of renewal and redemption, rejecting every cliché about a welcomed return. The Visitor's return can only be a visit to a house consumed by resentment and the dead. The living are, in a sense, dead also, at the least, dead to each other.

What makes Brennan's novel compelling is its story, yes, but also, and most important, the way it is written. The reader is not supplied "a back story," which writing workshops insist must be clearly set out. No, the story is learned by indirection and inference, and remains mysterious, with as many clues as readers need to know and no more. The father is recently dead, and one of Anastasia's reasons for returning home. Many years before, the mother had left him, taking young Anastasia with her. They flee to Paris—where literary characters, writers, and artists have run—and she dies there. Anastasia's father's mother, her grandmother, still lives in that hollow family house with her housekeeper, Katharine.

Without a cause-and-effect plot, the novel's movements are sometimes inexplicable, nothing is simple, and all of it unusual.

The characters might have behaved differently, which Brennan encourages readers to recognize, as she stages a family tragedy with disturbing subtlety and consequence. What is often called fate.

The novel is as complicated as anyone's lived reality, though far from a realist, kitchen-sink drama. Brennan's psychological novel articulates a cruelty particular to families, such as the fear of abandonment. The grandmother is relentless in blaming Anastasia. Their sadomasochistic dialogue isn't unusual to unhappy families, though rarely rendered in such beautiful language and with such exquisite style.

> "You are trying to drive me mad," she said distinctly. "I wish to God, and wish this every day of my life, that you would go away and leave me alone here. You cry, you're forever opening a door and coming into the room where I happen to be at the moment, and so on and on—"
>
> "I don't mean it."

Anastasia cannot defend herself, and, like any ingenuous masochist she hopes to please and appease her grandmother. In some quarters, this would be called "masochistic hope." You, reader, will want to have hope for her.

Brennan's thinking and attitudes arrive in surprising syntax and words. In this way her writing reminds me of Jean Rhys's, not because it is similar in style, but because with a few choice adjectives, each quickly shifts a mood from one sensation to another. Both writers attend to the ambiguities of friendship and love.

Anastasia's intense, uncanny interior monologue occurs throughout the novel, and, as she walks around the house again, she remembers its walls, rooms, and her young life in it: "Every turn in the stairs was a new blackness." Brennan's sharp turn left me breathless with admiration. That blackness, darkness in the rooms, is metaphorical and actual, and with "blackness" Brennan creates a duet of meanings.

When she was a child, Anastasia tells us, she used to "steal away from the fire and hide herself behind the heavy window curtains." Now as she moves around that same room, she walks to those curtains: "There was no one standing behind the curtains."

Again, a Brennan sentence stopped me. I felt its gravity, the weight of Anastasia's troubled mind. Anastasia doesn't see herself there. Then *The Visitor* turned into a ghost story without hyperbole, one that wasn't trying to be one, like a person who is funny without trying to be funny and more funny because of that.

Anastasia hopes and hopes. Katharine, the longtime housekeeper and companion to the grandmother, is kind to her as well as to an elderly and sick neighbor to whom Anastasia pays a visit. Brennan occasionally takes Anastasia off her grandmother's hook, allowing her, and readers, a brighter moment: The two women bolster her spirits, a respite from her grandmother's absolute emotional indifference.

What goes on in Anastasia's mind after each crushing incident, and how she apprehends it, perplexed and fascinated me. No psychoanalysis to aid her, she doesn't understand the aggression and can't do anything differently, the way any tragic hero cannot.

Anastasia's character unfolds, the story goes on, and she and it move into even stranger terrain.

I won't tell you more. Many introductions, from my point of view, while worthwhile and informative, tell a little too much. Their writers can't stop themselves, which I understand completely. This is Brennan's only novel, and there is much more to be said.

I had heard of her, but hadn't read any of her work, and now I can look forward to reading her stories and essays. To me, there's nothing more pleasurable than to know a great writer's work awaits you.

So, please consider this an invitation to read *The Visitor*. When you do you might wonder at the tale, the "whys" and "hows" of it, its special style. Questions and attendant thoughts might live in your mind. They absolutely do in mine.

Craig Owens Once Existed

> When writers die they become books, which is, after all, not too bad an incarnation.
> —Jorge Luis Borges

To be incarnated as a book may offer some people consolation, but not, I believe, Craig Owens, who lived only thirty-nine years.

Craig Owens was an influential intellectual, critic, teacher, and editor, a constant and consequential thinker. He was excited about art and ideas, he felt an urgency and pleasure about thinking itself, he took joy in it. Thinking was essential to him and who he was.

Craig was concerned, politically engaged, not a joiner, more a dedicated dissenter, and argued against complacencies of all kinds. His curiosity pushed him to study and learn most of the time, and he was fed by discussion, argument, theories, concepts, by the new and the old, by seeing art, ballet, films, opera, watching baseball—the Mets—football, by eating and cooking well.

Craig theorized about postmodernism and art, uniquely, generatively. Early on in his career, and in the early days of their careers, he thought deeply about the work of Sherrie Levine, Cindy Sherman, Barbara Kruger, Laurie Anderson. Through their art, he became aware and sensitive to issues others weren't addressing. In a seminal 1983 essay, "The Discourse of Others: Feminists and Postmodernism," Craig joined feminism, and alterity, to the debates in postmodernism and in art. His essays about identity, sexuality, gay politics, otherness, were challenging, critical, and complex. Craig's commentaries changed the discourse around contemporary art.

Craig Owens: Portrait of a Young Critic (2018) is based on a transcript of a video conversation between Craig and Lyn

Blumenthal. It stands as a succinct introduction to Craig's independent thinking, sense of play, his intellectual breadth, foresight, and honesty.

Lyn Blumenthal was an artist and a good friend of Craig's; their knowledge of each other, and trust, let Craig feel open and relaxed, even expansive. Their friendship enlivened the discussion. In a sense, Craig tells the story of his life up until that time, 1984, primarily considering his life as a learner, a young man interested in theater and art, a burgeoning intellectual. He elucidates how he came to think what he did, and why, and from whom, and when. It is, in a way, a mini-bildungsroman.

This book is also a contribution to primary research. The utility of documents from a particular moment that feature people speaking about their time and their thoughts should not be underestimated. It's not that the speaker holds the Truth because he or she was there. No. Primary research is a representation of lived lives, which allow us to comprehend better why people thought what they did and acted as they did, with what questions, and with what problems in their minds. Documents from participants and observers of events can be helpful in understanding also why we think what we do now, some of which is based on representations of the past. There are many misunderstandings or misreadings of acts, events, motives, and many versions, too. The present gets the past wrong, for one thing, because there is not only a single past, there are multiple points of view about any past. The interpretations and conclusions about histories might be seen differently, when different people reflect on and articulate what went before. Experience isn't Truth, but it suggests the unending variety of human consciousness.

The present needs to consider and reconsider why one story, say, is believed more than another. Craig tells us some of his version of events here.

Especially wonderful, and useful, is Craig's honest reexamination of ideas he had once absorbed, followed, and believed. Craig discusses how, without fully realizing its meanings and implications, he accepted what he had been taught, especially in imitation of important others.

Undoing was a piece of Craig's analytical mind. He was profoundly self-critical, and readers will notice this in his conversation with Lyn. Craig was asked, more than once, to publish a collection of his essays, and said no. He was insecure, true, as most of us are about our work; but he also knew some of his worth—he knew what he was capable of doing, that he could do more and better. Also, his sincere regard for intellectual life, books and writing, made him demur. Craig wanted to do the best he could, and he didn't feel he was quite there, yet.

Then there was no more time.

After people die, friends and colleagues step in. They may do what was not done, or what they can to keep the person's memory and work alive. After Craig died, Barbara Kruger, Jane Weinstock, Scott Bryson, and I edited a collection of his essays, disregarding Craig's resistance to publishing—there was no further chance for him to develop his work, or himself. In 1992, *Beyond Recognition: Representation, Power, and Culture* was published by the University of California Press, and is still very much in print. I urge readers who appreciate *Portrait of a Young Critic* to read it.

Craig's arguments in *Beyond Recognition*, and in this conversation, anticipate and engage current debates. In the 1970s and 1980s, political and cultural issues about representation, for one, followed on the impact of ideologies, psychoanalysis, structuralism and poststructuralism, especially, and, of course, from the great wave and ferment of the 1960s caused by the women's movement, the civil rights movement, and gay liberation. These issues remain contemporary, with different shadings and inflections, with new meanings and practices, but with many similarities.

Two weeks before his death, Craig told me enthusiastically that he was reading and thinking about—wanted to write about—Fassbinder, Pedro Almodóvar, and Derek Jarman. Their art nourished and thrilled him right to the end.

Craig Owens died in the early hours of July 4, 1990.

The process of an intellectual, like that of an artist, builds from one set of ideas, or series of works, to another; then to analyses of the work accomplished, relying on the capacity of the thinker, critic, artist, to reject what doesn't work, to reconsider it.

To change a position is no simple matter. Craig Owens, had he lived, would have revised and rejected his ideas, and found new ones to champion, dismiss, question, and rail against. He would have reversed, shifted, upended theories and opinions. I often wonder, "What would Craig have made of _______?" His responses and opinions were unpredictable. He was truly an independent thinker, often a contrarian, sometimes contradictory. A human being.

Rethinking is thinking, and thinking is not simple, and it must, of necessity, be its own endless goal. In our time, with its populist scorn for higher education, intellectuals, serious scholarship, and learning for its own sake, once called the pursuit of knowledge, when all of this is considered "elitist," one might consider what Craig Owens wrote and thought and taught, what he did in the thirty-nine years he had, and learn from him. Even take heart.

Craig wasn't a hero. And, as Barbara Kruger has proposed, we don't need another one. Craig dedicated his life to his passions, to the mind and its vicissitudes, to pursuits that mattered to him. He had jobs, he had to make money, and he also lived as much as he could in the way he wanted.

Craig Owens's kind of life, his decisions in life, should be cherished.

Lines, Gaps, Shapes, Strokes, Jokes, Colors, Holes . . .

To writers, words are material, their matter, their only stuff. Words have value in themselves, tricky beasts, relished, debated, hated. Amy Sillman values words. Her essays are literary incitements, they're exciting, and felt. Sillman confers untested, nonconsensual, verbal experiments on art, to visual ideas and compositions, to locate newer meanings. Let's say, Sillman seeks to describe the indescribable, which is all the more strange because she is primarily responding to visual forms and matters, there, supposedly, in plain sight. But they aren't, not without examination and engagement. That is, with a desire to apprehend more.

In a Sillman essay, words have their own weight, which is inestimable.

Her remarks on color weigh color on several scales, from the actual weight of pigments, to her consideration of how color weighs in the imagination and sensibility of painters. "Color is a material," she writes, and comes from other matter whose origins remain invisible, but not to her. One might say, the way labor is invisible in a commodity. Color, Sillman explains, is regularly separated from form as if it were negligible. But to her, for instance, pigments become "characters," a personification that creates more weight in a composition. So, viewers can now weigh paintings with an awareness of these elements.

It's exceptionally hard to articulate what color is, because the signified is incommensurate with its signifier. Like tongues to sex to bodies. Handling color affects an artist, substances encourage variations in practices and the sensibilities of artists. As they do in her paintings, Sillman's written descriptions of color pulse.

"The nomenclature of paint is all beautiful adjectives. You don't say 'pink,' you say *dianthus* pink, *hematite* purple, *flake* white . . . consider the esoteric feeling when working with stuff like the color carmine . . ."

An ambivalent disposition to conventional wisdoms, with pro and con attitudes to aesthetic theories, animates Sillman's mind. She tests and retests ideas. Rationality, explanation, and logic about art, the many theories about it, go so far, but will be confounded and troubled by the making of it—by artists' experience, subjectivity, knowledge of its history, sensibilities, repressions, sensuality, gender, psychology, et al. There are inevitable contradictions.

Sillman's emphasis lies in the importance of process, and how making creates meanings. There is a refusal—Sillman is a joyful refusenik—of false antinomies, distinctions, categories, binaries. She professes, here, that art is a coalition of materials, visual thinking, objects, theories, bodies, physical and psychical activity, of dailiness, and, urgently, of lived lives. No to privileging theory over making.

(Painting communicates, it is information, and it is also a form of knowledge. I once wrote, in defense of stories, or narrative, against those who said they were dead: "Stories are a way to think." Sillman might accept this premise.)

Gertrude Stein famously wrote, "I am I because my little dog knows me."[1] Let's say that little dog is art. What if art doesn't know you; the artist doesn't, and the work changes, maybe radically—Philip Guston is usually cited here (about whom Sillman has also written). What happens to ideas about art, is a fixed idea fixing you? Change disarms armed positions.

In psychoanalytic theory, "working through" means that, through the process of analysis, neuroses are addressed; and, worked through sufficiently, emotions and intellect fuse. "Neurotic unhappiness" will be released or experienced differently with understanding. It will be, to some extent, disenabled, so that the analysand achieves "ordinary unhappiness." (I'm bemused by scholars who disdain the practice of psychoanalysis and use the theory in their work.)

There is no cure, only understanding.

Doing their work, artists experience the necessity of change, and work through ideas, visual and cerebral, while they work. There is no one solution, Sillman shows. That is, there is no cure for art, it's not neurotic, rather it proceeds with and without direction and intention as it goes along. "What urge makes you want to do something that pushes further, on toward contingency, clumsiness, strangeness, or even brutality?" Different responses may be required, since stasis is no answer to a predicament.

Sillman's emphasis on process promotes the exposure of difficulties in art-making, the demands it makes, as the artist herself evolves, always in relationship to the world outside. The personal is political, yes, but the political is also personal, to Sillman. These evolutions, everywhere, make art evolve.

In "Some Thoughts on John Chamberlain," Sillman analyzes Chamberlain's car-crash sculptures, insisting on the significance of his use of color. "Palpable material that you mold and crush. . . . The colors in Chamberlains ooze and spread across parts, and do all the things that color does in painting." She reveals the syntheses in his body of work that have been overlooked.

Reading this essay, I remembered an exhibition of Chamberlain's sculptures, curated by Donald Judd, I saw not long ago at The Chinati Foundation in Marfa, Texas. I had seen his "car crashes" years before, perceived shapes, thought about destruction, and Warhol's car-crash images. But Judd's curation opened up these sculptures. The work hadn't changed, I had, in time and with time. Time in all senses conditions perception, and is inalienably part of it, along with subjectivity.

Sillman's desire to contend with Chamberlain's under-seen, under-acknowledged, checkered career derives from two realizations: that he was "hidden in plain sight" and that "an artist could become a cliché *and* remain simultaneously under-known." Her insights on Chamberlain sparkle with her motivation: to grapple with his uneven, partial reputation, one that many good artists suffer—for instance, Meret Oppenheim, so famous for her fur teacup and saucer (*Object*, 1936), was known for little else, a great frustration for her. Oppenheim once satirized her place in art history by making a tourist version of the teacup and saucer.

In "Some Thoughts . . ." Sillman scopes Chamberlain's career thoroughly, and registers the reasons for this paradox. Doing it underscores her compassion for an artist's shifts and departures over time. Or, in their truths. She delineates Chamberlain's variances, his approaches to high/low, his choice of materials, junk, and, finally, through him, she shows an appreciation for vulgarity, which aligns with others of her favorites: awkwardness, jokes, cartoons, and more.

Pictures of body parts, filth, sex acts, excrement, all that stuff, will be called vulgar. It's revelatory how meanings change. The Vulgate was the fourth-century Bible, written in Latin; *vulgata* also means common language, while *vulgaris* means of the common people. "Vulgar" should be descriptive, not a value judgment.[2]

But oh how words can't be held down. Words "live in the mind"; words "are highly democratic . . . uneducated words are as good as educated words, uncultivated words as good as cultivated words," as Virginia Woolf reminds readers.[3]

Sillman has declared her own dedicated class war in which high-mindedness, "cultivated" art, has nothing to do with art. There's a carnival of things in the carnival of life. Her aesthetics (pace Whitman) contain multitudes.

"I mix paint more than anyone I know," she writes. "My work is partially determined by the colors I buy." Those colors, pigments, I now know, are extremely expensive. Sillman's statements about her process strike me the way her paintings do—frank, disarming, open, bold, working through and embodying ideas and practices that have a necessity to her. All of her essays are highly informed, grounded in knowledge of her subjects, in art history, etc. They are cerebral, philosophical, and they are personal. The artists she discusses, the art, theories: All are close to her. But her revelations are not confessions, she is not whispering secrets, exposing what should not be known. In fact, it is what should be known about her practice, ideas, and what is at stake to her, what has profound meaning for her.

Sillman has skin in this game.

In "Why Amelie von Wulffen Is Funny," Sillman wonders, after writing that comic strips are printed in newspapers, "What 'news' does vW's work bring?" Which also comments, I think, on the province of, and degradation of, fiction—painting, novels, poems, movies. In her aquarelles, von Wulffen's characters "endur[e] the same tedium, tribulations, and triumphs that we occasionally do." Her work "links image to narrative, it is wed not to a saga or epic, but to a cheap novella. And to a critique of bourgeois subjectivity, these cartoons would answer: *What else is there?*"

Von Wulffen's scenarios "mirror our lives." Sillman doesn't make much use of the mirror metaphor; in my reading of her essays, its appearance is unusual. So with it, I infer Sillman's appreciation of certain kinds of representation, the love-side of her ambivalence toward representation. And there's her ambivalence toward abstraction. She does both and neither. She wills herself to, and does, defy categories, and so admires the inclusiveness and combinations in von Wulffen's art, which uses stuff most artists don't.

Holding a mirror up to life, when it reflects its brokenness, absurdity, comedy, and sadness, is not to make idealizations. The mirror is art that must be cracked and shown the fissures of so-called reality. Her essay on Rachel Harrison's complex work, in "A Few Remarks on Rachel Harrison's Use of Color," shares a few of the qualities Sillman ascribes to von Wulffen. She refers to Harrison's "farcical situations": "Absurdity generally prevails over gravitas. . . . She throws in merchandise, manufactures, surfaces, and jokes to further scrapple with the proceedings." Von Wulffen's work confronts painting: "She hobbles linearity with collage, overlay, interruption, fragmentation, glitch and omission. . . . Within this painterly fracture, drawing appears as if it were glue, a form of recuperation, a way to hold things together."

"Drawing as a form of recuperation" is a fascinating concept. Drawing things in, drawing us and it together. Sillman is devoted to drawing, to the line. Drawing is a first cousin to writing—that mark-making on cave walls. Maybe the two married. Sillman's involvement in the line would relate to her intense investment in words, their value, their weight. And vice versa.

In cartoons, lines are both visual and textual.

Sillman's essay "Further Notes on Shape" expands on and explicates her thinking toward curating the exhibition *The Shape of Shape* at The Museum of Modern Art, New York, in fall 2019. This essay is "round," a roundup of her concerns and their intersections, augmented primarily and significantly by a realization: "I barely knew anything about shape." Sillman takes us along, as she delves into the "holes" and "gaps" in art history, and digs at them. She points to absences and dismissals and rhetorical positions that still mark and impress themselves upon contemporary art and theory.

So, composition versus construction: Sillman traces the schism to the Russian constructivists who saw composing as "re-inscrib[ing] the values of a privileged bourgeois class, whereas to construct was the way to make a new society." Here, set historically in the crosshairs of this binary, Sillman's consideration of drawing returns, "an activity not founded on logic but made up of contingencies."

The dictum against composition, from the early twentieth century, maintains its grip, she argues, though "a singular position is precisely what radicals would have argued against." Her research into the complexity of these theoretical positions takes her to the sculptor Philip Pavia, editor of *It Is*, a 1950s artist-run magazine. He believed only through "'drawing, drawing and more drawing' could an artist perform a vanguard inquiry."

Like her essay on Chamberlain, "Further Notes on Shape" is thorough and concise, building a different narrative for complex issues in art history and art-making. Considering shapes, I wondered: Is a shape empty or full? Half empty, half full. Shapes shape patterns of thought, and ways of seeing. Which led to my recollecting the tools of childhood, its plethora of coloring books and jigsaw puzzles. These instruct with a particular logic—to color inside the lines; make objects fit neatly into spaces, and form alignments. But what if that wasn't how children learned; then, uncertainties, sketchiness, and impulses might not be contained or controlled easily. What if overflow was encouraged.

Compositions and drawings, Sillman postulates, and "artists fussing over shapes," have their own means of "register[ing] protest"; for one, "they make gestures of care and repair." The sense and suppositions of Sillman's proposals, in this essay and others, register her own protest against, say, the renunciation of bodies, hands, gestures, experience, materials, craft, and more, with an immense sensitivity to possibilities and to roads not taken.

In these scintillating essays—and each deserves its own essay—Amy Sillman excites, provokes ideas, plunders and aggravates language, detonates words with innovation, the way she does paint, pencil, color, line, stroke, mark, etc. She uniquely renders words to foreground pictures and picture-making, and builds avenues, pathways to lead to other ways of apprehending art.

So, she appreciates Laura Owens's paintings, because of, and not only, their "rejection of rejection" of painting. The rhetorical dismissal "painting is dead" annoys the hell out of Sillman, and with good reason, because painters are not zombies. She begins her review of the painter Carroll Dunham's *Into Words: The Selected Writings of Carroll Dunham* focusing on his most frequently used word, "weird," followed by "perverse." "Takes one to know one," she writes, and employs a blizzard of adjectives to describe his texts. She says, "No one writes about art like this." And, when Sillman grapples with and interprets his texts, she writes: "Reading this book, one also senses a drive to a psychic singularity, a mysterious black hole located at the center of his thinking . . . and the sheer tactile craving to wrap the mesh of language around the mystery of art-making, to respond to art's forms with language's invisible force."

I can't imagine a better way to end my essay than to use her words about desire in writing: "A tactile craving to wrap the mesh of language around the mystery of art-making."

Sillman's mind is full, her drive powerful, she does wrap, unwrap, make and unmake art, and in her essays, it is all here.

Notes

1 Gertrude Stein, "And Now," *Vanity Fair* (September 1934), p. 35.

2 Warhol wanted pop art to be called Common Art. A religious Catholic, he certainly knew that "vulgar" meant "common." His art enraged the class that wanted art to show their good taste and distinguish them from common people.

3 Virginia Woolf, "Craftsmanship," BBC radio broadcast, *Words Fail Me* (April 29, 1937); reproduced in *The Essays of Virginia Woolf, Volume VI*, ed. Stuart N. Clarke (London: Hogarth Press, 2011).

Of Its Time

What happened in 2012?

Otto Muehl, the Viennese Actionist, once kept a diary. A whole year was represented by this line: "Extreme Hatred for the Mayor of Vienna." Stealing from Muehl, about 2012 I could note: "Impulse to Slap All Birthers." Through our annus horribilis, or the US presidential campaign, some comfort came from thinking about history: People have always been stupid, wrong. Smart people, with generative ideas, occasionally prevail. This cheered me up.

I tend to believe that, before total annihilation, this clever/dumb species will design ingenious devices to ameliorate the poisonous effects of previous ones. I predict: The end is not near. Believing it, though, could be as reassuring to some as my recourse to history.

Future beings will laugh at us; each generation does about its predecessor. It's an endless competition. The chunky, clumsy, slow things they devised—electrical wires, sockets. Coming soon—tiny memory implants, iWands.

But let's not forget forgetfulness: A normal amnesia overwhelms most of any lived life. Recalling a year, last month? Stray scenes can return in startling dreams we usually forget; vague images surface, slip away.

In 2011, with millions, I watched Egypt's revolution on television: "I'm watching history; history is being made." But what does that mean, to watch an event that will be recorded, remembered, but not to have been in or of it? Anything could have happened in Tahrir Square. Normal disappeared. A few Americans told me they'd have liked to be part of their revolution. I thought, but didn't say: A revolution doesn't send out invitations. The Egyptians weren't "having a revolution." They were the revolution.

2012 rode in on the back of chaotic, thrilling, frightening political events: the clamoring will of people in the Middle East; the fragility of hope, and rebellion spreading; the instability of the euro and Greece's desperation; the Occupy movement's impact; now, street-by-street fighting in Syria, a government slaughtering its citizens, and no stopping yet.

In 2012, on May 1, I gave a reading at the KGB Bar in the East Village, with fellow writer Colm Tóibín. Afterward, a bunch of us had dinner. About 11 p.m., in a funky bar on Second Avenue, I heard a guy, who was peering into his iPhone, whisper: "Bin Laden's been killed." What? The bar turned dead quiet. He said, louder: "Bin Laden's dead." The bartender switched on the television. "Bin Laden's been killed." Colm and I walked outside, told passersby, or they told us: "Bin Laden's dead." I admit to shock, excitement, but more a rush of relief. "Admit" because I didn't expect relief; I didn't know that particular anxiety was lodged in me. What else didn't "whoever I was" know that might inflect or form "my positions" and "my ideas"?

Unique characters, like Marshall McLuhan, envisioned the future, and speculated brilliantly. But no one knows exactly what's coming, or the consequences that will follow. No one knows what artists will do next, either, or why. Maybe perceptive, ludic, didactic, inspiring, or dull art, film, writing. Contemporary work usually responds obliquely to its time, which necessarily includes the past, hidden or disguised. I didn't expect relief at bin Laden's death, and artists may imagine and describe a surprising object from and of its time, with no obvious source.

In 2012, I saw an exhibition of work by Anna Molska at the gallery Broadway 1602 in New York. I remember her video *The*

Mourners (2010) in part because it caught me—thematically, formally, psychologically—and made present what I hadn't expected. Molska asked seven Polish women to participate in a "social experiment." The women were friends, who also had a folk-singing group, and sang songs at funerals. Molska invited them to use a gallery, once a greenhouse, to do in it what they wanted. She provided neutral-colored parkas as costumes; and, in the windowed, spacious gallery, one wide bench and a white sheet, which became props.

In about twenty-five minutes, the women created a play: enacting a funeral, singing to the dead and the living, they danced, roughhoused, and laughed. They discussed God and the Devil, telling folk tales and their own stories about dying people. Very early in the improvised drama, one woman said, as if out of nowhere: "The Germans thought they were so smart; but they were stupid." Suddenly the past joined the present and framed it.

Molska's camera observes the group, usually in medium shots; close-ups study their happy, impassive, mournful faces. It watches them listening to each other or fashioning the white sheet into a corpse, which they position on the bench. The women sing to it and, as they sing, an unnerving seriousness settles. Their eyes close. Their voices sound like the only music possible for lamentation. Later, World War II returns, when a woman mentions her father being sent to a camp, and her sympathy for orphans. Tears come to their eyes. The work includes much more than I can report.

What happened in 2012?

The Horse's Eye

I

Writing and reading happen incrementally, one word, another; the speed of a reader, or writer, doesn't count, really. A writer might draw a line through a word or phrase; she might keep the first word visible under the new one, like a palimpsest or background reading. In writing, a superimposition doesn't fuse layers the way it does in films and photographs. A painting's surface compares better, when, say, its first or second layer shows through it.

In writing, shapes or structures for a composition build while the writer works. Paragraphs suggest idea shifts; line breaks and punctuation, breath, pauses, full stops, and starts. Gertrude Stein resorted to periods, though she didn't like them much: She knew their necessity though—things always come to an end. But that first written word might be, in the end, at the end. A writer begins somewhere, there's an unavoidable linearity.

Visual compositions are different. In painting, the frame, or the scale of the canvas or other surface, comes first. Drawings may have preceded the painting—they often do in Carroll Dunham's work. The size or scale of a painting will usually be considerably larger than a drawing for it. So, the paint-composition begins as a shape, with its limits and characteristics—square, rectangle, hexagon, etc. A painting could exceed its perimeter by dripping onto the floor or onto a wall beside it, but rarely does.

Painters address various parts of the surface, at different times. Every element unsettles or resolves a composition—work in one corner affects the entirety. Painters think variously, spatially, for one, and spatial order has its own exigencies, which compel adjustments and responses, painting over, overpainting, erasures.

Carroll Dunham visualizes ideas, thoughts, feelings. His approach to composition has shapes. In the *Now and Around Here* series (2011–2015), for instance, he chose recognizable forms—people, animals, birds, leaves, trees. He worked on linen with mixed media, and used vivid colors. Dunham covered the entire canvas. He drew and painted, because in his paintings line matters. His surfaces might show underpainting or pencil lines, like a writer's first thoughts.

II

> Don't explain, only describe.
> —Ludwig Wittgenstein

Close readings aren't popular, but I like doing them. In film, counting seconds between shots; in photography, noticing what the frame excludes, where it sits; in sculpture, measuring negative space, and the eye's movement through shapes, front, sides, back, if a piece has them; in dance, counting time between movements, and, in music, beats, rhythms, noting a singer's range, what sounds are amplified. Noticing musical stops. What's left out in writing is key.

I don't usually think about what's outside a painting's frame. I might think, This space is art, the empty space beside it is not. I ask myself what that inference about art's impact means. I notice where I look—first, second, third. I pull the painting apart, mentally: colors, textures, thickness or flatness of paint. There's a sense of the visceral, of feel, a hand might or might not be involved. I note the presence or absence of representational forms, look at the sides of a painting, because sometimes they're painted, sometimes left alone. I always wonder about that decision. And even though the material might bleed off its sides, nothing has been excluded from a painting, or everything has been.

With a close reading, even by "only describing," artworks are interpreted. The language chosen by a critic characterizes the elements she sees, because words have their own specificity, and, as important, associations and connotations. A synonym, close to a chosen word's meaning, inflects meanings with a difference.

Interpretations are parenthetical to a work. I mean, an interpretation is not the work. An interpretation can be a simile or metaphor, say. In writing, anything parenthetical can be removed from a sentence, not disturbing the sense of a sentence. It can be lifted out, without change. In fiction, I hardly ever use them, because of that. One day, I hope to use many, in a story.

I wonder whether a description is an interpretation is an explanation. I prefer not to explain, but contend with inevitable and annoying slippages.

III
Descriptions of Carroll Dunham's Paintings

Horse and Rider (My X) (2013–2015)
Two naked asses—horse's and woman's—occupy center stage. (They make me want to laugh.) The dark-haired woman's (which resembles a pair of melons) is poised on the brown horse's broad one, while his genitals hang down (like overripe fruit).

The woman rider looks away from the center, toward a yellow sun above her head, rounder than her ass. Her gray-white arms, lightly outlined in black, are thrown up and out. (In abandon, or maybe as V for victory. If she is victorious, I wonder what her victory might be.)

The horse's head, poised below the woman rider's outstretched arm, faces out, and looks at me or any viewer. His eyes peer (steadily, unnervingly) from the painting at the space before it. (The horse is reminiscent of Velázquez's painter, who looks out from the court scene, in *Las Meninas*: Both figures situate the viewer. Both are seeing and also being seen.)

He stares ahead, his brown pupils dot the middle of the whites. (I fall into the horse's eyes, where there is such benignity. Or, unblinking surprise, maybe compassion.) Painted like that, the eyes appear to follow a viewer wherever she might go. (I keep looking back, to check.)

The long-haired rider, her back straight, arms open, is going forward. Her pose looks exuberant. (Her exuberance defies sadness, for one, and she might be experiencing joy, in life. There's so little joy to feel, and yet here it is.)

A tree rises from the ground on the other side of the rider, parallel to the horse's face. It's a tree but it also isn't, though green leaves sprout, seemingly, from it; they're drawn with a light, gay hand (as Matisse might).

Tree, telephone pole, fence post, the brown shape complicates Dunham's picture. Its branches, if they are, have been chopped off; they haven't fallen off. The "trunk" is literally truncated, a visual pun that unsettles the "fate" of the horse and woman. (It suggests other double readings, such as, is this a tragedy or a comedy?)

The rods appear to enter the woman's body, but stop short of impaling her, only to emerge on the other side of her, piercing the horse's neck. That might have just occurred, since time in a painting is always, in a sense, in the present tense.

(And, just now the horse's eyes register shock, or hurt and pain.)

The broken tree or pole has sawed-off parts, boughs. It is just not a tree. (Maybe a fence whose planks police the space.) Horse, woman, the ambiguous structure—here a bough, there a rod—breaks up the space. (Or breaks it down.)

At the bottom of the picture, a fallen bough presents an obstacle to the horse, who has a lifted hoof. (Otherwise, the horse would trip, bolt, or ride up in fear. Then the woman would fall to the ground.)

Game (2013–2015)

A naked woman swings (like a circus performer) from the top branch of a faux tree. (Sawed-off branches or rods is a trope in Dunham's *Here and Now* series, appearing in all of them.) This woman, maybe "My X" (X marks the spot; X as in ex), is powerful, has great upper body strength. She is parallel to the ground, her legs thrust forward, and her nipples and vulva colored a deep, bright red. (The nipples extrude, erect; the vulva and labia are a heart shape. A valentine or V, for victory?)

A large black bird, a crow, sits on the same bough as the one from which she swings. Three others fly or are suspended near her; they might be looking in her direction or at the other crow. Again, the yellow sun rests above a woman's head, off-center. If *Game* has a center it is a line running across it horizontally; the space might be divided in quadrants. The lowest crow's head is on a line with the woman's vulva.

(Disorienting, this game, if it is one, and if it is, what is the game? There's a chance of losing, a sense of winning, or at least trying is important in these paintings. Survival is winning. Must be. Or, maybe its title is not a noun but a verb: "I am game for this." Or, is he gaming me? The painter may be playing a game. Later, Carroll Dunham tells me, There's a third sense. They're game for each other, crow and the woman, they're both prey. That hadn't occurred to me at all.)

The woman is swinging forward, her body is parallel to the ground; the birds flightless, or stuck in motion; a turquoise-blue sky envelops them all. It is impossible to know where in space this painting is: There is no definite ground. (I wonder if the faux trunk shoots into the sky, if it has a connection to the earth, or is entirely disconnected. The earth may have been deserted.)

Now and Around Here (1), (2), (3) (2011–2015)
This is a group of three paintings.

In *(1)*, a man's gray-white body, like the X-woman's, outlined lightly in black, is at the base of each. Headless, erect red nipples, his legs spread, his penis rests between his thighs. He is lying on his back. (And not playing an active "male" role; he is an observer in and of the landscape/scene.) Squiggly black lines, drawn gaily, represent his chest hair.

Red flowers, yellow leaves, green grass, a round yellow sun, all are within his purview. The brown boughs pierce the purple sky, two boughs entering from both sides of him, at the level of his knees. (This curious, possibly dangerous, and endangered "tree" behaves differently in each painting, though always in position to cause a threat to the other bodies. If this is meant to be Nature, Nature isn't behaving neutrally; and, a sense of "the natural" is under scrutiny. While primary colors usually signal exuberance and presence, and they also do in these paintings, the colors are blunted or leavened by damaged Nature or its threats. The colors spell "unnaturalness.")

In *(2)*, central again, the dark-haired woman's round ass. She is a full figure, naked, back to the viewer, one of her arms reaching out (beseechingly?), the other hanging by her side (no exultation). She looks into the distance; above her and off-center, a very large, round, bright yellow sun. She is standing in a field of blue (water, pool, lake, ocean); the blue rises above her knees. A lime-kelly green is background to her and the sun. (No sky here, or it's green from pollution. Or, it's a painting not at all about a natural setting.)

The man is supine, though his legs appear to be spread apart farther than in *(1)*. He is looking at her, seeing her, who stands, in the distance, and from his point of view, as if between his legs. A purplish-blue flower seems to be sprouting under him, emerging from him, and it is near or touching his genitals. (Or it is taking over.)

The faux tree's boughs hang in or protrude into the green "sky," separately. (Like cut ups, or as in a collage, seemingly glued on.) There are three purplish-blue flowers and six leaves, four the same type, green ovals; two, a lighter green, whose tops are straight-edged. (Maybe they are dead, or from a different kind of tree.)

In *(3)*, except for the yellow sun and dark-brown boughs or logs, the colors in this painting have changed (dramatically. I feel I'm looking at rust). The sun may be setting (impossible to ascertain, except that it seems to be). The man is again supine, but his nipples are dusky pink, and near his genitals, three yellow-brown objects rise (plants, fingers, growths, sprouts, other penises?). There are many of these, four rows of them; the boughs or logs enter the space from every side, except where the man lies. Some are crossed, thick rods; some narrow, and some are sticks. Brownish-pink flowers (maybe daisies, dried and dead) hang from the top of the painting. (One looks like a badminton shuttlecock.)

A brown dog, with eyes painted like the horse's, sits off-center, as if between the man's legs. The sun is directly above the dog, off-center also. The background or sky is tangerine orange (it might be sunset). The dog is just sitting, looking out of the painting to any viewer or space. (Or, might be waiting for its "master" to arise and play, go for a walk. But maybe the man is lifeless, sunset of his life, his nipples so pale. Has the blood left him, is his body cold?)

Three variations on a theme: A naked man lies or rests at the bottom of the three paintings. The picturing is from his point of view. (I see what he is seeing. Or, imagining.)

The male and female figures do not see themselves. The man sees her. She does not see him or look at him. They are objects in different picture planes. The horse's and dog's eyes matter, because the humans don't have eyes. The man doesn't have a head. The woman's eyes are indicated not articulated. Eyeless human beings, somehow they seem to be looking at something. The dog and the horse are looking out of the painting, at the viewer, and the dog may be looking also at the male figure.

A headless, male body, with arms, legs, feet, penis, nipples. Does he have a mind? He is a match to a Dunham female, though no female is headless. Does she have a mind? If so, what are they both thinking about. Or, rather, they are not thinking, or I can never know their thoughts. What do the paintings make a viewer, me, think about? The ubiquitous binaries, nature/culture; artificial/organic; male/female; life/death. Adam/Eve: banished from Paradise into a living hell.

And, also they raise a persistent, devilish issue: Is the female in art always, or merely, an object of male desire? Is she an object in ways a male nude could not be? Painting nudes in a time of easy-access porn—is the effect on the practice or product different? Does the sex, or sexuality, of the artist who paints or draws—nudes—matter? Some of Dunham's contemporaries: Lisa Yuskavage, Nicole Eisenman, John Currin, Jeff Koons. Or, earlier artists Picasso, Bonnard. Or, in another register, R. Crumb and Aline Kominsky-Crumb.

In Dunham's paintings, these Eves and Adams play other parts, rebel against traditional roles. His nudes—overblown, comic, ironic, unrealistic—may be metaphors, in an allegorical setting, that refer to newer realities, about gender, for one. His female is active, the male, passive, antithetical to stereotypes of femininity and masculinity. The figures exist inside bright colors, but the scenes are disturbing. They are in disrupted spaces. The female—arms outstretched, swinging from a fake tree: triumphant, capable, strong? The male—subdued, maybe defeated, or resigned, only there to observe this new world? Dunham may be portraying a female world in which males have been redefined and relocated.

I wander into Dunham's field of inquiry, don't settle my thoughts, and pursue the pleasures of possibility.

I can't explain Dunham's paintings.

Interpretation is not explanation.

The reader of any art is a second responder. The maker, the first responder, the thing's first intended and dedicated audience.

I recall Churchill's famous phrase, "Victory in our time." During World War II and the Battle of Britain, Churchill spoke over the radio and gave the British, still fighting the Nazis alone, hope. The woman's V is different. In Dunham's settings and in these times, if the female is triumphant over, say, patriarchy, her victory has many shadings. Some think women have gained what has been lost—I mean, that she triumphs over scorched earth, to succeed during permanent wars, and to witness nature in peril or destroyed. She might be restorative or also destructive. A pessimistic reading, this, and, I'm being literal, which can, in part, result from close readings.

To paraphrase Freud, sometimes a cigar is just a cigar; sometimes it's a penis. Now I rejig and consider: A supine male figure may also be an artist who created this—who "takes" this lying down. From this position, he observes the state of things, imperturbable, upset, resigned, or content.

Culture as a Verb (2013–2015)

People, bodies, are gone. The palette is three colors: rosy red, pale tan pink, and brown. The tree is facing out, its cut-off branches shooting toward the viewer. The thirteen leaves are a deep red: It could be fall. (It could be the aftermath of the Fall, when Adam and Eve were banished. It's hard for me to avoid the allegory of the Garden of Eden.)

Culture as a Verb is a leading title, like a leading question. (I can't stay away from its implications.) "To culture" is to cultivate, bring into being, to educate. It is an active, ongoing process. To cultivate may entail mixtures and choices, determinations about ways to produce what kind of cultures. Culture then is not a process, but a product of many determinations. (Is the painting addressing the process of making "culture"? Maybe.)

A mass of swirling rosy red covers or entangles the bottom half of the painting. The mass surrounds nine brown sawed-off branches or rods that point at the viewer. This (confrontational) pose or stance is unique in this series of paintings. In the background, behind the rosy-red mass, Dunham's trope: a faux tree, with cut-off branches hovers. Swirling, the mass is dynamic, an object in movement.

(The red mass threatens to advance. It looks like an armored vehicle—a tank. The brown rods are the main guns. Now the tree might be the turret of a tank, with more main guns or cannons. What is being cultured might explode or shoot to kill, what is being cultured is active and destructive, and intimates future human-made disasters.)

Big Bang (actual size) 1, 2, 3 (2012–2015)

A group of paintings—three variations on its eponymous title. All bright orange and golden yellow, with some black, abstract and loosely figurative, a roundish shape is central. Its perimeters change, the roundness expands as if pulled like taffy at its sides, but still keeps its globe-like shape, cosmos, world, universe. (The orange might be flames or represent internal explosive events that affect the look and shape of things—the order of things.)

The universe began, physicists say, because of the Big Bang. In Dunham's paintings, he pictures the wildness, the bizarre reality of everything beginning—true for each of us, a beginning, in life. Multitudes of relationships, of nations, religions, identities, wars, the natural order, everything begins.

Before the Big Bang, scientists say there was nothing. I want to be able to see nothing. I try, often, and find it impossible: "What" is nothing, a vastness of nothing, forever: If nothing is there, I can't see nothing, which can't be "there." An infinity resides in this tautology, or any tautology. A belief in God seems convenient and comforting, because a transcendent, omniscient God is always, and was always, and so there never was nothing. Even a few physicists believe that God, or a first or prime mover, caused the Big Bang, and "created" the universe. So, maybe rocket scientists also find "Nothing" impossible.

The Big Bang is a fact. In 1964, the sound of it was accidentally discovered by a horn antenna developed and built, by two scientists, for Bell Labs in New Jersey. The first photons released after the Big Bang, its afterglow, exist in the cosmos as radio waves. The horn antenna captured this sound, similar to a hissing noise, and recordings of it have been made. This seems as if it shouldn't be actual, but it is: The beginning of the universe is still around, in the atmosphere, as sound. It can be heard. I find this entirely startling.

IV

People live with abstract ideas, absorb (or reject) complex concepts, often referred to, with amusement, as "not rocket science." Which means even a nonscientist should understand.

A painting is not considered rocket science, but can be difficult, because it might refer to or represent what isn't immediately accessible or understood, and needs a viewer to see it, to complete it. This requires projections, identifications, and a feeling of necessity—

to understand it or understand what one is looking for. Looking, I am not just looking at something but also "for" something. Then I see it a certain way. I might be drawn or repulsed, and wonder: What is it I am apprehending. I doubt my perceptions, which aren't "natural," but educated. What is it addressing? What is it making or "seeing," what is it about, that I may not "see"? I often ask myself what I believe are the hardest questions, about necessity: Why is it there? Why do I look at it? These often can't be answered.

Paintings are fictions, human-designed constructions. Even when referring to actual events, like the Big Bang—fiction. This seems obvious: Art is made, not born. Some fictions seem truer than others: That is, some speak less indirectly to conditions and feelings, or present a greater verisimilitude—an awareness of the relationship to what is outside it.

Dunham's paintings, abstract and figurative compositions, conjure everyday realities as both more and less than real; the so-called ordinary is unfamiliar, new terrain, politically, sexually, environmentally. Fictional portraits of the known moving into an unknown, they show vivacity, even about the incapacity to know the future. I mean, they have vitality, these frank, beautiful misfits, or funny, smart, bold disturbances. Not stories but wordless pictures, the paintings ask a viewer, like me, to draw or write her own conclusions.

Human beings are devouring machines, Dunham's paintings suggest, competing with the natural world and carelessly upending it. Human beings don't perceive the damage they do, as it happens; they will turn a blind eye, adapt, go on, and live in peril. People will themselves to survive; they will do whatever it takes to survive. People don't get the big picture, because they're in it.

Inevitably it's said: Artists address the human condition. But the human condition is unstable, in flux—human-made. Art also represents—and has always—the inhuman condition, inhuman acts, wishes, circumstances, commissions of horror, of terror, even in the name of humanity. But then humans named it humanity.

I look at Carroll Dunham's paintings, and think about being alive. I'm alive now, and then I won't be, but I don't know when. Life is always endangered, by death, for one. In Dunham's paintings, there are no condemnations, there's no shame; jeremiads would lose me. I think about Samuel Beckett: "Dance first. Think later. It's the natural order." The paintings may be cautionary tales, but there's some dancing in them. And, the painter is fully aware he is part of the picture.

Paying Attention is in memory of an exceptional person, friend, and uniquely great artist, Susan Hiller. I miss her brilliance, the sound of her voice, her acuity, her growing up in Florida, her laugh, her startling integrity, her future work, her brave independence. Susan did it her way, and saying it like that would make her laugh. I miss her intensely.

Acknowledgments

I wish I could acknowledge every person who has encouraged me over the years, from my first-grade teacher who became my eighth-grade teacher; to all of my dear, unwavering friends; new and old friends; friendly acquaintances, colleagues, and random strangers. You moved me past futility, which is my psychological métier.

I am grateful to the artists who have felt that my writing aligns with their work and, more, that there is a relationship between my writing and their work. Many have helped me carry on writing, and just carry on. I especially want to acknowledge Elizabeth C. (Betsy) Baker, who was editor in chief at *Art in America* and who daringly published, beginning in 1986, many Madame Realism fiction/essays. Her belief in them began my art writing career. I want to thank all of the editors at various journals, magazines, and presses. There are too many to cite. The great ones know who they are, and know that I loved working with them and still do.

For this collection, I want to acknowledge my enormous admiration for its editor, Elizabeth Schambelan. I relied on her acuity and intelligence completely. Elizabeth's writing is brilliant, her ideas so resonant and generative. I am very fortunate to have had her eye and mind. I am grateful to my friend, the artist and iconoclast Paul Chan for his brilliantly ludic drawings for the cover.

I want to thank David Zwirner for having established this important art press, and Lucas Zwirner for his enthusiastic support of this collection. I want to acknowledge David Zwirner Books's extraordinary publisher, Doro Globus. She took this book on, wholeheartedly, and, along with it, me, its writer. Doro is a wise and kind person, also a writer, and generous. I can't thank David Zwirner Books's editor Elizabeth Gordon enough. She is a miracle editor and I believe can do anything and solve every problem. She kept every detail in mind, every change noted; discussing the contents and design of the book with her was illuminating and also fun.

I couldn't have hoped for a better press or better people for this collection.

Being a good or bad writer is uncertain and not up to the writer. Any artist's life has disappointments, everyone's life does. Rejections come hard, and subtlety is rare in our treacherous zeitgeist, with its obscene uses of power and violence sadly unavailable to "cancellation." Shaming has no power against the very powerful.

Making art and writing, making your way in this world—words fail, and I wish I could fail better. Most people try to go on, some can't, many have no freedom. I want to acknowledge them, also.

Bibliography of Essays

"Absence Makes Art" was first published in *Jim Hodges: This Line to You*. Exh. cat. (Santiago de Compostela, Spain: Centro Galego de Arte Contemporánea; Xunta de Galicia, 2006).

"An Afternoon with Stanley Whitney" was first published in *Stanley Whitney: Afternoon Paintings*. Exh. cat. (London: Lisson Gallery, 2019).

"Alex Harsley: The President Resigns" was first published in *OSMOS*, no. 12 (Summer 2017).

"All About the Writing, All About the Writing" was first published in Gertrude Stein, *Dix Portraits* (New York: David Zwirner Books, 2022).

"Art of His Time" was first published in *On Kawara*. Exh. cat. (Potomac, MD: Glenstone Museum, 2018).

"Beyond Good and Evil" was first published in *frieze*, no. 238 (October 2023).

"Blame It on Andy" was first published in *frieze*, no. 141 (September 2011).

"Blue Shores" was first published in *Stephen Shore: Selected Works, 1973–1981* (New York: Aperture Foundation, 2017).

"Cindy Sherman: Character of Characters" was first published as "Cindy Sherman" in *The Broad Collection*, ed. Joanne Heyler (Los Angeles: The Broad; New York: DelMonico Books, 2015).

"Correspondences" was first published in *Roni Horn: Gurgles, Sucks, Echoes*. Exh. cat. (New York: Matthew Marks, 1995).

"Courtly Love" was first published in *Bookforum* (December/January 2019).

"Craig Owens Once Existed" was first published in Lyn Blumenthal and Kate Horsfield, *Craig Owens: Portrait of a Young Critic* (New York: Badlands Unlimited, 2018).

"Cut Up Life" was first published in Charles Henri Ford, *Water from a Bucket: A Diary, 1948–1957* (New York: Turtle Point Press, 2001).

"Dana Schutz's *Boatman*" was first published as "Boatman" in *Dana Schutz* (London: Phaidon, 2023).

"Death Drive" was first published in *frieze*, no. 188 (June–August 2017).

"Decade-ism" was first published in *frieze*, no. 155 (May 2013).

"Don't Cry: Work" was first published in *Art and Artists* 8, no. 7 (October 1973). This text has been edited by the author for this volume.

"Drawing from a Translation Artist" was first published in *Drawn from Photography*. Exh. cat. Drawing Papers 96 (New York: The Drawing Center, 2011).

"Early Years of the New Museum: An Intellectual Reminiscence or Pieces from a Consciousness" was first published in *40 Years New* (New York: New Museum, 2017).

"Etel Adnan: Glorious" was first published as "Etel Adnan" in 4Columns, December 4, 2020, online edition.

"The Experience of Time" was first published in *Ad Reinhardt: Color Out of Darkness*. Exh. cat. (New York: Pace, 2023).

"Feeling Tuymans" was first published in *Luc Tuymans: Nice* (New York: David Zwirner Books, 2024).

"A Fictional Past" was first published in *frieze*, no. 163 (May 2014).

"Fighting Talk" was first published in *frieze*, no. 159 (November/December 2013).

"The Final Plot" was first published in *The Inevitable: Contemporary Writers Confront Death*, ed. David Shields and Bradford Morrow (New York: W. W. Norton, 2011).

"Generation Gap" was first published in *Granta*, no. 166 (Winter 2024), online edition.

"The Hardest Thing" was first published in *frieze*, no. 149 (September 2012).

"Hilary Harkness: Queer Visions" was first published in *Hilary Harkness: Everything for You* (London: Black Dog Press, 2024).

"Homage to Homage" was first published in *Steve Locke: Homage to the Auction Block*. Exh. cat. (Boston: LaMontagne Gallery, 2020).

"Home/Not Home" was first published in *Do Ho Suh: Anatomy*, ed. Amie Corry and Louis Rogers (London: MACK, 2025).

"The Horse's Eye" was first published in *Carroll Dunham: Drawings 1982–96*. Exh. cat. (New York: Gladstone Gallery, 2016).

"An Imagined Peace" was first published in *frieze*, no. 212 (July/August 2020).

"Imagined Places" was first published as "James Welling: Portfolio" in *Artforum* (May 2001).

"Introduction to *Closer*" was first published in Dennis Cooper, *Closer* (London: Serpent's Tail, 2023).

"Invitation to *The Visitor*" was first published in Maeve Brennan, *The Visitor* (London: Peninsula Press, 2025).

"It's So American" was first published in *Nate Lowman* (New York: David Zwirner Books, 2023).

"A Knowing Look" was first published in *frieze*, no. 169 (March 2015).

"The Last Words Are Andy Warhol" was first published in *Grey Room*, no. 21 (Fall 2005).

"The Life and Deaths of Jane Bowles (or, Reputation)" was first published in *The Bodies That Remain*, ed. Emmy Beber (Santa Barbara, CA: dead letter office/punctum, 2018).

"Life Less Ordinary" was first published in *frieze*, no. 157 (September 2013).

"Lines, Gaps, Shapes, Strokes, Jokes, Colors, Holes . . ." was first published in Amy Sillman, *Faux Pas: Selected Writings and Drawings* (Paris: After 8 Books, 2020). Expanded edition published in 2022.

"Love Story" was first published in *Art in America* (January 1987).

"Nothing and Everything to See Here" was first published in *Anne Collier: Eye*. Exh. cat. (Lismore, Ireland: Lismore Castle Arts, 2023).

"Oblivion" was first published as "Drinking to Forget" in *frieze*, no. 184 (January/February 2017).

"Of Its Time" was first published in *frieze*, no. 151 (November/December 2012).

"On Clint Eastwood's *Unforgiven*" was first published in *frieze*, no. 200 (January/February 2019), expanded version online.

"On Influence" was first published in *David Wojnarowicz: Brush Fires in the Social Landscape* (New York: Aperture Foundation, 2015).

"*Parts of Some Sextets* in Parts or as Yvonne Calls It: Mattress Monster" was first published in *Remembering a Dance: Parts of Some Sextets, 1965/2019*, ed. Yvonne Rainer and Emily Coates (New York: Performa; Hartford, CT: Wadsworth Atheneum Museum of Art; Milan: Lenz Press, 2023).

"Past Shock" was first published in *frieze*, no. 29 (June–August 1996).

"Playing Both Sides" was first published in *Raymond Pettibon: A Pen of All Work*. Exh. cat. (London: Phaidon; New York: New Museum, 2017).

"Point of View" was first published in *frieze*, no. 143 (November/December 2011).

"The Potter" was first published in *Nicole Eisenman: Maker's Muck* (New York and Zurich: Hauser & Wirth Publishers, 2024).

"Presence" was first published in *Pat Steir: Snow and Waterfall*. Exh. cat. (Philadelphia: Locks Gallery, 2023).

"Real Life and Living Memory" was first published in *Aperture*, no. 248 (Fall 2022).

“Reconsidering the Genius of Gertrude Stein” was first published as “Two Books” in *The New York Times Sunday Book Review*, January 29, 2012.

“Remember You Are a Body” was first published in *Adam Pendleton: Blackness, White, and Light*. Exh. cat., mumok – Museum moderner Kunst Stiftung Ludwig Wien, Vienna (Cologne: Walther and Franz König, 2024).

“Screen Presence” was first published in *frieze*, no. 177 (March 2016).

“Simply Profound” was first published in *Making Strange: The Chara Schreyer Collection*, ed. Douglas Fogle and Hanneke Skerath (New York: DelMonico Books, 2021).

“Soft Pink Light” was first published in *Granta*, no. 156 (Summer 2021).

“Still Moving: Eight Stories” was first published in *Justine Kurland: Highway Kind* (New York: Aperture Foundation, 2016).

“Stories Tell Stories” was first published in *Joan Jonas Is on Our Mind*, ed. Frances Richard (San Francisco: CCA Wattis Institute for Contemporary Arts, 2017).

“Stranger Spaces” was first published in *Laurie Simmons: Big Camera/Little Camera*. Exh. cat. (Fort Worth, TX: Modern Art Museum of Fort Worth; New York: DelMonico Books, 2018).

“Susan Hiller’s Wildnesses” was first published as “Susan Hiller” in *Aperture*, no. 237 (Winter 2019).

“Try Again” was first published in *frieze*, no. 145 (March 2012).

“21 TV Tales” was first published in *Barbara Kruger*. Exh. cat. (Bulleen, Australia: Museum of Modern Art at Heide, 1996).

“Warhol, Existentially” was first published in Donna De Salvo, *Andy Warhol–From A to B and Back Again*. Exh. cat. (New York: Whitney Museum of American Art, 2018).

“What Makes a Celebration?” was first published in *Aperture*, no. 246 (Spring 2022).

“A Woman I Once Knew” was first published in *Granta*, no. 168 (Summer 2024).

Index

D

E

W

Y

Z

Paying Attention: Essays on Art and Culture
Lynne Tillman

Published by
David Zwirner Books
520 West 20th Street, 2nd Floor
New York, New York 10011
+1 212 727 2070
davidzwirnerbooks.com

Editors: Elizabeth Schambelan,
Elizabeth Gordon
Copy editor: Clare Fentress
Proofreaders: Anna Drozda, Clare Fentress
Indexer: ARC Indexing

Design: Bonnie Briant
Production manager: Luke Chase
Printing: L.E.G.O., S.p.A.

Typeface: Adobe Caslon Pro
Paper: Coral Book White, 80 gsm

Great care has been taken to credit the first place of publication in the bibliography, on pages 458–460, correctly. In cases of errors or omissions, please contact the publisher so that corrections can be made in future editions.

Distributed in the United States and Canada by
Simon & Schuster, Inc.
1230 Avenue of the Americas
New York, New York 10020
simonandschuster.com

Distributed outside the United States and Canada by
Thames & Hudson, Ltd.
6–24 Britannia Street
London WC1X 9JD
thamesandhudson.com

ISBN 978-1-64423-174-6

Library of Congress Control Number:
2025948534

Printed in Italy

Front cover: Paul Chan, *plaudern, die Plauderi, der Plauderer (to chat, chat, talker) #1*, 2024. Ink on paper, 17 × 14 inches (43.2 × 35.5 cm)
Back cover: Paul Chan, *plaudern, die Plauderi, der Plauderer (to chat, chat, talker) #2*, 2024. Ink on paper, 17 × 14 inches (43.2 × 35.5 cm)

FSC
www.fsc.org
MIX
Paper | Supporting responsible forestry
FSC® C023419